COLLECTING PHOTOGRAPHICA

COLLECTING
PHOTOGRAPHICA

COLLECTING PHOTOGRAPHICA

The Images and Equipment of the First Hundred Years of Photography

GEORGE GILBERT

Copyright © 1976 by George Gilbert.

For information contact: Elsevier-Dutton Publishing Co., Inc., 2 Park Avenue, New York, N.Y. 10016

Library of Congress Catalog Card Number: 75-28698

ISBN: 0-8015-1408-8 (cloth ed.)
0-8015-1407-X (paper ed.)

Published simultaneously in Canada by Clarke, Irwin & Company Limited, Toronto and Vancouver

10 9 8 7 6 5 4 3 2 1

Hawthorn/Dutton

For information contact: Elsevier-Dutton Publishing Co., Inc., 2
Park Avenue, New York, N.Y. 10016

Library of Congress Catalog Card Number: 75–28698

ISBN: 0-8015-1408-8 (cloth ed.)
       0-8015-1407-X (paper ed.)

Published simultaneously in Canada by Clarke, Irwin & Company
Limited, Toronto and Vancouver

10 9 8 7 6 5 4 3 2 1

Contents

Acknowledgments

This book would not have been possible without the generous cooperation of a number of individuals and families whose interest in photographic history and the collecting of photographica goes far beyond the ordinary norms for pursuit of a hobby.

Both the hospitality and expertise of Matt Isenberg of Hadlyme, Connecticut, America's foremost collector and specialist in the earliest days of photography, and of Eaton S. Lothrop, Jr., editor of the *Photographic Collectors' Newsletter* and author of *A Century of Cameras*, were of special value to me. Their generosity included the loan of photographs and data from the librarylike files that these individuals maintain.

Photographs from the outstanding collections of Allen and Hilary Weiner of New York; from John and Valerie Craig of Simsbury, Connecticut; from Alan and Paulette Cotter of Santa Barbara, California; from Mike and Gladys Kessler of Lakewood, California; and Ernest Conover of Aurora, Ohio, were of extreme value in assuring coverage in a number of areas where difficult-to-locate equipment would have made it nearly impossible for me to provide the excellent photography that these photo-history teams made available.

I owe a special debt to a unique pioneer in the modern study of photographic history, Don Blake of Wilmington, North Carolina, who created *Graphic Antiquarian*, a publication seeking to broaden general interest in the collecting of photographica, who opened the files of his publication and offered access to the many valuable photographs that he has collected for his publication since 1970.

I am indebted to a broad variety of individuals who contributed their time and knowledge to assist in one or another of the chapters or who permitted elements of their own writings and research efforts to be incorporated in some of the material of this book. I especially thank Alfred Lowenherz, president of the Camera Club of New York and an early officer of the Photographic Historical Society of New York; Jerome and Shirley Sprung, president and treasurer, respectively, of the Photographic Historical Society of New York during the year in which this work was assembled; and Arthur Rothstein, director of photography of *Parade* magazine who helped make this project possible.

The painstaking research effort by Louis S. Marcus of West Hempstead, New York, in creation of the massive chronology of photographic history for the pages of *Photographica*, monthly periodical of the Photographic Historical Society of New York, was of tremendous help in the creation of the collector-oriented chronology presented here. I thank him for his permission to select liberal segments from his copyrighted materials.

To my wife, Ruth, who gave me her support during hundreds of hours of writing and editing, I hereby vote a permanent niche in the annals of photographic history.

To the numerous friends near and far who loaned illustrations, photographs, and other aids to this project, I express the hope that the credits for their use are a permanent expression of my gratitude for their magnanimity expressed in countless helpful ways.

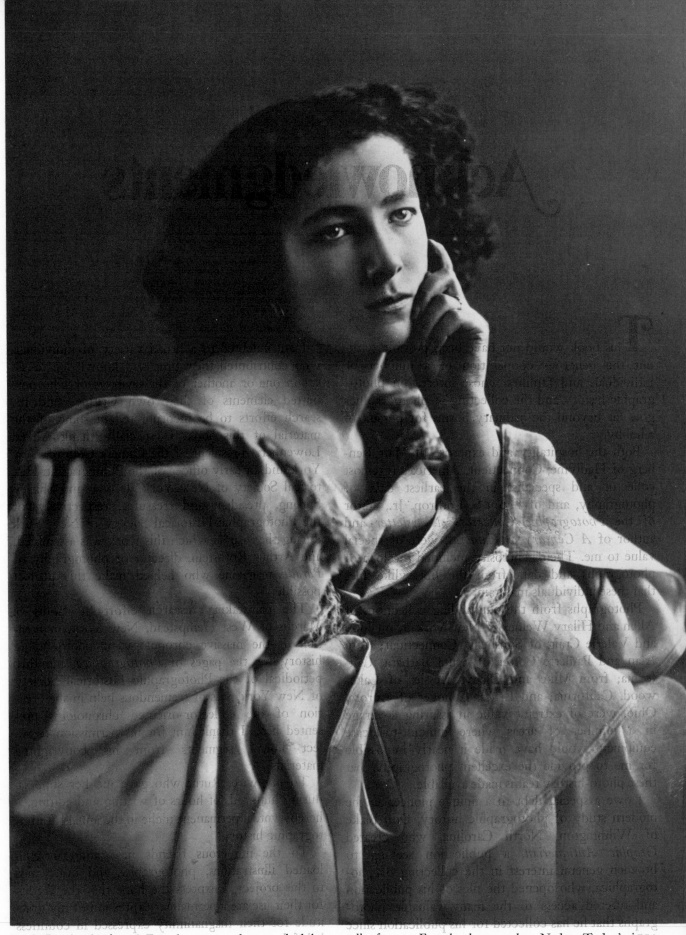

Sarah Bernhardt, famed French actress, photographed by equally famous French photographer Nadar. Today's image collector seeks the famous on both sides of the camera. *(Photograph courtesy of Masterpiece Collection of the Photographic Historical Society of New York)*

Introduction

The generation of Americans who searched for first-edition books in locked trunks and forgotten barrels and boxes up in the attic has been replaced by a new group of sleuths: the camera bugs. Young or old, as readers of the popular photographic press, they have been quick to learn that grandpa's old camera could have some value—even as much as thousands of dollars. And it's true—if grandpa had a special interest in the candid photography of the turn of the century—his concealed camera in the shape of a group of books, or in a cane handle, or even hidden in a cravat could sell today for $2,000 and more.

More likely though, the attic wreckers will find, if they're lucky, a pre–World War I camera, possibly one of the Panoram-Kodaks introduced between 1900 and 1910 that permitted the average family photographer to take a horizon-to-horizon panoramic photograph. Or perhaps he or she will find one of the tiny, all-metal cameras that resemble a railroader's pocketwatch. Eager camera collectors seek the popular Expo, or the English version known as the Ticka, and if the finder is really lucky, it will be a rarer Photoret. But it could be the more common family camera in a folding style, aimed from the waist, worth a lot less but just as important in the story of the growth of photography in American life.

An estimated 5,000 to 10,000 Americans are in the forefront of the collecting movement, which made itself known in the early 1970s. In 1969 there was but one organized group of photographica collectors meeting regularly to pay homage to trophy hunters who had found hidden game

in antique shops, thrift shops, pawnshops, and, of course, in attics. That group was centered in Rochester, New York, and drew upon history-minded engineers and staff people of Kodak and other photo companies in the upstate New York photographic capital. In 1974 the first national organization had its first annual symposium and elections in New York, and by 1976 there were nearly thirty collectors' groups across the country.

Amateur and professional photographers living in and near New York; Boston; Chicago; Pasadena, California; Columbus, Ohio; St. Louis, Missouri; and other major cities have learned to watch for antique-photography fairs where bazaars of booths and stalls displaying cameras, lenses, sepia images, and early literature of the photographic art are lined in rows. Dealing is sharp, for only at these counters can one locate a viewfinder, a plateholder, or a lens-shutter combination of the style no longer available in the Main Street camera store.

In between these semiannual and annual fairs, a coterie of antique dealers specializing in photographic vintage items are as diligently scouring America for photography's artifacts as the dealers in rare books, Tiffany glass, or Shaker furniture. As in the art field, many of these dealers have been commissioned by investment-minded individuals who have seen the advantage of a hedge against inflation in the images of the Daguerrean era (1839-1855) or in the Victorian era's rare cameras. These collectors especially seek the cameras of photography's first days, along with the lenses, specialized darkroom devices, and other evidences of the long-gone process of an image without a negative, made directly on a highly polished silver-coated copper plate.

Whereas owners of the rifles of the Civil War period dare not test-fire their weapons with modern gunpowder, collectors of early cameras, do occasionally field-test cameras that are apparently light-tight after fifty and more years. In some cases, today's studio sheet films can be fitted into yesterday's holders. The first roll-film cameras, however, defy easy testing, especially if they are of the folding-bellows design. Only recently the Eastman Kodak Company announced discontinuation of the #122 roll film, which fit the millions of postcard-size cameras made as late as 1945. As late as 1970, Kodak revealed it had demand for about six thousand rolls a year, too low a quantity to permit manufacture and shelf storage of a dated emulsion material. Today the owners of postcard cameras are limited to testing their early cameras using as film a single piece of photo paper loaded into the camera.

Home museums and occasional displays at seminars, such as the October 21–23, 1972, unique event in New York's Hotel McAlpin (which drew about five hundred enthusiasts on a rainy weekend), are where collected cameras are proudly put on display. A home collection may be as small as a choice half dozen items owned by one Park Avenue collector couple (with no item having a value of less than $2,000). But most of the existing societies have a dozen or so members who can display 200 to 300 cameras and the related accessories, many of which have been acquired as gifts or for a few dollars.

Most old cameras have little dollar value at this time. Mass-produced and without special technical features, they nonetheless reflect the growth of photography in their variety. Many collections are made up of large numbers of these cameras with great nostalgia interest but with little marketplace or trading value.

As in book, coin, or stamp collecting, the experienced collector is a specialist. He enthusiastically seeks out models from a specific country or era or the varieties within a camera type. The photographic equipment for the stereography (three-dimensional effect) enthusiast; or the long-lensed cameras of the nature photographer; the high-speed action cameras of the press photographer; the sealed cameras of the underwater photographer; the wide-angle cameras of the panoramist; or the concealed cameras of the spy crowd are but some of the varieties in equipment which whet the collector appetite of the aficionado.

For a long time I have collected camera imitations and fakes, which as in art, have a little world of their own. When the Leica camera became a means of exchange in the aftermath of World War II, "Leica" was tooled into many Leica-look cameras originating, for example, in Russian factories. There were also Leica look-alike cameras made in England, Italy, France, Japan, and even the United States either during or after the war. The Leica collectors, like Wedgwood collectors or Tiffany collectors, live in a collector world of their own. Their own organization. Their own national publication. Their own seminars and swap meets.

Other collectors of photographica eschew the hardware; they seek the images of the past, especially by those photographers whose names have outlived their subjects. Auctions of prints by the photographers of the nineteenth century and increasingly of the twentieth century have been conducted by Sotheby's and Christie's in England and at Sotheby Parke Bernet in New York, all monitored by a growing group of collectors who know that names like Cameron, Frith, or Stieglitz are money in the bank, like Picasso, Braque, or Matisse. Early albums have sold for as much as £40,-000 in England; in America, a single Daguerreotype of Edgar Allan Poe has sold for a reputed $38,000.

The fires of the collecting mania are being stoked by a new, younger generation whose training grounds have been the campuses of American universities. The study of photography has become routine at over five hundred institutions, sometimes as an art elective. Where photo history is included, the new young photographers are having face-to-face meetings with local collector-experts who bring rare cameras to the classrooms. For these students, a first-time encounter with a string-pull Kodak or a Civil War wet-plate camera is the start of a new collecting effort.

To the family with an attic but without a family photographer to guide the hunt; to the new young photographer with a curiosity about photography's past explained in terms of the development of its technology, this book is hopefully a helpful guide to some of photographic history's most exciting moments.

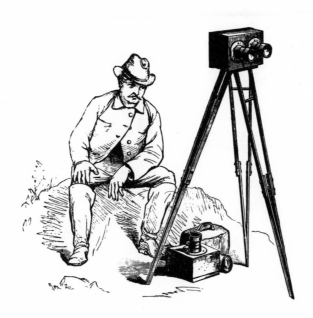

COLLECTING PHOTOGRAPHICA

Most eagerly sought Daguerrean images are those of outdoor scenes and work themes. Gold mining photograph reveals tremendous detail of interest to historians. (From the collection of Jerry and Shirley Sprung)

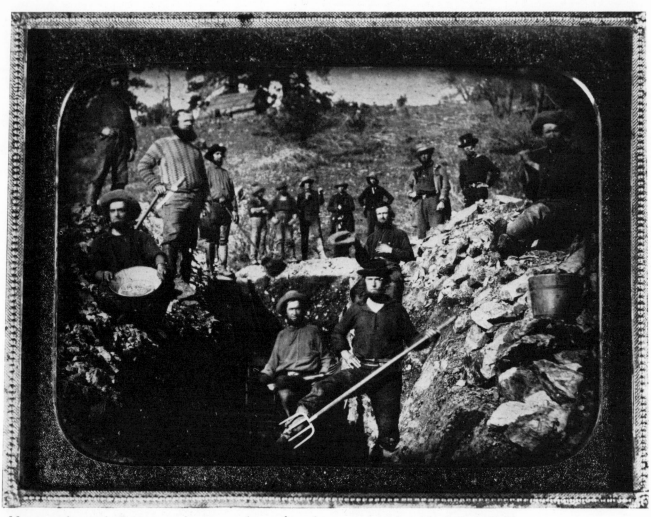

Most eagerly sought Daguerrean images are those of outdoor scenes and work themes. Gold mining photograph reveals tremendous detail of interest to historians. *(From the collection of Jerry and Shirley Sprung)*

1
Collecting Images

- A single Daguerreotype (see Glossary) of Edgar Allan Poe sold at auction for $9,250 and shortly thereafter was resold to a private collector for the equivalent of $38,000.

- A photographic album, containing primarily photographs by Julia Margaret Cameron of England, sold at auction for $123,000.

- A 1907 print, "The Steerage," by Alfred Stieglitz, sold at auction for $4,500.

- A pair of cartes de visite (see Glossary), the photographic calling cards of Alfred Tennyson, realized $300.

- A set of six Daguerreotypes purchased in a flea market for $18 were sold a few months later to the Library of Congress for $12,000.

- A group of stereo cards that went begging at 5¢ each back in the 1950s include many now selling for $10, $20, and $50.

The search for early America's photographic images is on.

During the late spring of 1975, a young man from a small community on the West Coast joined a few thousand Californians for an afternoon at a flea market. He purchased a few photo prints on paper that were part of a cardboard box full of photo images of all sizes and subjects: people, pets, landscapes, the usual run of miscellany. It was a case of "Your choice: $1."

He went through the box carefully after one of the early prints he spotted had been set aside. By the time he was down to the bottom of the box, he had chosen five prints. He paid the $5 and left.

California's earliest days may have been Indian and Spanish. It is not well known that there was a substantial English settlement in California in the mid-1800s, perhaps spurred in part by the Gold Rush, which had brought tens of thousands of Americans across the prairies or around the Cape by boat. It was a family of wealthy Englishmen who originally may have brought those five prints to America, because well over a hundred years later, these prints, brought as part of the family's reminiscences of Britain, were worth about $2,000 each.

The young photo collector had spotted what he realized were calotype prints (see Glossary), ex-

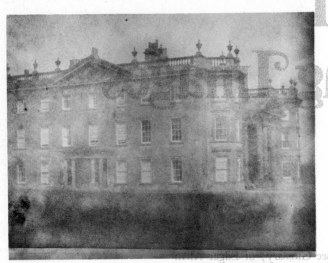

Recently discovered calotype by William Henry Fox Talbot, famous English inventor of negative–positive photography, from the experimental days, pre-1840. (*Photograph courtesy of* Photographica)

amples of the earliest known photography on paper, the English process (ca. 1839–1860) developed by William Henry Fox Talbot during the same period that Louis Jacques Mandé Daguerre in France was completing experiments that led to successfully accomplished images on silver.

Another West Coast photographica collector is Mike Kessler, a graphics designer and a recognized authority on the cameras of the 1880s and 1890s. All America benefited when, in 1972 at a San Francisco flea market, Kessler and a friend found on a table a group of Daguerreotypes which he bought as a set of six for $18.

The Daguerreotypes that are most readily located in the antique shops and flea markets are family portraits, usually of unidentified men, women, or children. Two kinds of Daguerreotypes are especially sought by collectors: large-size Daguerreotypes and outdoor Daguerreotypes (hurry to your neighborhood flea market; one may be waiting).

The scenes that instantly excited Kessler were all outdoor scenes, and, even without further identification of the subject matter, could be sold individually to collectors of this earliest period of photography (1840–1855) for $50 to $100 per image. Those that Kessler obtained were not just Daguerreotypes of some buildings; they are among the very earliest known photographs of the construction of the Capitol in Washington, D.C. They were soon sold to the Library of Congress for $12,000, so that today's and all future generations of Americans will have this dramatic evidence of the building of our nation.

Kessler may have gotten to the images just in time; their original protective cases had long been sold separately for use as small boxes for coins or cuff links; the delicate Daguerrean images were protected only by their original glass covers, which were sealed to the silver-coated copper plates with paper tape.

Rare Daguerreotype of the nation's Capitol was among a small group found in a San Francisco flea market, later purchased by Library of Congress for $12,000. (*Photograph courtesy of Mike Kessler and Darrell Dearmore*)

THE EARLY DEMAND FOR PHOTOGRAPHS

There probably isn't a family in America that does not have a box, a drawer, or an album or two of family photographs that is occasionally pored

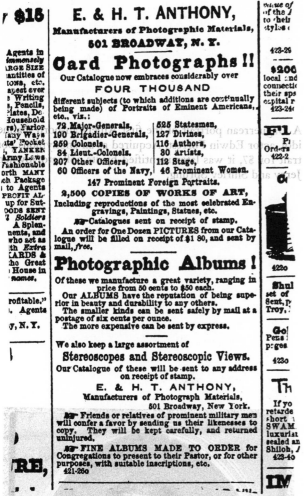

Pre-Civil War newspaper ad offered prints for collectors of images of famed Americans much as fans today seek movie stars or baseball heroes.

shops to acquire images suitable to today's home decor. But in 1840 the only *printed* image was a woodcut, lithograph, or an engraving; there was no way at the time to reproduce the detailed photo image with its tonalities from white to dense black onto the printed page.

As Daguerrean photography spread across America, families began to own these more personalized images. Some were suited to framing and display on the wall; the smaller ones in the protective cases were stored in drawers. There was as yet no need for the concept of a storage album, which would become a patentable item in 1860. That development awaited the change in photographic technique that made possible photographic prints on paper. The international acceptance of the French-developed photo print and card known as the carte de visite in the size of a small playing card made it possible for one drawer to store hundreds of photo images in the space required for a dozen Daguerrean cases.

The mass-production potential of the negatives from which these cards were made opened doors to a new collecting fervor. E. & H. T. Anthony & Co. in New York, which was supplying photographic aids to the professional studio itself, established a photofinishing capability enabling mass manufacture of cartes de visite and stereo cards. They offered to the general public photographs that could be privately owned: portraits of the government's highest officials, generals, diplomats, actors, painters, writers—anyone whose name was in the news.

During the Civil War, army officers who were battle heroes were already catalogued as available portraits that could be seen at Anthony offices or in the centers in other cities where Anthony had established agents. Photos could be purchased by mail and new subject matter could be provided to Anthony to permit further distribution of popular images. Today, the vast market that has existed for posters and the phenomenon of hero worship that made an industry of baseball cards for children and fan magazines for teen-agers and adults continues. The novelty of photography has long worn off, but the need to "own" a folk hero has not.

These purchased prints were usually stored in the drawer with other prized photos, and when al-

over when discussing how big the children have grown, how great a vacation had been, how lovely they looked as a couple "back then." Photographs, after all, are the most personal of heirlooms and the most accurate memory stimulators.

American families were already assembling boxes and photo albums by the time of the Civil War and earlier. The first Daguerrean parlor in New York City (1840) was not a photo studio. It was a display center for the French Daguerrean photograph, and people came in to buy a landscape, a photocopy of a famous painting, a water view, or some other subject that caught their fancy much as people today visit art galleries and print

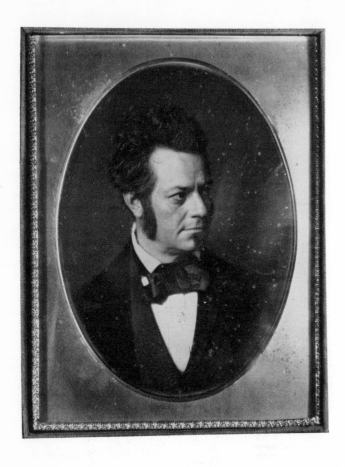

A Daguerrean portrait of the first American-born matinee idol, actor Edwin Forrest. Acquired as an anonymous portrait for $7, it was later identified by its collector-owners, Jerry and Shirley Sprung.

Another anonymous Daguerrean portrait was later identified as James Harper, an early mayor of New York City. *(From the collection of Jerry and Shirley Sprung)*

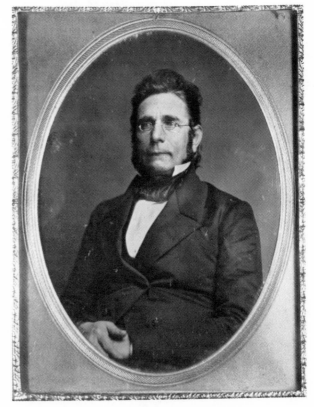

bums became the popular way to store and occasionally display the family's collection, these purchased prints were set into panel niches along with photographs of the family itself. Today when we locate a Victorian album, it is not unusual to find images of generals, circus freaks, actors, and other public figures alongside the pictures of great grandma and great granddad. Many an American family claiming a Civil War general as a long-lost relative because his portrait was on the same page as the dearly departed of that period can only be sure that there was a hero worshipper in the family (and *maybe* a general). After the Civil War, col-

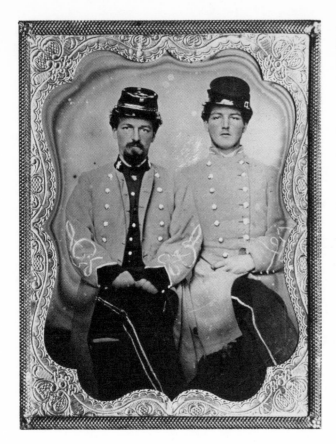

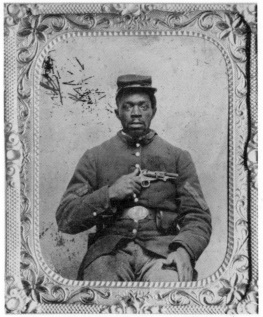

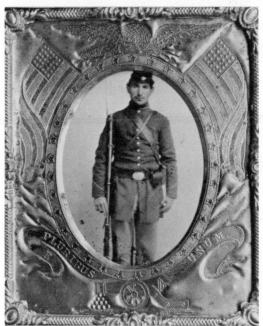

Collectors of Civil War mementoes compete with collectors of photographica for evidences of Civil War soldiers, uniforms, and equipment. (*Photograph courtesy of Herb Peck, Jr., and* Photographic Collectors' Newsletter)

lecting continued, as there was special interest in the cabinet-print–size portraits of actors and actresses by photographers José Maria Mora and Napoleon Sarony, for example.

Photographs were made in the nineteenth century on paper, on silver-plated copper, on glass, on lacquered iron sheets, and even on such exotic materials as leather and mica. They are mainly found as positives, but on occasion as negatives, often still in the storage boxes of the original photographer, dated and identified.

Prints in boxes, in frames, in albums—nearly anywhere—are of different photographic periods and techniques which can be used for identification. The following chart, by types and techniques, is a general guide to most of the kinds of materials used in photo processes.

TYPES OF PHOTOGRAPHS

(Originally published by George Eastman House, Rochester, New York, now International Museum of Photography)

MATERIAL	TECHNIQUE	PERIOD	COMMENTS
I. *Direct Positives*			
Metal			
Copper, silver-plated.	Daguerreotype	1839–ca. 1855	Silver tone before 1842; brown tone after 1841.
Iron, japanned black.	Tintype (ferrotype, melainotype)	1854–ca. 1900	Gray-black image; chocolate colored after 1870.
Glass	Ambrotype	1854–ca. 1870	
II. *Negatives*			
Paper			
Uncoated, often waxed or oiled.	Calotype	1841–ca. 1855	Extremely rare in America.
With gelatin surface.	Eastman paper negative	1884–ca. 1895	Rare, usually of poor quality.
Glass			
Thick, edges often ground, coating grayish, uneven.	Collodion	1851–ca. 1880	Not used to any extent in America until ca. 1855. By ca. 1860 universal.
Thin, edges sharply cut, coating black, very smooth and even.	Gelatin dry plate	ca. 1880–ca. 1920	Occasionally used today as in electron microscopy, astronomical photography.
Gelatin			
Looks like "film," but completely gelatin; brittle; edges uneven.	Eastman American film	1884–ca. 1890	Used in Kodak No. 1 (1888) provided circular image 2½"; Kodak No. 2 (1889) provided circular image 3½".
Clear plastic (nitrocellulose)			
Extremely thin, curls up, and wrinkles easily.	Roll film	1889–1903	
Somewhat thicker (after 1903), coated on both sides with gelatin to prevent curling.	Roll film	1903–1939	**CAUTION** Flammable.
Machine-cut sheets, exactly rectangular, edges stamped "Eastman."	Sheet film	1913–1939	Test by cutting small piece from corner, putting in ashtray, touching with lighted match. If it flares, base is nitrate.
Clear plastic (cellulose acetate)	Sheet film	1939–present	
Marked "SAFETY" on edge.	Roll film		
III. *Prints on Paper or Board*			
Paper			
Uncoated, brown to yellow-brown tone.	Silver print	1839–ca. 1860	Also called salted paper.
Coated paper, extremely thin, brown image, high gloss, usually on mount.	Albumen print	1850–ca. 1895	"Printing upon albumenised paper seems to be dying a slow but natural death." *Amateur Photographer*, August 3, 1894.

MATERIAL	TECHNIQUE	PERIOD	COMMENTS
Sizes of Mounts (on Board)			
Carte de visite	4¼″ × 2½″	Introduced in Europe in 1854; in U.S. ca. 1859	
Cabinet	4½″ × 6½″	Introduced to U.S. 1866	
Victoria	3¼″ × 5″	Introduced 1870	
Promenade	4″ × 7″	Introduced 1875	
Boudoir	5¼″ × 8½″	Date introduced not known	
Imperial	6⅞″ × 9⅞″	Date introduced not known	
Panel	8¼″ × 4″	Date introduced not known	
Stereo approx.	3″ × 7″	Introduced to U.S. 1859; introduced in Europe ca. 1854	
Stereo approx.	4″ × 7″	Introduced to U.S. 1870; introduced in Europe ca. 1854	
Gelatin Papers			
Coated, thickness of writing paper, yellow-brown to purple image.	Collodiochloride Gelatinochloride Aristotype Solio P.O.P. Proof	1888–ca. 1910	"Aristotype introduced a year ago." *American Amateur Photographer*, October 1889.
Uncoated, usually drawing paper, often pebbly surface, delicate gray image.	Platinotype	1880–ca. 1930	Became popular with art photographers upon its commercial introduction in 1880 by the Platinotype Company.
Similar	Palladiotype	ca. 1914–ca. 1930	Similar in all respects to platinotype, except salts of palladium used.
Uncoated, brilliant blue	Cyanotype Blue print	ca. 1885–ca. 1910	Invented 1840 but rarely used until ca. 1885 when its ease of processing appealed to amateurs.
Uncoated, usually drawing paper; various colors; resembles a wash drawing.	Gum bichromate	1884–ca. 1920	Used only for "artistic" photography.
Smooth, usually heavy paper; rich image in various tones	Carbon	1864–ca. 1900	Although invented earlier, first widespread use followed introduction of the transfer process in 1864.
Coated, semimat or smooth, black-gray-white.	Velox Azo D.O.P.	1893–present	All present-day printing processes are based on this so-called gaslight paper. Old prints often "bronzed" or with metallic silver sheen.

THE IMAGE MARKET TODAY

Today, as in the first days of photography, there are centers where one may shop for photographic images, current and of the past. In New York, outside Detroit, in Chicago, and elsewhere, galleries that historically began as centers for American graphics have become sales centers for photographic images. These centers encourage visitors by establishing exhibits that are advertised and publicized in the art columns of local newspapers.

The larger galleries maintain picture files from which one may select Daguerreotypes, ambrotypes, cartes de visite, albumen prints, platinotypes, gum prints, and carbon prints (see Glossary for explanation of these terms). Prices for prints depend on subject matter, rarity, size, and similar considerations. Many galleries will have a box of photo postcards where one may acquire a worthy print for as little as 50¢. If you see a rarity, such as the 1907 photograph by Alfred Stieglitz known as "The Steerage", you might keep in mind that a print of this photograph sold at auction in February 1975 at Sotheby Parke Bernet for $4,500.

There are numerous opportunities to acquire excellent examples of lesser photographers than Stieglitz in large sizes suitable for framing for $50 to $500. There are also photogravure prints (litho-like prints) from the locomotion series by Eadweard Muybridge (1830–1904) or from Edward Sheriff Curtis's studies of American Indian life in the $100-to-$150 range. There are now reproductions of the works of important photographers coming on the market, just as there are reproductions of Picasso or Degas. Reruns of Curtis prints were offered in 1974 for $60 per print almost at the same time that a mass-reproduction printing house was creating duotone reprints of suitable-for-framing quality that were being sold through art outlets in many cities—for $5 to $20.

The galleries that specialize in American photography are making major sales to the museums all

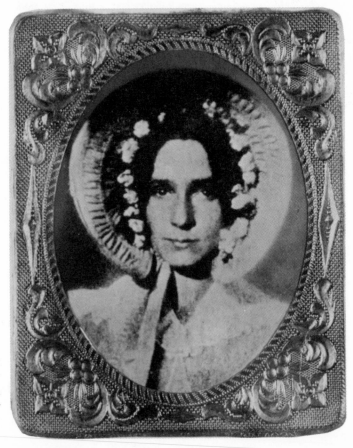

The portrait that has long been believed to be the first photographic portrait taken in America: Miss Dorothy Catherine Draper taken by her brother, John William Draper, early in 1840. The original was then sent to Sir William John Herschel in England. *(Photograph courtesy of Eastman Kodak Company)*

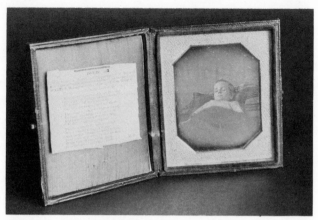

Death portraits, especially of infants, who had a high mortality rate up to the age of five, were commissioned by many American families. This Daguerreotype was found with a newspaper obituary. *(From the collection of Matthew R. Isenberg)*

over America who have themselves only recently entered into photo collecting on a large scale. The new generations of curators are as aware of the impact of photography on our culture as the young people who have made photography so much a part of their lives.

According to Lee Witkin, one of the leading gallery owners specializing in photographic images, nearly 50 percent of his sales are to museums.[1] They are buying the presently available images from the nineteenth century: Julia Margaret Cameron of England, Eugene Atget from France, Edward Weston of America. But "too many collectors want to buy only the old masters of photography. People should buy photographs because they like them—not as an investment commodity," remarked Tom Halstead, a Birmingham, Michigan, dealer in photographic images in the *Museum News*,[2] which in 1975 explained the photo-collector–gallery operations to museum officials.

Visiting the galleries or reading the literature provided by these galleries opens the doors to the beginnings of image collections with bona fide materials on the subject of your interest. By seeing many examples of work, one learns the nuances in

style, changes in photo periods, facts relating to the photographers, and similar information that helps guide print and image hunts in flea markets where a calotype could be mixed in with modern prints in a $1 box. The "stumble factor" should not be ignored by even the most novice collector, who can return home with a photo treasure from almost anywhere and say: "I stumbled on it!" Knowledge of prints and their periods makes it possible for the novice collector to participate in the mail-order auction and sales where one-paragraph descriptions, and possibly a postage-stamp–size reproduction, alone guide the decision to bid.

The search for early prints is underway every minute of every day as galleries, print collectors, publishers, museums, historical societies, and even industrial libraries endlessly cull through public and private collections seeking an image relating to their actual current or projected future needs.

One of the greatest sources for actual photographs of the Civil War or of famous people or important events in American history is the Library of Congress. Tens of thousands of negatives have been catalogued for the public; prints in 8-by-10-inch and larger sizes are available (not always from the original negative) for a few dollars. A catalogue of print services can be obtained by writing to Photoduplication, Library of Congress, Washington, D.C. 20540. One of the catalogues offered by this division is for Civil War photographs; it is sold to the public for 75¢.

In the 1970s, the Photographic Historical Society of New York, Inc., announced two portfolios of early photography, providing excellently made prints, each 11 by 14 inches, in sets of ten produced from specially made negatives of subjects on two themes: representative masterpieces of English, French, German, and American photographers, which included such portraits as Sarah Bernhardt (by Nadar: Gaspard Félix Tournachon) and Sir John Herschel (by Julia Margaret Cameron); and a group of photographs dating to the Farm Security Administration of the 1930s in which cameramen took a documentary approach to the changing social scene. The FSA photographers represented include the well-known photographers Arthur Rothstein, Walker Evans, Dorothea Lange, and Ben Shahn. The Society portfolios are sold for $48

[1] "A Bright Spot in the Art Market," *Museum News*, May 1975, pp. 27–31.

[2] Ibid.

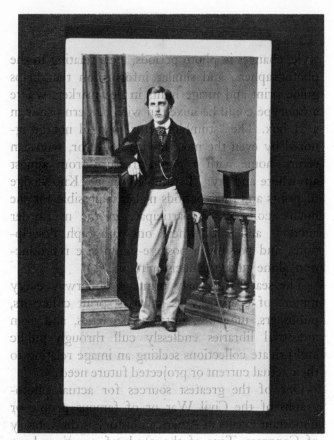

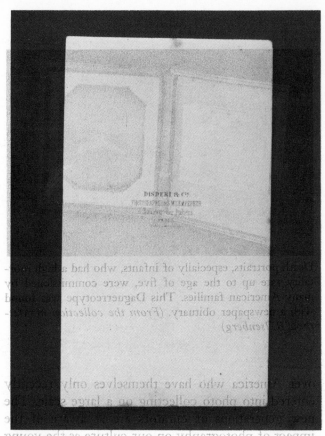

Front and back of actual carte de visite by French photographer Disdéri who is credited with popularization of the card-size portrait, starting in America about 1860. *(From the collection of the author)*

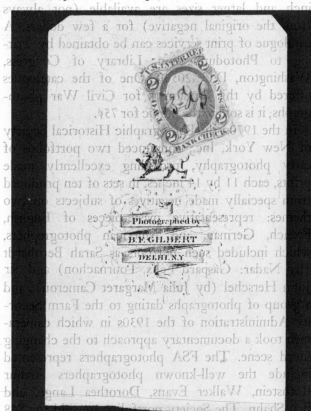

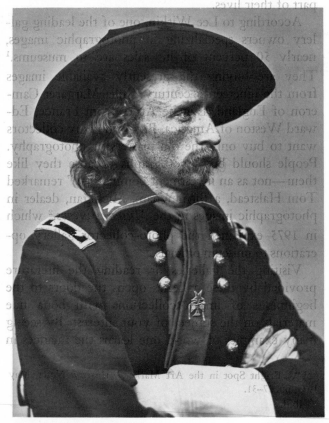

Tax stamps on the back of photographs date photographs to period of the tax law, 1864–1866. *(From the collection of the author)*

Portrait of Custer by Mathew B. Brady is part of the negative collection at Library of Congress. *(Photograph courtesy of GAF)*

Imprint on reverse of a carte de visite from the Brady studios. Brady led the photography effort during the Civil War.

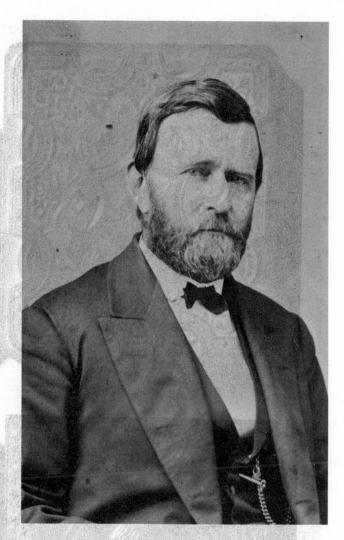

A carte de visite by Brady's National Photographic Portrait Galleries of General and President U. S. Grant with Brady studio identification. *(From the collection of the author)*

plus $2 shipping and can be obtained by writing to the Photographic Historical Society of New York, P.O. Box 1839, Radio City Station, New York, New York 10019. These prints have been acquired by museums and educators who recognize in these images the foremost examples of both early and contemporary photography.

Even a bookstore may be the source of excellent photographic collectibles—if the bookstore also sells used magazines. A single copy of the magazine, *Camera Work*, fifty issues of which were published during 1902–1917, edited by Alfred Stieglitz, is worth over $100. Print collectors have learned that each issue contains one or more specially made photo prints, any of which is worth $100 or more in today's print market.

Stereo-card collecting adds a further dimension of excitement, since these widely available "dimen-sional" photographs (see Chapter 5, "Stereo Cameras and Stereography") may be found at many antique shops and flea markets along with the boxes of ordinary postcards. One stereo card may be worth only the 25¢ or 50¢ asked. The very next one in the stack may be an Anthony scene of New York or a Langenheim of the 1850s which could be worth $10 or more.

Collectors of photographic prints inevitably find photography itself as the subject in fine art etchings, often by famous artists. The pages of *Chari-vari*, a French newspaper of the 1800s, are the source for Honoré Daumier lithographs, many of which show the role of photography in the life of the bourgeoisie. A number of Daumier illustrations poke fun at the subjects who expect to be aggrandized; others poke at the foibles of the photographer-artist himself as in the well-known Daumier

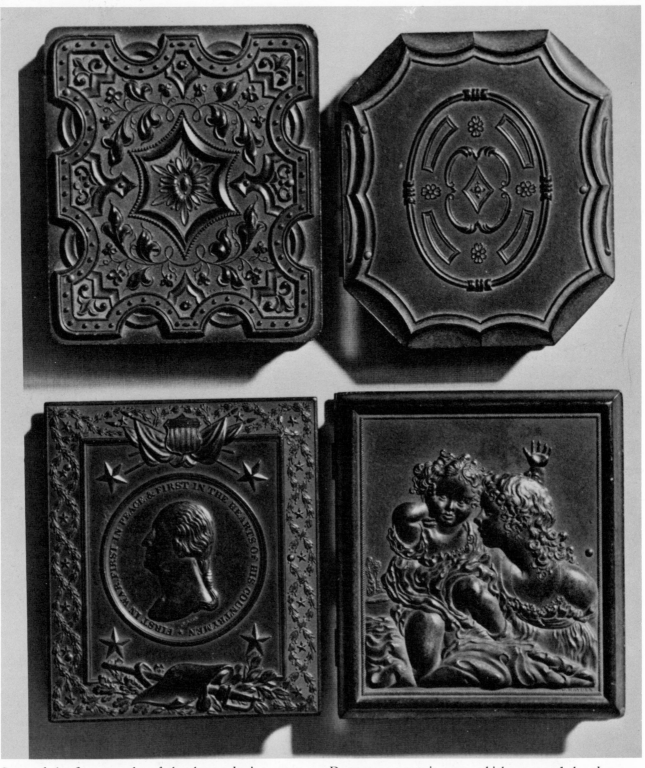

Some of the first examples of the thermoplastic process are Daguerrean portrait cases, which protected the glass-covered silver images on copper plates. Many case designs are rare today, and collectors will spend hundreds of dollars for choice examples of hard-to-find designs. *(From the collection of Alan and Paulette Cotter)*

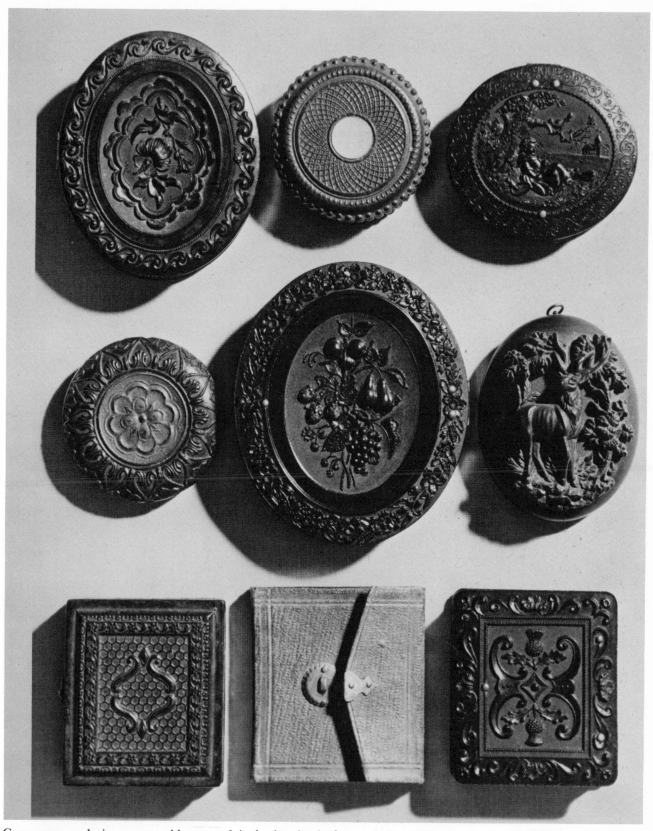

Cases were made in squares, oblongs, and in leather book-closure designs. The round cases (called Oreo cookies by today's collector) are threaded sections which must be unscrewed. *(From the collection of Alan and Paulette Cotter)*

15

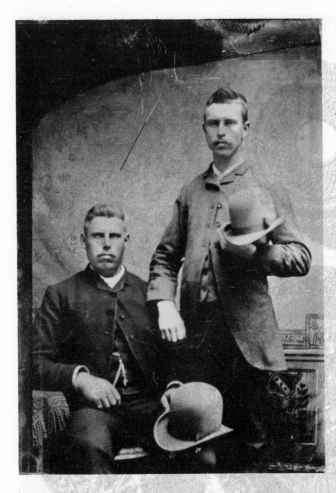

Tintypes, photographs on black-lacquered thin iron sheets, remained a popular and low-cost photographic process for the years from the Civil War to the 1930s. *(From the collection of the author)*

Mementoes of the circus included photographic novelty cartes de visite of the sideshow. Admiral Dot was a midget whose photograph was distributed by E. and H. T. Anthony & Co., photo suppliers, and the "Wild Men of Borneo" pose tranquilly for the Barnum circus portrait. *(From the collection of John Dobran)*

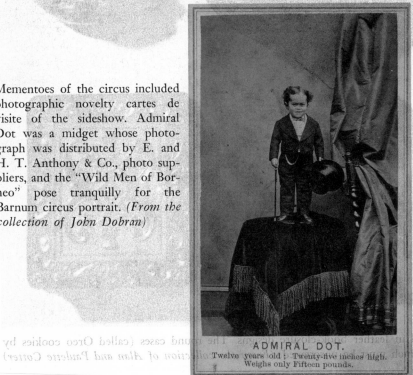

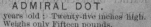

ADMIRAL DOT.
Twelve years old ; Twenty-five inches high.
Weighs only Fifteen pounds.

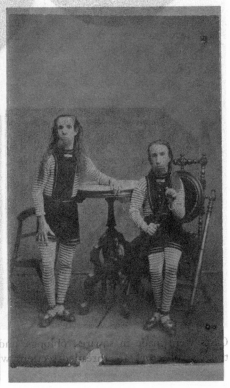

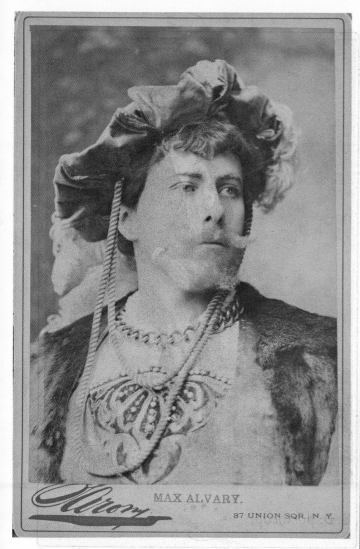

MAX ALVARY.

87 UNION SQR., N.Y.

One of America's early theatrical photographers was Napoleon Sarony who photographed Shakespearean actor Max Alvary. *(From the collection of the author)*

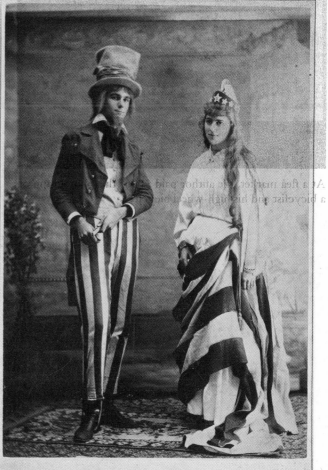

601 Fulton St, Brooklyn, N.Y.   *Durand and Moore*   34 Cherry St, Rahway, N.J.

The most popular photograph size of the late nineteenth century was the cabinet photo, 4¼ by 6½ inches. This costume portrait was possibly for a school play. *(From the collection of John Dobran)*

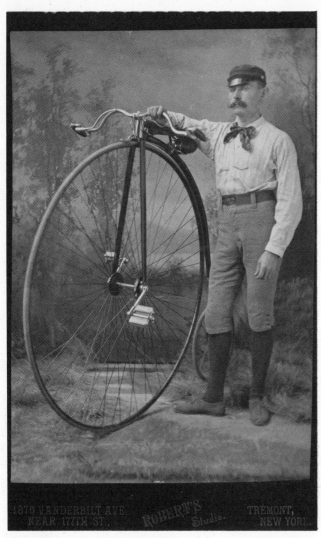

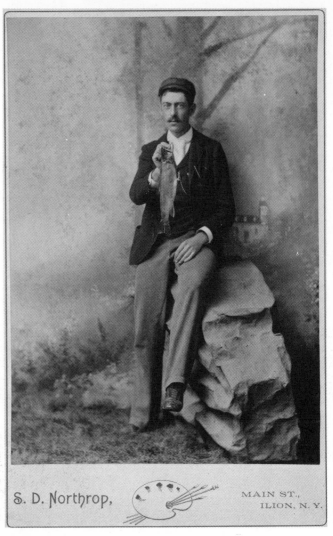

At a flea market, the author paid $1 for this photograph of a bicyclist and his high-wheel bicycle.

Most props in studio photographs were hats, canes, or Bibles. This is an unusual cabinet photo. *(From the collection of the author)*

(FACING)

The Steerage by Alfred Stieglitz (1864–1946), one of the most famous of early twentieth-century photographers, has brought as much as $4,500 in a recent auction for a single signed print. *(Photograph from the Masterpiece Collection of the Photographic Historical Society of New York)*

18

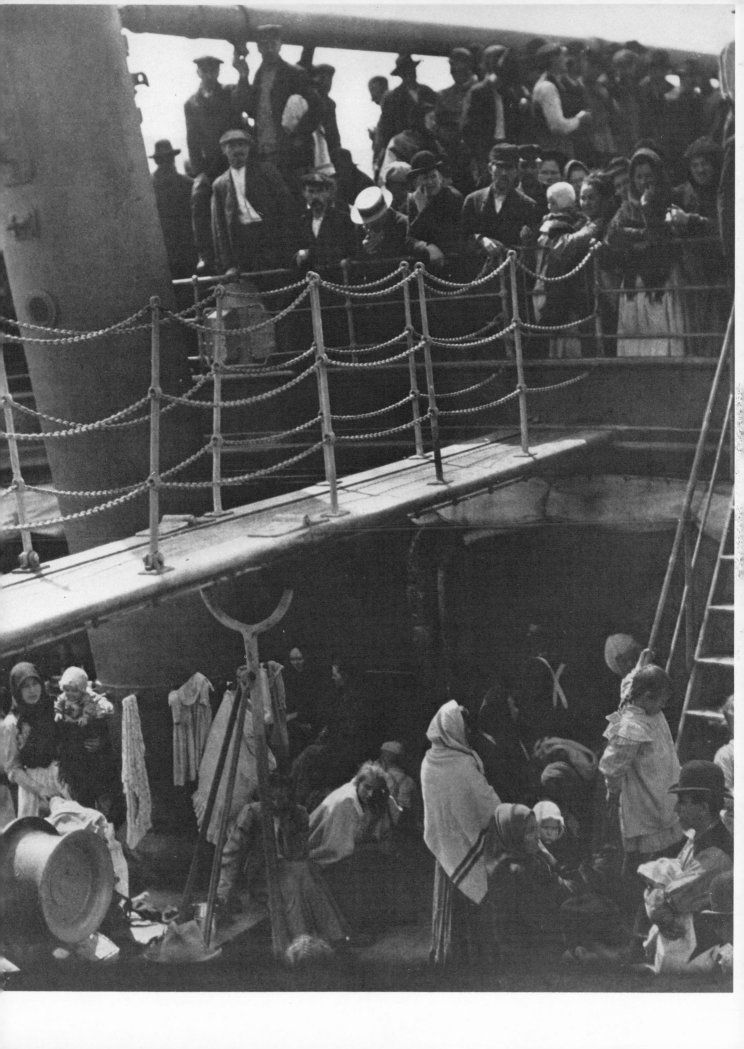

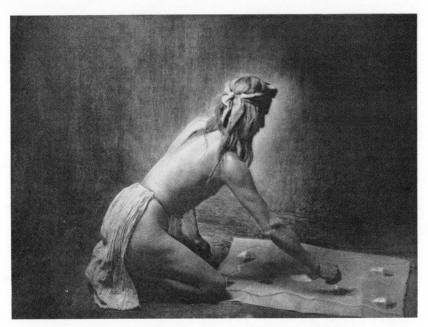

Financier J. P. Morgan commissioned photographer Edward S. Curtis to document the Indian tribes of America. *Apache Medicine Man* is one of over 100,000 negatives. Today collectors will pay over $100 for a single page from the photogravure prints from the volumes of the project. Recent new prints from the plates are sold for $60. Photocopies in duotone (by the offset process) are selling for $6 in art stores. Now collectors are asking: Where are the original prints? *(Photograph from the North American Indian, Inc., Westport, Connecticut)*

widely reproduced in photo-history books: Nadar in the balloon taking the famous aerial photos of the city of Paris before 1860.

Anyone collecting photographica will ultimately acquire one or another image: a Daguerreotype portrait, a Civil War albumen print, a post-mortem photograph (portraits of deceased family members, very often infants); and these images make it easier for anyone collecting photographica to explain the role of the camera in terms of the kind of photograph it makes possible. (For example, certain features of stereo cameras make stereo photographs possible, etc.)

For a fun start in photo collecting, there's a way to begin with fun images: the images of the tintype (see Glossary) photographer. Many people today remember the jolly day at the beach that more often than not included a visit to the tintype parlor. There, for 25¢ or 50¢ a merry portrait was taken against a silly seaside backdrop—a perfect souvenir of the occasion. Tens of thousands of these tintypes are available at this very minute at every flea market in America. You are looking for a photograph on a bit of "tin" (lacquered iron) about the size of a playing card or smaller; the cost is 50¢ or a dollar. It can be your start of a collection of genuine Americana. Look hard; the man in the picture might be your uncle.

Full (whole) plate	6½ × 8½ inches
Half plate	4¼ × 6½ inches
Quarter plate	3¼ × 4¼ inches
One-sixth plate	2¾ × 3¼ inches
One-eighth plate	2⅛ × 3¼ inches
One-sixteenth plate	1⅝ × 2⅛ inches

While there were cases for the half- and full-plate sizes, many were framed under glass in ornate carved frames for the wall. The most popular of the smaller size Daguerreotypes are believed to be the one-sixth size plates most commonly found in antique shops today. Daguerrean images were also made in round shapes about the size of a quarter. For protection the images were inserted in a special round case with screw-apart lid and base or a woman's locket or a man's pocketwatch. Smaller sizes were made to fit into rings and cuff links.

Picture size was arranged by choice of lens and manipulation of masks in the camera back or within the plate-holder with the subject advising the photographer beforehand of his choice of size (as this usually also determined the final cost). According to Robert Taft's *Photography and the American Scene* a typical price paid for photography was indicated by the records kept by Utica, New York photographer D. D. T. Davie, who kept a careful account of his business. In 1853 Davie averaged $2.53 for the one-sixth–plate size and $4.35 for the quarter-plate size.

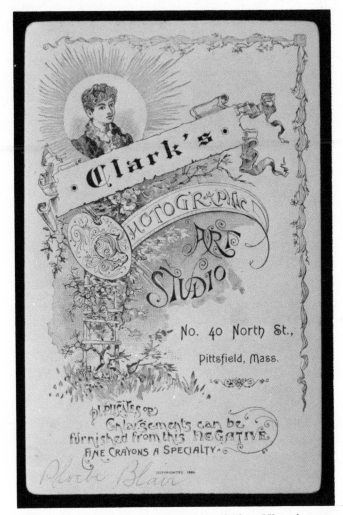

Rear side of cabinet photographs display Victorian art, often of interesting line and itself displayable. (*From the collection of the author*)

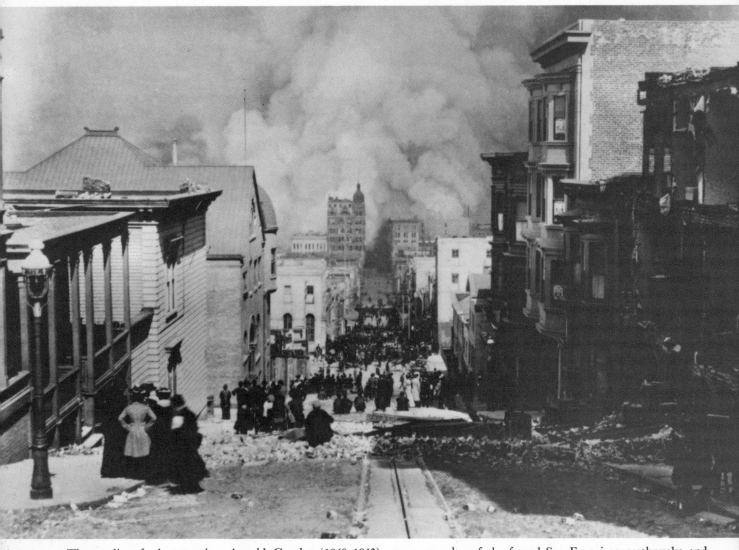

The studio of photographer Arnold Genthe (1869–1942) was a casualty of the famed San Francisco earthquake and fire. The photographer borrowed a small folding camera and produced some of the great documentary photographs of the event before he went onto a career photographing the famed personalities of art, dance, music, and politics in the 1920s. (The San Francisco Earthquake *from the Masterpiece Collection of the Photographic Historical Society of New York*)

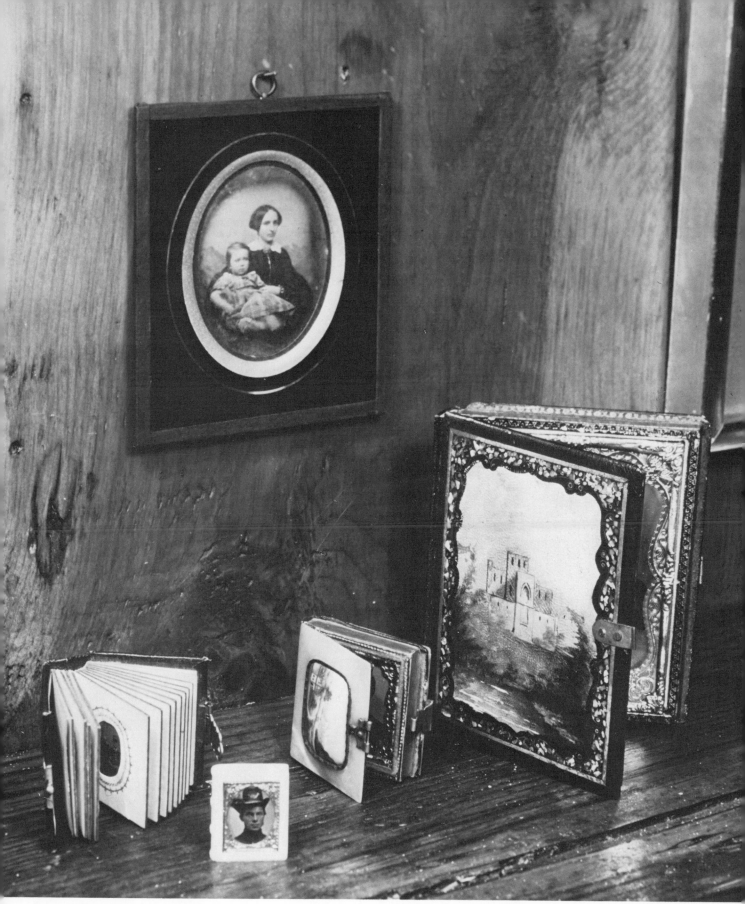

During the nineteenth century, photographic processes developed which put the photographic image on wood, porcelain, ivory, metal, paper, glass, and other materials. Photographs became a part of decorative items, vases, jewelry, and other personal items. *(From the collection of Matthew R. Isenberg)*

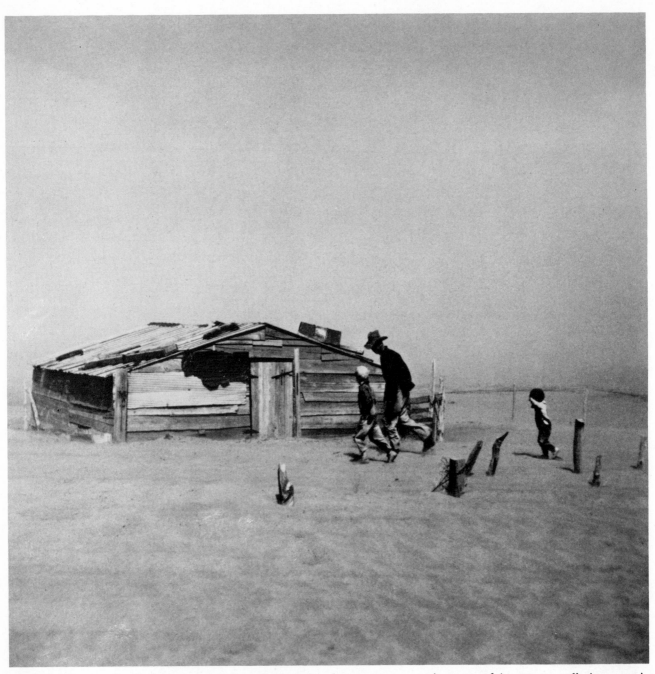

Collecting the work of contemporary photographers has become a new major area of interest as galleries open in major cities. Modern collectibles are such photographs as *Dust Bowl* by Arthur Rothstein. *(Photograph from FSA Photographers' Portfolio of the Photographic Historical Society of New York)*

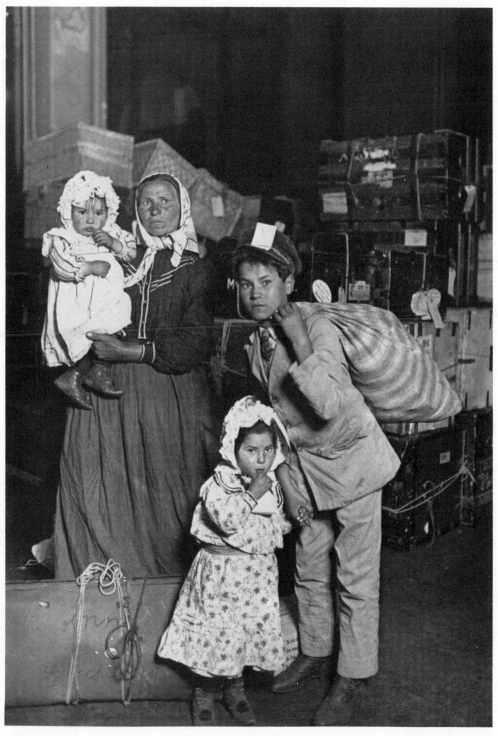

Work scenes and social documentaries by such photographers as Lewis W. Hine or Margaret Bourke-White are usually only available today from galleries and at auction. *Italian Family at Ellis Island—1905* by Lewis W. Hine is from his documentation of immigrants in the early part of the twentieth century. *(Photograph from Masterpiece Collection of the Photographic Historical Society of New York)*

25

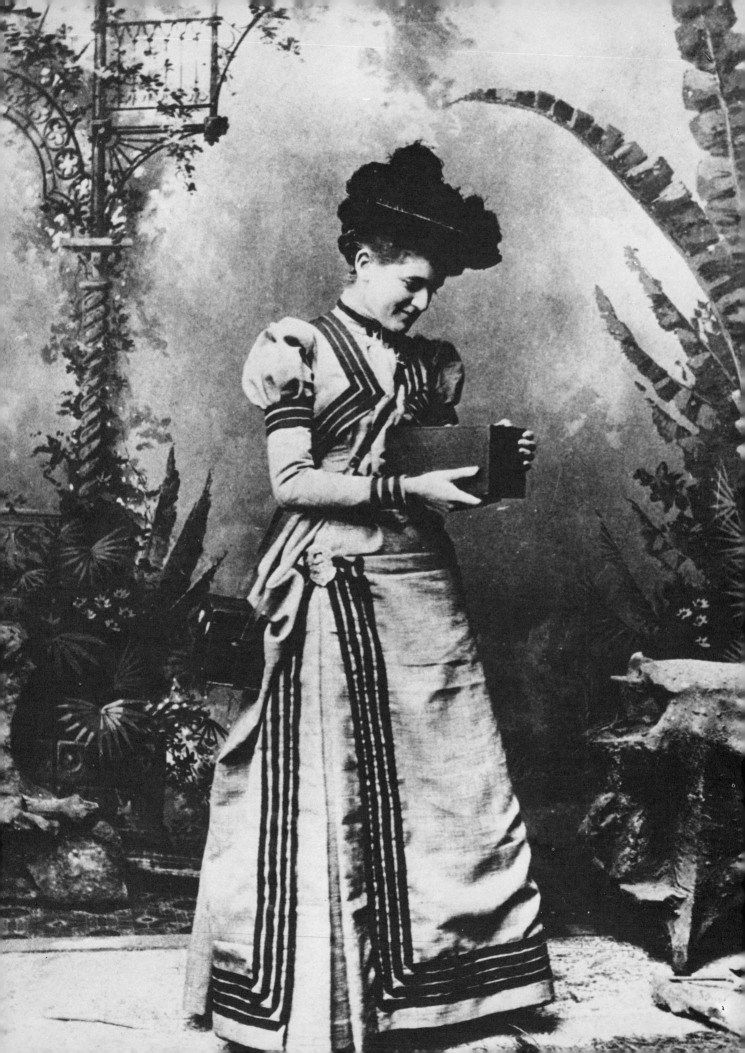

2
Box Cameras

- The prephotography camera obscura, which was mother to the need for the invention of photography, was a box.
- The first camera (Nicéphore Niépce, France, 1816) was a box.
- The first commercial camera (for Daguerreotypy, 1839) was a box.
- The first mass-produced practical family camera (Kodak, 1888) was a box.
- The most popular economically priced panoramic camera was a box.
- The tintype camera used in the parks and on the streets of America in the first half of the twentieth century was a box.

This list could go on and on. The box camera, with its simple lens up front and film or plate at back, with its black leather strap to hold a wood, paper, cardboard, metal, or plastic box, was the workhorse of American family photography starting in the 1880s and continuing to the present tiny drop-in–load candy-bar–shaped cameras of this generation.

DRY-PLATE PHOTOGRAPHY

The contribution in America of George Eastman was to present to the world an existing box-camera format comparable to the detective cameras (see Chapter 4, "Detective Cameras and Later Novelty Cameras") but preloaded with a 100-shot roll of film.

(FACING)
The Kodak, first roll-film box camera by George Eastman. *(Photograph courtesy of Eastman Kodak Company)*

For developing, one returned camera, film, and all to the factory. The starting point for this incredibly simple system ("You press the button; we do the rest," said the Kodak ads of the time) was the simple-to-build leather-covered wooden box. But Eastman had numerous existing box cameras to study before patenting his smaller preloaded one.

In the period prior to the Kodak camera, an important development in photographic chemistry had made a revolutionary change in the photographer's working procedure. New developments made possible the dry plate (see Glossary), successor to the wet plate, (see Glossary), which had been the material for the universally employed photographic process from about 1854 to the late 1870s. In this cumbersome method, photographers afield carried tents in which they could prepare their light-sensitive emulsion, flowing it in liquid form onto clean panes of glass, then rushing the still tacky-wet newly sensitized plate into cameras

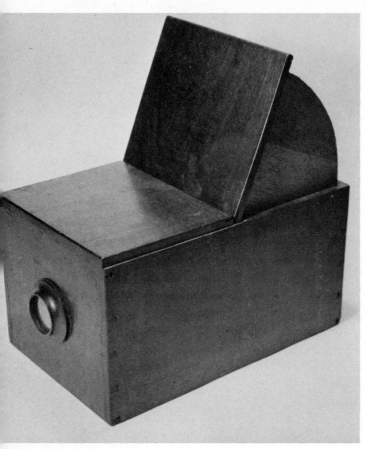

Camera obscura from the collection of Allen and Hilary Weiner.

It was in the making of the dry plates in 1881 that Eastman started his career with the first of his companies, the Eastman Dry Plate Company. He learned of wet-plate photography while getting ready for a Caribbean vacation, and then he learned of the simpler dry-plate process that was available to English practitioners. He never traveled to the Caribbean; he went to England instead and returned to America to invent a machine that would coat a glass plate with an even layer of the new emulsion. He conducted his experiments on his mother's kitchen table.

The new dry plates manufactured by Eastman and others who saw the future of photography in the potential of the dry-plate process were not only more convenient, they eventually offered a greater sensitivity to light than the "home brew" of the wet-plate era. Exposures could not only be shorter, they could be instantaneous in bright daylight conditions. The new dry plate set the stage for a camera

for exposures of a few seconds up to a minute, depending on light, lens, and subject matter. Back in the tents, the newly exposed wet plate would be immediately processed and finally air-dried on the site before returning to the city or studio.

The dry plate, a factory-coated pane of glass with a durable sensitized emulsion, could be loaded into holders prior to any photo excursion and then developed upon the photographer's return. Except for Polaroid photography, this "shoot first, develop later" procedure is followed today for those portions of photography that still depend on the blackening of silver to create a photographic image, as in studio portraits that are not in color. To the new generation of photographers working with electronic cameras and instant replay of tape-recorded full-color images, even dry-plate photography is as primitive as the wet-plate process, which died of time exposure one hundred years ago.

Artist's Sketching Camera. Given for one new name.

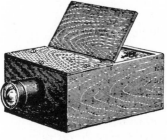

This cut represents a boy in the act of sketching a landscape with the camera. It can be used out of doors as well as in the house. This is one of the most attractive premiums we offer. We have used several thousand of these cameras, and they give great satisfaction.

With it boys and girls can sketch any landscape, or any object both near and far, in a few moments. It does not require previous practice. The Camera is 8 inches long, 5½ inches wide and 4 inches high. Below we show a diagram that will make its working plain.

The rays of light proceeding from an object at the point A will pass through the Lens and Tube at B, and will strike on the mirror placed at right angles at C. From the mirror they will be reflected up, and the picture will be distinctly seen upon the ground glass at D. Place a sheet of paper over the glass and with a pencil trace the picture.

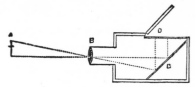

Given for only one name. **Postage and packing, 21 cts.**

We offer it for sale, including the payment of postage by us, for $1.25.

Advertisement for a camera obscura from *Youth's Companion*, ca. 1885.

28

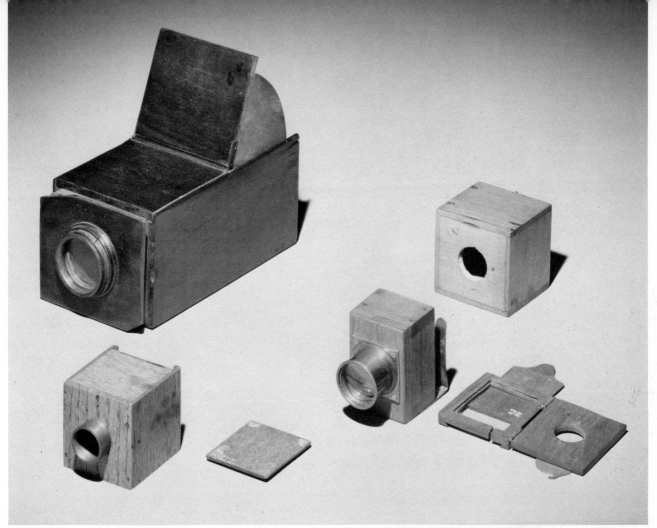

The principles of the camera obscura *(top left)* were created in primitive box cameras of William Henry Fox Talbot (1800–1877), father of the on-paper negative-positive photographic process (calotypes, Talbotypes). Mrs. Talbot referred to her husband's experimental cameras as his "mousetraps." *(Photograph courtesy of Eastman Kodak Company)*

that would no longer be immobile on the tripod; it could be hand-held for the brief exposure.

A new kind of photography was born along with the new photographic plate. While professional photographers were able to load their existing view cameras with the new films, a new camera design was born that could permit the first "candid" photography. The new camera did not announce itself as a camera with the familiar bellows, tripod legs, and protruding brass-mount lens. The new camera for the new plate was an innocuous box.

"A bewildering array of hand cameras appeared on the market in the 1880s. Many held several plates in a magazine, so that the photographer could take a dozen or more exposures without reloading," pointed out Beaumont Newhall.[1]

Many of this group were deliberately designed to mask their true function, built to resemble a workman's toolbox, a lunchbox, a doctor's satchel, and even in completely hidden forms such as hats, books, and even walking sticks.

One of the most popular of the hidden camera forms was R. D. Gray's Patent Concealed Vest Camera of 1886, which was a round metal can that was hung under a vest. It took pictures through a buttonhole of the vest. (See Chapter 4, "Detective Cameras and Later Novelty Cameras.")

[1] *The History of Photography from 1839 to the Present Day*, p. 89.

29

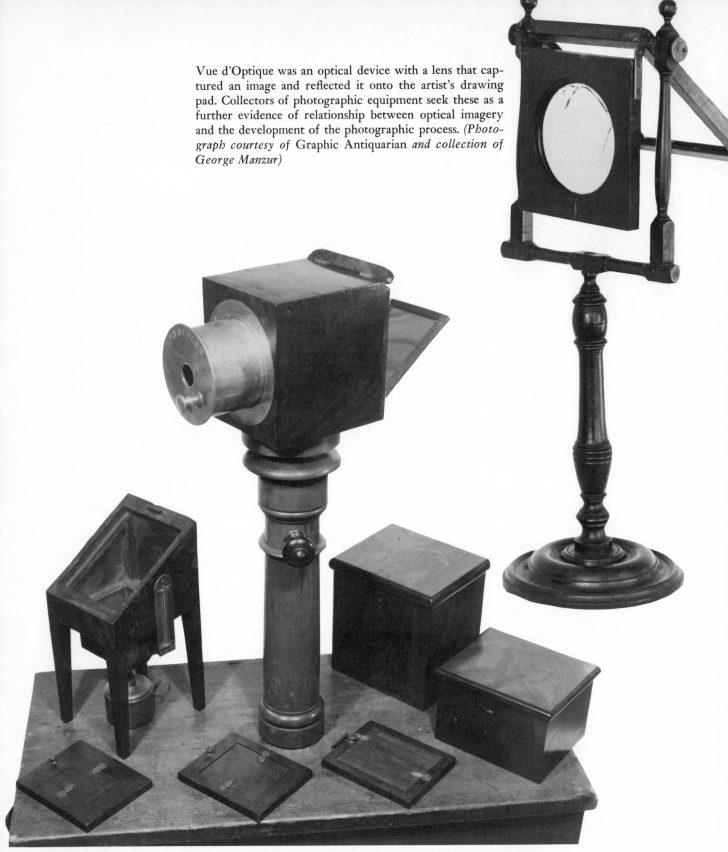

Vue d'Optique was an optical device with a lens that captured an image and reflected it onto the artist's drawing pad. Collectors of photographic equipment seek these as a further evidence of relationship between optical imagery and the development of the photographic process. *(Photograph courtesy of* Graphic Antiquarian *and collection of George Manzur)*

One of the most exciting finds in Daguerrean equipment is this complete portable Daguerrean system, New York-made (ca. 1843) by William H. Butler. It includes a quarter-plate camera, iodine and bromine sensitizing box, mercury fuming chamber, spirit lamp, and the unipod which permitted the camera to be taken on location. The outfit was found by Jerome Sprung in an antique armaments shop just outside New York City where it was displayed as Civil War equipment. *(From the collection of Jerry and Shirley Sprung)*

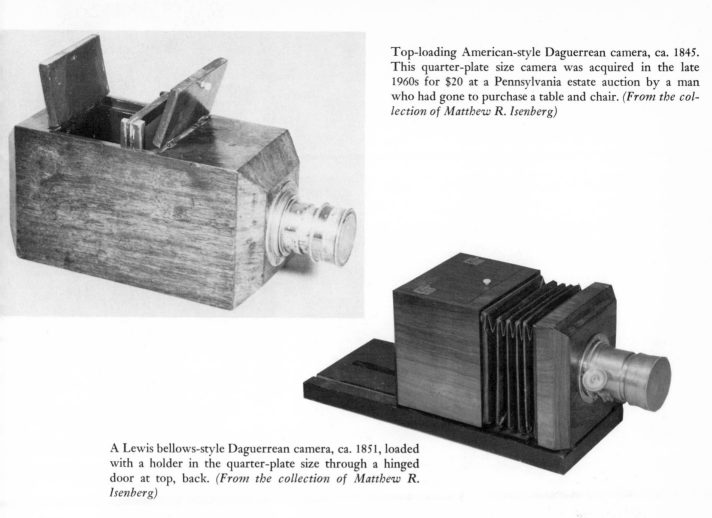

Top-loading American-style Daguerrean camera, ca. 1845. This quarter-plate size camera was acquired in the late 1960s for $20 at a Pennsylvania estate auction by a man who had gone to purchase a table and chair. *(From the collection of Matthew R. Isenberg)*

A Lewis bellows-style Daguerrean camera, ca. 1851, loaded with a holder in the quarter-plate size through a hinged door at top, back. *(From the collection of Matthew R. Isenberg)*

Thus, the gentleman standing at the corner watching the children at play or the ladies pausing at a window display photographically captured his subjects, who were totally unaware that at a moment of lull in their boulevard perambulations, a shutter had surreptitiously *clicked* to capture the moment. The detective-camera era had begun; and the most typical detective camera was a box!

The box-shaped detective cameras were made by every camera manufacturer of the day for a dozen years (1883–1895), usually in large sizes to permit the use of large plates for large-size contact prints. Prominent among these are now long-gone historic names as the Blair, the Waterbury, the Peerless, the Anthony PDQ (Photography Done Quickly), the Hetherington, the Premier, and the Hawk-Eye. Many were made in handsome woods; others were hidden in satchels of leather. The first models were loaded with glass plates from holders stored in the side or at the rear of the longish box. Models appearing before 1890, such as the Hawk-Eye of 1889, introduced after Eastman had revolutionized the photographic world with his smaller camera and its 100-shot load, were also to be used with flexible film loaded into the roll holder in a darkroom.

The Hawk-Eye was, according to advertisements of the period, the "$15.00 Detective and Combination camera . . . containing a coil of sensitized film for taking 100 different pictures without refilling, $25." A smaller camera for plates only, appropriately named the Lilliput, in the shape of a small satchel, was sold "complete with non-actobic lamp [a darkroom lamp] and 108 dry plates (2½ by 2½ inches)" for $25.

31

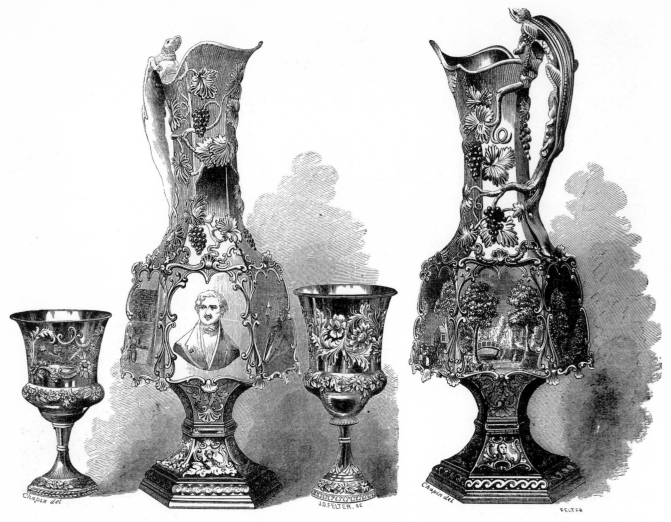

In the early 1850s, Edward Anthony, leading photographic supplier of the Daguerrean period, created these silver objects (a massive 20-inch-high silver pitcher with portraits of Daguerre and Niépce plus two goblets) as prizes in a contest for the best full-plate Daguerreotypes taken prior to November 1, 1853. This illustration is from *Gleason's Pictorial Drawing-Room Companion*, one of the papers announcing the competition. The first-prize winner was New York photographer Jeremiah Gurney; the second prize went to Samuel Root. Collectors today would like to know where these valuable silver prizes can be found. *(Illustration from the collection of the author)*

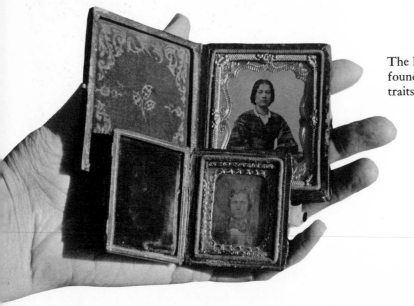

The Daguerreotypes and ambrotypes *(top)* most commonly found in antique shops today are unidentifiable family portraits, usually one-ninth and one-sixth plate sizes.

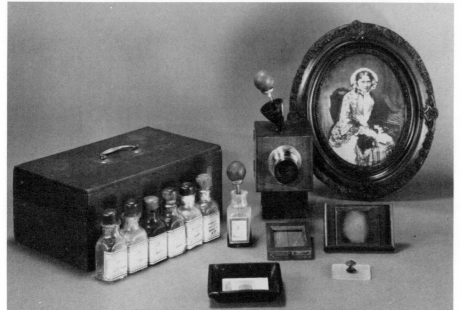

Collectors of nineteenth-century photographic equipment seek the Dubroni camera and its processing system, which permitted the photographer to develop the glass plate within the camera after exposure. The box-shaped camera resembles Daguerrean equipment but actually dates to the early 1860s. *(Photograph courtesy of Agfa-Gevaert-Foto-museum)*

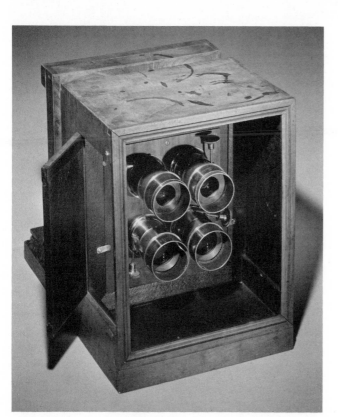

A studio camera, ca. 1870, with four lenses permitted four exposures on a single full plate to obtain four quarter-plates. *(Photograph courtesy of Eastman Kodak Company)*

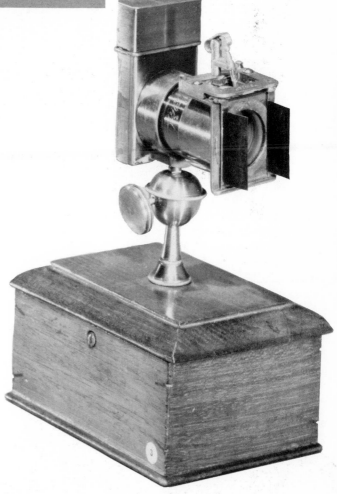

English miniature wet-plate camera of the 1850s: the *Pistolgraph* by Thomas Skaife. It reputedly nearly caused his arrest when he pointed it, gun-fashion, at Queen Victoria. *(Photograph courtesy of Eastman Kodak Company)*

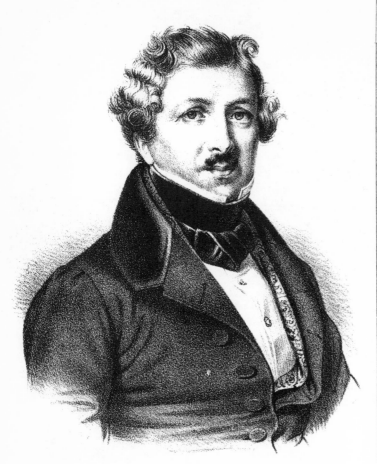

Louis Jacques Mandé Daguerre (1787–1851). His partnership with experimenter Nicéphore Niépce finally permitted a fixed image on silver-coated copper. Without a negative, his inflexible process crumbled when photography on paper, later on glass, became the processes that led to photography's rapid growth.

Early newspaper account of first exhibit of Daguerreotypes in America.

Billboard by a traveling photographer offers "likenesses of Adults" in cloudy and clear weather. Children (less able to hold still) were photographed in high-noon light only. *(From the collection of John Dobran)*

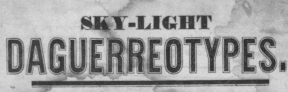

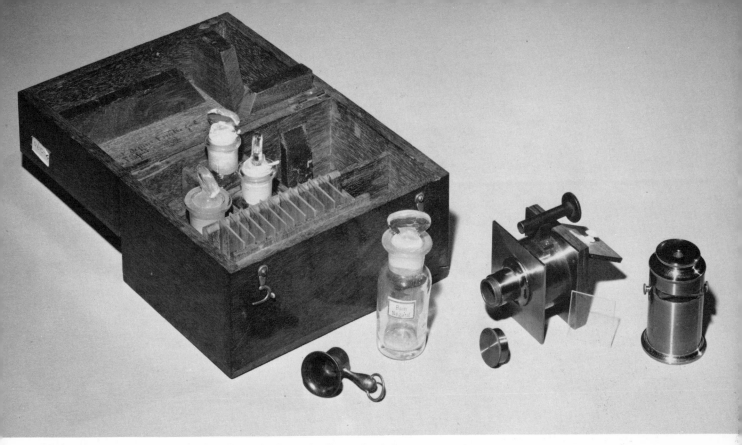

In the 1860s, a camera system in a box, the Bertsch all-metal miniature, took pictures on 1-by-1-inch glass. *(Photograph courtesy of Eastman Kodak Company)*

THE KODAK LAUNCHES FAMILY PHOTOGRAPHY

In most cases before the development of the Kodak camera of 1888, the most common detective camera was a box camera, often a foot long or longer, always bulky and inclined to being heavy when loaded with holders full of glass. So when Eastman's company announced a detective-styled but smaller camera in 1888, the photographic world took instant notice. He called it the Kodak camera and showed it in the hand to make the point of its small size, only 3¼ by 3¾ by 6½ inches. Said his introductory advertising:

It is a magazine camera, and will make 100 pictures without reloading. The operation of taking the picture is simply to point the camera and press a button. The picture is taken instantaneously on a strip of sensitive film, which is moved into position by turning a key.

Fifty years later, the Kodak cameras were essentially the same in numerous Brownie, Hawk-Eye, and other Kodak-owned versions. Press a button—and turn a key. With this concept, a new possession joined the list of family-owned luxury items, along with the bicycle, the typewriter, the binoculars, and other evidences of family prosperity.

The first design was made available in two sizes. The very first Kodak camera took round pictures, each 2½ inches in diameter mounted on a neat permanent board of the type used by professional portrait studios of the period. The second model was a larger camera called the Kodak No.2. Its 4½-by-5-by-9-inch box was factory loaded for 60 exposures, each of which was returned after processing as a circular picture 3½ inches in diameter. Film was available for loading this model with a 100-exposure roll, which was the same capacity of the first model. Collectors can still find these circular photographs in the postcard boxes and print boxes of antique shops, where they are sold for $1 to $2 each.

The flexible film that was loaded into the camera at the factory and then processed by Eastman's plant at Rochester, New York, was a gelatin-supported emulsion on paper. But after 1889 the film was actually on a clear celluloid.

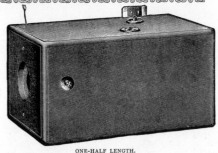

Size:
3¼ x 3¼ x 6½ inches.

Weight:
1 lb. 10 oz.

Price, $25.00.

Loaded for 100 pictures, including Sole Leather Carrying case with Strap.

Size of Picture:
2⅝ inches in diameter.

ONE-HALF LENGTH.

The Kodak Camera.

ANYBODY who can wind a watch can use the Kodak Camera. It is a magazine camera, and will make 100 pictures without reloading. The operation of taking the picture is simply to point the camera and press a button. The picture is taken instantaneously on a strip of sensitive film, which is moved into position by turning a key.

❋ ❋ A DIVISION OF LABOR. ❋ ❋

After the 100 pictures have been taken, the strip of film (which is wound on a spool) may be removed, and sent by mail to the factory to have the pictures finished. Any amateur can finish his own pictures, and any number of duplicates can be made of each picture. A spool of film to reload the camera for 100 pictures costs only $2.00.

No tripod is required, no focusing, no adjustment whatever. Rapid rectilinear lens. The Kodak will photograph anything, still or moving, indoors or out.

❋ ❋ A PICTURESQUE DIARY ❋ ❋

Of your trip to Europe, to the mountains, or the sea-shore, may be obtained without trouble with a Kodak Camera, that will be worth a hundred times its cost in after years.

 ❋ A BEAUTIFUL INSTRUMENT ❋

Is the Kodak, covered with dark Turkey morocco, nickel and lacquered brass trimmings, inclosed in a neat sole leather carrying case with shoulder-strap—about the size of a large field-glass.

Send for a copy of the **KODAK PRIMER** with Kodak photograph.

The Eastman Dry Plate and Film Co.

Branch, 115 Oxford Street, London.   ROCHESTER, N. Y.

George Eastman brings a simple-to-use roll-film, factory-loaded camera to the American family in 1888 with this announcement of the Kodak (a coined word he thought people would easily remember). Another camera of the period was called the Knack.

All of the Kodak box cameras of the period that followed took either rectangular or square photographs. All of the first cameras from 1888 to 1892, with the exception of the low-cost "ordinary" wooden-box Kodak model, repeated the trim, black, oblong look and the neatly black-leather–covered appearance. The successor models were factory loaded with 48, 60, or 100 exposures—even up to 150 exposures (see "A Brief History of Most Eastman Kodak Cameras" in Appendix C).

Eastman made it convenient for the camera to be returned to Rochester for the processing of the film, the printing of the successful frames, and the reloading with fresh film. The reloaded camera was then returned with the negatives and the prints to the camera owner, who had waited without a camera to see what the $10 sent to the Eastman Dry Plate and Film Company would bring. *Would the pictures come out?* This question plagued many, since the cameras had no "aiming" devices and focusing was actually a hit-or-miss proposition. But shortly after the camera was introduced, photographers with the skill to process their own films were given the option of processing and reloading the camera at home.

These earliest cameras, the factory preloads, are especially sought by the camera collector as the *pièce de résistance* of any collection of American or box cameras. The first camera, the Kodak camera, finished in "dark Turkey morocco" in clean condition and preferably with its over-the-shoulder case, is readily sold to a collector for $2,000 or more.

Collectors at auctions and flea markets are endlessly hoping to find these earliest Kodak cameras among the tens of thousands of black box cameras that appear on counters at flea markets on any weekend. These earliest Kodak products are most easily identified by the fact that they incorporate a string-set shutter. (A string emerges from a hole at camera top; it must be pulled before each exposure to cock the shutter mechanism. In the very first model of the very first Kodak camera, the pull of the string set the shutter for a series of exposures.)

Eastman's 1891 plan for a camera that could be easily loaded with film in daylight was a revolutionary one. Cameras would no longer be shipped to the factory by the family photographer; he would load the film in the camera himself. These new cameras were called the Daylight Kodak cameras. The film, in its light-protected cardboard carton, was called a cartridge. The first cartridges moved film in the camera from one lighttight paper box into another. The concept of a *roll* of film with a black paper leader feeding from one spool to another with a wide spool end (flange) to protect the film from the intrusion of light was introduced a year later in the Boston Camera Company's Bull's-Eye camera. This camera was loaded with film that had a paper backing on which were printed num-

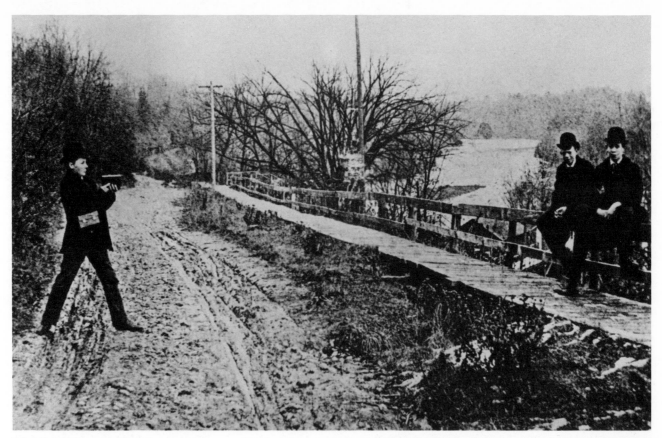

The Kodak could only be pointed—not aimed. There was no provision for a viewfinder or a ground glass for focus. *(Photograph courtesy of International Museum of Photography at George Eastman House)*

bers that could be viewed through the little red window in the camera's back.

This innovation was so important that in 1895, rather than continue to pay royalties, Eastman chose to buy the company making the Bull's-Eye. In that momentous year, Kodak introduced the Pocket Kodak, the Bullet, and their own version of the Bull's-Eye, all using the ruby window for viewing exposure sequence numbers. That system has held in one form or another to this day.

Film cartridges were made in a variety of sizes, since the newly emerging line of Kodak cameras were to be of different sizes. The range at first was from the smallest, which was to fit the smallest Eastman camera (the Pocket Kodak of 1895 and 1896, only 3¾ by 3 by 2¼ inches), up to the largest of the cartridges, films in rolls so large that the individual frame size was 5 by 7 inches (for the camera known as the No.5 Cartridge Kodak, a folding camera with pull-out bellows).

With the addition of a $5 camera to the Kodak line of box cameras, which had consisted primarily of $15 to $25 cameras, and with Kodak and Kodet* folding cameras appealing to a broad market, by the year 1896 the Eastman Kodak Company had already produced one hundred thousand cameras.

The pictures taken by the tiny Pocket Kodak camera may have been small for the time but their success was enormous. In the period of the detective cameras, Kodak had innovated with an unusually small box and a simple system of photography using film instead of plates. By 1895, Kodak was committed to broadening the market with small hand-held cameras in both box and folding styles. Large-size cameras were from then on only to be made for sale to professionals and the most serious amateurs. That tiny pocket camera, then, came to

* A cheaper version of a Kodak camera.

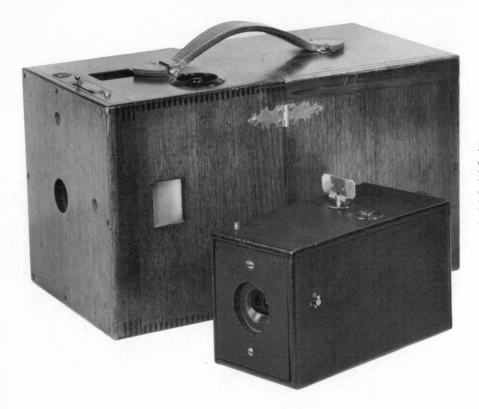

Much smaller than many of the detective cameras of the day, the Kodak looks particularly small compared to the popular Hawk-Eye of the period. *(Photograph by the author)*

At first the Kodak could only be loaded by returning the camera to the factory; later, film rolls were made available to photographers, but the processing of strip film was beyond the skill of the typical family. *(Photograph courtesy of Eastman Kodak Company)*

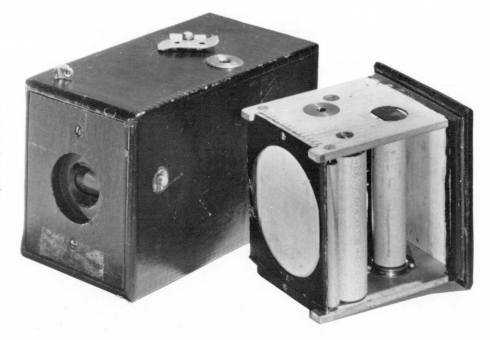

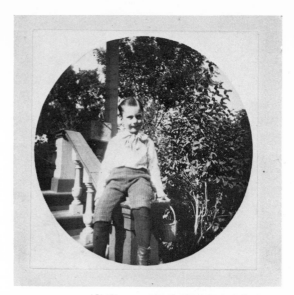

Collectors look for the readily identifiable factory-made prints from the Kodak: round images, each 2½-inch diameter, were mounted on heavy board.

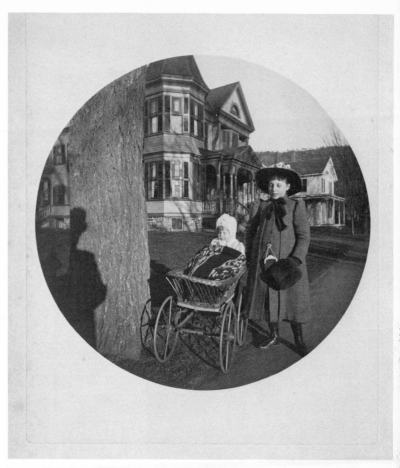

Later Kodak models offered a larger image as this 3½-inch-diameter picture from the Kodak No. 2.

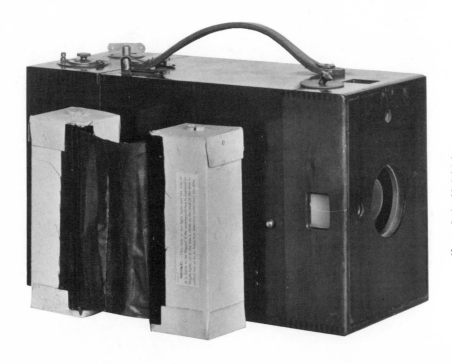

In 1891 Kodak introduced the Daylight Kodak, a camera that the family could load without a darkroom. The cardboard-box system of the time is like today's plastic one. *(Photograph courtesy of Eastman Kodak Company)*

Box cameras, which were glass-plate loaded, were made by a number of companies and as large as the 5-by-7-inch Anthony. *(Photograph courtesy of GAF)*

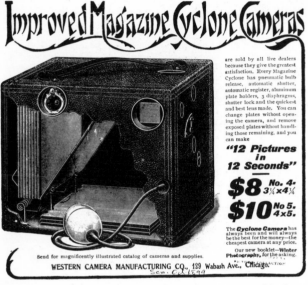

Box cameras incorporated novel features such as this drop-down plate system, which made it unnecessary for the photographer to carry plateholders, ca. 1888.

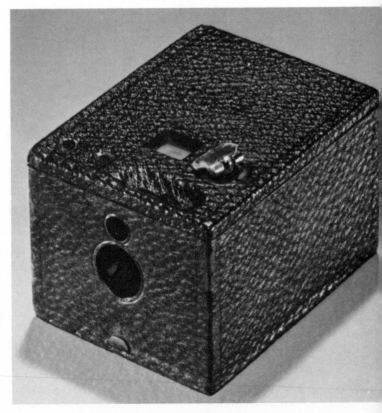

In 1895 Eastman introduced his next major idea in cameras: a still smaller, less expensive camera that could be loaded with roll film in daylight and frame advanced by watching for a number in a red window at the back of the camera. The Pocket Kodak of 1895 was born. It was only 2¼ by 3 by 3¾-inches. *(Photograph courtesy of Eastman Kodak Company)*

The "Bull's Eye."

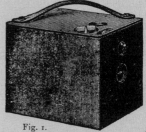

Fig. 1.

Here's Something New. *How would you like to own a Camera that requires no dark room, that can be loaded and emptied in broad daylight, that has an achromatic lens, set to take pictures at any distance from eight feet upward, no "focusing" being required; that measures about 5 x 4 inches, weighs less than two pounds, and costs (that's the wonder of it) only from $8 up to $15—the top price? A brief description may interest you.*

A light-proof cartridge protects the film from light when loading and unloading by an opaque covering, so that one may carry a number of cartridges and take as many pictures as desired, inserting the cartridge and removing after use in broad daylight anywhere — each cartridge containing film for twelve exposures, thus avoiding the winding off of a long roll of film before getting any results. Fig. 1 shows the instrument in its case, and in Fig. 2 the case is removed from the camera. The shutter is always set, and is operated by pushing the spring alternately to right or left. The pointers on the shutter, as seen through the opening through the front of the camera, show which way to push the spring. The shutter is exceedingly simple in construction and the action is instantaneous, though it may also be adjusted for time exposures. The films are numbered from 1 to 12 consecutively in white figures on the back of the black paper strip which covers the film, and this number can be seen through the opening at the back of the camera, thus showing the number that is exposed and enabling one to keep a record of the same.

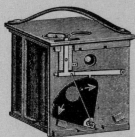

Fig. 2.

Fig. 3 shows the camera open to place the cartridge in position. The seal is cut, and resting the thumb against the cartridge, the end of paper is poked under cross piece, and drawn out about eight inches, as shown in cut. Then turning the camera over, so the reel will be on top and key toward you, pass the paper under cross piece, poke the end through the slot and turn key to left until the paper is secured. Slide the brass cover over the back and slip the camera into the case. A few more turns of the key winds up the opaque material to where the film begins, and camera is then ready for use. A "finder" is provided to locate the view properly, and one has only to aim camera and press the shutter spring for each picture, turning the key to bring a fresh part of the film into position. Fig. 4 shows manner of cutting off films in a dark room preparatory to development; but it is not required for the user to do this, as after removing the cartridges from camera they may be mailed to the factory to have the pictures finished and returned. In the cut the film is shown under the black paper on which the numbers are seen, and the position of each exposure is shown by white marks on the edges of the black paper.

Fig. 3.

Simplicity is the dominant characteristic of this camera, and it is due to this and the improved American methods of grinding lenses by machinery that it is possible to sell a camera giving such a large percentage of good results, and finished in the best possible manner, for a moderate price. The makers issue a fully illustrated book and instructions for operating the "Bull's Eye" camera, which they will be pleased to send, with sample of work, to any address on application. BOSTON CAMERA MFG. CO., 380 Tremont Street, Boston, Mass.

Fig. 4.

In 1892 the Boston Camera Company introduced the Bull's-Eye camera. It was the first to load with a numbered roll film and a red window at back to guide film advance. George Eastman later bought the Boston Camera Company in order to obtain the Bull's-Eye patents so that Kodak could offer cameras with this feature. (*Advertisement from* Century, *June 1894; reprinted from* Photographic Advertising from A-Z)

Any school=boy or girl can make good pictures with one of the Eastman Kodak Co.'s Brownie Cameras

Using the familiar imagery of the Palmer Cox "Brownies" (gnomes who make work easy), a $1 camera is aimed at America's youths in 1900. Collectors look for the various versions of the "first" Brownie which differ in back closure and finish details. The "first" of the first Brownies has a near half-inch-wide box end closing the camera, soon replaced by a thin lid with a metal closure as shown in this advertisement. Brownie packaging exploited the Palmer Cox images.

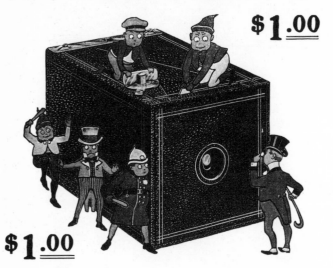

$1.00

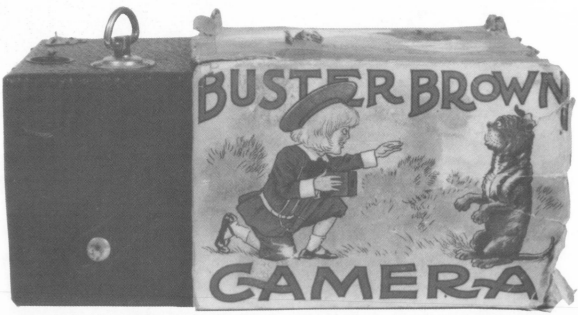

The successful Brownie soon gets look-alike competition: the Buster Brown of the 1900s. *(From the collection of Robert Lesser; photograph courtesy of Stefan Congrat-Butlar)*

signify Kodak as a camera for the family photographer.

The dramatic success of the Kodak cameras was not lost upon its competition. To begin with, Eastman Kodak introduced its own competition to the Kodak camera line with the Flexo and Bullet cameras, which helped to weaken the competition while guaranteeing the circulation of more cameras using Kodak film. E. & H. T. Anthony was aiming at the newly opened family market with a camera called the Buck-Eye. These all were loaded with the important film that Kodak was making available for its own cameras: roll film on a transparent base.

Other companies were introducing smaller box cameras (smaller than the relatively large detective cameras) that were loaded with glass plates. Examples of these are the Anthony Magazine camera (1892) taking 24 pictures, each 4 by 5 inches, and the Magazine Cyclone cameras produced from 1898 to 1907 in different sizes and selling for $6 and up to $10.

The distinguishing feature of these box cameras, whose exteriors were essentially nondescript leather-covered black boxes, is not evident to the visitors to antique shops and thrift stores. There box cameras may be lined up on a shelf, looking like brothers and cousins, often without identification marks on the outside (but usually well marked once the rear lid has been opened). However, they do have a distinguishing feature, and it is simply the fact that these cameras were loaded with glass plates. Some of the cameras were made large enough to store three or more double-side plate-holders of the type common to the professional photographer's view camera. Others, such as the Cyclones, stored glass plates within the body of the camera, with ingenious systems of changing plates, differentiating one camera from another. In the more interesting variants, gravity systems were used to "drop" the exposed plate to the floor of the camera while a spring pushed the fresh plate into the film plane. In one camera, the Velox, the camera was turned upside down after each exposure to "drop" the plate.

If people were going to buy plate-loaded box cameras, then Kodak could not ignore the market in which it had first begun its now-growing empire.

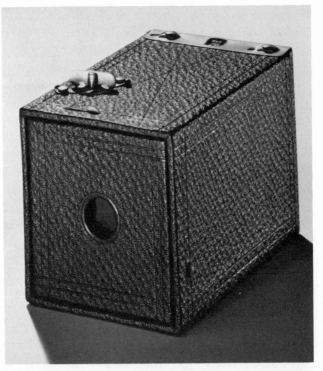

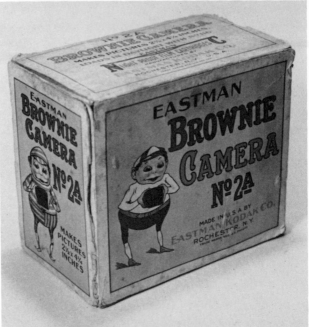

Eastman bids for the youth market with a $1 camera loaded with a roll of 15¢ film. He names it Brownie; it becomes one of the most famous trade names in United States history.

Kodak continued to make and offer such glass-plate–loaded box cameras as the No.2 Eureka (1897), which took 3½-inch-square glass plates and sold for only $4. Using the same size plate, the Blair Company's Hawk-Eye Jr. (1896) was selling for $8.

The more typical glass-plate– or cut-film–loaded cameras of the period (up to about 1900) were such cameras as the Adlake, the Montauk, the Monroe, the Niagara, the Night-Hawk, the Premier, the Premo, and the Quad. Sears, Roebuck & Co. offered the Seroco. Camera buyers were also offered the Trokonette, the TAKIV ("take-IV"), and the Sunart cameras. The Daylight Loading Tourist Vive for $5 in the final days of these glass-loaded boxes advertised that it could be loaded "using either cartridge roll films, cut films, or glass plates of any make." A stereo-model Vive sold at the time for $12 "taking 50 stereo or 100 single pictures at one loading."

Any of these box cameras might be found almost anywhere today in the United States. In the circles where camera collectors meet to swap stories and oddities, a plate-loaded box camera is available at $20 or $25. If it is a stereo model, it could sell for five times or even ten times that sum.

One of the most remarkable and smallest of the box cameras produced in those years was the Kombi, easily one of the most amazingly conceived cameras in the photographic history of America. This tiny (only 1⅝-by-2-by-1⅝-inches) all-metal camera was loaded with a 25-exposure roll of film. It sold first for $3 and later for $3.50, and it was introduced in time for the 1893 Columbian Exposition in Chicago.

Remarkable? Amazing? Without question. It was a system camera akin to the Leica and the Hasselblad professional system cameras of today. How? Why? This $3 camera featured a section containing the film that could be slid off so that a preloaded second back could be immediately attached (exactly as with the Hasselblad, which costs $1,200 today). The aperture stop could be removed from the lens so that the camera would be reversed to serve as a hand-viewer magnifier of rolled lengths of positives (transparencies) of the photographer's own photos or from a library of rolls offered by its maker, the Alfred C. Kemper

Company of Chicago, who made available a strap that secured the camera to a specially made tripod. Finally, the camera was designed to make either round or square pictures by use of a slide-away mask in the film holder.

Advertised as a combination camera and graphoscope (viewer), it was attractive in its oxidized-silver finish (a gun-metal black). A system of special darkroom aids was developed to simplify development of the new tiny roll of film. As one of the most ingenious cameras in its period, it has caught the fancy of collectors of both box cameras (the smallest) and novelty cameras (the most extensive system design). No wonder then that today the Kombi usually is sold for more than $100—when a seller can be found. In flea markets and antique-shop circles it is only a small metal camera, an undistinguished little black box. In a midtown New York antique shop, I was able to find mine—for $7.

Today the Kombi is an unknown name outside collector circles, but the Brownie, the $1 box camera that was announced in 1900, is a name that even nonphotographers instantly identify.

THE BROWNIE IS BORN

If George Eastman made history with his Kodak camera of 1888, he learned that he had only scratched the surface of the potential market when in 1900 he introduced the amazing $1 box camera that could be loaded with "transparent film cartridge, 6 exposures, 2¼ × 2¼ . . . 15¢."

Until its debut in 1900, the word *brownie* was a synonym for a hard-working sprite or elf who performed, according to the original Scottish legend, household chores of butter churning or wheat thrashing. This friendly diminutive little fellow had become well known at the turn of the century because of the development of the now-familiar and then popular Brownie* cartoons and stories created by artist Palmer Cox.

---

* To this day there is no firm corporate knowledge of the true roots of the use of the name *Brownie*. There was an executive of the Kodak plant at the time, F. A. Brownell, and some believe it is possible that the new project was "Brownie's camera."

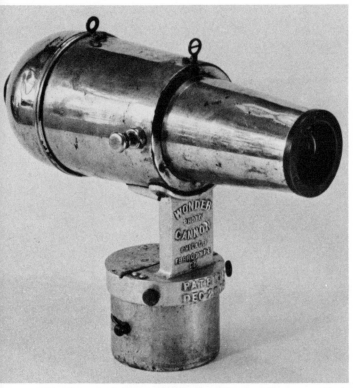

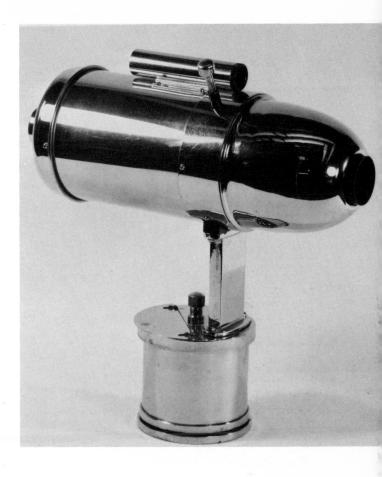

Photo button cameras like the Wonder Cannon and the Errtee were popular at resorts and seaside centers. *(Photographs courtesy of Allen Weiner and Matthew R. Isenberg)*

In popular magazines of the day, such as *The Cosmopolitan*, full-page ads announced:

ANY SCHOOL-BOY OR GIRL CAN MAKE
GOOD PICTURES WITH ONE OF THE
EASTMAN KODAK CO.'S
BROWNIE CAMERAS $1.00
BROWNIES LOAD IN DAYLIGHT WITH FILM CARTRIDGES FOR 6
EXPOSURES, HAVE FINE MENISCUS LENSES, THE EASTMAN
ROTARY SHUTTERS FOR SNAPSHOTS OR TIME EXPOSURES AND
MAKE PICTURES 2¼ × 2¼ INCHES

A $1 camera when everyone knew the Bullet and Buck-Eye cost $6 and $10? Six pictures for 15¢ worth of film? At once the newest part of the market—America's youth—was given an opportunity to participate in the emerging family hobby of photography.

Brownie cameras in a variety of sizes entered the American home, and the word *brownie* changed in the American lexicon: It was no longer a name for an elf; it was the synonym for a camera. Is there an American home without one somewhere forgotten on a shelf?

The new Brownie motivated further developments. Now anyone seeking entry into the profitable camera business had to provide a low-cost camera with a roll-film capability in a design that permitted the camera to be loaded in daylight. Along came the Ansco, the Buster-Brown, and the Kewpie from Sears, Roebuck. Each was as "boxy" a box camera as the competitors could produce. And there were others—Zar, Little Puck, and Mystic, for example.

The new small $1 Brownie was the fulfillment of an Eastman idea to "bring Kodakery to every schoolboy or girl." The idea of the small hand-held box camera had been fully realized in the Pocket Kodak of 1895 and 1896, and the competition's small cameras like the Blair Baby Hawk-Eye (1897),

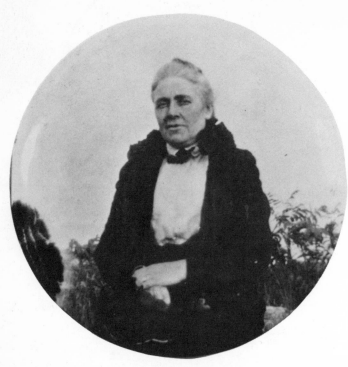

Photo buttons are usually found in jewelry trays of antique shops and flea market stalls for a dollar or two.

"which could be safely loaded and unloaded in broad daylight," already hinted at a taste of things to come with a mass-market potential. The Blair camera directly anticipated the move to the youth market in advertising for the Baby Hawk-Eye, which claimed that it is "so constructed that a child can readily understand the method of making exposures."

Collectors obviously want one of the first Brownies of 1900, but few know that there is more than one "first" Brownie. Only six are known of the actual first Brownie, a camera with a back cover like a shallow lid (perhaps ½ inch deep). It evidently was not a successful means of insuring a lighttight fit; a new back was designed, and a metal clip secured a flat lid onto the camera's back in the succeeding model. This second "first" Brownie is identifiable by its very smooth exterior leatherlike finish. A third "first" Brownie is the commonly available mass-production model illustrated in the famous Brownie introductory advertising: The metal clip locks the camera back to the body; the exterior finish is a coarse-grained leatherlike paper covering.

The next important advance in box-camera variants was the film-loading simplification made pos-

sible by the Rochester Optical and Camera Company introduction early in 1903 of the so-called film pack: a flat canister holding flexible film in sheets in a system that made possible cameras without rollers, wind knobs, or the little ruby window at back. The film-pack–loaded camera is most typically represented by the boxlike Premo Film Camera. It was the simplest version, taking 12 exposures in the way common to film packs that are provided for a variety of cameras in use today, such as the Kodak Recomars or Plaubel Makinas or Graflex cameras. Later in 1903 Premo became a Kodak-owned trademark. Film packs could be loaded into adapters that made this convenient film-handling system available to owners of a variety of other cameras. Cameras designed only to be used with film packs are available at flea markets and elsewhere in the $5 to $25 price range, depending on condition, terms of the sale, etc.

There are interesting collectibles that incorporate amazing technical innovations. The 3B Quick Focus Kodak camera is one. Box cameras, by their rigid and low-cost construction, were not generally adjustable for distance. Users were taught to expect acceptable results by limiting the range to "middle" distances, never closer than five to six feet. But in the 3B Quick Focus Kodak of 1906, the distance could be set on a scale once the photographer had estimated the number of feet to his subject. The camera front was spring-loaded to move out away from the film to adjust for near or far photography. Since it sold for $12 at a time when folding cameras were available at that same price, it was never very popular, as compact, folding styles were more easily carried about. Today, this novel box camera is not easy to find; but the pop-open front makes it a true collectible.

PANORAMIC BOX CAMERAS

The next group of cameras that deserve special attention are those designed for the very unique

(FACING)

The street photographer is nearly gone in America but he may still be found in many European and South American countries using his special box camera. *(Photograph by Don Hunstein)*

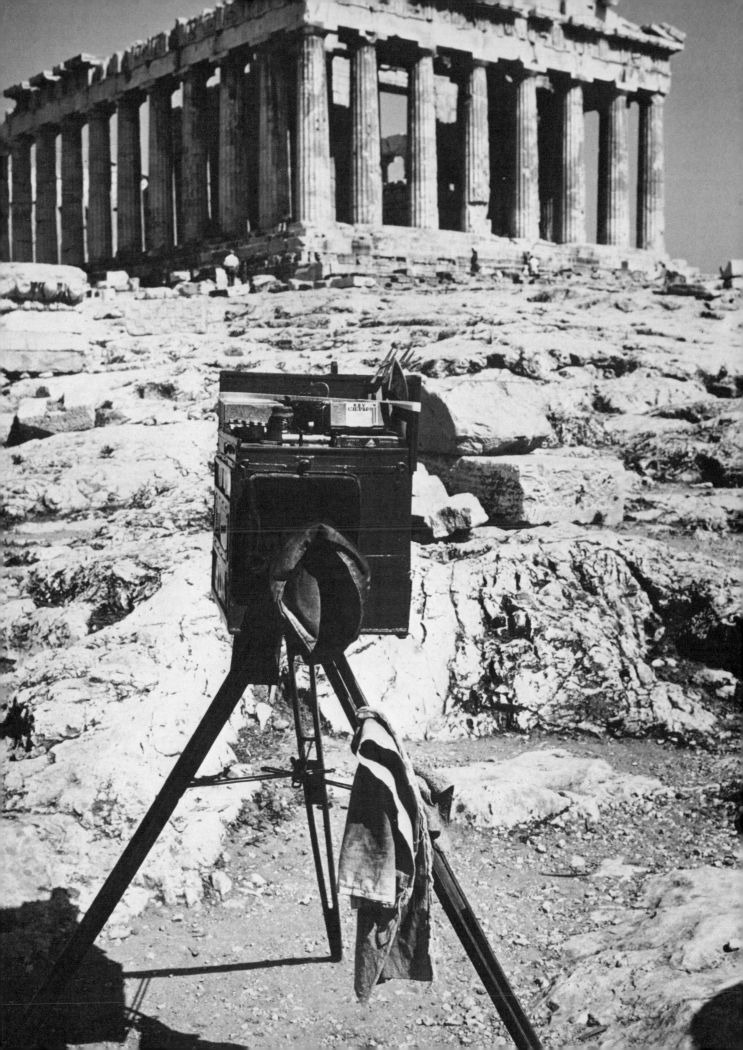

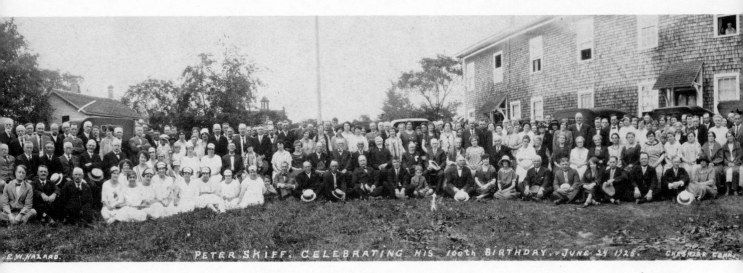

Typical panoramic photograph is a memento of special festive occasions. This was a 100th birthday party in 1925 honoring Peter Skiff of Connecticut. *(From the collection of John Dobran)*

idea of taking a wider-than-usual photograph: the panoramic photo. Two Kodak models, Panoram-Kodak's models No.1 (1900) and No.4 (1899) are the first simple cameras that allowed amateur photographers to bring back professionallike vistas from their travels. The camera was held steady and aimed at a distant shoreline or skyline. The lens swung in an arc to create a 112-degree-wide (twice the ordinary coverage) picture that measured 2¼ by 7 inches on the No.1 and 3½ by 12 inches on the No.4. Competitor look-alikes were the rarer Turret Camera Company panoramic box of 1904 and the Al-Vista, aimed at the professional market, with a 180-degree sweep offered in models as early as 1896 (later to become the Conley Panoramics made up to 1912 for sale by Sears, Roebuck).

Loaded with standard roll film, the Panoram-Kodak cameras are even today occasionally used by photographers fortunate enough to own one in working condition. They are sold and traded in collector circles at prices just above and below $100 each. Film for the larger model is the no-longer-available size #103 (for postcard-size cameras). The smaller camera used 2¼-inch-wide #105 rolls.

The 3A Panoram-Kodak was introduced in 1926 and discontinued in 1928. It was loaded with the then-available #122 roll film.

STEREO BOX CAMERAS

While Chapter 5, "Stereo Cameras and Stereography," offers a complete discussion of stereophotography, it is worth mentioning here the special group of stereo box cameras. In their box shapes, invariably covered in black leather, they resemble ordinary box cameras at a first glance. Only the fact that two lenses may be seen in the two round portholes at the camera front indicate their stereo capability. The No.2 Kodak Stereo was the prime example, which sold in the early 1900s for $15. It was loaded with 3½-inch-wide roll film so that contact prints could be mounted in cards and enjoyed in full stereo relief in the millions of existing hand-held home stereo viewers. A Conley (Sears, Roebuck) stereo box camera and the Stereo Magazine Vive, which loaded with glass plates, were also offered at the turn of the century. But these were not even pioneering efforts in America. In 1900, Montgomery Ward was already selling the glass-plate–loaded Quick-Shot Stereo Magazine camera, a black box with two "eyes" at front to capture dual images in stereo relief on one glass plate.

By the 1930s, the English Stereo Puck (from Thornton-Pickard) and the German EHO were box cameras that took stereo pairs on the readily available #120 roll film.

Regardless of the model, any stereo box camera of the early (pre-1930) period has a collector value in excess of $100. The two apertures for lenses about 2½ inches apart make these cameras instantly identifiable by anyone.

BOX CAMERAS OF THE STREET PHOTOGRAPHER

An amazing variety of cameras were produced in the closing days of the nineteenth century and early days of the twentieth century which gave birth to a new profession: the street photographer. He walked the streets of London, Paris, and New York City, and later in other eastern American cities with a pony to attract children to the thrill of a seated moment on the saddled back of a pavement-wearied pinto. His product was any of a range of photo products from a tintype to a paper print, from a photo button to an instant bit of photographic jewelry. With his product selling from 25¢ to $1, even today his counterpart in the tourist-traveled historic sites throughout the world still offers the one truly personalized memento of any trip.

The street photographer with his bucket of water for a quick rinse of the hyposaturated print was a familiar sight in parks and playgrounds and on boardwalks where a Sunday crowd often gathered round to see the photographer's hand emerge from the magic black box with a print to be dropped for a minute or two into the wash-water bucket at his feet.

Today the street photographer's camera is likely to be a Polaroid. Before and after World War I, it was more likely the box camera made in Chicago by the three Mandel brothers. Loaded with tiny photo cards when the camera top was opened, this camera carried its own tiny bucket of a mix of developer and fixer. This monobath process required a direct-positive paper (the twentieth-century equivalent of the tintype), and while these papers are now used primarily in the darkroom for direct prints from color transparencies, their earliest versions in small card and postcard shapes, and even in roll form, could be loaded into a variety of Mandel-made cameras.

The Mandel cameras are readily identified by their labels (Chicago Ferrotype Co.) and also by their unusual construction features. In most models, the top was lifted open by unlatching the larger snap latches found on trunks. A hole (large enough for the hand to fit into) at camera back was light sealed with a rubberized black cloth with a rubber-banded closure.

Cameras were loaded with light-sensitive petite postcards which were developed in a direct-positive (no negative) procedure. Following a quick rinse in a bucket of water, the damp-dry print was given to the waiting customer.

One famous camera of the period, the Wonder Photo Cannon, of the Chicago Ferrotype Company, looked like a torpedo. It took a tintype that snapped into a button-with-pin. The cameras known as the Mandel and the Mandel-Ette were paper loaded, as was the Day-Dark.

The 1930s saw a version of the street photographer's box camera called the PDQ, which, like all of these cameras, also required a tripod. It loaded with a roll of paper and was an ingenious combination of camera, attached developing tanks, and a cutting knife within to separate the newly exposed paper section from the supply spool.

Collectors seek street-photography cameras for the nostalgia and also for the unusual in-camera processing system that the camera contained. The simplest Mandel cameras, taking pictures about 2 by 3 inches, are sold at photographica trade fairs for considerably less than $100; larger and more complex models sell for $100 and more.

There are versions that loaded with actual sensitized tintype materials, with a magnet within the camera holding the tin sheet in the focal plane. Cameras have had lots of strange aiming and focusing systems and weird shutters, but a magnet to hold the film? That's an irresistible collectible for the irrepressible.

One of the most important of the collectible tintype cameras was the all-wood NoDark, "a developing tin-type camera" sold in about 1900 with a slogan that sounds strangely familiar to the photographer today: "Finished picture in a Minute."

This handsome box was a long box camera in the

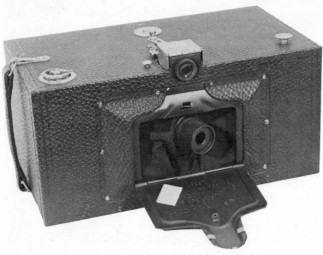

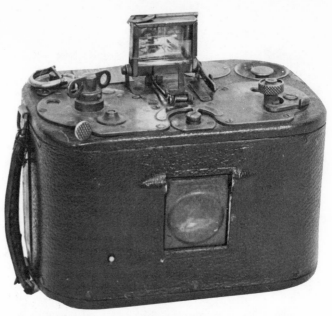

Special-design box cameras like the Panoram-Kodaks used the same roll film of box cameras of the day. A swinging lens exposed the wide scene onto the extra-width of the wide-shape camera. *(Photograph courtesy of John and Valerie Craig)*

The box camera with the highest shutter speed in history: A press shutter made possible photographs at 1/1000 second in the No. 0 Graphic, which found few buyers and has become a limited-edition collectible of today. *(Photograph courtesy of John and Valerie Craig)*

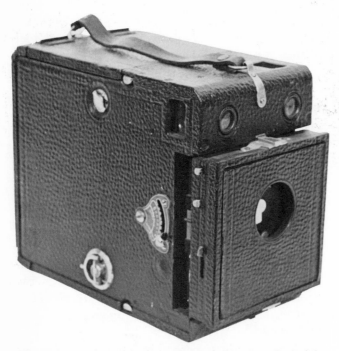

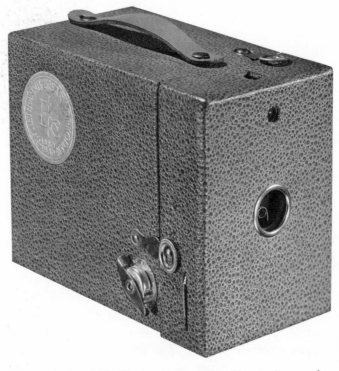

The box camera with the pop-out front: the 3B Quick-Focus Kodak, which was spring activated to snap open to the desired focus, ca. 1910. *(Photograph courtesy of John and Valerie Craig)*

The tan-colored Kodak Anniversary Box Camera is one of history's most astonishing box cameras. Approximately 400,000 were given away *free* to United States children to honor the fiftieth anniversary (1880–1930) of the founding of the Eastman companies. *(Photograph courtesy of Eastman Kodak Company)*

Mothers – this Camera FREE to any Child Born in 1918!

(Any Child whose 12th Birthday falls in 1930)

Go to a Kodak dealer and accept one ... complete with Roll of Kodak Film, FREE!

PAY NOTHING, BUY NOTHING

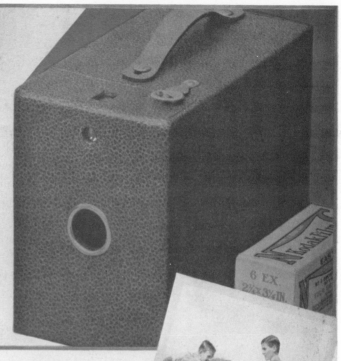

A Gift of 500,000 Cameras
to the Children of America

in Commemoration of the 50th Anniversary of Kodak

with the compliments of

George Eastman, Chairman of the Board of the Eastman Kodak Company

MOTHERS!

Beginning on the first day of May, 500,000 cameras, as illustrated, are to be given to American Children whose twelfth birthdays fall in any month of the calendar year 1930.

If you have a child who reaches the age of twelve this year, take your child to a Kodak dealer's and accept one of these cameras, complete with roll of Kodak Film—free. Buy nothing; pay nothing.

The gift is made with the compliments of George Eastman, Chairman of the Board of the Eastman Kodak Company, to the Children of America to commemorate the 50th Anniversary of Kodak.

There are no reservations to the gift, except that no cameras will be given *before* May 1, or *after* May 31, 1930, and *none* after the original supply of 500,000 is exhausted. *To be sure of getting one, act early.*

The Gift's True Object

This gift is made to benefit both the giver and the children who receive it. Many eminent people hold that its

GEORGE EASTMAN
Creator of Kodak, which celebrates its 50th Anniversary by giving away 500,000 Cameras to American Children

acceptance is a duty every mother owes her child.

One leading educator declares that in developing *character, observation, appreciation of beauty and a depth of human understanding,* amateur picture-making is probably second to no other factor as an educational adjunct.

Another says that it brings a child in touch with every phase of life and nature, and implants *a clean interest* in the formative mind, during the dangerously impressionable years, when a wholesome pastime is

---

A GIFT of 500,000 Cameras

The camera—complete with one roll of Kodak Film—is to be given absolutely WITHOUT COST to any child whose twelfth birthday falls in any month of 1930.

500,000 cameras, as illustrated, are to be given to children who reach the age of twelve this year.

The gift is from the Eastman Kodak Company, with the compliments of George Eastman, Chairman of the Board, in commemoration of Kodak's 50th Anniversary.

Gift Cameras will be distributed May 1, 1930, by authorized Kodak dealers, and continued until the supply of 500,000 is exhausted. None after May 31, 1930.

To get a camera, simply take your child to an authorized Kodak dealer's. Pay nothing. Child must be accompanied by either parent or guardian.

---

most needed to safeguard the future of the growing child.

More and more, every day, thinking parents are regarding amateur picture-taking in that light.

* * * *

THIS GIFT IS MADE WITH TWO ENDS IN VIEW:

Sentiment: In appreciation of the grandparents and parents of today, who, as the picture-taking children of yesterday, played so important a part in the development of amateur photography and of the Eastman Kodak Company.

To place in the hands of their children and grandchildren an admittedly important character-building force.

Business: To interest hundreds of thousands more children in picture-taking. And thus to raise amateur photography among the coming generation to even greater heights than its present remarkable peak. For as amateur photography increases in popularity, the use of Kodak products will naturally increase with it.

Beginning on May 1

The Anniversary Cameras will be at Kodak dealers' everywhere on May 1—

Typical pictures, actual size, 2¼ x 3¼ inches, taken with the Anniversary Camera and Kodak Film

ready for distribution. None before that date. Take your child to one of these stores. Get the camera. No red tape, no delay, no cost.

The gift-giving period begins on May 1, 1930, and will extend into the month of May as long as the supply of 500,000 cameras holds out. Be sure of getting a camera for your child.

* * * *

EASTMAN KODAK COMPANY
Rochester, N. Y.

For a Noteworthy Expression from Mrs. Calvin Coolidge, as to the Significance of the Eastman Gift, See Page 151 of this Magazine.

The astonishing 1930 offer to give away 500,000 cameras. *(From the collection of Eaton S. Lothrop, Jr.)*

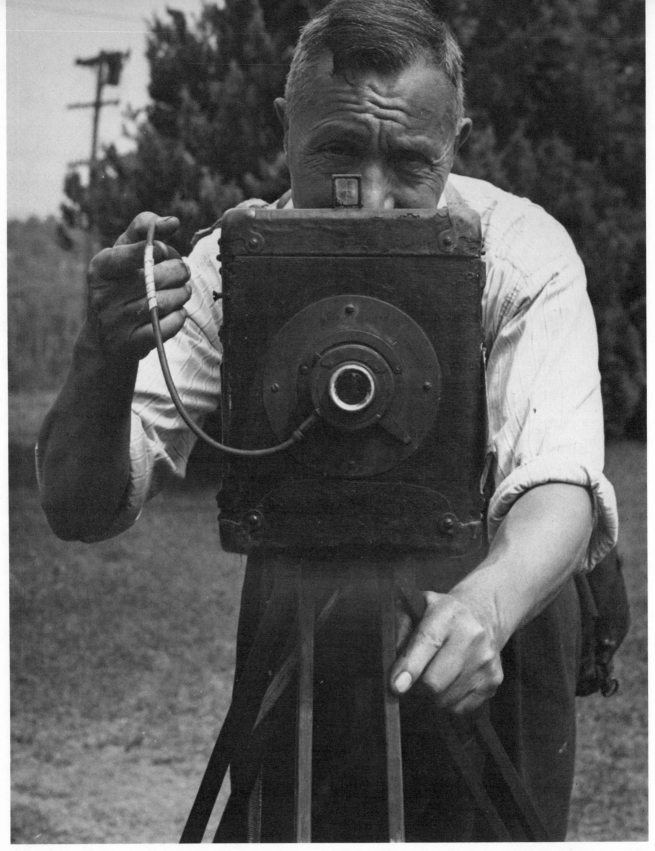

Box cameras for the street photographers were made in large numbers by the Mandel brothers of Chicago who built the tintype camera into a luggagelike case supported on a tripod. *(Photograph by Alfred Lowenherz)*

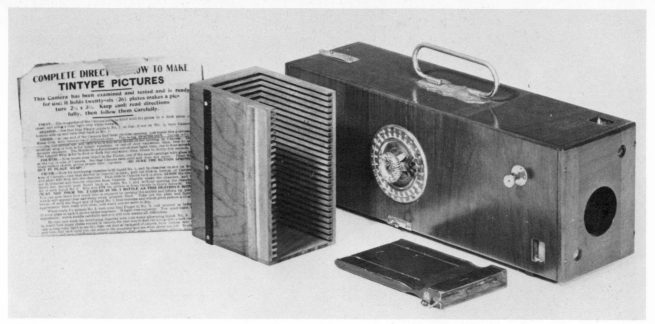

This camera offered "finished pictures in a minute" in 1900. It was the NoDark, a tintype camera loaded with twenty-six tiny metal plates.

period when folding plate cameras were rapidly replacing all other cameras. It was loaded in the darkroom with 26 sensitized tintype plates, each precut to 2½ by 3½ inches, and contained within its body the entire system for processing the exposure immediately after the picture was taken. The camera was sold originally for $6; the plates were available at 75¢ for 26.

The Quta Photo Machine with tripod ($30) appeared in 1904, loaded with 36 ferrotype (tintype) plates, each 2 by 2½ inches. It resembled

two box cameras stacked one on the other with a bulb-activated shutter and lens in the top section. The bottom box, open to the rear, permitted the street photographer to store his developing tank on a working shelf.

To collectors of cameras that take pictures-in-a-minute, where is a better point at which to start? Answer: Find out all you can about Dubroni and keep collecting tintype cameras until one comes into your lucky, lucky fingers.

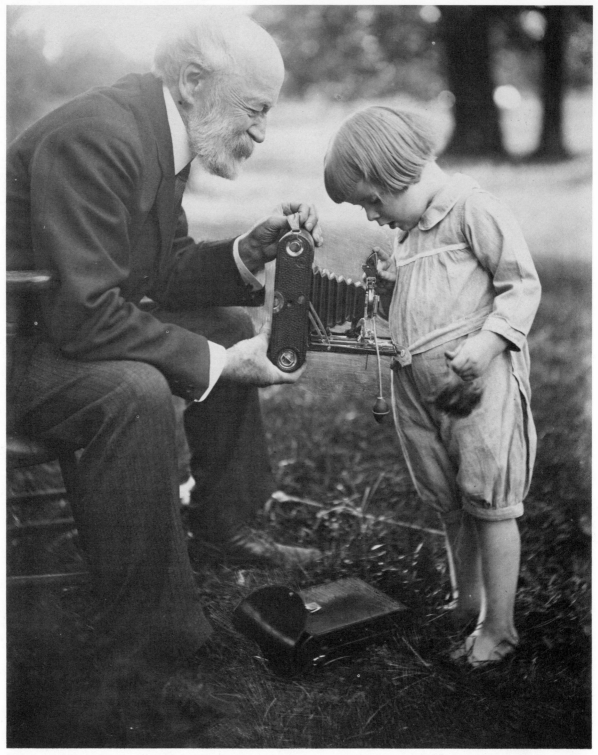

No. 4 Folding Pocket Kodak: a family-size roll-film camera which took 4-by-5-inch pictures. *(Photograph courtesy of Eastman Kodak Company)*

3
Folding Cameras

The camera's first shape was that of a box, a direct descendant of the camera obscura, which had been the artist's box with a lens.

Within ten years of the start of photography, especially with the development of the wet-plate collodion process, the photographer was ready to go afield. Afoot, on horseback, or in a wagon, he sought equipment that would be compact and light.

The view camera of 1850–1880s which replaced bulky all-wood design of the Daguerrean era (1840–1855) with the lighter weight and collapsibility of folded leather, was born, and the box shape of the Daguerreotype camera was generally retired for two generations. The optical industry created sharper, faster, wider, longer lenses. The rush to provide the improved technology for the quickly developing professional-photography market was a new industrial gold rush.

The cameras of the wet-plate era (1854–1880) were almost universally alike: wooden frames, leather or canvas bellows, a ground glass at back, and a brass-mount lens at front. No shutter; the lens cap was on and off for exposures of from four to forty seconds. But even with the development of the dry-plate system, cameras made fifty and sixty years later reflected few essential differences. Folding cameras for use outdoors were smaller, lighter, more graceful; cameras for the studio were larger, bulkier, heavier, and often integral to rolling tables, which held the photographer's accessories, loaded holders, and exposed holders. Collectors looking at worn view cameras are tempted to date these to the earliest periods, but design changes were few over the years, and few cameras bear either the maker's name or a model number. Usually only the lens has a name or serial number.

The cameras of the wet-plate era (pre-1880) are silver stained at the woodwork along the back bottom edge where the dripping plate could not be prevented from leaking some of the still-wet emulsion onto and into the camera (some studio-type tintype cameras from later on bear such stains). Wet-plate-era cameras are simpler in design and enjoy fewer brass knobs and rails than their later counterpart models. The backs of the wet-plate camera fold out and away or from the top down to permit the plateholder to be loaded into the camera.

The camera sizes popular for the period were most often of the full plate (6½ by 8½ inches was the actual size of the image) but were also available in smaller sizes and in larger sizes, even up to 24-by-27-inch monster cameras used for outdoor landscapes, loaded with 14-by-17-inch and larger sheets of glass.

In most cases, the lens board was removable so that the photographer could select a lens best suited to the subject. His lens for portraiture was a different optic than the one used for landscape photography, for example. Lenses were frequently imported from France (as the Darlot) or from Germany (as the Voigtländer), but American lens makers also got a good share of the business, especially for the smaller cameras.

One of the camera's lens boards might have two matched lenses so that the view camera could be

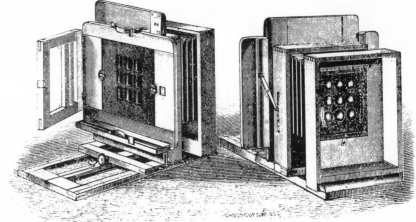

The Gem Box by American Optical Co. is a nine-tube studio camera for multiple exposure on a single plate. *(Photograph courtesy of GAF)*

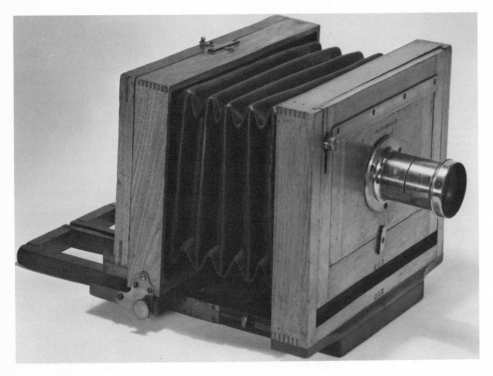

The Scovill 5 by 8, ca. 1885, one of many folding plate cameras for studio or field use. With an interchangeable lens board, it could be used for stereo photography too. *(From the collection of Matthew R. Isenberg)*

adapted for stereo-photography views. In many of the larger cameras, the back itself was interchangeable so that one camera body would serve many lenses and many film sizes (for portraits, landscapes, stereo views, etc.).

It was more commonplace at the time for the sales agent to identify the product with his retail store than for the manufacturer to incorporate his name or factory serial number in the body. As a result, even the most sophisticated collector may find it impossible to identify or date a nondescript view camera found without lens or carry case.

However, there were a number of major professional camera systems before the 1880s that are immediately recognizable to the experienced collector. By and large, an identifiable camera (by model, serial number, lens, or nameplate) is from the post-1880 period.

A choice item for any collector seeking at least one example of the wet-plate era would be the common E. & H. T. Anthony or Scovill 4-by-5-inch, 5-by-7-inch, or 6½-by-8½-inch view camera. Such a camera has a present value of $300 or more; yet its simplicity and lackluster appearance would

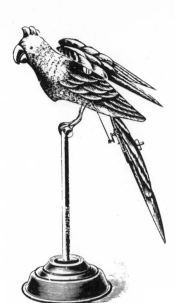

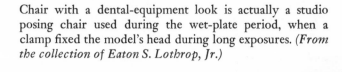

Chair with a dental-equipment look is actually a studio posing chair used during the wet-plate period, when a clamp fixed the model's head during long exposures. (*From the collection of Eaton S. Lothrop, Jr.*)

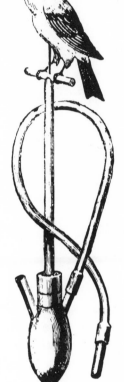

The "bird" from "Watch the Birdie!" Photographer blew into the tube to make a warbling sound to delight children. (*Illustration from the collection of the author*)

tend to make it an unpretentious item in a typical antique store. The black-silver staining in the woodwork at the camera back and bottom would confirm its likely use in the wet-plate period.

DRY-PLATE VIEW CAMERAS

The more readily located small view cameras, often boxed in wooden carry cases, date back to the early 1880s and 1890s when the success of the dry-plate photographic negative rushed the growth of photography. Photography had become so com-

monplace that a new social organization emerged, the camera club, largely made up of nonprofessionals who shared the wonder of a new hobby. The cameramakers encouraged the growth of this new market with such cameras as the Anthony Amateur Outfits in a variety of sizes starting at 4 by 5 inches with holders and lens for as little as $9. The camera body was made of mahogany; the lens was a single achromatic one, well suited to portraiture; and the photographer could get started with the one double holder provided. This loaded with two plates exactly as the holder commonly used in studio cameras to this day. A wooden tripod was $1 more.

Models were also available with shutters and in heavier designs for indoor (studio) use along with lenses especially suited either to portraiture or for stereo photography in a 5-by-8-inch size for $16.50. The 5-by-8-inch size was especially popular since stereo photography required a camera larger than the 4-by-5-inch plate size.

The smallest camera model of the period, in most cases, was the 3¼ by 4¼ (quarter plate). One

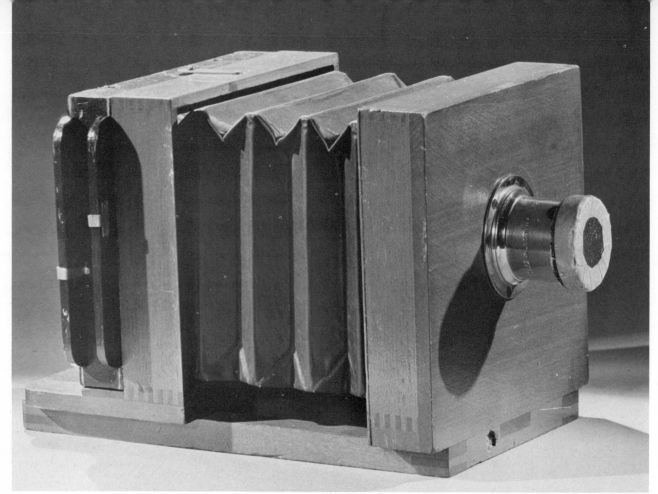

Scovill and Adams 4-by-5-inch folding camera is equipped with brass-mount lens without shutter. Typical studio and field camera for time exposures, ca. 1888. *(Photograph courtesy of GAF)*

model, the Bijou, was advertised by James C. Cummins of Baltimore, who was the area agent for Anthony photo products and others. The 1888 catalogue described it as "the neatest, nattiest and altogether nicest camera of its kind ever made." The plate size was the same as that of the lantern slide used in magic lanterns, so "slides can be made from them by contact printing in an ordinary printing frame." It sold for $9 without a lens.

The Anthony catalogue of the time also listed "Fairy Cameras: The most attractive and elegant piece of apparatus of its kind ever offered." They were handsomely made in walnut and lavishly accoutered in brass fittings with focusing gears in the camera bed and other adjustments of the lens and film back to make them worth the $40 to $50 (depending on size).

THE SATCHEL/FOLDING DESIGN EMERGES

It was in modification of the boxy detective-camera shapes that the first major innovation in folding cameras emerged in America. The detective

cameras (see Chapter 4, "Detective Cameras and Later Novelties") used satchel shapes and shoulder-bag designs to disguise the fact that the bags were, in fact, surreptitious cameras.

Using the satchel-style case as the basis for a design, Kodak introduced a line of "glass-plate folding Kodaks," which were offered in 4-by-5-, 5-by-7- and 6½-8½-inch plate sizes. Closed, they were over-the-shoulder-slung box satchels in black leather. Opened at what appears to be the side of a case, a lens, shutter, and bellows emerged ready for use. The case was opened at the top to load in glass plates or the special roll holder, the Eastman-Walker Roll Film Holder, which Kodak had developed and patented earlier in the 1880s. The roll holder enabled all view cameras to be loaded with Eastman's "American" film, a film-on-paper system that was discontinued with the emergence of transparent film.

The economy folding model from Kodak arrived in 1894 with the folding Kodet camera in models that sold for $12 and $15 when Kodak's own larger No.4, No.5, and No.6 Folding Kodak cameras were being offered for $60, $75, and $100 respectively.

KODAK CAMERAS BEGIN TO GET SMALLER

With the success of the tiny Pocket Kodak, it was clear to the Eastman Kodak Company that there was room in the market for smaller folding cameras using smaller film sizes. After the Folding Kodet and Folding Pocket Kodak cameras were introduced in sizes as small as the No.0, which took pictures 1⅝ by 2½ inches; and then in slightly larger models 1 and 1A, taking pictures 2¼ by 3¼ and 2¼ by 4½ inches respectively. The next size, the No.2, took square pictures 3½ by 3½ inches; the No.3 and No.3 Deluxe took the 3¼-by-4¼-inch

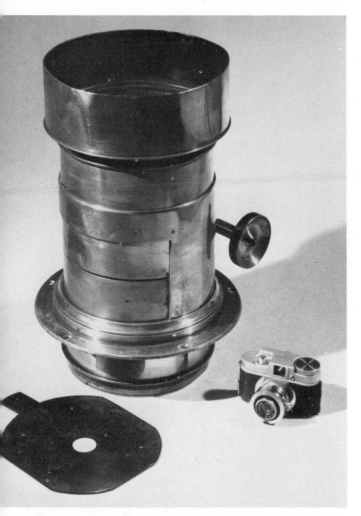

Brass-mount studio lenses are a collectible for many interested in the nineteenth-century period. A low-cost subminiature camera, ca. 1950, is shown alongside to emphasize lens length. *(From the collection of the author)*

size; the popular No.3A took pictures 3¼ by 5½ inches; and the No.4 took pictures 4 by 5 inches. The even larger model 4A took pictures 4¼ by 6½ inches. Since many of these cameras were available with different lenses and shutters, they were priced at many levels.

Cartridge Kodaks, with their daylight-loading capabilities, were folding cameras introduced first in 1897. With these and the Folding Pocket Kodak cameras that followed, the ground glass that permitted focusing and composition disappeared (except for a few special Kodak cameras). Owners were then required to guess the focus distance, a satisfactory procedure if the subject was five or more feet from the photographer.

The Blair Camera Company, makers of the Hawk-Eye Detective camera, brought out its competition model to the folding Kodak cameras: their Tourist Hawk-Eye for $9. There were other models of the Hawk-Eye available from $5 to $50.

In this same period (1890–1898), a plethora of folding plate cameras, most loading with glass plates, came on stage. Such names as the Poco, the Premo, the Ascot, the Century, the Graphic, the Hawk-Eye, the Ray, the Seneca, the Conley, and the Snappa (which was unique in that it was magazine loaded with up to 24 plates and designed to change films with a push-pull motion as in some European stereo cameras).

These cameras were offered in a range of models, usually starting with the small size (4 by 5 inches) and, infrequently, as small as 3¼ by 4¼ inches. Those with shallow backs were aimed at a newly emerging hobby of bicycling with a camera on bicycle. Some of these "cycle" cameras were the Cycle Poco and Cycle Graphic. These thinner, lighter cameras were soon to dominate the plate-camera market. Kodak literature of 1897 promotes the use of Kodak folding cameras as well suited to bicycling. Presumably they could be used off the bicycle, too.

The exterior leathers of most of these cameras were most often black; but many of these have become red-purple with age. The dried leathers of these and others can be treated and refreshed as described in "Treating Old Leathers," in Appendix E.

The interiors of these cameras often include beautifully varnished cherry or mahogany woods

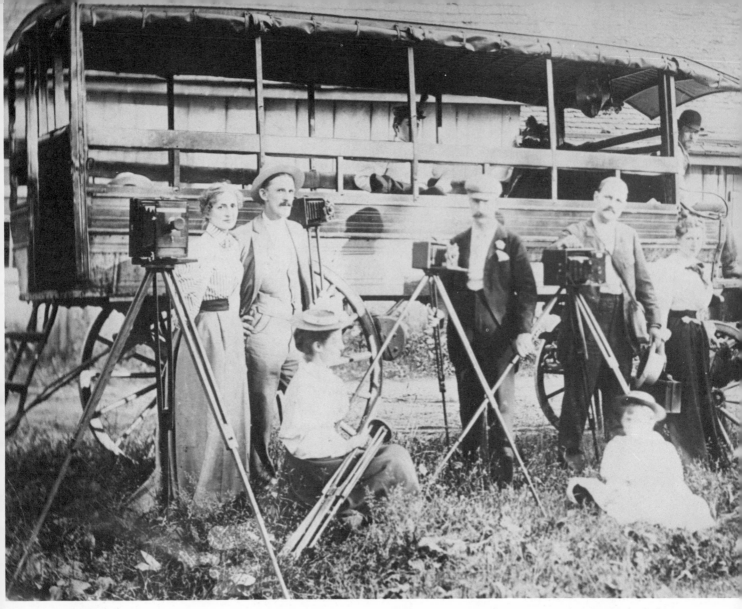

A Sunday outing for amateur photographers who in the 1880s formed the first societies in the United States to share a new avocational interest. The dry-plate era has opened photography to thousands as a leisure pursuit. *(Photograph courtesy of Eaton S. Lothrop, Jr.)*

with impeccable woodwork of a sort only rarely seen today. Since these cameras have invariably been stored in a closed and often encased condition, the finish of the camera interior is unmarred; the exterior leather may be dried and scuffed, belying the beautiful interior.

The lenses of all of these cameras range from the simplest single-element designs with stops in a rotating dial for aperture control. The shutters cover the designs of the time, spring-loaded or air-activated. Shutter speeds commonly range from less than a second up to $\frac{1}{100}$th of a second.

These cameras could be aimed in one of two ways: by viewing through the ground glass before inserting the camera plate, or by using the tiny on-camera waist-level viewer usually built onto the camera bed near the lens.

The main American folding plate camera of this type to continue after World War I was the Speed Graphic, which had become the near-exclusive possession of the press photographers. The Korona and the Century studio cameras were the equipment for the portraitists and commercial photographers. There were special giant cameras for the

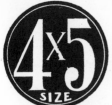

CONLEY
IMPROVED COMPACT CAMERA

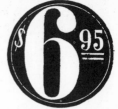

$6.95

THE 1908 MODEL

IS MADE WITH

DOUBLE RAPID RECTILINEAR LENS.
WOLLENSAK SENIOR AUTOMATIC SHUTTER.
RACK AND PINION FOCUS MOVEMENT.

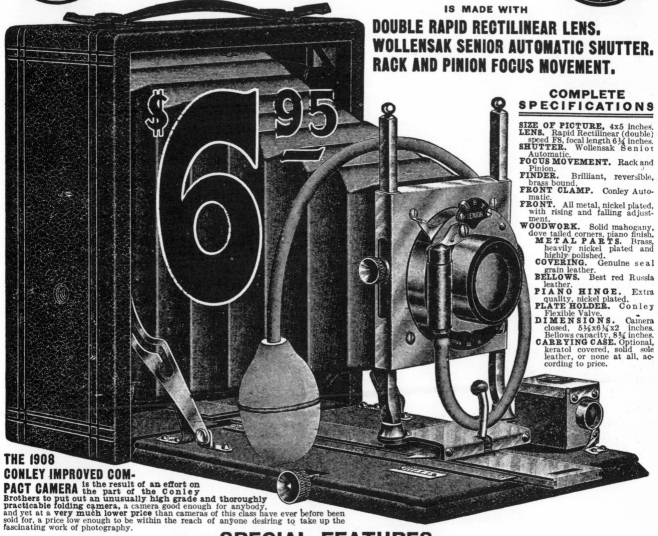

COMPLETE SPECIFICATIONS

SIZE OF PICTURE, 4x5 inches.
LENS. Rapid Rectilinear (double) speed F8, focal length 6¼ inches.
SHUTTER. Wollensak Senior Automatic.
FOCUS MOVEMENT. Rack and Pinion.
FINDER. Brilliant, reversible, brass bound.
FRONT CLAMP. Conley Automatic.
FRONT. All metal, nickel plated, with rising and falling adjustment.
WOODWORK. Solid mahogany, dove tailed corners, piano finish.
METAL PARTS. Brass, heavily nickel plated and highly polished.
COVERING. Genuine seal grain leather.
BELLOWS. Best red Russia leather.
PIANO HINGE. Extra quality, nickel plated.
PLATE HOLDER. Conley Flexible Valve.
DIMENSIONS. Camera closed, 5⅛x6¼x2 inches. Bellows capacity, 8¾ inches.
CARRYING CASE. Optional, keratol covered, solid sole leather, or none at all, according to price.

THE 1908 CONLEY IMPROVED COMPACT CAMERA is the result of an effort on the part of the Conley Brothers to put out an unusually high grade and thoroughly practicable folding camera, a camera good enough for anybody, and yet at a **very much lower price** than cameras of this class have ever before been sold for, a price low enough to be within the reach of anyone desiring to take up the fascinating work of photography.

SPECIAL FEATURES.

THE 1908 CONLEY IMPROVED COMPACT CAMERA is made with rack and pinion focus movement, making it very easy to quickly and accurately focus the Camera. It is equipped with the Conley automatic patent front clamp, the most convenient and satisfactory front clamp ever devised, the exact same front clamp that we use on our highest grade Long Focus and Double Extension cameras. The front of this camera is constructed entirely of brass, nickel plated and highly polished, and is made with rising and falling adjustment for regulating the relative amounts of sky and foreground. Besides the rack and pinion focus movement with all metal rising and falling front, Conley automatic front clamp and other special features, this camera is equipped with an extra quality reversible brilliant view finder, nickel plated piano hinge, highly ornamental side arms, strong leather handle and spring actuated ground glass focusing screen with mahogany back panel.

THE DOUBLE RAPID RECTILINEAR LENS which we furnish with the 1908 Conley Improved Compact Camera is exactly the same grade of rapid rectilinear lens that is used on cameras costing from three to five times the price we ask for the Conley Improved Compact Camera. It is a lens that possesses unusual depth of focus and great covering power, and it works with great rapidity, making the camera especially suited to instantaneous or snap shot exposures. This lens is guaranteed to cover the entire plate to the extreme corners and produces an unusually clear cut and snappy negative.

THE WOLLENSAK SENIOR AUTOMATIC SHUTTER with which we equip the 1908 Conley Improved Compact Camera is arranged for instantaneous exposures and bulb or time exposures of any desired length. This shutter is exceedingly easy of adjustment and works very smoothly, without the slightest vibration. It is an automatic shutter, by which we mean that after each exposure it automatically resets itself for the next one and is thus always ready for instant use. It is not necessary to set it before an exposure can be made. This shutter can be operated either by finger release or by pneumatic bulb. It is provided with a fine iris diaphragm for regulating the size of the opening, and is in every way a high class, reliable and satisfactory shutter.

THE RACK AND PINION FOCUS MOVEMENT is a feature usually found only in cameras sold at much higher prices and it is an adjustment that contributes greatly to the ease and convenience of operation. The speed and accuracy with which the camera is focused by this rack and pinion movement adds to the efficiency of the instrument and insures a larger percentage of perfect pictures.

MATERIALS AND WORKMANSHIP. In manufacturing the 1908 Conley Improved Compact Camera we use only the very highest grade materials, the exact same style and quality of materials that we employ in our highest grade cameras. The best quality of carefully selected, thoroughly seasoned and kiln dried mahogany is used for all of the woodwork, and the covering is a high grade of seal grain morocco leather. The bellows is made from the best red Russia leather lined with lightproof, black gossamer cloth. All metal parts are of brass, nickel plated and highly polished. The workmanship in every way is thoroughly first class, these cameras being put up by the same workmen who put up our highest priced cameras. The same leather workers put on the covering; the same finishers give to this camera its beautiful piano polish; the same skilled workmen assemble the cameras, putting together the different parts as they come from the various departments of the factory, and every Conley Improved Compact Camera that leaves our store is just as carefully inspected and guaranteed to reach the purchaser in exactly the same perfect condition as the most expensive cameras that we sell.

PRICES.

No. 20K111 Conley Improved Compact Folding Camera, 4x5, with one Conley flexible valve plate holder, without carrying case, exactly as illustrated and described on this page. Shipping weight, 3½ pounds. Price..................................... **$6.95**

No. 20K112 Conley Improved Compact Folding Camera, 4x5, complete with one plate holder, same as No. 20K111, but with substantial keratol covered (imitation leather) carrying case, containing space for the camera and four plate holders. Shipping weight, 4¾ pounds. Price.......... **7.45**

No. 20K113 Conley Improved Compact Folding Camera, 4x5, complete with one plate holder, same as No. 20K111, but with solid sole leather carrying case, containing space for the camera and four plate holders. Shipping weight, 4¾ pounds. Price........... **8.40**

Sears, Roebuck & Co. catalogue of 1908 offers a 4-by-5-inch plate camera with lens for $6.95.

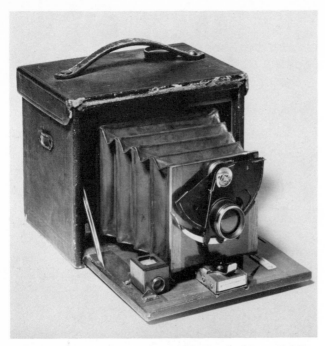

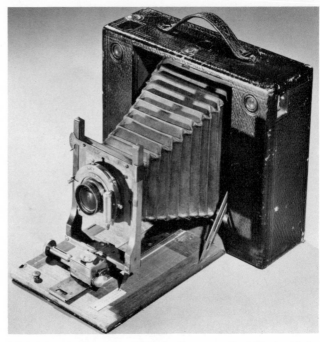

The first folding camera from Kodak, the No. 4 Folding Kodak, is built into a luggagelike case, ca. 1890. *(Photograph courtesy of Eastman Kodak Company)*

The No. 4 Cartridge Kodak Camera of 1897 could be loaded optionally with roll film or glass plates. *(Photograph courtesy of Eastman Kodak Company)*

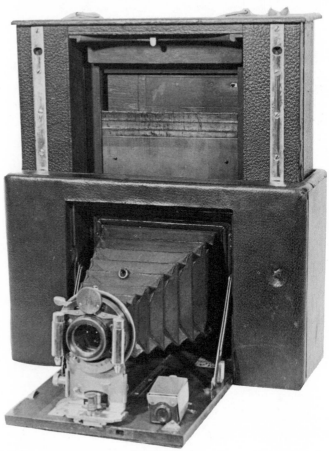

The Blair Convertible, ca. 1896, had a drop-in back, which was loaded with film, positioned after focusing on a ground glass. *(Photograph courtesy of John and Valerie Craig)*

banquet photographers and special-purpose panoramic folding cameras like the Cirkut for the field photographers.

The era of roll film led to the death of the hand-held or tripod-mounted small view camera as well as the American folding plate camera. Not until the development in Germany of the all-metal folding view-type cameras, such as the Linhof and the Plaubel Makina, would the average nonprofessional photographer consider the possible advantages of a view camera as opposed to the other types of equipment available to him as the twentieth century began its inexorable move towards miniaturization.

ROLL-FILM MODELS

The folding bellows cameras became smaller with the introduction of the cartridge Kodaks. They lost their ground glass with the introduction of the Folding Pocket Kodak in 1897. These new Kodak cameras addressed themselves to the family market.

Selling for $10 and taking a picture 2¼ by 3¼ inches, the pop-open–front Folding Pocket Kodak camera offered the load-in-daylight feature that Kodak had already introduced earlier in its boxy Daylight Kodak, but this camera was loaded with a roll of film instead of the paper-box system of the Daylight Kodaks. One could own a Folding Pocket Kodak for as little as $6 or could pay as much as $75 for the No.3 Folding Pocket Deluxe equipped with a Bausch and Lomb Plastigmat f/6.8 lens, covered, according to Kodak's 1907 advertisement, with "selected Persian morocco, a leather with a beautiful natural pattern in soft brown tints. The bellows is covered with brown silk. On each instrument is a solid silver nameplate and with each one is included a hand-sewed carrying case of Persian morocco with silver trimmings." Films for the No.3 Folding Pocket Kodaks were available in rolls as short as 4 exposures for 25¢, 6 exposures for 35¢, and 12 exposures for 70¢. Kodak's box cameras without ground-glass aiming and focusing (advantages of the majority of the boxy detective cameras) showed that the public was ready to accept a simple camera idea. The Folding Pocket Kodak

camera brought this idea to a new and higher level of reality.

By 1902 the camera had been made even more "pocketable"; a smaller model (the new No.0 Folding Pocket Kodak camera) took 1⅝-by-2½-inch pictures on a 6-exposure roll of film that sold for 15¢. An earlier box camera, the boxy Pocket Kodak camera of 1895, had already shown that there was a market for smaller pictures.

Kodak brought out a model with the same design in a larger size too: the model 1A of similar appear-

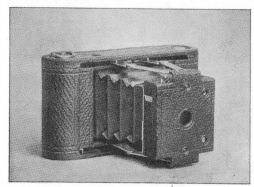

PHOTOGRAPHIC OUTFITS

If it isn't an Eastman it isn't a Kodak.

Picture Taking with

The Folding Pocket Kodak

means a full realization of the charms of photography without the drawbacks of burdensome apparatus, without bulky plate holders or heavy, fragile glass plates.

The Folding Pocket Kodaks have the finest meniscus achromatic lenses, our automatic rotary shutters, sets of three stops and accurate view finders. They are, in short, equipped for the finest photographic work, and like all Kodaks they use our film cartridges and

Load in Daylight.

Folding Pocket Kodak No. 1, for pictures 2¼ x 3¼ inches, - - - - - $10.00
Folding Pocket Kodak No. 1 A, for pictures 2½ x 4¼ inches, - - - - - 12.00
Folding Pocket Kodak No. 2, for pictures 3½ x 3½ inches, - - - - - 15.00

Kodaks $5.00 to $35.00.

EASTMAN KODAK CO.

Catalogues free at the dealers or by mail.   [1900]   Rochester, N. Y.

The start of the folding cameras for the family from the Eastman Kodak Company was launched with ads like this one of 1900.

63

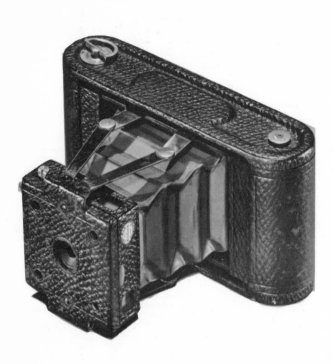

The No. 1 Folding Pocket Kodak: a roll film fold-together camera for the family of 1898. (*Photograph courtesy of Eastman Kodak Company*)

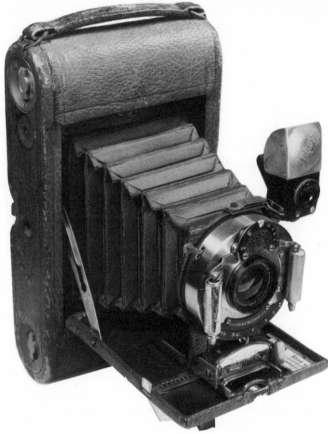

No. 3 Folding Pocket Kodak Special: an elegant camera with silk-covered bellows and silver details, ca. 1903. (*From the collection of Jerry and Shirley Sprung*)

ance, taking a larger roll of film than the other. All of these cameras may be obtained today for $1 to $10 at flea markets, garage sales, and in thrift shops. Each one probably works as well today as it did over seventy years ago.

An improved line of Folding Pocket Kodak cameras in a range of sizes appeared in the early 1900s with the lens protected behind a drop door—a return to the folding-camera design of the 1890s, which was continued on all folding Kodak cameras until the 1950s.

Since it was the intention of the Eastman Kodak Company to sell film, they introduced the lower-cost Brownie line of cameras, which would accept the same films as the costlier Folding Pocket Kodak models. With the success of the Brownie cameras, similar cameras emerged from competitors, and such cameras as the Buster Brown and the Hawk-Eye appeared along with the Ansco. The Hawk-Eye was the product of the Blair Company, which in

the 1890s had been marketing both detective and folding cameras typical of the plate-loaded cameras of that vintage. Blair's success in the folding-camera field led to still another Eastman Kodak Company acquisition; Hawk-Eye became the trade name of still another Kodak manufacturing facility and has been retained to this time as the brand name for Kodak-made cameras that are generally not sold through retail stores. Hawk-Eye cameras are sold directly by the factory to companies sponsoring contests in which cameras are gifts and in similar premium uses.

One of the more unusual and early novel folding cameras of the period was not a Kodak product, and it is an especially sought-after model: the $10

Try Before You Buy

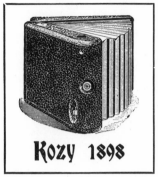

Kozy 1898

WE will send you a New Pocket Kozy Camera on 10 days' trial; we make Kozy converts that way—scores daily. The Kozy tells its own story best; that's why we want you to try it. If you don't like it, sent it back; if you do, pay for it—cash, or a little every month. **We don't want your money unless you want the Kozy.** This seemingly reckless offer is safe, because the camera is exactly what we claim. **Kozy superiority is making Kozy sales.** Our factory, now doubled in capacity, is running overtime on orders; demand unprecedented, satisfaction universal. Therefore, our 10 days' trial offer is continued until July 1. You will never know real camera luxury until you try the

New Pocket Kozy Camera

THE SMALLEST MADE THAT TAKES LARGE PICTURES ON A DAYLIGHT FILM

❧ ❧ ❧   The One You Can Try Before You Buy   ❧ ❧ ❧

Slips Into the Pocket like a Book.

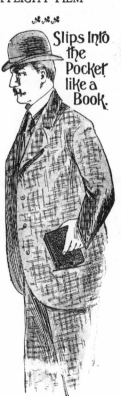

YOU CAN'T TELL whether a camera will exactly suit you, or not, until you try it; but you needn't be in doubt as to the Kozy. We **know** it has no equal at its price, and **for that reason** are entirely willing to send you one

ON 10 DAYS' TRIAL

Test it thoroughly indoors and out—snap-shots or time exposures. **Prove our claims by your own experience.** You will find that the Kozy is the neatest, strongest, lightest pocket camera in the market—1⅝ in. thick, weighs 16 ozs.; takes 12 large pictures on each cartridge film; loads and unloads with perfect safety in **broad sunlight;** is mechanically simple—a child can operate it; does work equal in quality to cameras twice its size and many times its cost. It has every convenience other cameras have. **Demonstrate these facts by your own experience.** Then, you can make

Easy Monthly Payments

to balance your account, or save a liberal percentage by paying cash in full. If the Kozy **isn't** what you need, you can send it back, and no harm done. **That's fair enough.**

> JUST THE THING for Bicyclists, Tourists, Canoeists, and all Camerists who must economize space, time and money . . .

THIS IS OUR LIBERAL OFFER

Good until July 1.—Read Carefully

You will find Kozys in the stores as soon as we can get them there; mail orders are pushing us just now. Ask your dealer for the Kozy; if he hasn't it, send us your name and address, with **$1.00** as a deposit, mentioning this magazine, and stating occupation and references. The Kozy will be forwarded, **charges prepaid.** For ten days after its receipt, test the camera to your satisfaction. If, at the expiration of that time, you decide to keep it, send us **$9.00** more, making a total payment of **$10.00**, in full; or send **$2.00,** and thereafter **$2.00** a month for 5 months, making a total payment of **$13.00.** Understand, if you are not entirely satisfied after ten days' trial, you may return the camera to us, charges prepaid, and we will immediately refund your deposit of $1.00. **This offer is good until July 1.** Illustrated catalogues and full particulars **free** on application. We refer to Mechanics' National Bank, Boston, as to our responsibility. Address, to-day,

KOZY CAMERA CO., Dept. 33, No. 44 Bedford St., Boston, Mass.

Advertisement for the book-shaped Pocket Kosy of 1898, a folding camera of novel design much sought by collectors today.

Pocket Kozy camera of 1897–1901. The camera was advertised to "slip into the pocket like a book"; it also opened for use like a partially opened book and in some ways looks like the revolutionary folding camera of the twentieth century, the SX-70 Polaroid, which also retained the bellows to permit a flexible body design. Today's collectors are happy to pay $400 or more for a Kozy in clean condition.

Stereo Folding Cameras

While the stereo era was past its high-water mark, the photographic industry was creating stereo cameras for the family photographer. Kodak and others were hoping that widely available roll film and this new folding camera would rekindle the interest in the dying embers of the stereo blaze, which had burned fiercely only years earlier in the entertainment-dry Victorian parlors of American homes. Foremost examples of the stereo folding cameras, in a horizontal format to create the necessary side-by-side pictures on 2¼-inch or slightly wider film, make all of the competing cameras look like mold mates from the same factory. Whether as in the Stereo Hawk-Eye, which was produced in various models, or the more popular Stereo Brownie Kodak, the cameras all had the same drop front and red leather bellows pull-out feature.

All of the stereo folding cameras of the early 1900s have the near-identical configuration, since all loaded with roll film that was stretched across the back of the camera during the loading process (Americans had already learned this in the earlier cartridge and Folding Pocket Kodak cameras). All of the cameras opened the same way; a door in the side of the camera dropped to a flat position. Then the camera's owner reached in to pull out the double set of bellows and the standard which supported two lenses. Since many of the shutters for these cameras were air-actuated, a squeeze-bulb on a short length of red tubing was provided. With a firm squeeze of the bulb, a rush of air actuated the shutter on the camera which was of necessity held still for a horizontal photograph. The result was two near-identical negatives on the film—if the photographer remembered to advance the film the full seven inches to bring the fresh film from the roll into the film plane behind the lenses. If he didn't, his next shutter trip would "double-expose" the second picture over the first, ruining both sets of exposures.

Autographic Cameras

In 1914, a new development was featured on the folding camera that awarded Kodak differentiation from its competitors and that also has become a point of interest for collectors. An inventor sold the Eastman Kodak Company a simple idea for $300,-000: a way to "write" on the film edge while the film was still in the camera. A trap door was built into the backs of Kodak folding cameras starting in 1914. The new folding "autographic" cameras were born. A stylus, which was removable from the camera, was the "pencil." Said a typical Kodak announcement ad in *The Literary Digest* of October 10, 1914:

Just release a stop and a little door opens in the back of the Kodak; write whatever notation you want on the red paper of the Autographic Film Cartridge with a pencil or stylus; expose from two to five seconds; close the door and you are ready for the next exposure. On the margin between the negatives will appear a permanent photographic reproduction of the notation you made.

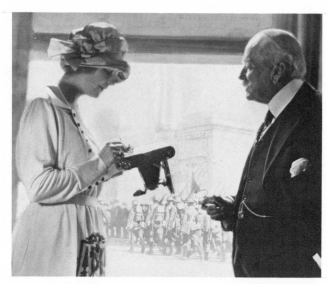

The autographic feature permitted easy identification of the photograph. (*Photograph courtesy of Eastman Kodak Company*)

The *Autographic*

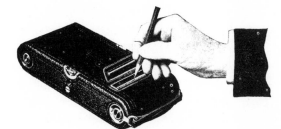

KODAK

You can now date and title your negatives, permanently, and almost instantly at the time you make them.

EVERY negative that is worth making is worth a date and title. The places you visit—interesting dates and facts about the children, their age at the time the pictures were made—the autographs of friends you photograph—these notations add to the value of every picture you make. Architects, engineers and contractors who make photographic records of progressive work, can add greatly to their value by adding notes and dates permanently on the *negatives* by means of the Autographic Kodak. The amateur photographer who wants to improve the quality of his work can make notations on his negatives, of the light conditions, stop and exposure.

Just release a stop and a little door opens in the back of the Kodak ; write whatever notation you want, on the red paper of the Autographic Film Cartridge with a pencil or stylus ; expose from 2 to 5 seconds ; close the door and you are ready for the next exposure. On the margins between the negatives will appear a permanent photographic reproduction of the notation you made. It is not a part of the Autographic plan to have this writing appear in the print itself, but simply that it be kept as a record of date and title on the negative. It is obvious, however, that it is no trouble to include it on the print when desired.

The greatest photographic advance in twenty years.

No. 3A Autographic Kodak, pictures 3¼ x
 5½ in.,   -   -   -   -   -   - $22.50
No. 3 Autographic Kodak, pictures 3¼ x
 4¼ in.,   -   -   -   -   -   - 20.00
No. 1A Autographic Kodak, pictures 2½ x
 4¼ in.,   -   -   -   -   -   - 17.50

EASTMAN KODAK CO.,
At all Kodak dealers'.   ROCHESTER, N. Y., *The Kodak City.*

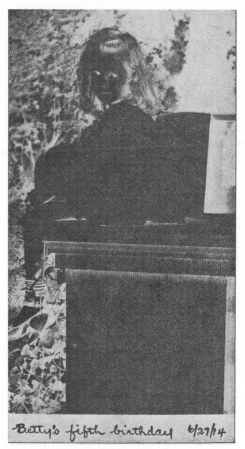

AN AUTOGRAPHIC NEGATIVE.

The 1914 announcement of Kodak's exclusive autographic system. Advertisement from *Photographic Advertising from A-Z.*

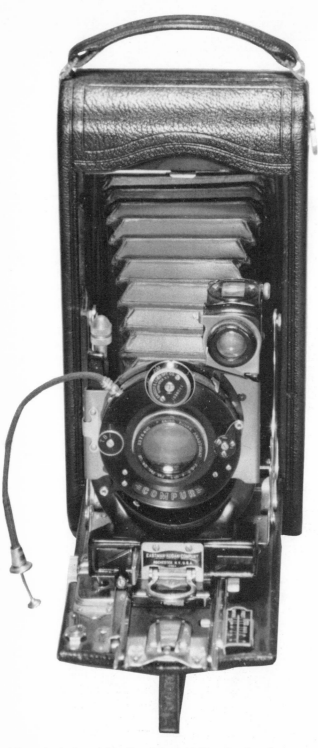

The 3A Autographic Special of 1917: a landmark among collectible cameras from Kodak. It was the world's first camera with a built-in range finder to end guess focusing.

The patented feature was made available only on Kodak and Brownie cameras. Collectors of American cameras seek these autographic cameras, which were sold by the thousands and thousands in many Autographic Kodak models (see Kodak and Brownie listings in Appendix C).

In the early days of folding cameras, the most prestigious folding camera was the 1901 No.3 Folding Pocket Kodak Deluxe with morocco leather and silver trimmings in a hand-sewed carrying case. But in 1916 it was a technical feature and not morocco leather that distinguished the prestige 3A Autographic Kodak camera of 1916: It was the first camera in the world to incorporate a built-in optically precise range finder. It was an invention that had long been necessary, especially for the faster lenses that had begun to appear on the press cameras, since at wide-open apertures the in-focus zone was often measured in inches, not feet. It was this feature, coupled to the press camera, that made it possible for the bulky Graflex cameras to be dropped in favor of the eye-level finder-aimed Speed Graphic cameras. It was this feature that made possible the rapid success of the Leica and Contax cameras with interchangeable lenses, any one of which could be quickly and accurately focused even at the amazing apertures of $f/2$ and even $f/1.5$ at a time when lenses four to eight times slower were in general use.

Other Advanced Kodaks

The overwhelming bulk of folding cameras had the shutter system located up front with the lens. One company developed and stayed with a more difficult shutter: It was located at the *back* of the camera in what is known as the focal plane. This type of shutter is thus called the focal-plane shutter. It operated like a window roller curtain, with a thin slit across the shade rolling at high speed past the film. This shutter, unlike the front-shutter sytems even of the present era, provided a low-cost and accurate way to achieve shutter speeds up to 1/1000 second, necessary for high-speed sports action. It also made possible on the folding camera

The Krauss Takyr of 1906, a French camera, incorporates a back-of-camera (focal plane) shutter and a magazine for quick change of 9-by-12-cm plates. *(From the collection of Dr. R. H. Krauss)*

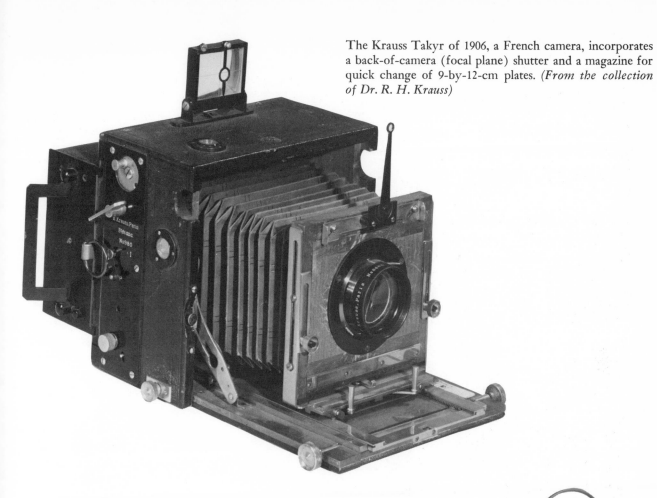

The Graphic folding plate camera of the 1890s became the Speed Graphic of the 1900s with the addition of a built-in back-of-camera (focal plane) shutter. *(From the collection of Matthew R. Isenberg)*

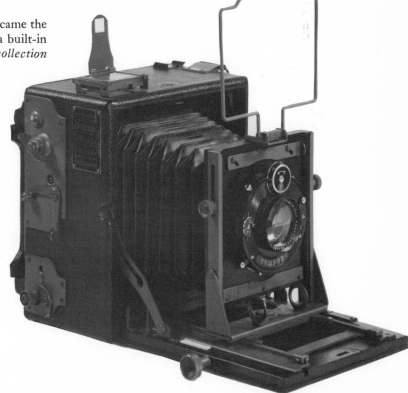

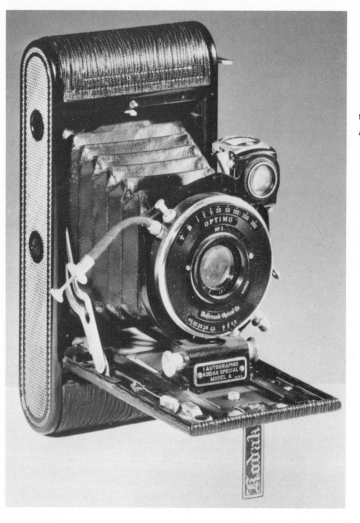

1A Autographic Kodak Special of 1915 offered shutter to 1/300 second and lens to f/6.3, a superior combination for the folding cameras of the time. *(Photograph courtesy of Eastman Kodak Company)*

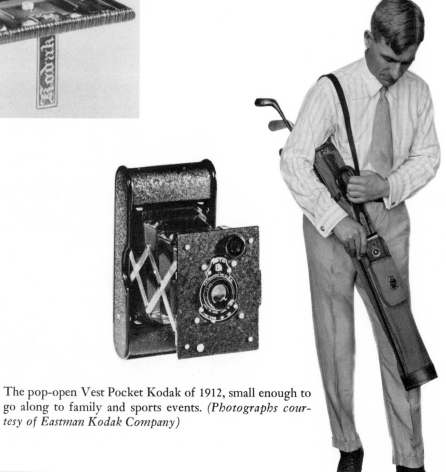

The pop-open Vest Pocket Kodak of 1912, small enough to go along to family and sports events. *(Photographs courtesy of Eastman Kodak Company)*

the advantages of lens changing, which had been part and parcel of the professional's view-camera system.

The camera maker was Folmer & Schwing Mfg. Co. in New York. They had started with the common folding plate cameras of the 1890s and had made the Graphic one of the important cameras in that format. The shutter, which they made available for many cameras, became the basis of a Graflex (see Chapter 6, "Single-lens Reflex Cameras"), with built-in shutter, and then of the Graphic, which became the press camera. It was the Graflex that won press attention until the coupled range finders made available as an accessory in the late 1920s brought the Graphic folding camera back into favor.

In 1908 and 1909, Kodak entered two cameras into competition against these plate-loaded cameras with a roll-film camera with high-speed focal-plane shutters: the 1A and 4A Speed Kodaks for 2¼-by-4½-inch and 4¼-by-6½-inch pictures. Each was furnished with f/6.3 lenses, moderately fast for the time but not uniquely so. The Speed Kodaks incorporated the Folmer & Schwing (now Kodak-owned) focal-plane shutters, but they enjoyed only limited success, possibly because they were roll-film loaded and had no precise means for focusing and viewing. The available sheet-film–loaded camera of the period was of more interest to the cameraman likely to require the high shutter speeds. They were discontinued in 1913, shortly after the introduction of the No.0 Graphic, a smaller, boxy camera with a high-speed shutter that enjoyed modest sales until the 1920s. Today they are only rarely seen and are in great demand by the collector market, selling for over $100 when available.

It was the focal-plane shutter, in both English and German cameras, that was to be the basis for some of photography's most dramatic camera de-

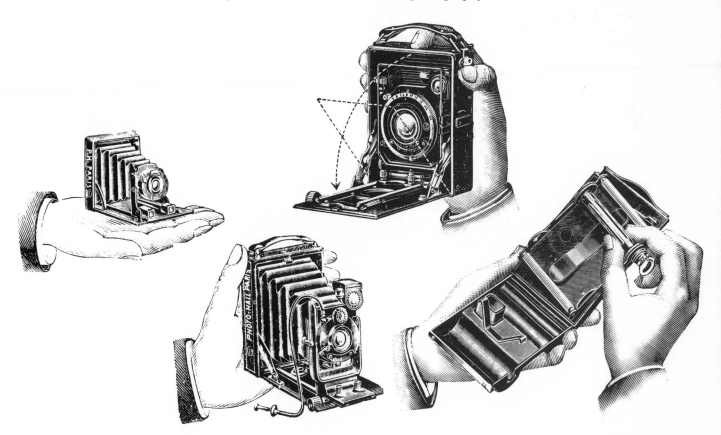

Germany became the center for all-metal folding cameras loaded with cut film sheets or roll film between 1910 and 1930. Most were in the small sizes for family use.

velopments. An outstanding example would be the Ermanox camera of the Ernemann Company. This camera was made in a number of sizes for plate-loaded holders, and it was the smallest Ermanox, loaded with plates only 4½ by 6 centimeters (about the size of a pack of cigarettes), which was equipped with the super-fast f/1.8 or f/2 Ernostar lens, that startled the photographic world in the early 1920s.

This high-speed lens permitted indoor photography without flash, and it gave birth to the second great wave of candid photographs; the first wave had been the candid street photographs made by the cameras of the detective-camera era before the twentieth century (see Chapter 4," Detective Cameras and Later Novelty Cameras"). The Ermanox in the hands of a skilled photographer, Erich Salomon, brought to the world scenes within the halls of the League of Nations made in the unposed manner that would become the hallmark of photography only a decade later when the miniature camera conquered the world. The Ermanox will always be identified with Salomon; today no one can remember any photograph or photographer associated with the 1A or 4A Speed Kodaks.

THE VEST-POCKET ERA

Before World War I, Kodak had launched a new smaller-size line of folding roll-film cameras: the vest pockets (smaller than the Folding Pocket Kodaks). It created a photographic negative of a new size, only 1⅝ by 2¼ inches (the 4½-by-6-centimeter size of smaller cameras in England and Germany), which was offered in a new film number, #127.

The camera became known as the Doughboy's camera since it was a flat, easy-to-carry-in-the-tunic pocket camera for the soldier of World War I. A Seneca version in this style was even called the Military Vest Pocket Seneca. By the mid-1930s, there had been so many models of Kodak cameras, plus Brownie cameras, plus Hawk-Eye and smaller cameras of other manufacturers that they provided a torrent of new film sales for the Eastman Kodak Company.

The VP cameras of Kodak and its competitors were offered in pop-out and later fold-down front cameras like the first Folding Pocket Kodaks. Models were offered with the most simple shutters but also in advanced designs. For instance, in 1921, the Vest Pocket Kodak Special offered a Kodak Anastigmat f/6.9 lens, which made possible portraits at three feet without the need for accessory (closeup) lenses. By then, the phenomenon of the autographic performance, an incorporated feature, was only an afterthought in the advertising, which stated: "A remarkably compact camera—likewise an unusually efficient camera, autographic, and richly finished." Like all cameras of this basic pull-out–bellows design, large and small, the camera was held at the waist to be aimed through a tiny reflex finder.

It was in the 1920s that Kodak began to lose its leadership as the maker of the bold photographic innovations (except in the cine area). Despite the internal postwar troubles in Germany, it was there that new superior cameras emerged in a growing tide that was only to be shut off by World War II.

There was a whole new concept of smaller folding plate cameras that could be hand-held developed in lightweight metals. The leading camera stores of the United States became display centers for numerous boxy, black, all-metal plate-loaded folding cameras that had drop-down doors and pull-out lens-shutter systems. These snuggled into the closed case and then opened to be the finest corrected lenses of the period with the most advanced shutters. This was especially true of the Compur. While the great Voigtländer camera had its own lenses, bodies made by lesser-known camera companies often featured the preferred Zeiss lenses, which were considered to be the symbol of lens perfection for that decade. These early cameras of the post–World War I period were reaching the United States shores in the smaller sizes of 6 by 9 centimeters and 9 by 12 centimeters. They have been generally ignored by collectors as too alike in their appearances and too innocuous in their mechanical or optical detailing to be of interest. But

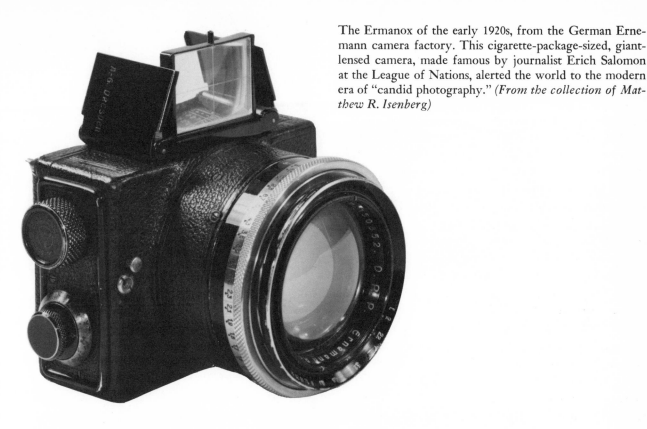

The Ermanox of the early 1920s, from the German Ernemann camera factory. This cigarette-package-sized, giant-lensed camera, made famous by journalist Erich Salomon at the League of Nations, alerted the world to the modern era of "candid photography." *(From the collection of Matthew R. Isenberg)*

some, such as the Bentzin and the KW Patent ETUI, are marvels of compactness in design.

Almost simultaneously, these cameras were offered in roll-film models without the advantages of the ground glass. These cameras with fine optics, priced in most cases lower than the similar-size Kodak cameras of the period, won great family interest. Where there was innovation, it was in the direction of miniaturization. A number of cameras, for example, were designed to accept the now widely available #127 film, which in the United States provided 8 pictures on the roll in the typical vest-pocket Kodak of the time. The German innovation was to create a camera that made possible 16 pictures on this same roll of film.

In the same way, cameras were designed that could accept the equally widely popular #120 roll film, which in most U.S. cameras provided 8 pictures, each 2¼ by 3¼ inches. The German cameras won attention by permitting (optionally, before loading the roll) a choice of 8 or 16 pictures on the roll. Other models offered only 16 pictures

on the roll, and these cameras won wide success both for their low price and their compactness.

When these cameras became an important factor in the mid-1920s, Kodak began to review its own product line. One step was ultimately to employ a leading industrial designer, Walter Dorwin Teague, to assist in improving the appeal of the Kodak product.

One of the leaders in the new Kodak dress-up was the Kodak Vanity camera aimed at the women of America. It was offered in combination with a matching lipstick in 1928. In 1929, the followup was with the Kodak Petite camera: a vest-pocket camera offered in such colors as green, gold, rose, gray, lavender, and blue. It was in the same period that Ford Motor Company executives were still boasting that you could buy a Ford in any color you wanted—so long as it was black. Kodak was not the first with the vanity camera; Ansco had already created an ensemble with a hidden camera in the case (see Chapter 4, "Detective Cameras and Later Novelty Cameras").

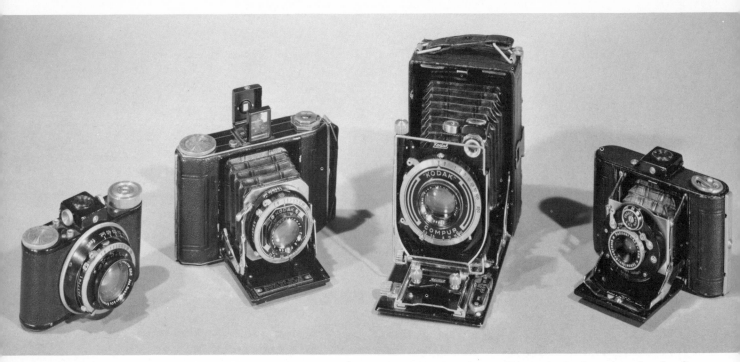

In the early 1930s, Kodak took over the Nagel-Werke in Stuttgart, Germany, and brought back to America the first German-made Kodaks. *Left to right:* the Pupille, Duo Six-20, Recomar, and Vollenda. There are collectors of all variants of the German Kodak line. *(Photograph courtesy of Eastman Kodak Company)*

The next major news from Kodak was to come from Europe. It was as if someone had decided that "if you can't beat 'em, join 'em." In 1932, Kodak acquired the Nagel camera factory, and now there were Kodak cameras that had the compact design, the 16 images per roll, and the move toward miniaturization. Ten years after the Germans had opened the market in America for 6-by-9-centimeter and 9-by-12-centimeter plate-loaded cameras, Kodak announced their German-made Kodak Recomars Nos.18 and 33.

An outstanding and typically German folding camera of the German Kodak works was the Kodak Duo Six-20, which was introduced in 1934. It was the first Kodak camera to take 16 pictures on roll film originally designed for 8 photographs. The numbering system on Kodak paper backing on the film now had to be altered to accommodate cameras that could take 8, 12, or 16 pictures on a roll. The location of the little red window at the camera back determined which number series could be seen by the photographer when he advanced the

film between exposures. Part of the decision was surely the effects of the depression. Kodak was saying: Get more pictures for your film dollar.

These smaller cameras were among the first cameras for the family's picture-album photographer from Kodak in this period that could be aimed by being held up to the eye. (Thirty years earlier, the 1A Speed Kodak could also be aimed this way.) From this time on, almost without exception, no Kodak camera was designed that was not to be used at eye level, with the exception of certain box cameras.

THE AMERICAN-MADE FOLDING CAMERA COMPETITION FADES

The cameras of the World War I period and beyond which bore such names as Seneca, Ingento, Buster Brown, and others from mail-order companies, had disappeared one by one. Ansco, before 1930 an acquisition of the German Agfa camera and film company, was the major domestic competitor to Kodak camera sales. For the non-Kodak camera to attract attention, it had to offer never-before-seen features. Thus, in 1925 Ansco introduced an atypical roll-film camera that brought the photographic industry to its feet in applause: The film rolled itself to the next position at the touch of a button! The camera included a spring-loaded wind-up system for the 6-exposure roll. It was called the Semi-Automatic Ansco and was launched in the popular 1A size for 2½-by-4¼-inch pictures in $30 and $40 models. The Automatic Ansco advanced the film upon clicking the shutter.

In 1926 Ansco introduced the first popular American-made 35-mm camera: the Ansco Memo (see Chapter 8, "35-mm," page 135). All of these cameras are a must for the collectors of the Ansco cameras, and the Semi-Automatic and Automatic are classics for the collector of auto-advance cameras. Memo cameras are widely offered in collector circles for under $50; the rarer Semi-Automatic and Automatic are seen only occasionally, and their owners will not be tempted to sell or trade for less than $100 in value.

In 1926, the roll-film camera was taken one step

Kodak bids for the woman's market in the late 1920s with cameras in color-coordinated feminine cases. Note the Art Deco design emblazoned on baseplate. *(Photograph courtesy of Eastman Kodak Company)*

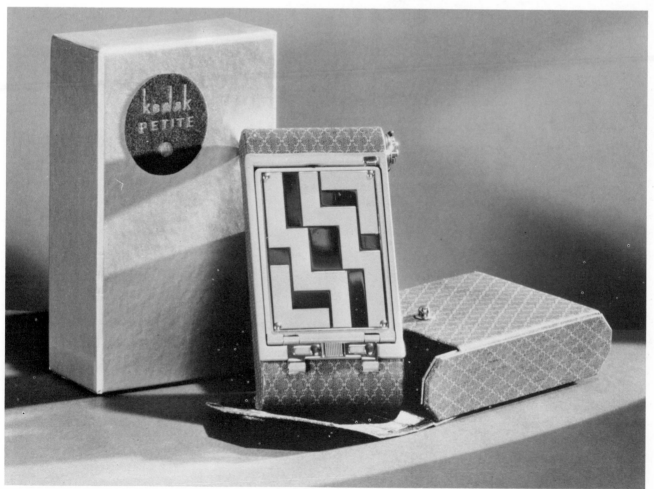

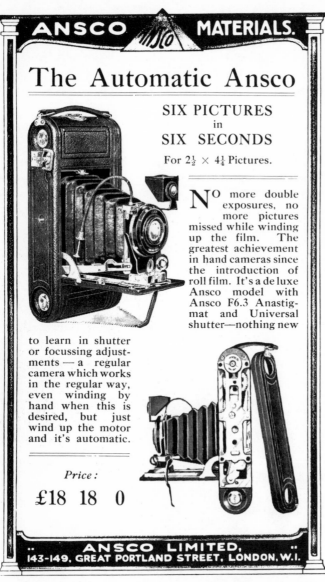

The Automatic Ansco

SIX PICTURES
in
SIX SECONDS

For 2½ × 4¼ Pictures.

NO more double exposures, no more pictures missed while winding up the film. The greatest achievement in hand cameras since the introduction of roll film. It's a de luxe Ansco model with Ansco F6.3 Anastigmat and Universal shutter—nothing new to learn in shutter or focussing adjustments — a regular camera which works in the regular way, even winding by hand when this is desired, but just wind up the motor and it's automatic.

Price:

£18 18 0

ANSCO LIMITED,
143-149, GREAT PORTLAND STREET, LONDON, W.I.

Ansco makes history with an undistinguished-looking folding roll-film camera in 1925 called the Automatic Ansco. Its spring-wound motor advanced film after exposure. (*Advertisement from* British Journal Photographic Almanac)

The German camera makers threw their hats into the American ring in the same period with their revolutionary 35-mm cameras: the Leica and the Zeiss Contax. No wonder they quickly won the reputation as being the leaders in the field of camera development. It was in the mid-1930s that the Germans produced what were surely the most remarkable roll-film cameras ever to come into being. Zeiss produced their Ikonta line in an improved group known as the Super Ikontas. They lived up to the "super" with such features as built-in range finders, precision shutters, and superior optics; and finally, in the model called the Super Ikonta BX, Zeiss engineers included an on-camera electric exposure meter that even guided the photographer to the correct exposure. No American camera of the time offered this advantage. Even today, the unquestioned roll-film camera king from a technical point of view is the Super Ikonta BX in

Kodak launched a new roll-film size (#828) in 1935 with the compact, molded Bantam camera. (*Photograph courtesy of Eastman Kodak Company*)

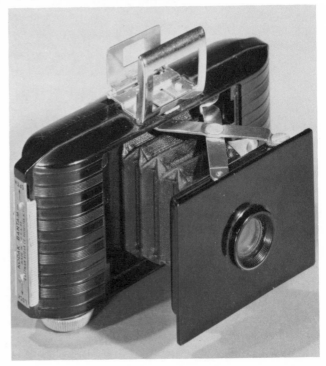

ahead by the Palko. This amazing camera had provision for a ground glass (not unusual since this had been available in the 1890s in the Cartridge Kodaks, for example), but it included a built-in system for adjusting picture size for up to 31 pictures on a 10-exposure roll of film. Palko cameras are among the most rare of roll-film cameras. They could be loaded with the popular #122 (postcard-size) film.

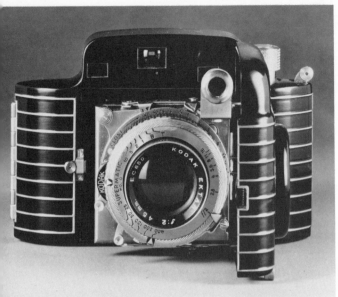

The landmark Bantam Special, delight of the collector with dramatic Teague design and f/2 lens, first offered in 1936. *(Photograph courtesy of Eastman Kodak Company)*

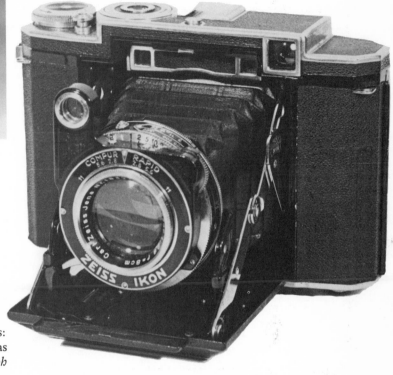

The landmark and high point in folding roll-film cameras: the Zeiss Super Ikonta B. No roll-film camera since has matched its features, boast collector-owners. *(Photograph courtesy of John and Valerie Craig)*

the model in which the range-finder window is combined with the aiming-viewfinder window. The similar-appearing Super Ikonta B was the same camera without the exposure meter.

Photographers are still glad to locate and buy this fine-quality camera of the 1930s for use with the readily available roll film on which it takes 11 exposures, each a square (2¼ by 2¼ inches).

America brought the flag of excellence back to America and to Rochester in 1938: Kodak introduced the Super Kodak Six-20. Photography was never again to be the same. This unusual roll-film camera actually set itself to the prevalent light to assure perfectly exposed picures regardless of the

experience of the owner. It was the first mass-produced camera with a built-in electric eye linked to the aperture control of the lens. It took 8 pictures on a roll, each 2¼ by 3¼ inches. With the advent of World War II, the production of this amazing photographic innovation was shut down. It was never made again and is listed as "discontinued, 1945."

Selling for nearly $250, the Super Kodak Six-20 never expected or achieved a mass market. Relatively few were made, so the collector today is fortunate to locate one. When one is offered in collector circles at $750, it is quickly sold. It has become an American classic along with the Model A Ford or the Cord automobile.

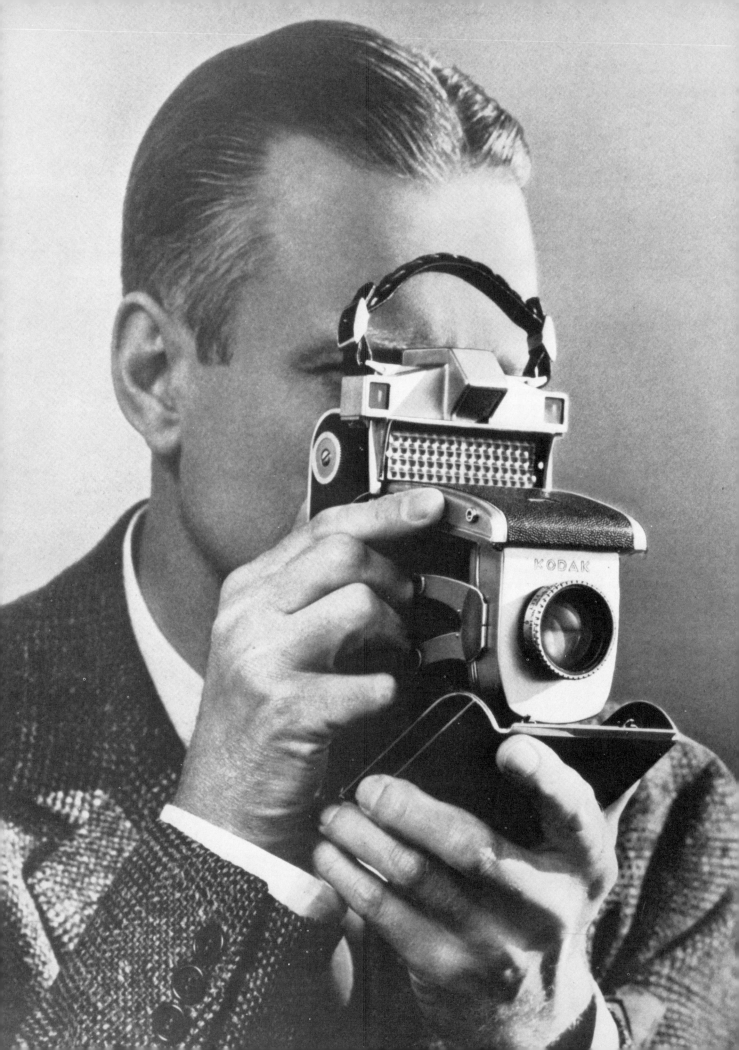

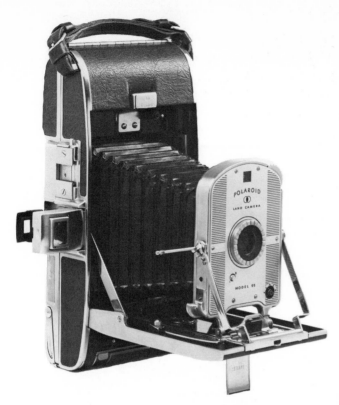

The Polaroid Model 95. First of the current generation of picture-in-a-minute cameras, this awkward and bulky folding camera introduced millions of families to the pleasures and excitement of instant photography in 1948. The Polaroid system started with quarter-plate (3¼-by-4¼ inches) near-sepia images; later other sizes and a high-quality black-and-white image was provided. Polaroid images in color followed a few years later.

As the first of the many Polaroid cameras in the nearly thirty years since the debut of the Model 95, it became a familiar sight wherever families of the 1950s gathered. Large for the size of image it captured (because of the need to provide for the over-size roll of film interleaved with photo paper and the pods of gelatinous chemistry, which processed both a negative and a positive simultaneously) the heavy and clumsy camera is already a collectible classic, one still readily available for a few dollars almost everywhere today. (*Photograph courtesy of Polaroid Corporation*)

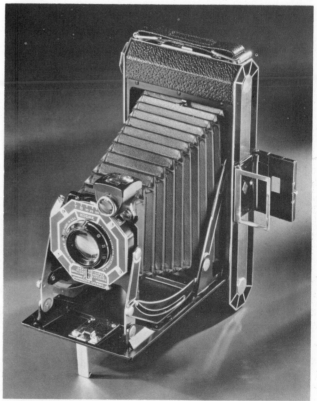

(FACING)
The Super Kodak Six-20 of 1938: a prized collectible for folding camera and Kodak collectors. It was the world's first camera with automatic electric-eye exposure control. (*Photograph courtesy of Eastman Kodak Company*)

Kodak Six-16 camera of 1932 was a modernized roll-film camera reflecting the Art Deco period. It added an eye-level viewfinder, which had long been part of German cameras of this general configuration. (*Photograph courtesy of Eastman Kodak Company*)

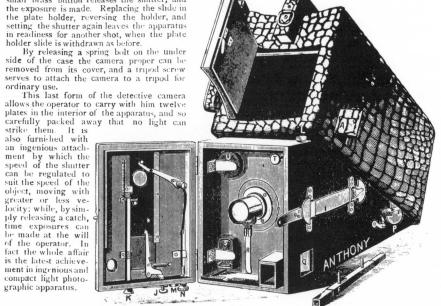
A rare detective camera accessory. The satchel for Anthony's Satchel Detective Camera alone would bring over $2,500 in the collector market.

4
Detective Cameras and Later Novelties

The successful emergence of the dry-plate process in the early 1880s eliminated the need for the photographer to enter a tent on site to ready his negative materials. The new plates immediately freed the photographer from the burdensome laboratory work in the difficult conditions out in the field. Almost just as quickly it opened the way to new design concepts in cameras.

The owner of the view camera with ground glass back for composing and focusing was able to load dry-plate glass into his earlier wet-plate holders. The development of sensitized emulsion on a flexible base (not glass) led to the development of the Eastman-Walker Roll Film Holder, which now made it possible for the view camera to be loaded with negative materials on flexible film. The idea of nonglass film was not new; the idea had been tried thirty years earlier in Europe but without success.

While the roll-film idea was trying to find its way into acceptance, the dry plates, which could be carried about in a box, were the beginning of a new period of photography in America. These first years of the dry plate up to just before 1900 have become known as the era of the detective camera.

The first of this new group of hand-held cameras in the United States was issued a patent in January of 1883. Referred to as a "photographic camera" (U.S. Patent 270,133) and patented as William Schmid's Patent Detective Camera, it was essentially a box camera that loaded at back with a glass-plate holder. "Anyone provided with this instrument can take photographs while walking along the street without attracting notice from the curious," stated *Anthony's Photographic Bulletin* in September 1883.

It was not a camera to anyone but the cognoscenti. To the world, it was a wooden box with a metal handle. There were no bellows, no protruding lenses, no tripod. The photographer did not stand behind it; he carried it in his hands and looked down at a tiny window to aim and shoot. It was in fact the first hand-held "box" camera.

It sold for the astronomical (at the time) sum of $55 and was available from E. & H. T. Anthony & Co. of New York. It took a quarter-plate photograph in its first model (3¼ by 4¼ inches), and by 1885 the Anthony catalogue advertised a 4-by-5-inch model for $60. Writing in *Photographica*, the periodical of the Photographic Historical Society of New York, in May 1973, photo-equipment historian Eaton S. Lothrop, Jr., points out that this camera was "at the root, so to speak, of the hand camera development (particularly in the United States)."[1]

A number of cameras emerged within the next years which aped the design concept—and the detective-camera era was on. In 1887, Anthony, which had made a success of the Schmid, introduced the Anthony Satchel Detective Camera, another box camera but with further concealment of its true function by a satchellike shell that fitted over the wooden box. Models were priced as low as $35 and up to $93 (the latter encased in genuine alligator and equipped with a superior lens). With-

[1] P. 11.

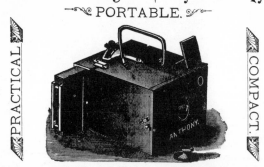
Ad announcing the first American detective camera of 1883.

out the satchel case, the Anthony Climax camera (see photograph on page 88) was sold for as little as $25.

By 1893, the Anthony Climax was no longer being offered, and by 1896, even the Satchel Detective Camera was no longer listed in the Anthony catalogue. And although in 1890–1891 the Anthony Company introduced the PDQ (Photography Done Quickly) in $15 and $20 models, they were discontinued sometime around 1891–1892. Clearly the problem was competition.

The competition to the Anthony cameras of the period came from the Anthony Company's traditional rival, Scovill Mfg. Co., which was later to merge with Anthony to form the world-famous Ansco company. In 1886 Scovill announced their own detective camera in the 3¼-by-4¼-inch and 4-by-5-inch sizes that loaded with double-plate holders. The availability of roll film permitted development of the Scovill Roll-Holder Detective Camera, which was furnished with a roll-film holder that was interchangeable with the more standard double–glass-plate holder. (Within two years, George Eastman would rock the detective-camera field with the Kodak camera, preloaded with 100 shots and requiring no holders. A year earlier, his Eastman Detective Camera, a 4 by 5, met with no interest.)

Other cameras of the period, in wood, even antique oak, and in the leather coverings that were to be the symbol of box cameras for the next fifty years, were the Waterbury, the Mascot, and the Knack, all from Scovill and available until about 1895.

Today's collectors avidly seek the larger detective cameras of the period like the Hawk-Eye Detective of the Boston Camera Company (later sold by Blair). These cameras, a foot long and oblong overall, had the bulk to store within their forms the

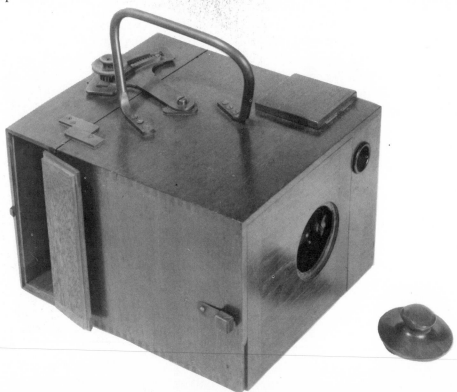

Actual Schmid camera of the inventor who started the phenomenon of the hand-held box-shaped camera.

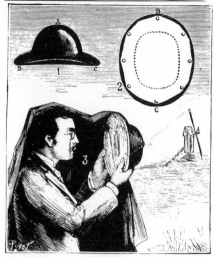

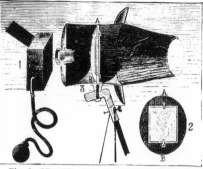

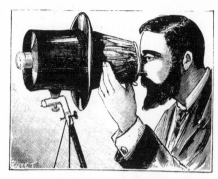

Cameras concealed in derbys, top hats, even cane handles developed from inventive imaginations in the 1880s and 1890s.

Fig. 1.—THE DERBY HAT AS A CAMERA OBSCURA.

Fig. 2.—BEAVER HAT CONVERTED INTO A PHOTOGRAPHIC CAMERA.

Fig. 3.—MODE OF USING THE APPARATUS.

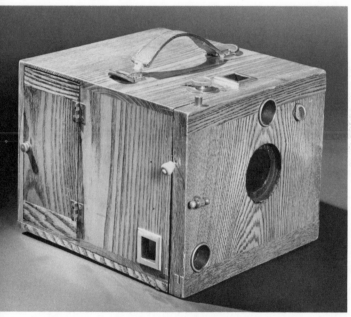

Blair Hawk-Eye of 1892 is a shoe-box-sized camera for photography on glass plates. *(From the collection of Marvin and Katrinka Kreisman)*

The Knack 4-by-5-inch plate detective camera was among the vast array developed with the advent of the dry-plate negative. *(Photograph courtesy of GAF)*

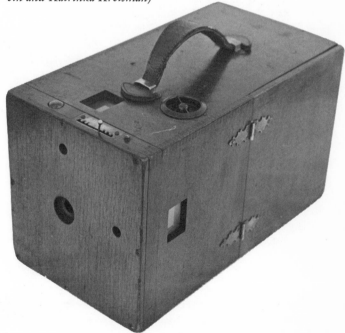

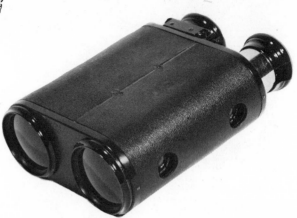

Rare Stereo Physiographe was a French binocular camera, ca. 1903. *(From the collection of Matthew R. Isenberg)*

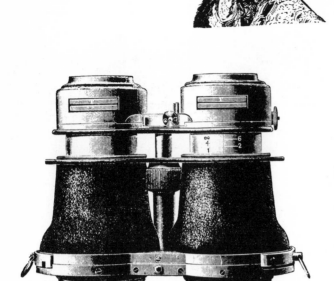

Goerz Photo-Stereo binocular of 1901 is literally unknown in America.

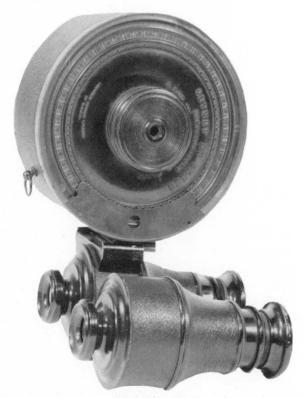

The binocular camera credited as the world's first detective camera: the Jumelle di Nicour of 1867. *(From the collection of Matthew R. Isenberg)*

additional glass plates that permitted the photographer to take additional exposures without returning to the darkroom. The Hawk-Eye remained available until 1898, and features that were developed as it evolved were incorporated in box cameras all the way up to 1915.

All of these detective cameras and the generation of boxy black cameras that followed, whether roll- or plate-film loaded, were in major competition with the lower priced ($25) and smaller (only 6½-by-3¼-by-3¼-inch) first Kodak camera of 1888. Then in 1895 Kodak dropped the other shoe by introducing a tiny box camera: the Pocket Kodak at $5.

In 1894, a camera so small that its advertisement warned, "it's not a toy," was the Kombi. The beginnings of truly small mass-produced and easy-to-use small cameras had begun, and the era of the novelty camera was launched. (The Pocket Kodak and the Kombi are discussed fully in Chapter 2, "Box Cameras.")

Cameras had been hidden in many shapes—pistols, binoculars, and the other unlikely forms—starting as early as the 1860s. In the late 1880s, one of the most ingenious and successful was R. D. Gray's (later C. P. Stirn's) Patent Concealed Vest Camera. This was a camera built as a flat, round metal drum in 6-inch and 7-inch diameters. It hung by a cord about one's neck, concealed under a coat or vest so that its lens could protrude through a buttonhole. Six round pictures could be taken on a

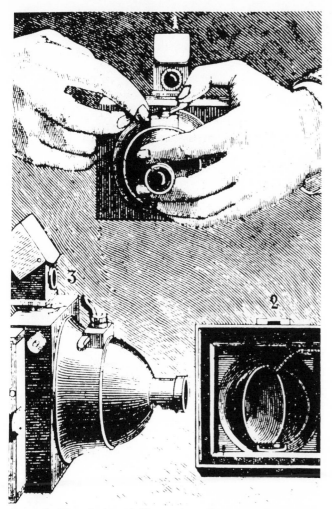

An early French (1890) illustration of the front, side, and interior view of the functionally designed Photosphere. *(From* Aide Memoire de Photographie, *1890)*

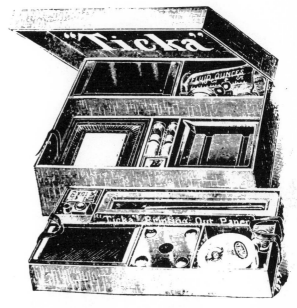

The Ticka Watch Camera was sold with a darkroom system with chemicals, darkroom aids, and photographic paper in England and France after 1903.

special round glass plate before the camera was opened in the darkroom. The maker advertised:

The only camera invisible to the eye; carried concealed under the coat or vest; takes 6 sharp pictures without a change of plate; always ready and in focus.

C. P. Stirn also made another amazing bit of photographic equipment: the Wonder Panoramic Camera, a true wonder in that while it measured only 4 by 4 by 6 inches, it made pictures 3¼ inches wide and 18 inches long! While the Stirn Panoramic is so rarely seen that it is hardly known by collectors, the Stirn Vest Camera, more publicized today and seen in many collections, is a very ea-

gerly sought camera, novel in its shape and in its use of a round glass plate.

The idea of a round camera became a popular one, as the collectibles within that framework indicate. In 1886, the British firm of Lancaster & Sons introduced their small, collapsible watch camera. The Photoret was also a round camera, but it was tiny, shaped like a pocketwatch. A film disc was shifted for each successive exposure exactly as in the Stirn.

The Expo Watch Camera and its English counterpart, the Ticka Watch Camera of the early 1900s, also took the shape of a railroadman's pocketwatch. Exposure was through the winding stem in which a

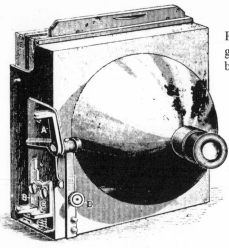

Ford's Tom Thumb camera of 1883. It loaded with square glass plates and is occasionally found in its original wooden box with plateholders.

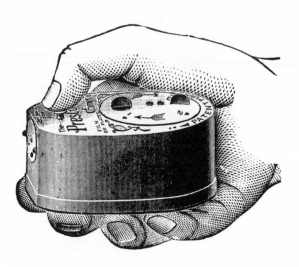

Just over 3 inches long and 2 inches wide, the tiny Pocket Presto was an amazing camera that could be loaded with glass plates or with a fifty-shot roll of film. (*From* Photographic Advertising A-Z)

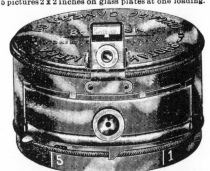

THE 1897 IMPROVED PHOTAKE

Has Every Feature Desired by Amateur Photographers.
Has a Brilliant View Finder.
Has a Superior Achromatic Lens.
Time and Instantaneous Safety Shutter operated without resetting.
It is made of seamless metal beautifully finished.
Its circular form makes it small in size and large in capacity
Takes 5 pictures 2 x 2 inches on glass plates at one loading.

WHY Buy a camera and before you can use it have to spend several dollars for appliances and lose a week's pleasure in delay. We send you the PHOTAKE CAMERA with complete outfit consisting of six dry plates, developing and fixing chemicals for same, paper to print 12 pictures, a Ruby light, and book of directions, postpaid to any part of the United States, for **$2.50**

Thousands now in use. Here's one of the many letters received daily:

"I have had two $5.00 cameras but I like the PHOTAKE the best, even if it does take a smaller picture."
W. J. DEAN, 74 South St., Biddeford, Me.

Every camera guaranteed as represented.
Send two cent stamp for Photake Booklet and sample picture.
CHICAGO CAMERA CO., 58 Fifth Avenue, CHICAGO.

Expo Police Camera

(The Newest, Smallest No-Bellows Roll Film Camera Yet Made.)

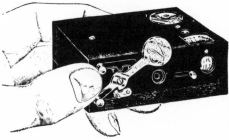

The Police Camera, the newest (patents 1911) and most unique small camera on the market, is, as its name implies, designed for instant use, without wasting the time or attracting the attention that is unavoidable in taking pictures, even with the smallest folding or bellows camera.

The Expo Police Camera was roll-film loaded and is among the smallest known box cameras, ca. 1915.

The tiny round Photake loaded with glass plates. (*From* Photographic Advertising from A-Z)

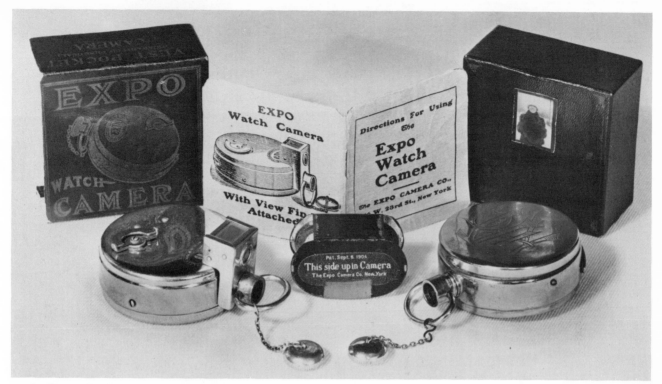

Look-alike collectibles: the Expo Watch Camera (United States) and the Ticka Watch Camera (England). *(From the collection of Alan and Paulette Cotter)*

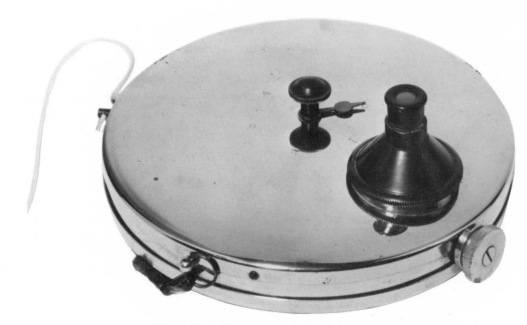

Stirn's Vest Camera of 1886. It hung around the neck on string, worn under a vest with its lens protruding through a buttonhole. *(Photograph courtesy of Asahi Pentax Museum)*

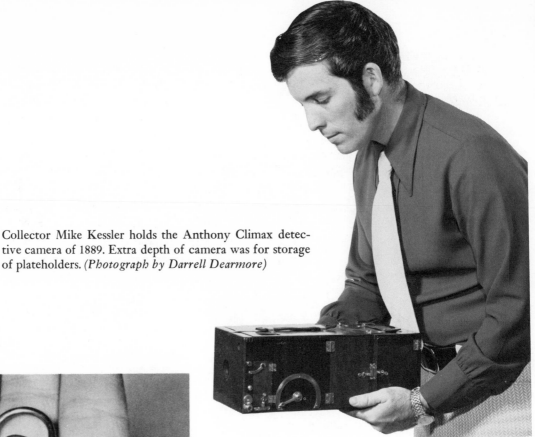

Collector Mike Kessler holds the Anthony Climax detective camera of 1889. Extra depth of camera was for storage of plateholders. *(Photograph by Darrell Dearmore)*

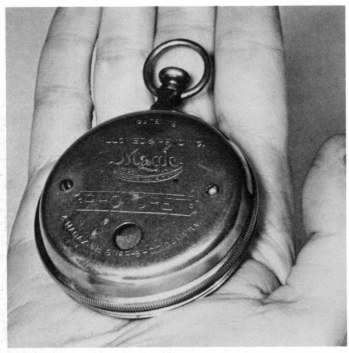

A rare watch camera, the Magic Photoret, ca. 1893, took photographs on a plate disc. *(From the collection of Alan and Paulette Cotter)*

lens was concealed. Each loaded with a cassette of film in some ways not unlike today's Instamatic #126 cartridge. Both of these cameras are well known to collectors and examples are usually to be found at most photographica trade fairs. Depending on condition, they can be had for about $100 each.

The Photake, also a round camera, was unusual in 1896 in that it loaded with glass plates so that its owner could take five exposures before changing plates. This is an exceptionally rare example of a tiny novelty camera of the period. Its proponents advised prospective owners that they need not put up with "kinky" roll film of the time.

By the period of World War I, a further model had been added to the Expo camera line: the Expo Police Camera. This was a small flat box that never achieved the popularity of the Expo Watch Camera. Its simple shutter and film-winding arrangement make it almost a boxy version of the proven round Expo design. But because so few were sold over the years, collectors will pay two and three times the price of the Expo Watch Camera for the Police model.

One of the most interesting of the novelty and detective cameras was particularly amazing and was aimed at the female market of 1926. At that time Ansco introduced the Photo Vanity, a small travel case for the woman who wanted lipstick, powder, rouge, and a mirror (in the case lid) to provide a complete makeup capability. A boxlike section within the vanity concealed a camera that was aimed and used when the travel case was closed, resting on a table or held in the hands. The camera is known only to the most sophisticated collectors and would have a value over $500 to the detective/novelty camera collector.

Kodak brought out its own vanity cameras in colors and with makeup ensembles starting in 1928; none of these was based on a *hidden* camera. Kodak's final effort in the market was the Kodak Coquette, an ensemble of a Kodak Vanity camera in color with a matching lipstick and compact introduced in 1930. These are eagerly sought, and few ensembles are found intact today.

MINIATURE NOVELTIES

In the 1930s, one of the most dramatically tiny and effective cameras in the history of photography was developed in Riga, Latvia, by a brilliant engineer, Walter Zapp. He took his stainless steel cigarlike camera all over the world to interest photo dealers in the idea of ultraminiaturization: the Minox was born. It took a picture on Europe's new smaller motion-picture film (9.5 mm, unperforated) to make a negative no larger than a pinky nail (8 by 11 millimeters).

But the idea of miniaturization was not a new one. One hundred years earlier, William Henry Fox Talbot had created photographs in tiny box cameras, which his wife referred to as "mousetraps." The cameras took pictures only slightly larger than postage stamps. These prototypes were for his own experimentation and were never mass-produced. The originals are in the British Science Museum where they are treasured for what they are—the world's first miniature cameras.

The Minox had barely become known when the events of World War II and the bloodbath in Europe was to make this unusual tiny camera a welcome tool for military-espionage purposes. In the years that followed, the Minox became a prestige novelty camera of the upper echelons of the financial world, sparked by advertising in such magazines and newspapers as *Fortune* and the *Wall Street Journal*. The Minox of today is no longer stainless steel, and it is now a product of Germany, available with a fabulous range of special accessories and photo aids, which make this camera the basic symbol of ultraminiature success.

Perhaps the most unusual camera in the miniature field of the 1930s was the Compass, a design of

Cameras were hidden in book or made to appear like books, as is Dr. Krügener's Patent Book Camera of 1892. (*From the collection of Matthew R. Isenberg*)

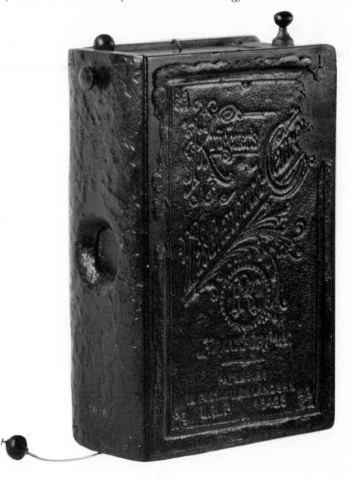

A 1889 advertisement for the Blair Hawk-Eye. *(From* Photographic Advertising from A-Z*)*

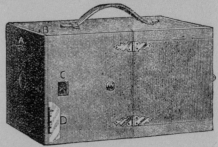
An 1890 advertisement for the P.D.Q. (Photography Done Quickly). *(From* Photographic Advertising from A-Z*)*

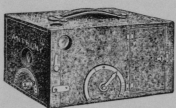

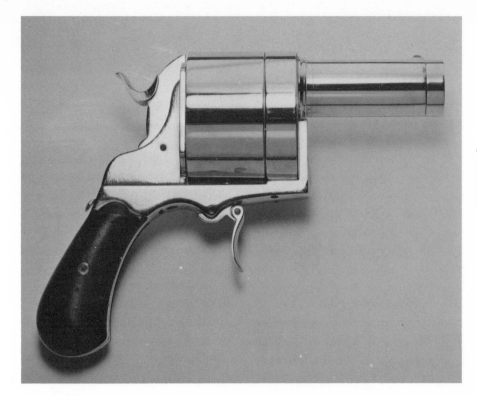

The Enjalbert Photorevolver of 1882. It took ten photographs, each postage-stamp sized. *(From the collection of Michel Auer, France)*

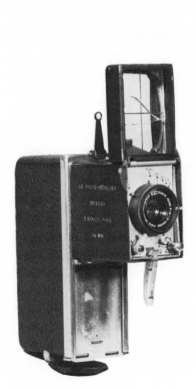

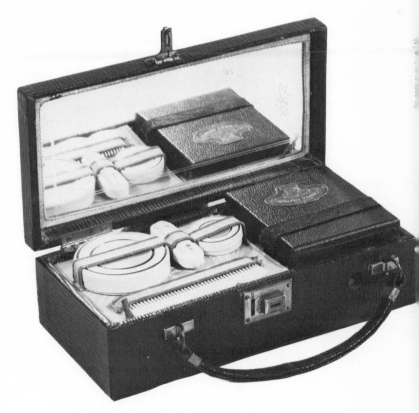

The Krauss Photo-Revolver of 1921 took a magazine for forty-eight plates or roll film for one hundred shots. *(From the collection of Dr. R. H. Krauss)*

The Ansco Photo Vanity of 1926. It carried make-up aids and hid within a camera loaded with #127 roll film. *(From the collection of Matthew R. Isenberg)*

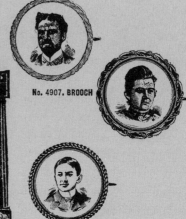
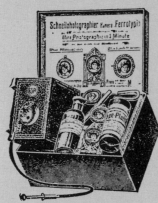
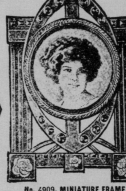
Minute Brooch Camera was sold in the 1920s with plates and miniature frames for the tintype process at $4.35.

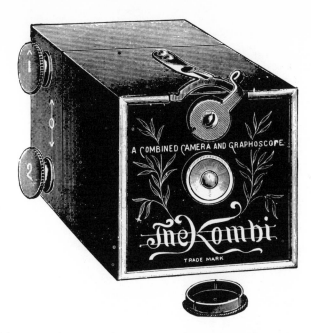

The Kombi (actual size) was an all-metal novelty camera of 1893.

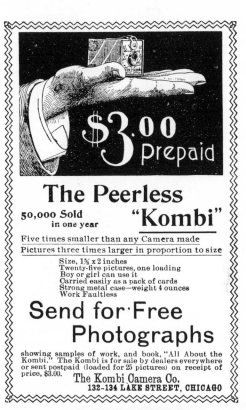

Advertised at $3, thousands of Kombis were sold in its first years. Today's collector pays $100 and more.

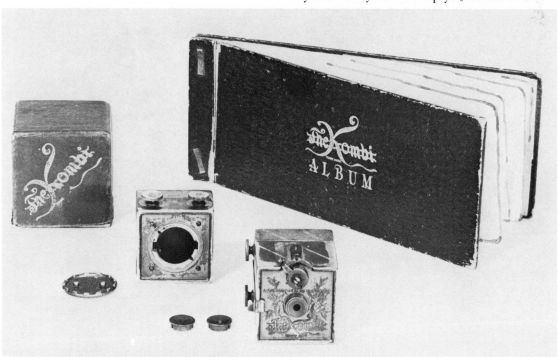

The Kombi and its interchangeable back, box, and a Kombi photo album. (*From the collection of Alan and Paulette Cotter*)

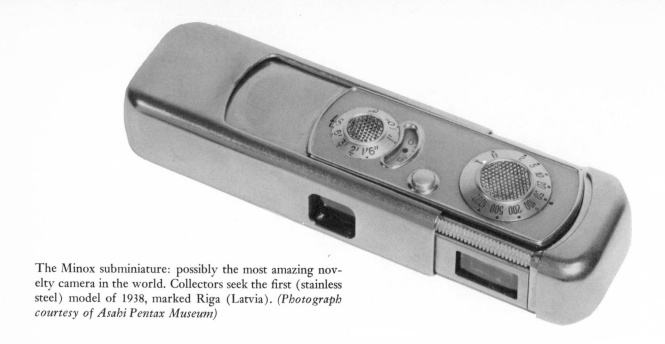

The Minox subminiature: possibly the most amazing novelty camera in the world. Collectors seek the first (stainless steel) model of 1938, marked Riga (Latvia). *(Photograph courtesy of Asahi Pentax Museum)*

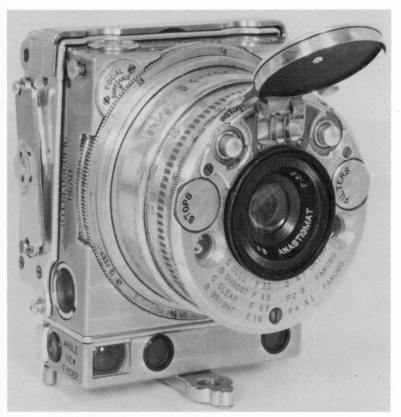

The English-designed, Swiss-made Compass of 1937 for plate or roll film with built-in exposure meter, angle viewfinder, and other ingenious capabilities. *(Photograph courtesy of Asahi Pentax Museum)*

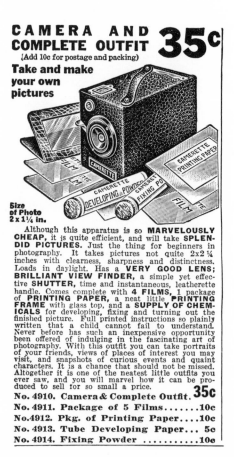

Numerous cardboard box cameras and plastic cameras of the 1930s were made to sell for under $1. Collectors seek examples as novelty cameras of the past.

an engineer, Noel Pemberton-Billing, in Britain executed by the prestige Le Coultre & Cie. watchworks in Switzerland. The Compass is about the size of a package of cigarettes. It is safe to say that per square inch and per ounce this is more actual camera than any camera in history. It loaded with a roll of cut film. It incorporated a coupled range finder; an extinction-type exposure meter; a focusing magnifier on a ground-glass screen; and even such aids as a stereoscopic head, a panoramic head, three built-in filters, direct and right-angle viewfinders, and twenty-two speeds from 4½ seconds up to 1/500 second. The lens was an f/3.5 and it took a picture 1 by 1½ inches.

Approximately 5,000 of this unique apparatus were made. For a collector of either miniature or novelty cameras, the Compass represents a truly special position in the imaginary Photographic Hall of Fame. Together with its amazing pocket tripod and enlarger-projector, it is included in most major collections of sophisticated equipment. No camera made since has offered within this size range such a system of photography for the connoisseur.

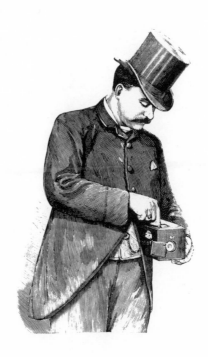

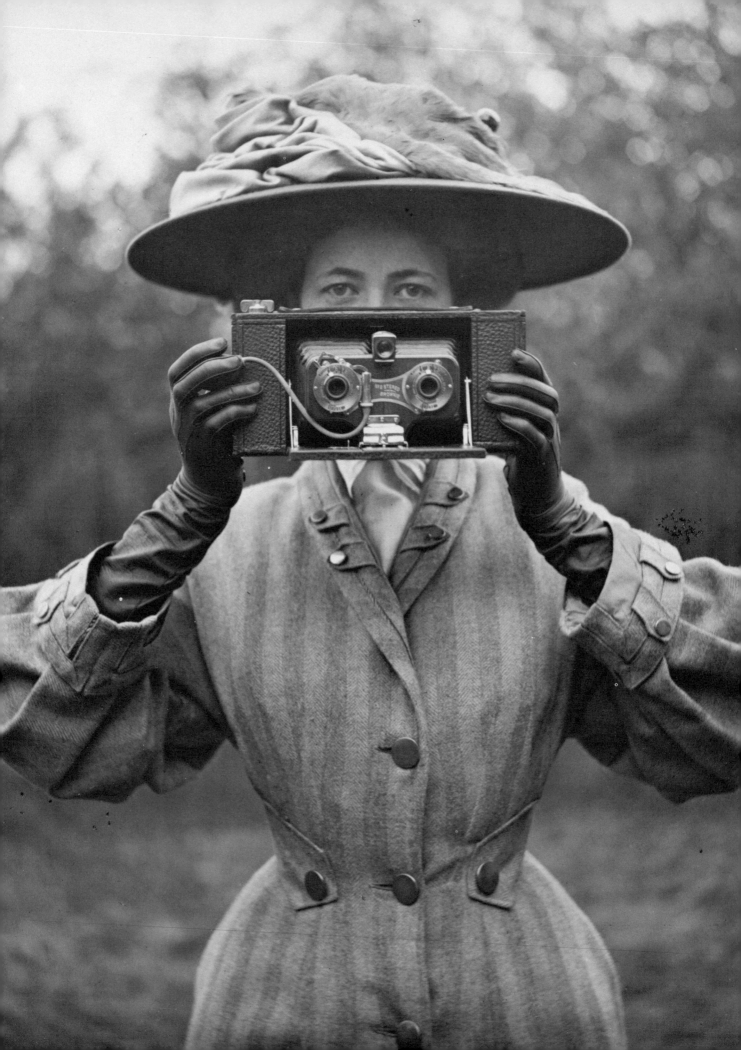

5
Stereo Cameras and Stereography

One of the most curious corners of the photographic cabinet began with an English invention that in its time had the shock value of TV images in the 1940s. Its inventor was Sir David Brewster (1781–1868) who in 1850 made an advance on an idea developed earlier by Sir Charles Wheatstone (1802–1875): The hand-held viewing stereoscope was born. The earlier Wheatstone device was too large to be held in the hands.

With the Brewster viewer it became possible for paired photographs to be viewed so that a world in depth leaped from the twin photographs into a three-dimensional reality whose foreground was "near" and skyline "far," an incredible look into space. "The stereograph creates its dramatic effect," explains Beaumont Newhall in *The History of Photography*,[1] "because it reproduces binocular vision. Normally we see the world with both our eyes. The image of each eye is slightly different; the fusion of the two in our mind is our most important method of depth perception."

By 1855, there were already three major kinds of photographic capabilities to provide the necessary left-and-right images for stereo: the Daguerreotype, which was being made all over the world from 1839 and nearly to 1860; the calotype (or paper-negative system), which would fade into obscurity as the "on-glass" negative capability developed; and finally, the newly developed wet plate, which was about to emerge as the practical system for mass reproduction of images (and as the progenitor of the contemporary system of photography).

[1] P. 74.

Oliver Wendell Holmes, America's poet-philosopher of that period, became an early propagandist of the new photography with the astonishing depth illusion. His enthusiasm led to his development of the popular hand-held viewer known as the Holmes-Bates. It is the viewer most commonly found in attics or in antique shops, today selling with a handful of representative stereo cards for about $25.

The first stereo photographers used the popular standard view cameras of the time, making two separate exposures, first with its lens to the left, then with lens to the right. This was satisfactory for landscapes where the subject was immobile. Paired cameras were also used. Within a few years, the lens board fitted with two matched lenses permitted the exposure of simultaneous images, and subject matter could include individuals who sat for the necessary four-second or even longer exposures of the wet-plate era.

These paired side-by-side images would be viewed through paired lenses to bring to life three dimensions for the viewer. The negative made by the wet-plate collodion process permitted mass reproduction of stereo cards, and a new industry was born on an international scale: Sets of stereoscopic views brought parlor entertainment and cultural education to every member of the family, exactly as TV today photographically transports the family to distant corners of the world. Just as the TV networks send cameramen to the far corners of the world, such companies as the London Stereoscopic Co. in England and E. & H. T. Anthony & Co. in America were directing photogra-

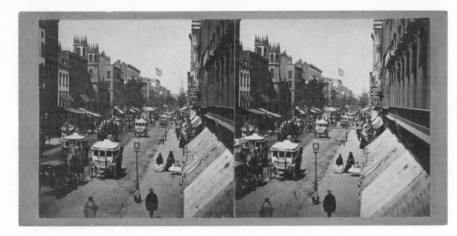

Early Anthony Stereo View was among the stereo cards that began a new era in parlor entertainment. *(From the collection of the author)*

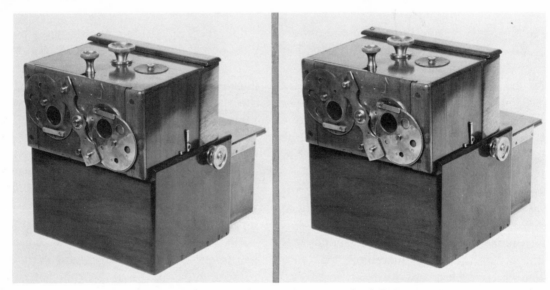

Stereo photo of the first commercially successful stereo camera, the J. B. Dancer Stereo Camera of 1856. *(From the collection of Matthew R. Isenberg)*

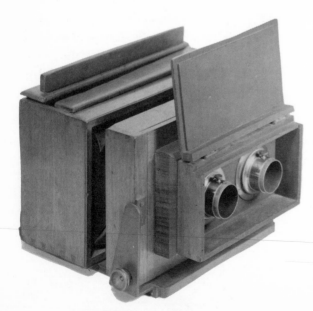

A popular stereo camera of the Civil War period made by John Stock & Co., New York. It loaded with wet plates 4 × 8¼ inches for studio and field use. *(From the collection of Matthew R. Isenberg)*

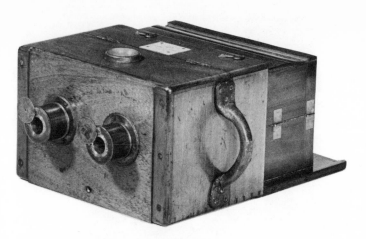

The Blair Collapsible Stereo Sliding Box Camera, ca. 1860. *(From the collection of Alan and Paulette Cotter)*

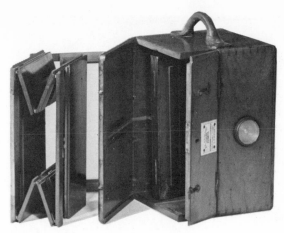

Partly opened to show inner storage area.

phers to distant places to create the stereo-card sets.

Very little has changed in stereoscopy since those first days. Some of the stereo cameras are still made and used today, though the age of stereo more or less came to an end in the 1930s despite a brief flurry of rekindled interest in the late 1940s and early 1950s. The smaller models of the stereo camera required that the lenses, like your eyes, be approximately 2½ inches apart when the scene was captured on film. The Mascher viewer of the Daguerrean era, a fold-up holder that protected two Daguerrean or ambrotype images and opened to reveal binocularlike lenses for viewing the protected images, has its twentieth-century counterpart in the all-metal viewers common in Europe in the 1920s.

The phenomenon of the stereo image and the industry that resulted has been carefully studied and researched by William Culp Darrah, a Pennsylvania academician who has designated six eras of history for the stereo views in his authoritative study, *Stereo Views*:[2]

The Pioneers	1850–1860
The Excitement	1860–1865
The Grand Flowering in America	1865–1873
Flooding the Market	1873–1881
Mass Production and Distribution	1881–1920
The Decline	1920–1935

[2] P. 9.

During those seventy years between 1850 and 1920, literally every village and city in America with a photographer had its own stereograph production with widely circulated views of the local historic sites, main streets, major buildings, and scenic features. Darrah believes that 95 percent of the total stereo views taken in America were actually produced by less than one thousand photographers and publishers. Whatever their source, millions of stereo cards were made and sold, and ultimately these have become one of the most familiar remnants of the Victorian Era, available by the boxful along with postcards at every antique shop and flea market even today.

Not only were individual cards produced, but the major entrepreneurs in Europe and later in the United States produced sets to be sold door to door by salesmen. They cover every imaginable theme, but especially travel, religion, and the great national news events that were the subject of the stereophotographer's lenses: the development of the railroads, the excitement of the expositions, the Russo-Japanese War, the Civil War, and similar epic moments in history were especially well documented for the waiting consumer. The opening of the West; the grandeur of the Rockies; humor in the bourgeois home; the gold fever in Alaska—they all became the basis for a salable product.

"The Terrible San Francisco Earthquake and Fire" could be "enjoyed" in the home in a special set of 60 "beautifully colored stereoscopic views, 60

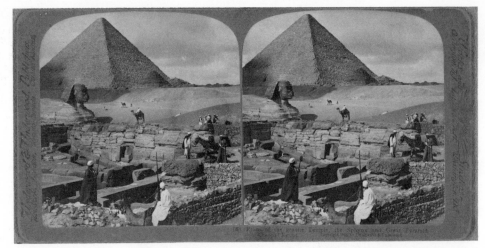

American families traveled to distant corners of the world by viewing Underwood and Underwood Publishers' stereo cards. This view is titled *Sphynx and the Great Pyramid. (From the collection of the author)*

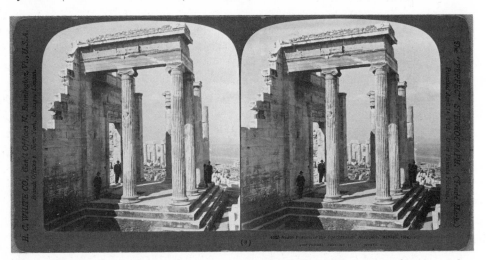

The H. C. White Company was another major distributor of travel sets for the parlor stereo enthusiasts. This view of the Acropolis was from a set depicting Greece. *(From the collection of the author)*

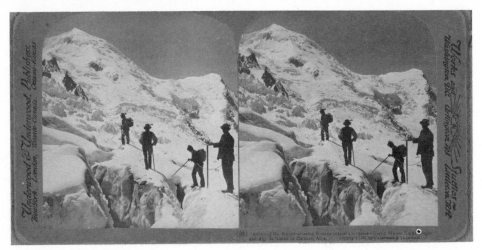

The Ascension of Mont Blanc is from a 1901 copyright Underwood and Underwood, Publishers' stereo card set. *(From the collection of the author)*

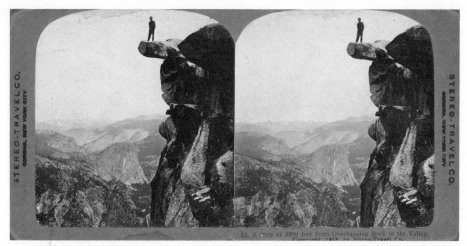

The Rockies of America's West were photographed for all sellers of stereo card sets. This is a 1912 view by the Stereo-Travel Company. *(From the collection of the author)*

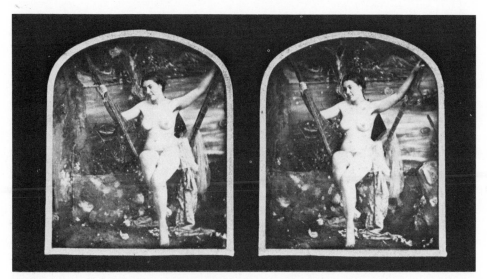

Early glass stereo pair (ca. 1850s, possibly French) is a rare type of stereo art form. *(From the collection of Alan and Paulette Cotter)*

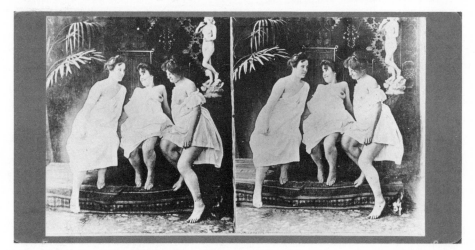

Stereo photography in a brothel, ca. 1900, possibly of French or German origin. *(From the collection of the author)*

historic descriptions printed on the backs, 1 leatherette case for the 60 views" for 75¢ from Sears, Roebuck in 1909. A 100-view set of hunting, fishing, camping, and Indian life studies was available for 85¢. One hundred views of the St. Louis World's Fair were 85¢, which could also bring the Siege of Port Arthur or 100 views of "Fair Japan." One hundred colored views of the Holy Land were also 85¢ at Sears, and the mail-order company even had a special plan for church administrators who could purchase stereo cards to give to a child, one per Sunday, to induce Sunday School attendance. The child was given a gift viewer of the Holmes-Bates type after receiving 15 stereo cards. Sears sold the viewers for as little as 24¢ each plus 6¢ postage.

The tens of thousands of stereo negatives necessary to meet the demand came from relatively large stereo cameras usually mounted on tripods. For home stereophotography and small-format commercial transparencies, there were cameras such as the Verascope of Jules Richard, Paris, which was about the size of a pair of binoculars. They took photographs on glass plates contained in special magazines, each of which permitted up to 24 pictures to be shot before it was taken to the darkroom, where the plates could be unloaded and processed. Thanks to the small stereo cameras of this size, it was possible for the stereophotographer to bring back the only photographs of the snow-covered passes to the gold fields of Alaska or of the rapids of the Colorado River, where it was not possible to attempt photography with a larger view camera on a tripod.

Underwood and Underwood, a firm that had absorbed many of the earlier leaders in the stereo-card–publishing field by 1901, was manufacturing 25,000 stereo views per day (more than 7 million a year) along with 300,000 stereoscopes (viewers) annually. At this time, only four companies were actively selling stereo-card sets door to door: Underwood and Underwood; Keystone View Company, which ultimately absorbed Underwood and Underwood's stereo operation; Griffith and Griffith; and the H. C. White Company. Darrah believes that the best cards published after 1898 were Keystone views. Boxed sets of such subjects as the Holy

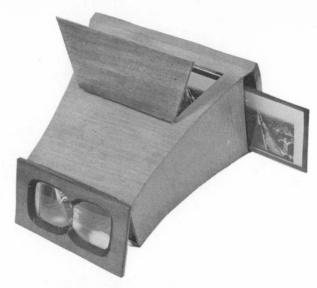

Brewster viewer predates the more popular Holmes-Bates "open air" type. (*Photograph courtesy of* Graphic Antiquarian *and Carole G. Honigsfeld*)

Land, the Spanish-American War, World War I, and travel subjects may still be found intact in the antique stores today.

It was Underwood and Underwood who, along with cards and viewers, also introduced another related collectible. This was the descriptive guidebook that supplemented the descriptive message commonly printed on the reverse side of the stereograph. This guidebook incorporated a specially prepared map that indicated where the camera was sited and indicating the field of view incorporated for each view. For a set of cards on Yellowstone Park, for example, it was possible for the armchair traveler to understand the location of major park features in relation to other points of interest.

The use of the stereo-card set was so well developed that card sets and messages were generated to meet the intellectual capabilities of primary or secondary school students in addition to family-entertainment card sets. In short, exactly as with TV fare, there was the "Sesame Street" program, "The Six O'clock News," and the adult humor for the evening hours when children were abed. There were nude stereo cards sold discreetly and even other cards that were never acceptable in the parlor. A recent stereo-card–set sale was made up of three hundred cards attributed to a bawdy house in

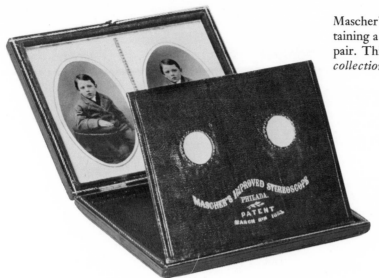

Mascher's Improved Stereoscope was a folding viewer containing a Daguerreotype, ambrotype, or later tintype stereo pair. This example is a ½-plate stereo tintype. (*From the collection of Alan and Paulette Cotter*)

Denver, Colorado, whose patrons could select from stereo views the lady of the evening he wished to meet.

To enjoy these views, a variety of stereo-card holders were developed. Since some views were made on glass as positives, some viewers are enclosed boxes in which the individual glass slide is viewed against a ground glass when held up to the light. The more familiar Holmes-Bates stereoscope, invented by Holmes and actually made in 1861 by a friend, Joseph L. Bates, was never patented. It had a hood to shield the eyes, and it provided for a sliding card holder to permit focus adjustment for each person.

As early as 1854, the first mechanized (rotary) viewer had been introduced in England. American versions in cabinets, some about 30 inches high with drawers to hold stereo views, were being produced as early as 1859 in the United States, says Darrah.[3]

Luxury versions in both hand-held and table-type viewers, including the versatile Stereographoscope, which permitted magnified images to be seen of the popular cabinet cards and also for one-at-a-time viewing of stereo cards, emerged in rose-

[3] Ibid., p. 10.

Ornate Brewster viewer is a rarer form of the box-like viewer for stereo cards or stereo glass pairs. (*From the collection of Allen and Hilary Weiner*)

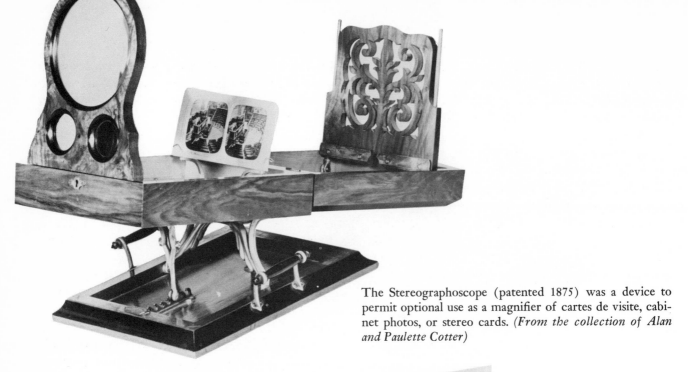

The Stereographoscope (patented 1875) was a device to permit optional use as a magnifier of cartes de visite, cabinet photos, or stereo cards. *(From the collection of Alan and Paulette Cotter)*

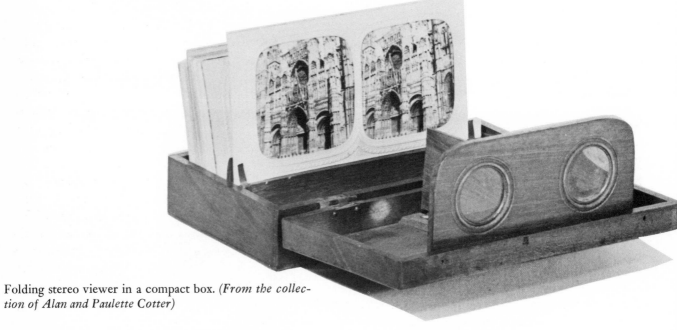

Folding stereo viewer in a compact box. *(From the collection of Alan and Paulette Cotter)*

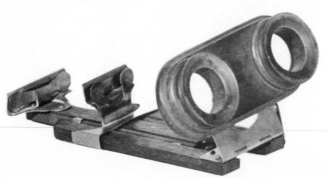

Unique folding stereo viewer held cards in a sliding clip. *(From the collection of Alan and Paulette Cotter)*

wood, cherry, and mahogany versions. Some of these were inlaid with ivory or mother-of-pearl. The hand-held viewers were sold for as little as 25¢, but elaborate versions could be purchased for as much as $23.

Those stereo viewers with aluminum hoods are likely to be survivors of the hundreds of thousands made from 1899 to 1901 in the shaded design. Twenty-five years later, an electrified model with a binocular look was introduced by the Keystone View Company.

There is hardly a flea market that does not have one or more versions of a stereograph viewer available for the new collector. Brewster viewers of the very earliest period are much harder to find. The Mascher Stereo Holder, which incorporates the twin Daguerreotypes, are among the most rare stereo-image hand viewers.

The stereo cards, which sold for 5¢ and 10¢ each in the 1950s, have become 25¢ to $1 items with some selling for as much as $100 each if they feature a famed Civil War general or are the identifiable rare card of an early photographer of such fame as Alexander Gardner or Mathew B. Brady.

In the earliest days the cameras that made this entire world of stereophotography such an amazing sociological phenomenon followed for the most part the designs of the most common nonstereo cameras. Later, German and French camera makers created especially innovative optical and mechanical features for photography on dry plates (glass) and then again on roll film. It is usually the all-metal and small black-finished stereo cameras (such as the Voigtländer Stereflektoscop and Rolleidoscop or Heidoscop of Germany of the 1920s or the blued-brass French Verascopes of Jules Richard, which began an amazing year-by-year continuous production of a basic compact design in metal and leather) that have become most eagerly sought by the stereo collector cognoscenti.

Stereo cameras were produced in small numbers overall, since the average family photographer who eagerly purchased stereo-card sets simply did not extend his family-photo effort to creating personal stereographs. However, by 1901 there did exist a box camera with stereo capabilities, and by 1905 a lower-priced version appeared under the Brownie name. Other American stereo cameras were the handsome folding Weno Stereo Hawk-Eye, the Korona, the Premo, and the now-rare Stereo Graflex. Both Sears and Montgomery Ward offered models under the names of Conley and the Quick-Shot, respectively, in box shapes using glass plates in the Conley and 4-by-7-inch glass plates in the Quick-Shot. The American families who had learned to purchase box and folding cameras only a few years earlier were not ready for the "quantum leap" to stereo.

Almost any stereo camera of that period has a collector price of $100 and up, though the small simple 45-by-107-millimeter French and German models of 1910–1925 are worth somewhat less. The Stereo Auto Graflex in 1910 sold new for $292; today it would sell for three or four times as much to the collector.

The stars in any stereo-equipment collection are more often the more readily available mechanically innovative compact European cameras. With amazing push-pull mechanisms changing one glass plate for another in a magazine that hung on the camera (so that it could be readily removed for positioning of a ground glass and then reattached), these cameras also included such convenience features as a bubble level for absolutely horizontal camera positioning, ingenious dual-shutter mechanisms, and overall compact shapes. The collector who locates a German Ica Polyskop or the Stereo-Deckrullo-Nettel or one of the French Gaumont Stereo Block-Notes or the Stereospido has found a fine camera gem. By comparison, the Stereo Kodak model No.1, which was first offered in 1917 and discontinued in 1925, is an easy-to-pass-up simple black folding camera.

Mass-produced German and French cameras were available from the 1890s. The German stereo cameras from the factory that became world famous for the twin-lens Rollei line were first the Heidoscop, which was plate loaded, and a few years later, the roll-film version called the Rolleidoscop. These cameras emerged in the 1920s as the stereo era was coming to an end, and the factory simply turned the side-by-side lens mount design on end to become famous for the Rolleiflex and

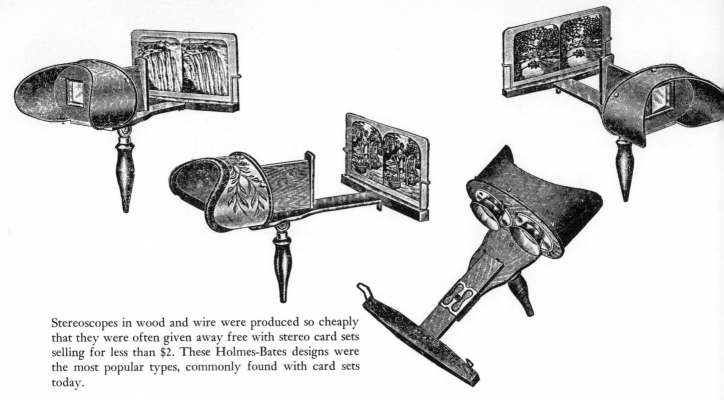

Stereoscopes in wood and wire were produced so cheaply that they were often given away free with stereo card sets selling for less than $2. These Holmes-Bates designs were the most popular types, commonly found with card sets today.

A typical catalogue offering of stereo cards during the height of the collection fever offered 100 cards for under $1. Themes as the Russo-Japanese War, "Fair Japan," the Holy Land, "Famous Cities of the West," and others were offered. (*From* Catalog of Sears, Roebuck & Company, 1908)

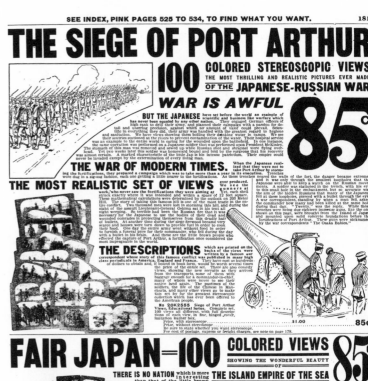

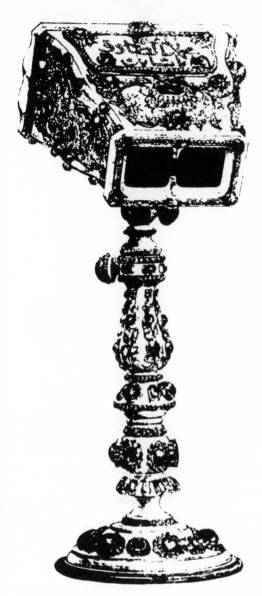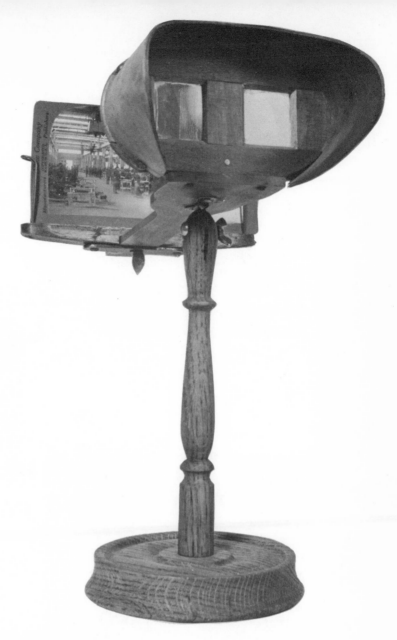

Ornate Brewster-type viewer was custom made for royalty; simpler Holmes-Bates viewer on a pedestal is far less common than hand-held type. (*Photograph courtesy of* Graphic Antiquarian *and Carole G. Honigsfeld*)

then the Rolleicord with lenses stacked one above the other (see Chapter 7, "Twin-Lens Reflex Cameras").

In the 1920s and 1930s a number of efforts to win a family audience with low-cost plastic stereo cameras included such a camera as the Stereoco of 1926, and even two Bakelite tiny box cameras were banded together into what was surely the lowest-priced stereo camera ever offered in America: the Duo Univex Stereo, priced at anywhere from 89¢ to $2.50. This tiny, inexpensive camera of the 1930s is as rare as some of the stereo cameras of fifty years earlier, say stereo collectors.

A flurry of interest was rekindled in the stereo idea from 1948 to 1955 based on 35-mm camera designs. Following World War II, thanks to the success of 35-mm photography, American and German stereo cameras were introduced to exploit the stereo interest of a new generation of Americans who were also being introduced to stereo in the nation's novelty-seeking motion-picture theaters. America's leading cameras in this field at the time were those offered by the David White Company of Milwaukee, Wisconsin—the Stereo Realists selling for nearly $200, and the Kodak Stereo camera, which sold for $84.50. Entries in the field under $75 were the Wollensak, the Revere, the Universal Stereall, the German Iloca, and others. But the re-

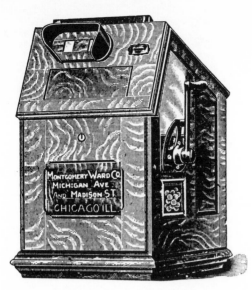

The coin-operated Quadruplex Stereo Picture Machine stored four sets of twelve stereo cards with the image illuminated through side glass panels, ca. 1900.

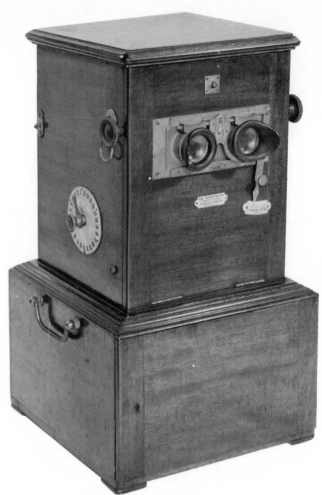

Le Taxiphote was a French-made crank-operated table viewer for the parlor. It showed twenty-five glass stereo views. *(Photograph courtesy of Asahi Pentax Museum)*

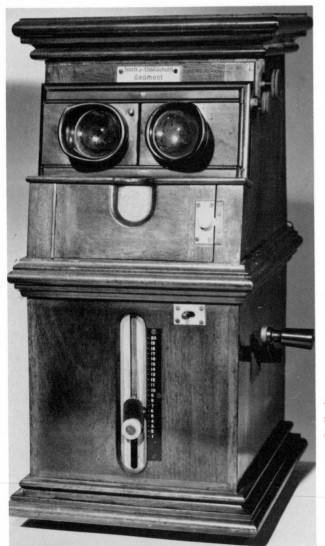

Gaumont French-made parlor stereo viewer stored twenty stereo cards and had a drop-feed mechanism. *(From the collection of Louis S. Marcus)*

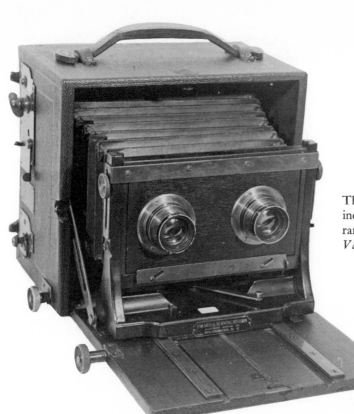

The famed Folmer & Schwing Stereo Graphic in a 5-by-7-inch size equipped for stereo, ca. 1910. A very large, very rare stereo camera. *(Photograph courtesy of John and Valerie Craig)*

Stereo Auto Graflex, 5 by 7 inches, from Folmer & Schwing was made between 1904 and 1922 and is extremely rare. *(From the collection of N. M. Graver)*

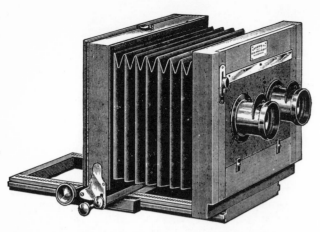

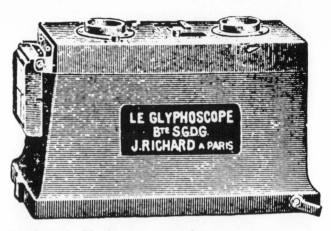

The 1899 Rochester Optical Company's New Model Stereoscopic Camera, 5 by 8 inches, was sold with matched lenses, tripod, and one holder for $22. It is typical of the stereo cameras of the field photographers.

French-made Glyphoscope was a low-cost stereo camera for glass plates with a detachable lens/shutter system to permit use of the body as a viewer. *(From the collection of Eaton S. Lothrop, Jr.)*

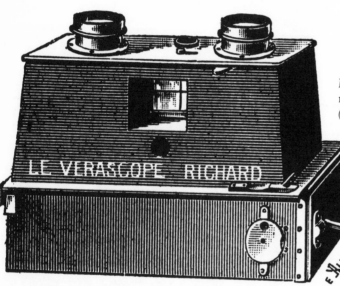

Magazine-loaded Verascope from Jules Richard, Paris, permitted plate changing with a push–pull on side handle. *(From the collection of Eaton S. Lothrop, Jr.)*

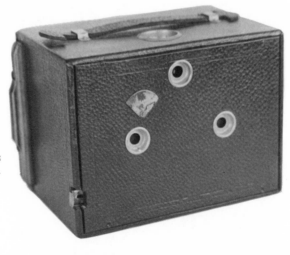

The 1902 Conley Stereo Box Camera loaded with glass plates. *(From the collection of Marvin and Katrinka Kreisman)*

emergence of stereo died; efforts by Hollywood and by the stereo-camera makers were equally disappointing.

CLEANING STEREO CARDS

Stereo views of the past are available in a number of forms, the most familiar of which is the slightly curved cardboard mount. This deliberate curve in the paper assists the simple lenses in providing a reasonable degree of sharpness across the image. If the card is overly soiled, which is the case more often than not, a soft art eraser or art gum may be used to carefully remove fingerprints or other surface soot. A damp cloth (not wet) may also be used to lightly wipe away the surface dirt without saturating the emulsion. A drop or two of ammonia in the near-dry damp cloth will help clean up especially dirty cards. Do not use any type of damp cloth on tinted cards, since it is likely that the tints are water soluble.

DATING STEREOGRAPHS

In *Stereo Views*[4] Darrah suggests these clues to dating of the stereo card:

Card mount flat with actual photos pasted on it:
    Corners square—1854 to 1870.
        Color white, cream or gray, lustrous: 1854–1862
        Color canary yellow thru chrome yellow: 1862–1868
        Color dull gray: 1860–1863
        Color blue-green, red, violet: 1865–1870
    Corners round
        Actual photographs, colors as above: 1868–1882
        Copied photoprints (with loss of detail): 1873–1878
        Printed (not photographs): 1874–1878
Card mounts curved (actual photographs):
    Buff mounts, thick card: 1879–1906
    Gray mounts: 1893–1940
    Black mounts: 1902–1908
Lithoprints, thin cardboard:
    Multicolored: 1898–1929
    Black and white: 1906–1925
Tissue cards (transparency-type):
    French: invented pre-1865 and available until 1875
    German and English: 1865–1875
    United States: 1895–1900

[4] Ibid., pp. 19–20.

Unidentified source, with doorways, windows, eyes pierced to allow light rays to go thru: 1868–1875
Glass Views
    United States scenes: 1852 (1851?)–1862
    European: 1850s to 1919
Daguerreotypes: 1850–1854
Porcelain: 1854–1858

Other Dating Guides

Darrah also offers information on dating stereo cards according to the label or imprints they might bear. Here are the criteria:

Langenheim (on a narrow strip on reverse): 1856
Anthony (on a broad white label): 1858
Langenheim, Barnum, London Stereoscopic Company (imprinted on card face): 1858–1864
Cards with label or imprinted with list of views with the subject of the card underlined or marked off: after 1868
Cards with revenue stamps (required by law from September 1, 1864 to August 1, 1866, to be affixed to card back, canceled by hand stamp or rubber stamp, often with actual date of sale): September 1, 1864 to August 1, 1866. The tax was 2¢ for 25¢ or less; 3¢ for any card selling for 26 to 50¢; 5¢ for any card selling from 51¢ to one dollar. This revenue-stamp dating confirms the period of sale but many views sold at the time were from negatives taken years earlier.

STEREO-CARD SIZES

Again, Darrah offers the following information on card sizes:

Most popular: 3½ by 7 inches
Also offered: 4 by 7, 4⅜ by 7, 4½ by 7
Glass slides (from Europe): about 1880 to 1920.
    45 by 107 millimeters and 6 by 13 centimeters. There were other (usually larger) sizes, too.

STEREO INTEREST TODAY

In January 1974, the National Stereoscopic Association was formed to assist those interested in any aspect of stereography. Within eighteen months, it had a membership of over 450 with dues-paying subscribers in the United States, Canada, Europe, and Africa. The organization publishes a

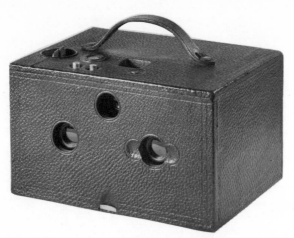

No. 2 Kodak Stereo camera was a roll-film box camera, ca. 1902. *(From the collection of Matthew R. Isenberg)*

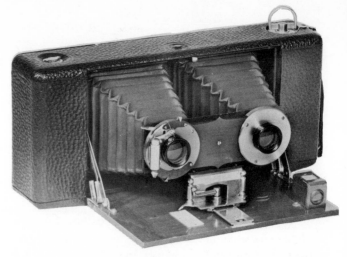

Stereo Hawk-Eye Model No. 3 was a folding roll-film camera for the family photographer, ca. 1910, taking paired 3½-inch square photos. *(From the collection of Alan and Paulette Cotter)*

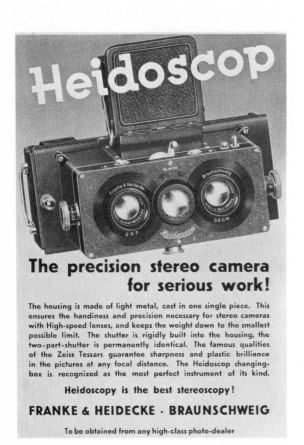

Heidoscop

The precision stereo camera for serious work!

The housing is made of light metal, cast in one single piece. This ensures the handiness and precision necessary for stereo cameras with High-speed lenses, and keeps the weight down to the smallest possible limit. The shutter is rigidly built into the housing, the two-part-shutter is permanently identical. The famous qualities of the Zeiss Tessars guarantee sharpness and plastic brilliance in the pictures at any focal distance. The Heidoscop changing-box is recognized as the most perfect instrument of its kind.

Heidoscopy is the best stereoscopy!

FRANKE & HEIDECKE · BRAUNSCHWEIG

To be obtained from any high-class photo-dealer

After World War I, Germany's Franke and Heidecke Company introduced the plate-loaded Heidoscop.

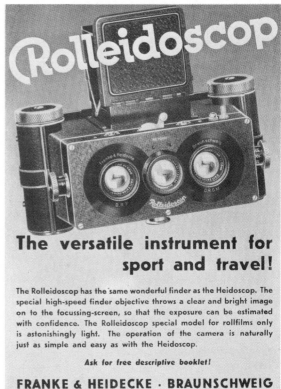

Rolleidoscop

The versatile instrument for sport and travel!

The Rolleidoscop has the same wonderful finder as the Heidoscop. The special high-speed finder objective throws a clear and bright image on to the focussing-screen, so that the exposure can be estimated with confidence. The Rolleidoscop special model for rollfilms only is astonishingly light. The operation of the camera is naturally just as simple and easy as with the Heidoscop.

Ask for free descriptive booklet!

FRANKE & HEIDECKE · BRAUNSCHWEIG

To be obtained from any high-class photo-dealer

Roll-film version of the Heidoscop was the Rolleidoscop, which followed in mid-1920s. When the stereo age faded, the company introduced its major success—the Rolleiflex.

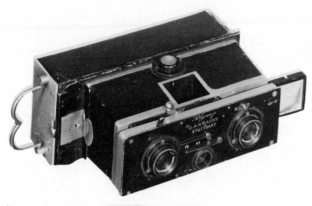

The 1906 German-made Polyskop offered Zeiss lenses and a rapid-change system for glass plates. *(From the collection of Dr. R. H. Krauss)*

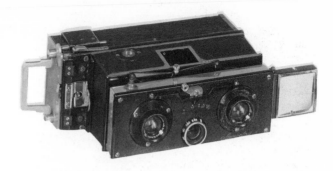

The 1921 Stereoplast retained features of earlier all-metal stereo cameras and added faster (f/4.5) lenses, a shutter speed of 1/300th second, and magazine load for glass plates. *(From the collection of Dr. R. H. Krauss)*

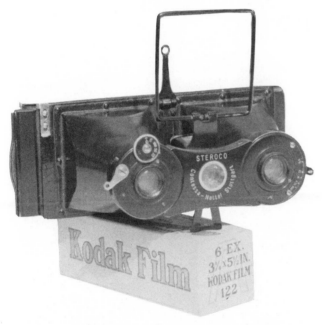

Low-cost Contessa-Nettel Steroco of 1926 was sold with a printing frame and a viewing box for glass positives for $25.

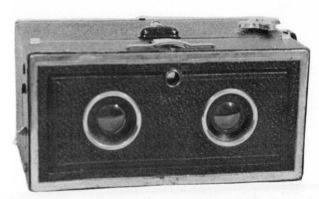

Roll-film loaded EHO low-cost stereo box camera was still sold as late as 1938 for family stereo photography. *(Photograph courtesy of John and Valerie Craig)*

bimonthly newsletter, "Stereo World," in furtherance of its purposes, which include the encouragement of the study of stereographs and stereo history as a visual record of over eighty years of American history. An annual convention presents speakers and the opportunity for stereo collectors to meet and trade both cards and equipment. Membership is $10 annually; the organization is headquartered at: R.D. #1, Fremont, New Hampshire 03044.

A BRIEF CHRONOLOGY OF STEREO PHOTOGRAPHY

1838 Sir Charles Wheatstone, English scientist, invents the stereoscope.

1840 Stereoscopic Talbotypes (see Glossary) said to have been exhibited at Brussels Royal Academy of Science.

1841 First stereo Daguerreotypes reported.
Calotypist Henry Collen takes stereoscopic portrait of Charles Babbage.

1849 Scottish scientist Sir David Brewster invents the hand-held stereoscope in a boxy form.

1850 The Langenheim brothers in Philadelphia introduce commercially made stereographs into United States.

1851 Queen Victoria at London Crystal Palace World's Fair is presented with a stereoscope by Duboseq & Soleil. This marks the beginning of the extreme popularity of stereo photos.

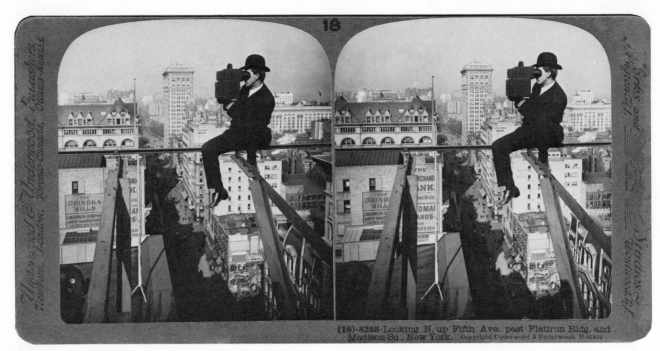

Twin-Lens Stereo Graphic is an exceedingly rare stereo camera, used by a press photographer during skyscraper construction over Fifth Avenue, New York, ca. 1902. The photograph is from a stereo card. *(From the collection of the author)*

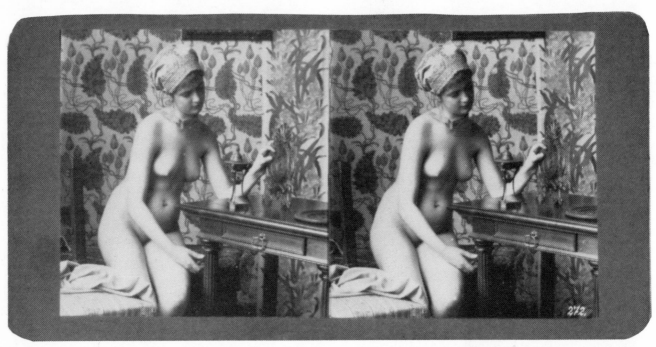

Stereography often extended to areas that were not quite acceptable for parlor viewing, as this piece for promotion for a house of ill repute suggests.

1852 Famous Daguerreotypist Antoine François Jean Claudet, working with Wheatstone since 1842, sends stereo Daguerreotypes of the Crystal Palace exhibits to the tsar of Russia.

1853 John F. Mascher of Philadelphia patents case for stereo Daguerreotypes with built-in viewer.

John Benjamin Dancer designs first two-lens stereo camera in Manchester, England. Production starts three years later.

1854 Albert Sands Southworth and Josiah Johnson Hawes of Boston patent a cabinet (Wheatstone-type) stereoscope for viewing 6½-by-8½-inch-size stereo Daguerreotypes.

George Swan Nottage forms London Stereoscopic Company; within a short time the company sells a half million viewers. He rises from humble origins to the Lord Mayor of London as a result.

1855 Claudet patents lenticular (see Glossary) stereo viewer with lenses in adjustable eye tubes.

1856 Introduction of the box-shaped stereo case; it resembles a flat cigar box with eye tubes at one end.

1857 Negretti & Zambra publish one hundred stereoscopic views by Francis Frith.

1858 Powell's Patent Stereoscopic camera uses single lens, which slides laterally in a track to produce a pair of independently taken stereo exposures.

The first book illustrated with photo stereographs is published in London: *Teneriffe* by C. Piazzi Smith.

Publication of *Stereoscopic* magazine is begun.

1859 Oliver Wendell Holmes writes in *Atlantic Monthly* about stereographs; he invents the compact "skeleton" model stereoscope (still called today the Holmes-Bates Viewer).

American firm of Anthony (later to become Ansco, then GAF) offers stereo views of scenic subjects for sale.

Alexander Beckers starts manufacturing table stereoscopes, which become very popular in the United States. They store and show stereo cards without using the hand-held viewers.

William England, staff photographer of the London Stereoscopic Company, travels throughout America and produces the first photographic views of the United States to become available in Europe.

1860 Introduction of the Rotary (or Revolving) Stereoscope.

1861 Dr. Coleman Sellers of Philadelphia designs the "stereo phantasmascope" (see Glossary), an early effort at a motion-picture effect.

1862 "Stereotropes" (see Glossary) mounted in revolving cylinder shown at International Exhibition in effort to simulate motion in imagery.

1863 Invention and patenting of the pedestal stereoscope: the Holmes-Bates–type viewer on a base.

Brady group photographs Civil War in stereo, financed by Anthony, using stereo cameras by John Stock, New York.

1864 L. M. Rutherford creates unique stereo pair of the moon, taking exposures first on September 15 and then on November 13. (Differences in the moon's relative position provide stereo relief effect.)

1885 Dry-plate stereo photography made easier with development of 5-by-8-inch view cameras offered by such leaders in equipment as Scovill, Anthony, and others.

1889 Patenting of the stereographoscope, which permits viewing of stereo cards and of larger cabinet photos; it Z-folds for storage.

1894 Introduction of the first model of the Verascope by Jules Richard, Paris, an all-metal stereo camera for 45-by-107-millimeter photos. With but slight changes, it is made continuously to the 1920s.

1892 Introduction of F. E. Ives's Kromscop; it optically reunites three stereo transparencies for 3-D and three-color effect.

1901 Kodak enters the field of stereography with the roll-film No. 2 Stereo Kodak box camera.

1904 Introduction of the Stereo Graflex loaded with 5-by-7-inch plates.

1905 The first folding stereo camera to be made by the Eastman Kodak Company: the No. 2 Brownie Stereo camera.

1913 Introduction of the first 35-mm camera for stereo: the Homeos by Jules Richard, Paris.

Introduction of the Voigtländer Stereflektoscop, a camera to take 45-by-107-millimeter photos on either plates or roll film.

1917 Introduction of the Kodak Stereo Model I.

1919 Introduction of the Stereo Lilliput, a collapsible miniature bellows camera for 45-by-107-millimeter plates by Ernemann.

1921 Introduction of the Heidoscop, a magazine-loaded camera for 6-by-13-centimeter plates.

1926 Introduction of the Rolleidoscop, a roll-film version of the Heidoscop, one of the final high-quality cameras at the end of the major interest in stereography.

1947 A brief flurry of interest, which will last about ten years, is created by the introduction of the 35-mm–loaded Stereo Realist. Its success leads to competitor 35-mm cameras and novelty-format cameras by a number of American and German companies.

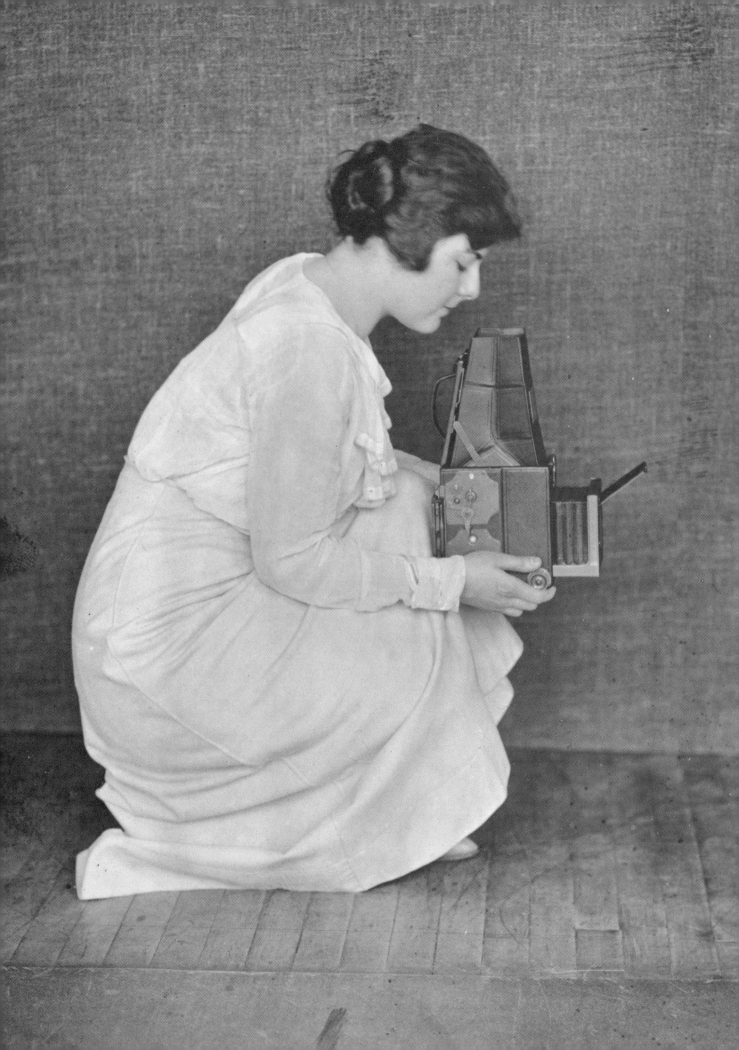

6
Single-Lens Reflex Cameras

If you were asked to select a few cameras that were as American as apple pie, any list from any photo historian would surely include the ubiquitous Graflex. This was the camera that for thirty years, along with its kid brother, the Speed Graphic, dominated the world of American press photography to the exclusion of almost any other camera of their times.

The amazing thing is not that it happened, but why it happened. Picture taking with the cumbersome one-eye monster Graflex cameras was far from a simple process. Perhaps its ability to capture the attention of the press photographers, and even of such creative giants as Edward Weston, was due to the excellent high-speed shutter, interchangeable lenses, and the convenience of looking down into a protected ground glass to see the picture before it was taken. In the view cameras of the period, a tripod was a must, but the Graflex could be held and operated without the need of the tripod.

The Graflex camera was the first widely successful single-lens reflex camera in America, but it was not the first single-lens reflex camera. That honor would have to go to the camera obscura (see Chapter 2, "Box Cameras"), which, equipped with an internal mirror, permitted the artist to aim a lens and to see an image, right side *up*, on its ground glass.

(Lenses turn the world upside down, as anyone who has peeked under the photographer's black cloth has learned with some surprise. A mirror captures the upside-down image and flips it to a right-side-presentation on the ground glass, but right and left are reversed in this observed image.) Nonetheless, the camera obscura of the eighteenth century was a functioning tool of the artist since it presented an image that could be traced on tissue paper on the ground glass (in order to establish accurate perspectives for drawings and paintings). To get the image large enough to be useful, about as large as the size of this page, the camera obscura itself had to be about the size of a small suitcase—too large to carry out into the fields. The compromise size that is most often seen in museums or private collections is 1½ feet long and permitted a tracing about 5 by 7 inches.

The cameras developed by Niépce and Daguerre in France and Talbot in England did not incorporate the mirror internally. These were all boxes with a lens at front and a ground glass at back. Amazingly, though the principle of the single-lens–reflex design had been developed by artists in the 1600s and 1700s, it was not until the 1860s that William Sutton in England patented the first single-lens reflex. Apparently only a small number were made, and only literary references to such a camera tell us of its existence. When the first one is found, perhaps in an English attic, it will make history in the collecting field.

In 1884, the first single-lens reflex camera was successfully marketed: the Monocular Duplex, an American contribution to the design of cameras.

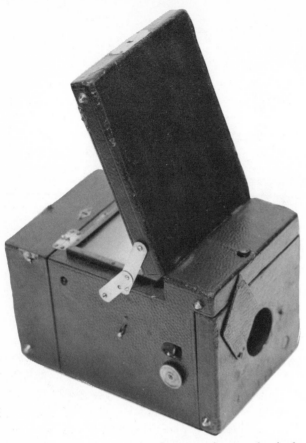

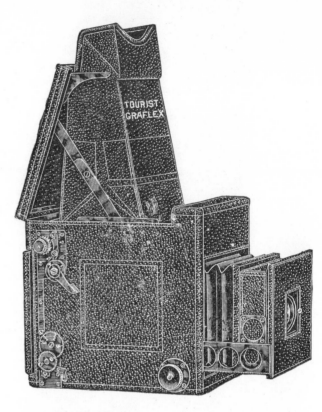

The Monocular Duplex, the first American-made single-lens reflex camera, ca. 1885. The only known example. *(From the collection of Matthew R. Isenberg)*

The Tourist Graflex of 1903. It simplified high-speed action photography. *(From advertisement in* Photo Miniature*)*

The rare Patent Reflex Hand Camera, ca. 1898, from the Reflex Camera Co., Yonkers, New York. *(From the collection of Matthew R. Isenberg)*

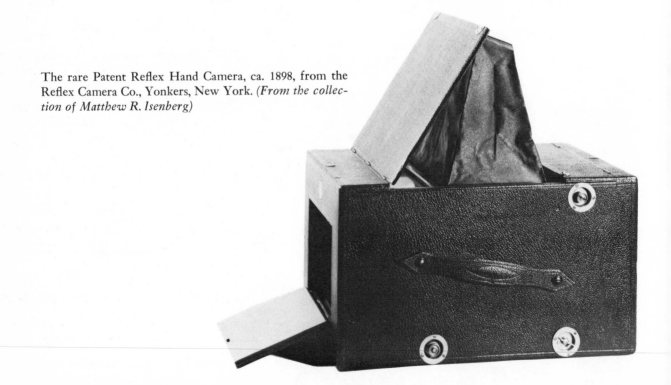

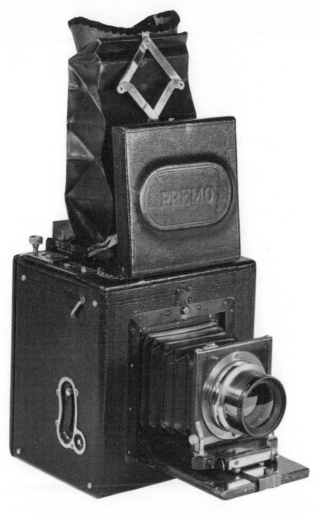

The Premograph, ca. 1906, a rare single-lens reflex camera from the makers of Premo folding-plate cameras. *(From the collection of Matthew R. Isenberg)*

There is only one known example of this first single-lens camera (in the collection of M. R. Isenberg), making it the most rare of significant American cameras.

The New Patent Reflex Hand Camera, a descendant of the Monocular Duplex, advertised as "the only hand camera made which can be focused without removing film or plates," was available in 1900 in 4-by-5-, 5-by-7-, and 6½-by-8½-inch sizes. Obviously, convenience was the feature that would bring light to the eyes of the newly emerging American professional: the press photographer. He could keep film ready in the camera while adjusting the camera for the moment of exposure.

But carrying and aiming the larger of the reflex cameras, which were made in Yonkers, New York,

is an awesome task, since the box was a bulky monster about 18 inches long that was held at waist level for aiming and focusing.

While there were some single-lens reflexes produced in Britain and on the Continent in the 1890s, they were never marketed in America.

An early advertisement of the New Patent Reflex Hand Camera is illustrated with an action at bat of a baseball scene, surely one of the first examples of the use of sports photography as an attention-getting device.

The single-lens–reflex (SLR) design was ignored by most other camera manufacturers in this period, and it took the New York City firm, Folmer & Schwing, which was making view cameras for the photographers who sought compact, easily folded, smoothly opened cameras, to enter the field. The Folmer & Schwing products were aimed at the bicycle market of the 1890s. At that time, all makers offered "cycle cameras" such as the Cycle Poco, the Wizard Cycle, and the Cycle Graphic. In 1897, Kodak brought out its own catalogue of bicycle cameras for those who would wish to spend a Sunday on wheels, carrying a camera in a special case attached to fit between the rider's knees and even with the camera mounted on the handle bars.

Folmer & Schwing was also making a novel device that was offered to owners of most view cameras. It was a roller-blind shutter that fit onto the camera back to permit photography at speeds from ⅕ to ¹⁄₁₀₀₀ second. The shutter replaced the entire camera back since there was provision to accommodate the double-plate holder common to the time. It was offered in sizes from 4 by 5 inches up to 8 by 10 inches. With the introduction of the Speed Graphic, the shutter was ultimately incorporated into the body of a Graphic camera.

When the company brought together its experience in making quality folding plate cameras, its experience in creating an American* back-of-the-camera shutter, and then, the concept of the internal mirror to direct the image up to the camera top, a revolution in photography was underway.

Lightweight models were called the Tourist Graflex (*graphic* plus *reflex* equals *Graflex*); Graflex

* The use of the back-of-the camera shutter was earlier popularized in Europe, particularly by Goerz with their Anschutz of the late 1880s.

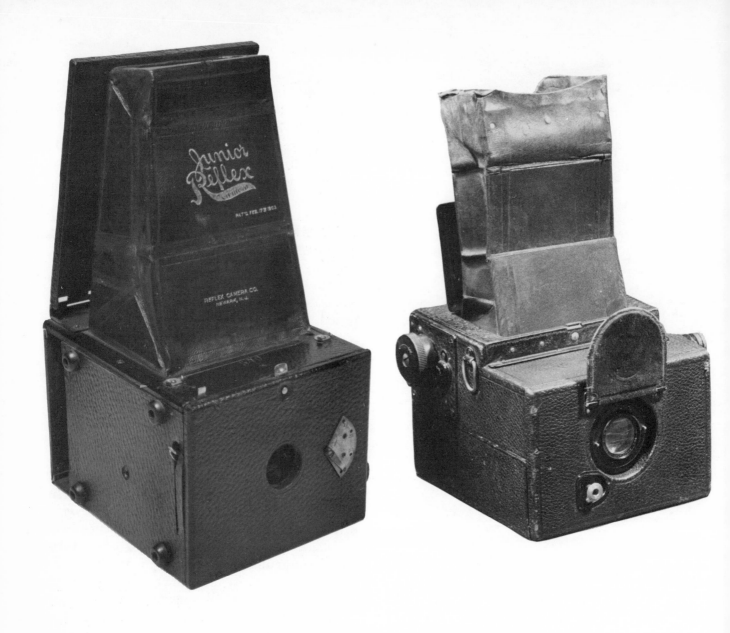

was also offered in telelensed models such as the Telescopic or Naturalist Graflex, in stereo models, and in Press Graflex models. Changes in lens focal length and film sizes created changes in overall size and weight, and each camera model found its own audience; the era of single-lens reflex camera photography in America was in progress.

In Europe before and after World War I, the design had its manufacturer proponents in England and in Germany. Few of these cameras reached America until the 1920s, when models from both countries made their commercial debut on the American scene. The Carbine Reflex camera (Butcher's Reflex Carbine from England) was being marketed in 1926 in America at Willoughby's, New York, for $25. In the same period such reflexes as the Mentor, Zeiss Miroflex, and Ernemann from Germany also entered the U.S. market.

But the market for single-lens reflex cameras in America truly belonged to Graflex, whether it was owned by Folmer & Schwing, or later on when it became the Folmer & Schwing Division of the Eastman Kodak Company. (Thus it is possible to find Graflex cameras that are made by Kodak.) The Folmer & Schwing focal-plane shutter was incorporated in the company's own Graphic cameras

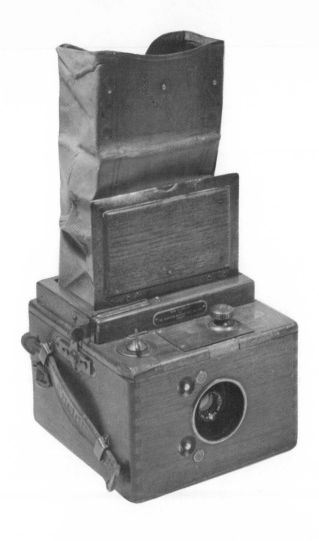

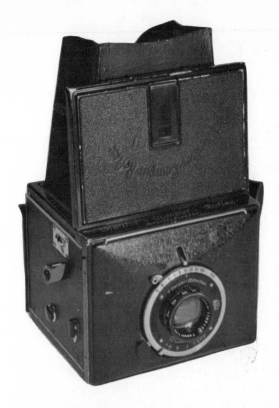

Four early twentieth-century SLR design cameras in the 6-by-9-cm format, precursors of today's modern SLR 6-by-6-cm quality SLRs. *From left to right*, chronologically: the Junior Reflex, ca. 1905 (United States); the Ensign Focal Plane Reflex, ca. 1920 (England); Ensign Tropical (teak) Reflex, ca. 1925; and the Mentor-Compur-Reflex, ca. 1930 (Germany).

during this period and also into such Eastman Kodak cameras as in the earlier 1A and 4A Speed Kodaks (see the section on Roll-Film Models in Chapter 3, "Folding Cameras").

The Rochester Optical Company, makers of the popular Premo folding and box cameras, before 1910 had added a simple single-lens reflex version of the Premo box for film packs with the Premograph. Smaller than any one of the Graflex cameras, costing only $10 at a time when the Graflex cameras were selling for $100 (for the roll-film–loaded 1A Graflex) and up to $292 (for the today-rare Stereo Auto Graflex with matched Goerz lenses), the Premograph was an attempt to capture a family market for the rather sophisticated box camera it offered.

The Premograph has the look of a black box camera, except that the top unfolds to reveal a ground glass. The owner looked down to see the

image captured at the moment of shutter release onto 3¼-by-4¼-inch film. The key that brought the mirror into position with a forward wind became the shutter trip when reverse wound. The main advantage of the costlier, sophisticated Graflex camera, that one could focus the lens for photography at any distance, was not available in this simple Premograph box camera–reflex camera since there was no provision for lens focusing. Since this lens was about f/11, the image on the ground glass was for aiming, not focusing. The design proved to be a complicated way to use a simple camera. The Premograph was among the least successful of all Premo cameras; this makes it one of the most difficult for the Premo collector or single-lens reflex camera collector to locate. A short-lived Rochester Optical Co. quality reflex, the Premo Reflecting Camera (1905–1906) is, though, even rarer.

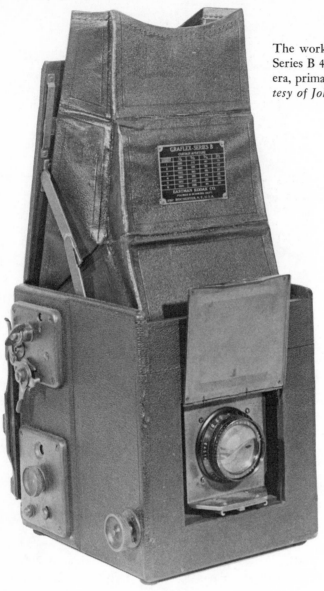

The workhorse of the Graflex system: The 1925 Graflex Series B 4-by-5, single-lens reflex was an all-purpose camera, primarily used by the professional. *(Photograph courtesy of John and Valerie Craig)*

Imported from Germany, the Paff Reflex, ca. 1922, was a roll-film (or film-pack) loaded single-lens-reflex box camera that sold for $15. *(From George Murphy catalogue)*

The Kodak Company made only modest efforts to interest the family photographer in the benefits of single-lens reflex photography with the 1A and 3A models of the Kodak-made Graflex for 2½-by-4¼-inch and 3½-by-5¼-inch (postcard) images. Nevertheless, this design was to become the most important camera type of the twentieth century following the popularization of 35-mm film and color photography. But then, they did own the Folmer & Schwing Division with its Graflex name from 1907–1926 until they were forced by a court decision to divest themselves of it in 1926.

Collectors seeking SLR-design cameras aimed at the family users are restricted to representative SLR cameras of the 1920s and 1930s that are English and German entries to the market. For example, the Pilot 6 from Germany, which was an excellent low-cost camera since it offered both a focusing lens and an adjustable shutter and diaphragm system. The Pilot 6 could be loaded with the widely available #120 roll film. In this same period, which saw the rapid rise to fame of the Rollei line of twin-lens reflex (TLR) cameras, Pilot also introduced a TLR model (see Chapter 7, "Twin-Lens Reflex Cameras"). An unusually small single-lens reflex of the 1920s from Germany was Ihagee's box-type Paff, which uses #117 film.

In the 1930s, faced with the import of successful single- and twin-lens cameras from Europe, and wanting to edge out the less expensive models of

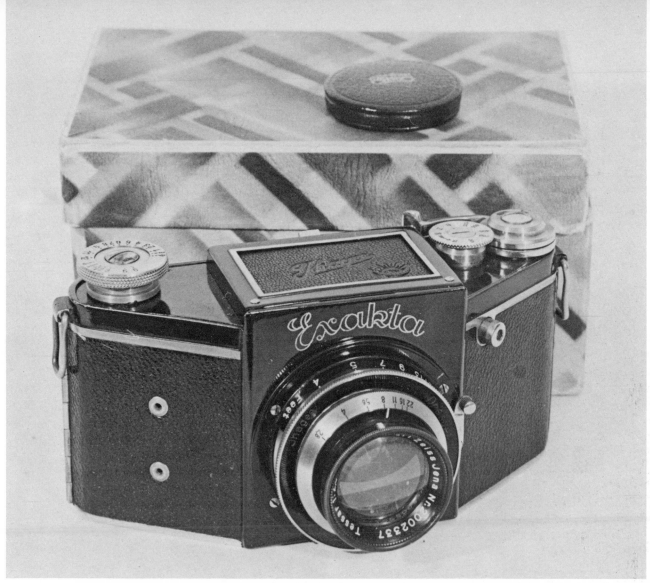

The Vest Pocket Exakta of 1936. Its proponents predicted the camera revolution into 35-mm SLR photography starting in the 1950s. *(Photograph courtesy of John and Valerie Craig)*

the Rollei, Graflex introduced the smallest Graflex cameras ever made: the National Graflex. These took 10 pictures on a roll of the popular #120 roll film. The last model added the advantages of interchangeable lenses and the high shutter speeds, which originally had attracted the American press photographer to the early Graflex.

The bulky Graflex cameras were being phased out in the 1930s as the press photographers moved over to the lighter, faster-to-handle Speed Graphic cameras. By the addition of the coupled range finder, which became an available necessity, this camera could be focused without looking into the dim ground glass. The Speed Graphic with a coupled range finger and a synchronized flashgun was

the "fastest gun in the West." A photographer could expose both sides of a double-plate holder, hand it to the waiting motorcyclist-messenger, and see his photograph in the printed newspaper by the time he arrived back at the office for his next assignment.

The Big Bertha Graflex cameras in 4-by-5- and 5-by-7-inch plate sizes were the necessary equipment for the endless coverage of baseball and football action from vantage points overhead or on the sidelines. With telephoto lenses and high-speed Folmer & Schwing shutters (identical to those from years before), these photographic cannons were unmatched in their ability to capture a slide into home plate or a tackle on the one-yard line.

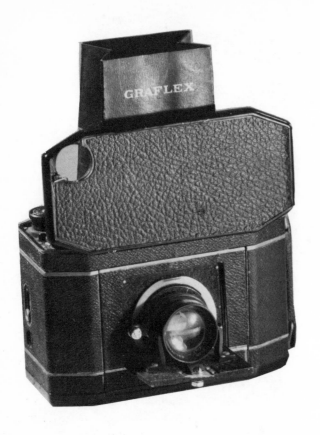

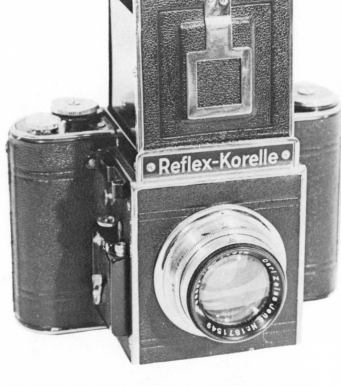

The miniaturized National Graflex of the 1930s tried to gain an American foothold in the growing small-camera field. *(From the collection of the author)*

The Reflex-Korelle from Germany loaded with roll film and offered a system of screw-in interchangeable lenses available on few other cameras of the time. *(Photograph courtesy of John and Valerie Craig)*

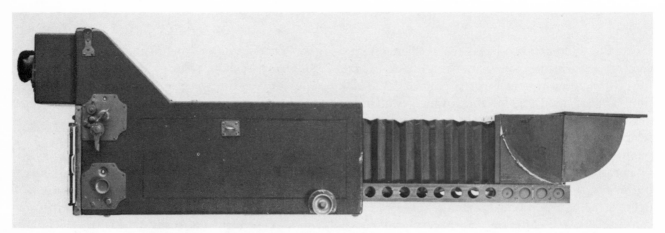

One of America's rarest SLR cameras, the Naturalist Graflex was designed for telephoto use with lenses showing 1/25th of the ordinary scene. *(Photograph courtesy of Ed Romney)*

With the market for larger Graflex cameras limited by the success of the Speed Graphics (from the same company), the Graflex designers hoped in the National Graflex Models I and II of 1932 and 1934 to attract an American family audience away from the German cameras. The effort failed, and Graphic cameras themselves would disappear twenty years later under the impact of 35-mm photography.

The single-lens reflex idea came into its own for the family-photography market with the appearance of one German camera: the Vest Pocket Exakta from Ihagee. The only thing "vest pocket" about it is the name, which derived from the fact that this unique camera loaded with the same film as the compact (when folded) vest-pocket cameras, #127 (see the discussion of the Vest-Pocket Era in Chapter 3, "Folding Cameras.")

The Korelle-Reflex of the period offered an interchangeable lens system for photographers who sought an SLR in a 6-by-6-centimeter format.

The Vest Pocket Exakta opened the door to the design of further Exaktas and a range of lenses that could be more accurately aimed and focused on the internal ground glass than through the peep-sight system of the Leica and Contax cameras. (These miniature cameras were at their best when used with lenses up to short focal length telelenses. For the longer telelenses or for ultracloseup photography where the Exakta excelled, the Leitz and Zeiss engineers introduced a mirror system to convert the basic eye-level camera into a crude single-lens reflex with dual controls to close the mirror and to open the shutter. Clumsy and expensive.)

With the introduction of the 35-mm Exakta cameras in 1937, there was now a German Big Three commanding the photographic leadership in the miniature feld, which America never matched, and which was finally conquered by the Japanese camera-industry growth after World War II. The last Graflex was made in 1957, and no quality single-lens reflex camera has been made in America since.

In 1884 the Monocular Duplex cracked wide a door that ultimately swung open to invite the American photographer into a world of more precision, more versatility, and more advantages than any other camera system in history. It would have taken someone with the courage to openly state that America would land a man on the moon in less than a hundred years and also to state that at the same time, Japan would be the camera factory for the whole world.

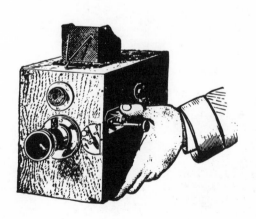

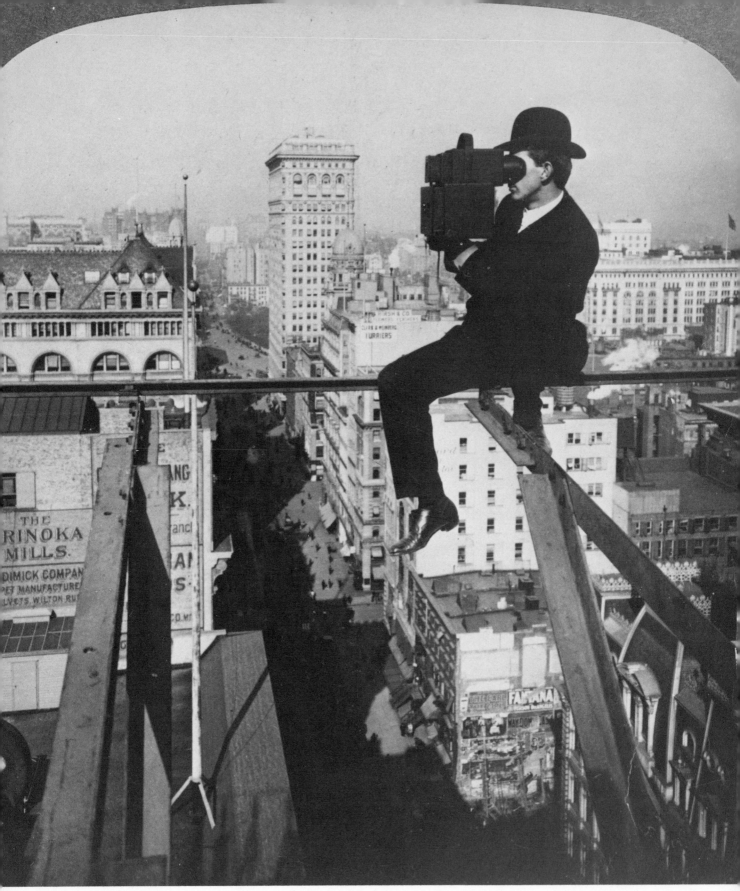

Stereo photographer documents New York's early skyscraper construction high above Fifth Avenue, using Twin-lens Stereo Graphic.

7
Twin-Lens Reflex Cameras

Among the most rare of cameras are the twin-lens reflex (TLR) cameras made before 1900. Most collectors don't even know they exist. Ask in a camera store or a professional photographer about the earliest of the cameras that had one viewing system atop the taking lens system (like two cameras, one atop the other). There is either the admission of guilt of noninformation or the (wrong) guess that it was a German invention of the 1920s, possibly even the well-known Rolleiflex or one of the German copies of that famous camera of the period.

Three American companies prior to 1900 tried in vain to interest photographers in the advantages inherent in focusing and composing on a ground glass while a matching camera below was charged and ready for the moment of shutter release.

G. Gennert, producers of the Montauk twin-lens camera at the very end of the detective-camera period (1883–1896); the Rochester Optical Company, makers of Carlton, which was practically unknown among the popular cameras of this company; and finally, one of the greatest camera makers in the first half of the twentieth century, Folmer & Schwing, who made the famous Graphic and Graflex cameras were the U.S. TLR makers. The Folmer & Schwing entry in the field was the Graphic Twin-Lens camera; only its illustrations seem to exist today. Moreover, no current photographers or collectors have ever seen or used the Carlton or the Montauk. We only know of them from their advertising and catalogues.

The failure of these designs to capture any significant sector of the camera market kept other camera makers from starting models. In their book, *The History of Photography*,[1] the authors, Helmut and Alison Gernsheim state that the first twin-lens reflex camera dates back to February 1880 with a camera specially made by an English company, R. & J. Beck, who constructed a model in which two lenses moved with the winding of one knob, taking 3¼-by-4¼-inch pictures.

In 1887, the Kinegraphe by E. Français (Paris) was announced to the Société Français de Photographie. The year 1889, however, saw significant TLR versions emerging in England, France, and Germany. The Cosmopolite was introduced that year by the French company that had earlier made the Kinegraphe; in Germany, Dr. Krügener's Simplex was a nonfocusing TLR all-wood box; and in England, the Ross and the Carlton (not the Carlton made by Rochester Optical) were shortly to appear. Models for the Ross, known as the Divided Camera, were offered in roll-film, plate, and magazine versions. Barely born, the system was thus ranging from very simple to very sophisticated formats.

In the ensuing years, London Stereoscopic Co. announced a variety of TLR models. The design idea captured modest attention for a bit more than a decade, but then the single- (not twin-) lens reflex cameras, which emerged in all countries, became popular and were made available in all of the medium and small standard camera sizes.

The emergence of the smaller-format twin-lens reflex camera was an outgrowth of the stereo age.

[1] P. 415.

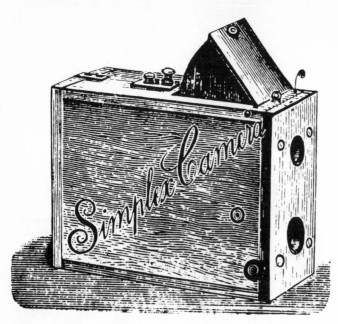

Dr. Krügener's Simplex-Magazin-Camera (Germany, ca. 1890) is box-shaped with an early twin-lens reflex design. (*From the collection of Eaton S. Lothrop, Jr.*)

The Franke and Heidecke Company of Germany had been successful in the 1920s with two basic stereo cameras (see Chapter 5, "Stereo Cameras and Stereography"). By adopting design features of these, the Rolleiflex was born in 1929. With this camera, the twin-lens reflex, smaller than most of the then-popular single-lens reflex cameras, not only offered miniaturization, it incorporated a fast-crank wind for film-advance simplicity and other conveniences. Its success was the beginning of the end for the larger, bulkier, more difficult-to-use Graflex cameras of America and their counterparts in England and Germany.

Within a few years of the demonstrated capability of the Rollei as a photographic tool, first Voigtländer and then Zeiss introduced their own versions: the Voigtländer Brilliant for the low-cost market and the Superb for the better camera shelf, and in 1938, the high-quality Zeiss Ikoflex.

In the 1930s, the Rolleiflex moved toward a mass market with a lower-priced version of the Rolleiflex, the Rolleicord. To meet the competition of the even smaller 35-mm cameras, a Rolleiflex in a smaller (4-by-4-centimeter) format became the smallest of the TLR cameras. The original Rollei-

flex took 12 square pictures on a roll of #117 film (soon changed to #120), each 2¼ by 2¼ inches. The smaller size Rolleiflex could be loaded with the #127 film of the vest-pocket folding cameras. These smaller Rollei cameras, first in black and later in warm gray leather versions with a chrome finish, are among the most handsome compact twin-lens reflex cameras ever built and highly collectible.

The miniaturization of the twin-lens reflex by Zeiss took a strange turn when the Zeiss engineers married their "roll-top desk" shutters and lenses of the Contax II to a twin-lens reflex camera that could be loaded with 35-mm film: the Contaflex of 1935. It is the outstanding TLR, since it offered interchangeable lenses, a built-in (not coupled) exposure meter, and shutter speeds to $\frac{1}{1000}$ second. Of all TLR cameras, this is the most sophisticated (and most costly[2] at $650) of the period, featuring the fast f/1.5 lens, which made it the fastest TLR in history. But it had a design flaw that has driven every Contaflex owner absolutely crazy: It could not be used to take a vertical-format photograph. Heavy, operable only by right-handed people, and—like all other TLR cameras—almost impossible to aim except when looking down (or up into) the ground glass, it was ideal only for wide pictures. Its weight and shape, and the fact that you had to look *down* into the camera to focus and shoot, defeated attempts to turn the camera on its side. You just couldn't photograph the Empire State Building with a camera of this design. Almost all of the other TLR cameras before and after the Contaflex, however, took square (or nearly square) pictures; in them there would have been no advantage in trying to change the camera position from horizontal to vertical viewing. A square is a square.

The Contaflex of the 1930s had everything going for it up front: fast lenses, built-in meter, etc. The Rollei cameras had everything going for it in back: interchangeable backs to use plates instead of roll film, and even provision for 35-mm photography. Most other twin-lens reflex cameras of the period were basically simple cameras with neither the svelte lines of the 35-mm camera or the conveni-

[2] *Fortune* magazine, October 1936, "The U.S. Minicam Boom" (unsigned), p. 160.

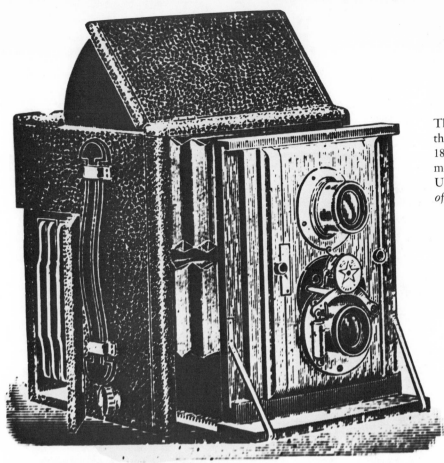

The Carlton Twin-Lens Camera from the Rochester Optical Company in 1895 is believed to be the first commercially produced TLR in the United States. *(From the collection of Eaton S. Lothrop, Jr.)*

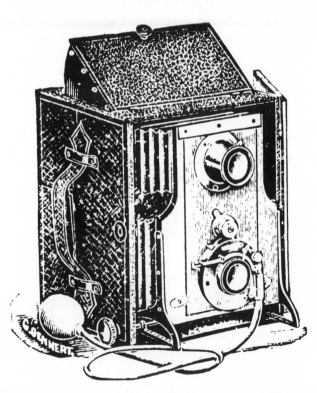

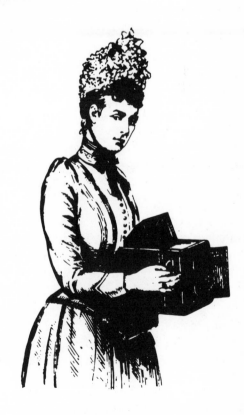

The Twin Lens Montauk by G. Gennert, ca. 1899, was among the three SLR cameras made in the United States before 1900 which collectors would like to locate; no known examples can be found in any of the major collections. *(From the collection of Eaton S. Lothrop, Jr.)*

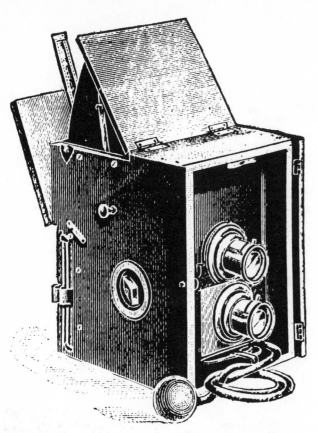

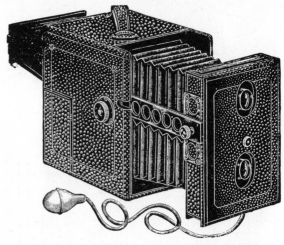

The almost unknown Twin-Lens Graphic Special of Folmer & Schwing Mfg. Co., 1901, placed the ground glass at camera rear. (*From the collection of Eaton S. Lothrop, Jr.*)

The RR 'Record' Twin-Lens Camera from Levi, Jones & Co. (England, ca. 1895) was among a number of TLR designs developing in Britain. (*From the collection of Eaton S. Lothrop, Jr.*)

ence and compactness of the folding models. But all sold well.

Such cameras as the Fothflex, Weltaflex, Zecaflex, Altiflex, and the Pilot offered either convenient price or an ingenious fold-up system to achieve a relative compactness.

Collectors particularly like the Rube Goldberg fold-away front of the Zecaflex, which actually incorporated a bellows and a finder that was above the taking lens. It sold for about $75 in the late 1930s—about half the price of the Rolleiflex, which offered automatic film winding and a greater degree of precision in construction.

The Pilot achieved a compactness when not in use by incorporating bellows but also by a design that used the #127 roll film of the Rollei 4-by-4-centimeter model. The essential difference in the Pilot that attracts collectors to this camera is the fact that along with the Contaflex, it is one of the few TLR cameras that does *not* take a square picture. The Pilot image is 3 by 4 centimeters (1³⁄₁₆ by 1⁹⁄₁₆ inches); and 16 pictures are taken on a roll of film. Thus, this camera offered a horizontal format and film economies. It sold for as little as $60 with an f/3.5 lens and for as much as $125 with an f/2 lens. Collectors are glad to pay $100 and more for almost any model, but the models with the fast f/2 lenses attract the most interest.

Before 1939, nearly a half dozen Rollei models had won acceptance in the American market, and collectors find the standard (1932) model and even the original Rolleiflex (1929) relatively easy to find in pawnshops and camera stores. Many are still in use today. Collector interest in the Rollei cameras in general has not been high. There is even less interest in the Ikoflex cameras, which were introduced in 1934 with different models in subsequent years. Nor is there any great demand for the near-primitive Voigtländer cameras which offered neither lens speed or shutter excellence to the owner-user. Collectors of TLR cameras do seek the Voigtländer Superb with its unusual parallax-correcting viewing lens (in which the top lens leans forward to look down at "near" objects).

In the hands of the experts, the Rollei cameras

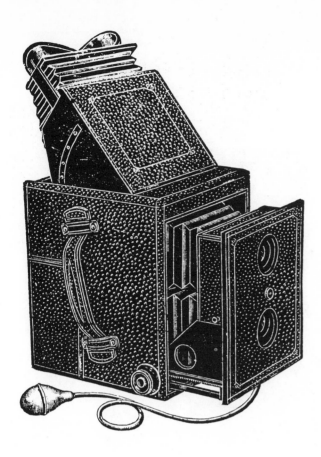

The Twin-Lens Graphic, 1901, provided an angled view of the ground glass, a forerunner of the many Graflex cameras developed by Folmer & Schwing Mfg. Co.

Easily the world's most famous TLR, the famous German Rolleiflex. Fast handling and compact with a crank to advance film, it raced ahead of all competition, starting in the late 1920s. Example shown: Standard Rolleiflex, No. 404142, ca. 1935. *(From the collection of Robert and Marilyn Goodman)*

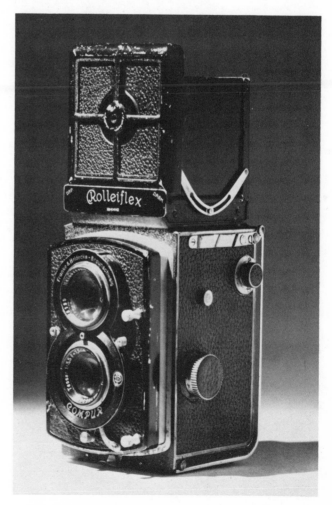

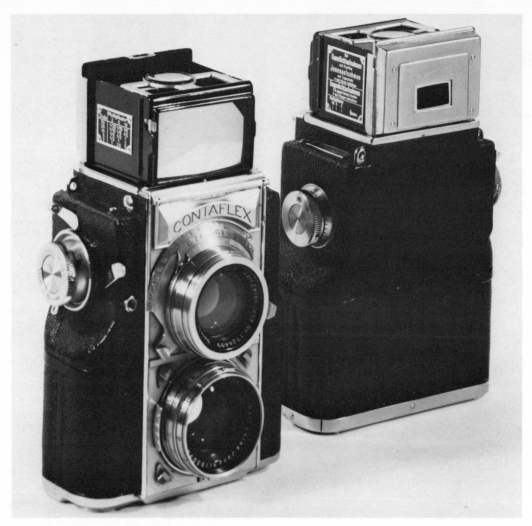

The ultimate in 35-mm twin-lens-reflex design, the Zeiss Contaflex (shown front and back), was first introduced in 1935. It offered total lens interchangeability and even a built-in exposure meter (non-coupled). *(From the collection of Matthew R. Isenberg)*

were excellent tools, bridging the distance between the slow-handling larger-format camera and the tiny negative of the 35-mm cameras. Some of the great portraitists, photo journalists, and fashion photographers of the 1930s proved that even without interchangeable lenses, the sturdy, high-precision 6-by-6-centimeter Rollei was a trustworthy workhorse. Their demonstrated excellence opened the doors to ultimate acceptance of the capabilities of the 35-mm camera, which began to be recognized only when issue after issue of *Life* and *Look* magazines rolled off the press with amazing photos by known proponents of the 35-mm–camera age, like Alfred Eisenstadt and Henri Cartier-Bresson. In that same period, Martin Munkaci, Fritz Henle, and Toni Frissell were creating a visual impact with the fast-handling Rolleiflex in the pages of *Vogue* and *Harper's Bazaar*.

A Kodak reflex and an Ansco competitor did not appear until after World War II. They came too little and too late; the move to 35-mm had become a stampede and the TLR would give way to a new generation of single-lens reflex cameras in 35-mm and 6-by-6-centimeter formats.

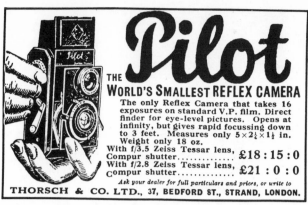

A typical advertisement for the Pilot Pocket Reflex—billed as "World's Smallest Reflex Camera." *(From the collection of Eaton S. Lothrop, Jr.)*

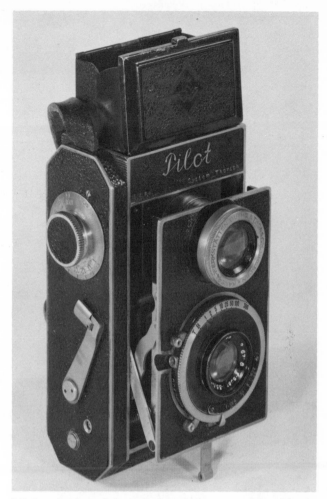

Miniaturization of the twin-lens design was achieved in the Pilot Pocket Reflex of Guthe & Thorsch (Germany, ca. 1930) which loaded with film of the vest-pocket folding cameras (#127) to take sixteen pictures, each only slightly larger than 35-mm double frame. *(From the collection of Matthew R. Isenberg)*

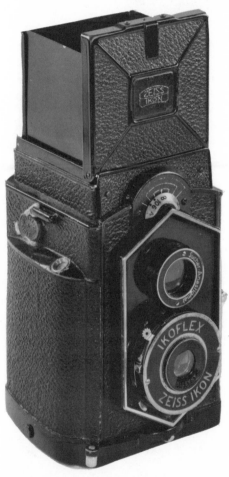

The Zeiss Ikoflex was a major German competitor in the mid-1930s to the two major German TLR offerings: the Rolleiflex/Rolleicord and the Voigtländer Superb and Brilliant cameras. *(From the collection of Matthew R. Isenberg)*

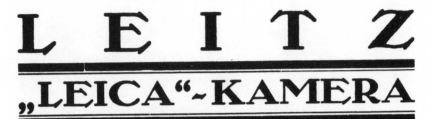

LEITZ
„LEICA"-KAMERA

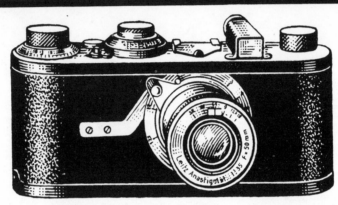

Ein neuer Kameratyp

für Normal-Kinofilm / 36 Aufnahmen 24×36 mm ohne Kass.-Wechsel

Leitz-Anastigmat „Elmax" 1:3,5

Vollendete Auszeichnung / Größte Tiefenschärfe
Hohe Vergrößerungsmöglichkeit

Schlitzverschluß

verstellbar u. verdeckt aufziehbar / Geringes Volumen u. Gewicht
Schnellste Aufnahmebereitschaft

III. Katalog „Leica Nr. 384" kostenlos / Lieferung durch die Photohandlungen

Ernst Leitz / Optische Werke / Wetzlar

A 1925 advertisement announces the history-making Leica camera (Model A). *(From the collection of Eaton S. Lothrop, Jr.)*

8
35-mm

If it hadn't been for the invention of motion pictures, there would not have been the phenomenon of the 35-mm camera, which has dominated the photographic scene for the last half of the twentieth century. The motion-picture camera and the projection device necessary for the showing of the film required a system that would permit the rapid advance of film frames, one after another, in endless procession with both accuracy and speed. The technical solution to the problem was the perforation of the film edges to permit claws to pull it—first in the camera, later in the projector—down to and then away from the frame area.

Since the film reels would be distributed all over the world to entertain audiences, there had to be a universal industry agreement on not only the size (width) of the film but also of the claw holes if films were to fit all projectors. The resultant film, today's familiar 35-mm film, became available as raw stock in every technologically advanced country. Ultimately still cameras were developed everywhere to be loaded with short lengths of the now widely available film material. Predictably, the first still cameras to take advantage of this perforated film are among the most eagerly sought cameras by collectors: the French Homeos stereo camera of 1913, for example; the American Tourist Multiple of 1914; or the German Levy-Roth Minnigraph of 1915.

Many of these first 35-mm cameras, and especially the prestige precision cameras from Germany, were costly and complicated. Some models of the Leitz Leica, the Zeiss Contax, and the Ihagee Exakta were produced in runs of only a few thou-

sand. Thus, as "limited editions," these have commanded a high degree of collector interest.

The first mass-produced 35-mm camera was introduced in America in 1926 (before the Leica). It was the Memo from Ansco (Binghamton, New York), merger of the E. & H. T. Anthony & Co. and the Scovill group of companies. But it was not until a major film breakthrough almost ten years later by the Eastman Kodak Company in 1935 that the stage was set for the major entry of 35-mm cameras onto the world photographic stage. The film was the revolutionary new film for color photography at a modest cost: Kodachrome. The metal cartridge created to house this film for the Kodak Retina I started a most amazing camera-design revolution.

Two more of the limited-edition 35-mm cameras were produced in the United States in the period just before World War I. The Tourist Multiple of 1914 with a boxy vertical shape held a fifty-foot coil of 35-mm black-and-white motion-picture film that could take 750 photographs before the camera was reloaded. The 2½-by-4-by-8-inch camera was priced at $175 and was aimed at the prestige traveler market. The owner was offered a projector to show his photos from positives by projection.

The Simplex Multi-Exposure was another camera loaded with a fifty-foot coil of the 35-mm film. Its innovations included the optional use of the camera for single frame (standard motion-picture film area) or double frame (the 24-by-36-millimeter shape of the 35-mm image of today). The owner could take 400 double-frame exposures or 800 single frames. It sold for $65, and its pictures

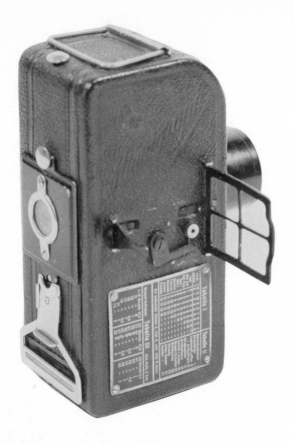

The rare Minnigraph, a pre-Leica 35-mm camera of Germany. *(From the collection of Matthew R. Isenberg)*

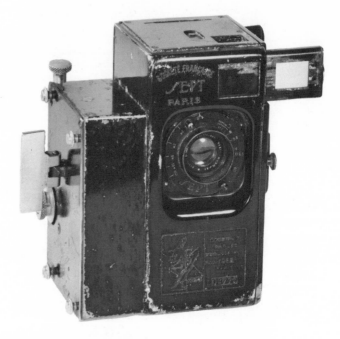

The Sept, a French combination motion picture and still camera (convertible to a projector), ca. 1923. *(From the collection of Matthew R. Isenberg)*

were meant to be projected as positives in a projector-enlarger offered by the company.

Reputedly less than a thousand of the Tourist Multiples were made and sold, which makes this a much-sought example of an early 35-mm camera. Evidently, even fewer Simplex cameras were made, and collectors often meet to discuss why no one has been able to find more than a half dozen examples as evidence of its existence.*

* Some cameras are dated by the patent application, while others have been dated by such evidence as the first public notice (advertising or news stories) or by the dates of catalogues in which these products are listed. This can obscure the real date of first appearance of a piece in a collection. A perfect example of this is the confusion relating to the order of appearance of the Tourist Multiple, the Homeos, and the Simplex, all cameras loading with 35-mm film. The patent application was made for the Tourist Multiple in 1912 and for the Homeos in 1913; but the earliest known literature for the Tourist is 1914, while dated literature is available for the Homeos during 1913. The Simplex of the same period is shown only in literature of 1914.

After World War I the Ansco Company conceived of the idea of a lower-cost version of a camera combining the Tourist Multiple and the Simplex. The camera was to be smaller and lighter like the Minnigraph. Since Ansco was a film manufacturer (as it is today as GAF), it could and did design a tiny metal canister to hold a 50-picture (not 50-foot) length of film that could be pulled down by a claw mechanism, exactly as in a motion-picture camera, from one tiny can at camera top to its mate at camera bottom. Its picture area was "single frame": a match to the standard set around the world for cine frames (1 by ¾ inch).

For the Ansco Memo, which sold for $20, there are a half-dozen kinds or variants: first run with un-

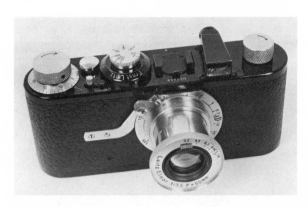

The first of the famous Leica system of cameras, the *Leica A* with the "hockey stick" on the face. *(Photograph courtesy of Jim Lager)*

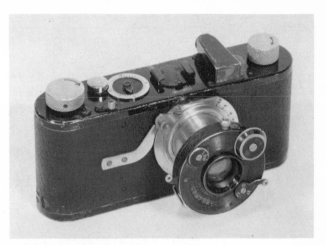

Easily identifiable Leica B has its shutter at the lens instead of at camera back. Ca. 1927–1930; now quite rare.

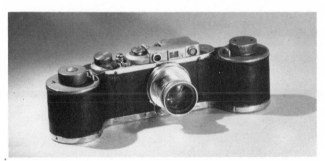

Barrel end identifies the Leica Reporter (model FF or 250). Model shown is a Russian copy. *(From the collection of the author)*

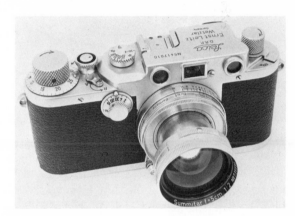

Leica IIIc of the 1930s included interchangeable lenses and coupled range finder. *(Photograph courtesy of Jim Lager)*

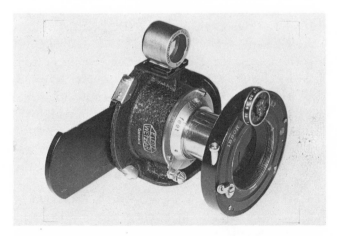

Special laboratory Leica (single-shot). *(Photograph courtesy of Graphic Antiquarian; from the collection of Francis B. Paca)*

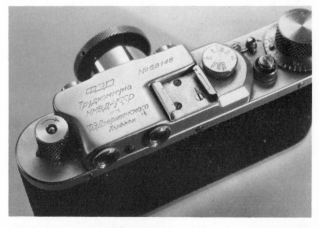

Russian Leica copy (FED) of 1930s. Leica was also copied in England, United States, Italy, and Japan. *(From the collection of S. D. Clark)*

French EKA loaded with non-sprocketed 35-mm motion-picture film, ca. 1924. *(From the collection of Dr. R. H. Krauss)*

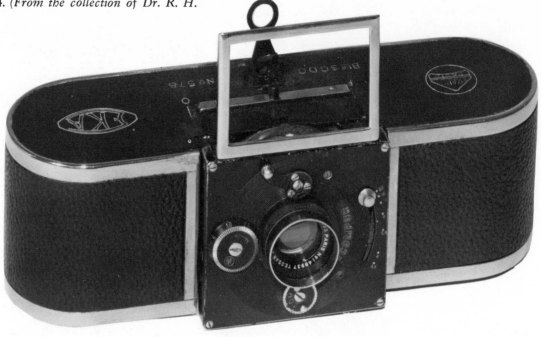

protected shutter release; second run, which became the major run, with protected shutter release; models in black; models in all-wood (as tropical); the Boy Scout model; the unsubstantiated Camp Fire Girl and Girl Scout models; models with f/6.3 lenses; and models with f/3.5 (focusing) lenses, etc. The camera, thirty-five years after the Kombi, was a system camera, carrying the system idea to new highs: There were not only matching Memo closeup lenses and Memo filters, but there were also a Memo projector, a printer, a copier, and an enlarger to handle this motion-picture film in the noncine darkroom. The French Sept camera of the same period could be used for movies or still photography, and it even converted into a projector.

Limitations of the film quality and the chemistry made it difficult to capture the kind of 35-mm image that fifteen years later was to shock and excite the American readers of *Life, Look,* and other emerging picture magazines of the pre-TV world.

Obviously, this camera or one stemming from it was the starting point for an American move into the 35-mm field on a worldwide basis. It was over a decade before it would happen.

In the meantime, it took the makers of such precision optical equipment as microscopes, telescopes, binoculars, and similarly sophisticated engineering to create the camera systems that would give birth to the "candid camera" photography, action-packed and emotion-laden photographs taken indoors and out without flash by the century's greatest photographers.

In 1925, E. Leitz of Germany began to distribute what was to become one of the great classic cameras of the twentieth century: the Leica A. It required the photographer to load cassettes with his own film since there was no factory-packaged film in a cassette shaped for this new camera. Its f/3.5 lens was no faster than lenses on many other all-metal cameras that had been pouring out of Germany in the 1920s, on larger bellows cameras or roll-film–loaded folding cameras, or very large reflex cameras, or such miniature versions as the Ermanox line of cameras.

Within the next seven years, the new improved Leica models were to incorporate the features that would make the Leica system of photography the worldwide standard for photographic perfection in a miniature camera for camera makers and photographers to this day. A German film firm, Perutz, then made film in daylight load cartridges available for the growing world-wide Leica market.

The new Leica cameras (see "Dating the Leica," pages 250–251 in Appendix B) included faster lenses that permitted action photos indoors; a built-in range-finder system to assure precise focus even in dim light without the guesswork focus of most other cameras of that era; and accessory systems that made this new, small precision equipment applicable to the demands of the scientist, the educator, the traveler, the portraitist, and the sports photographer. New lenses made possible wide-angle photography and telephotography with quick replacement of one lens for another by a screw-in system.

Despite the American depression, by 1936, twenty-five thousand Leicas had been sold to the wealthiest Americans, who paid nearly $100 for the simplest model and up to nearly $300 for the costliest version with the fast f/2 lens. (At that time a new Plymouth automobile sold for $375–$400.)

In the same period, two other camera companies were launching their own ideas in cameras that could be loaded with the 35-mm film: Zeiss and Ihagee. Zeiss, who competed with Leitz in the microscope and binocular market, introduced three models of the Contax by 1936. With the pioneering already completed by Leica, even the first Zeiss Contax had provision for interchangeable lenses and a military-type built-in range finder that automatically engaged each lens for its required focus adjustment. The second model, the Contax II, added the sparkle of chrome and moved shutter controls into the body at the camera's top. The Contax III of 1936 took a step Leica did not follow for another two decades. It provided a noncoupled exposure meter on the body of the camera to guide the photographer in the frustrating problem of how to set the lens and shutter to assure proper exposure. (The first mass-produced camera in the world with the capability of automatically setting the proper exposure was not to appear until Eastman Kodak introduced the Super Kodak Six-20, a folding roll-film camera in 1938.)

The Zeiss marketing people and engineers did everything they could to step ahead of the Leica people. Theirs was the camera with the faster lens (the Zeiss Sonnar f/1.5 competed with the Leitz Summar f/2). Theirs was the camera with the fastest shutter speed: The Contax offered $\frac{1}{1250}$ second

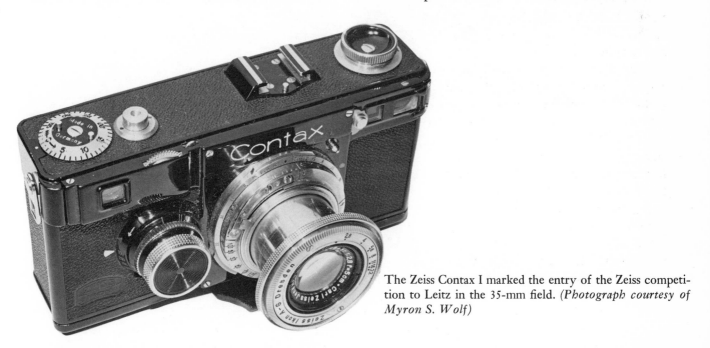

The Zeiss Contax I marked the entry of the Zeiss competition to Leitz in the 35-mm field. (*Photograph courtesy of Myron S. Wolf*)

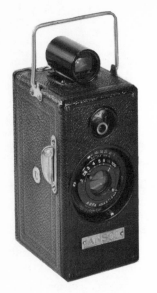
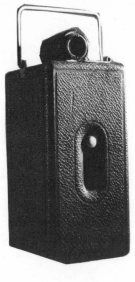

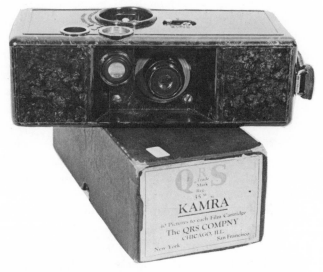

America's first mass-produced 35-mm camera was the Ansco Memo of 1926. Shown here are the front and back of the 1927 model. A claw mechanism advanced film as in cine cameras. *(From the collection of the author)*

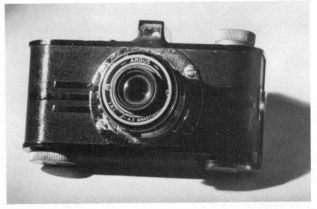

QRS Kamra loaded with forty-shot cartridges of 35-mm film. It had the shape of the French EKA. *(Photograph courtesy of John and Valerie Craig)*

The Argus A opened color photography on Kodachrome to millions of Americans. *(From the collection of the author)*

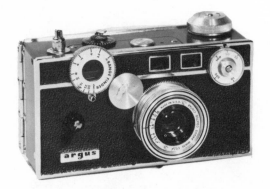

The Argus C–3 with its brick shape was a design landmark in 1939. *(From the collection of the author)*

as opposed to the $\frac{1}{1000}$ second featured only on the most expensive models of the Leica. Theirs was the first with the built-in exposure meter, while Leica owners carried a Leicameter accessory in their pockets.

The Zeiss people went one step further: They married the Contax to a twin-lens reflex design and in 1935 introduced the Contaflex, which sold for the startlingly high price of $650 (in depression dollars)—more than the price of a brand new Plymouth, Ford, or Chevrolet. (This Contaflex is not to be confused with the post–World War II single-lens reflex Contaflex.)

The Zeiss innovations were not enough to recoup the seven-year head start of the Leica. Leica stayed ahead by a sales factor of six to one. This has made the Contax less available to collectors, but the magic of the Leica reputation has made this system so popular that collectors of the Leitz products have their own organization in the United States, the Leica Historical Society of America, which meets and publishes to explore little-known details of the camera, its makers, the optics, etc. (see listing in Chapter 9, "Collecting Photographica.") There is no parallel group for the Zeiss Contax collectors, or even for collectors of Kodak products, the most widely collected photographic line in the U.S.

The Leica collectors center their searches on a number of the most obscure Leica cameras, three of which are totally different in their design and background and indicate some of the interest in Leica lore. One is the Leica B, a model with a front-lens shutter; all other Leicas have shutters within the body. The second is the Leica FF (or Leica Reporter), first made in 1933, a special model that had barrellike ends to hold a coil of twenty-seven feet of film, enough to take 250 exposures before the camera was reloaded. So few "reporters" or others wanted this strange Leica with its bizarre configuration that only 1,250 were produced, making it a limited-edition collectible. (Stranger yet, the Russians, who were not signatories to the International Patent Agreements and who unselfconsciously therefore copied all technical equipment of interest, also made a copy of this unmarketable Leica, one of which ultimately arrived at a camera

shop in Florence, Italy, where it was acquired by the author, thanks to a friend, for $25 in 1967.) The third group of Leicas eagerly sought by collectors exists in a greater abundance. These are the gray-covered Luftwaffe Leicas, the wartime cameras made for the German Air Force. They were marked in various ways to indicate that they were official military equipment, in some cases with a letter *K* for *Kugellager* ("ball-bearing") after the serial number to indicate that the shutter was designed for use in below-freezing temperatures. (The *K* does not stand for *Kaltefest* ["coldproof"], as most collectors believe.)

There are other eagerly sought Leica cameras and special Leica camera aids sought by collectors: The single-shot Leica, the Leica rifle (gun), certain lenses as the Thambar (for soft portraits), early viewfinders, darkroom aids, etc.

In the period when Zeiss and Leitz were vying for the growing American miniature-camera market, the Exakta camera system was introduced by Ihagee (Chapter 6, "Single-Lens Reflex Cameras"). It immediately found favor with the medical profession since it provided a simple-to-use system for closeup photography of the teeth, the skin, the eye. It was just as superb in long telephotography, where the Leica and the Contax were relatively awkward to aim and use. The Exakta became a favorite with the nature photographers who admired the ease of telephotography of birds and closeup photography of flowers and insects.

The Exakta camera, with a number of unusual features in its very first model, used the widely available vest-pocket film (#127). The model using that film has been called the Vest Pocket Exakta. The name for the camera loaded with motion-picture film? The Kine-Exakta. A variety of Exaktas followed after World War II. Collectors seek these variants and especially the Exakta with the fast lens: the Night Exakta with the Biotar f/2 lens, the optical equal to the popular Leica lens in speed.

The one thing that the three major systems from Germany—Leitz, Zeiss, and Ihagee—shared was their high cost. The American earning $20 to $30 a week (see Comparative Value of Early Cameras in

Appendix) during the 1930s (if he was working at all) was not in a position to acquire a camera costing over a month's salary. (At times 25 percent of the working population was unemployed.) Nonetheless, the candid-camera craze launched by the owners of these cameras whose work was published widely in the picture magazines was not to be denied. Using the plastic of the time (Bakelite), a new breed of low-cost cameras that could be loaded with the new Kodachrome and priced starting from $9.95 (later $12.50) were announced in early 1936. In the first few weeks, the makers of the Argus A sold as many cameras as the number of Leicas sold in the prior ten years. By the end of 1941, Argus enjoyed sales reaching into the millions.

The Color Breakthrough

The search for a practical means to color photography had long intrigued the photo scientists, and there are successful experiments which date back to the Daguerrean era. A variety of systems involving cameras with the capability of exposing the three primary colors in nature onto three films had begun to exist before the 1890s. They reached their finest technological development by the middle 1930s in a group of cameras known to professionals and never seen by any but the most sophisticated of amateurs as "one-shot cameras." These were registering color-filtered photographs on glass plates to assure identically sized images after processing. They were heavy, costly, and were literally museum pieces as they were created.

A major breakthrough in film made the special camera for color photography an instant dinosaur. The film was Kodachrome, a multilayered emulsion which was developed in the early 1930s by two young photochemists who had contracted their development services to the Eastman Kodak Company. The ability to produce a film with many layers ended the need for cameras which would "color-separate" (establish the three primary colors of red, yellow, and blue) as the film itself did this.

Any camera could now take color pictures in slide form. The application of the new principles made it easy to later make color prints available for the family album. As a result, by 1974, over 98 percent of photographs sent to photo laboratories by amateurs were in color; black-and-white photography for the vacationer or family photographer of the baby's first birthday has all but disappeared.

Color-slide photography, a new kind of photography for the American family of the 1930s, had been made possible by the identical concept as that of the Kodak of 1888: a simple-to-use camera and factory processing to assure perfect results. The low-cost Argus camera had a fast lens for the price (f/4.5) and a shutter to $\frac{1}{200}$ second. In a second model, the AF (F for "focusing"), the photographer was given control of closeup photography without accessories. But the most important model

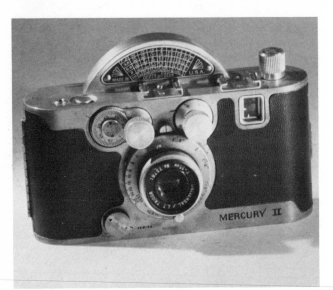

The Universal Mercury II; a metal, 35-mm camera, ca. 1940, with a shutter to 1/1000 second at a fraction of the price of the Leica. (*From the collection of the author*)

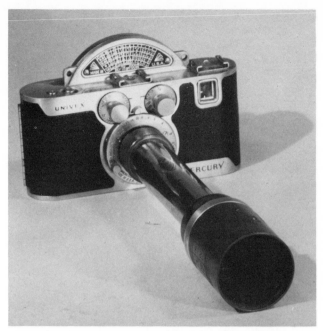

First model Mercury with handmade, long telelens. This one was found in a pawnshop in 1965. *(From the collection of the author)*

was the "Brick" (the Argus C), and especially the more advanced model of the C group, the C-3.

Possibly only with the exception of the French Verascope stereo camera, first made in the 1890s and made continuously from then on to the mid-1920s, no independent camera maker had ever achieved the marketing success of the Argus C-3. It sold over 2 million oblong, boxlike cameras during the next twenty-five to thirty years. (After World War II, Polaroid had such success in the over-$100 camera field that Polaroid Corporation claimed it sold more cameras than all other makers of over-$100 cameras combined.)

The amazing Argus was sold for far less than $50. It looked like the "candid camera" in cartoons. It was held to the eye like the Leica, whereas most cameras of the time were box and folding cameras usually aimed from the waist by checking the reflected image on a tiny ground-glass "finder." Remember?

The Argus camera was loaded with film that Kodak made widely available at the time for the cameras it was introducing for the quality market: the folding-type Kodak Retina cameras, made by Kodak in Germany (see Chapter 3, "Folding Cameras").

Unlikely as it seems today with the success of 35-mm film in Instamatic cartridges, Kodak elected not to use the perforated Kodachrome motion-picture film for the mass-market cameras of that period. Instead, the engineers suggested that by totally removing the perforations from one edge, a slightly larger film area could result (1⅛ by 1⅝ inches as opposed to the common 1 by 1½ inches). A new line of cameras called the Kodak Bantams were now introduced, using the 35-mm film in its strange format and perforation set-up (one perforation per film frame to permit film winding with an automatic "stop" after each frame). The new film (#828) was packaged with a paper backing for loading in daylight without the use of the tiny metal canister system of the regular 35-mm film rolls.

There were a wide range of Kodak Bantam cameras made during the next twenty-one years, starting with 1935. The Argus cameras of the same period were all loaded with 20- or 36-exposure rolls of black-and-white or color films. The Bantam cameras were loaded with an 8-exposure roll of film in color or black-and-white. Slides made from the exposed Kodachrome were mounted in 2-by-2-inch cardboard mounts, which fit all projectors of the period. Kodak aimed its cameras at the family that they believed was not interested in exposing more than a few pictures on any one outing. There was more than a little truth in this belief, since many

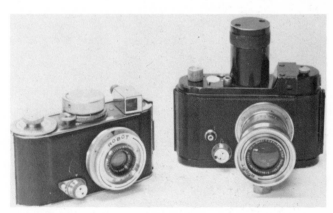

Pre-war and wartime (Luftwaffe) Robots. They loaded with 35-mm film and took photographs 1-inch square in sequence fashion. *(Photograph courtesy of* Graphic Antiquarian*)*

owners of the Argus cameras and the 35-mm–loaded Kodak Retinas did complain that film from summer pictures was still in the camera when it was time to take the annual family portrait at the Christmas tree.

While collectors find it easy to locate early examples of the Argus and Bantam cameras of the pre–World War II period, only one model has dramatically captured the collector fancy. Perhaps all others are too common and too recent to have become a collectible. The one exception is the prestigious American camera of the period: the Kodak Bantam Special, finest of all Bantam models, designed by the industrial designer Walter Dorwin Teague. Like the Leica A and the Contax I, it has become one of the classic cameras of the period. Its brightly enameled die-cast body opened from an easily pocketable size to reveal a brand new Kodak lens, a 45-mm f/2 Ektar, and possibly the world's finest shutter of the time, the Compur Rapid, made in Germany with shutter speeds from 1 second to $\frac{1}{500}$ second. A fine split-image range finder and an eye-level viewfinder made focusing quick and easy. It had no interchangeable lenses or systems of aids and accessories that had made the Leica, Contax, and Exakta cameras of the period such stand-out successes. Nonetheless, it is not uncommon after thirty-five years to find these cameras at auctions almost bringing the $110 of the camera when new. One leading collector, Allan Weiner in New York, began his collection with this camera, which he acquired at the Sotheby Parke Bernet auction of 1970—for $100.

The earlier Kodak quality miniature cameras, the Kodak Retinas, which sold at the time for $110 and up to $140, have never achieved the degree of interest that the Kodak Bantam Special has won. They had neither the speed (f/2) nor the stylishly handsome appearance of the Teague design. They enjoyed only modest success in their own time and a little less than that to the collector audience today; except for the Retina IIIc, which commands its original price today.

Two especially interesting 35-mm cameras from Germany in the mid-1930s were the Zeiss Tenax and the Robot. While these were loaded with 35-mm film, they were created to fill the special need

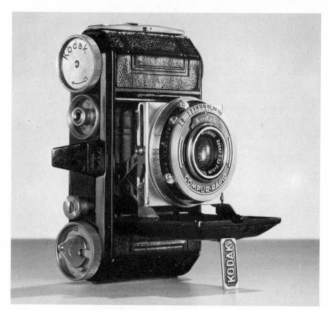

Kodak enters 35-mm field in 1935 with Kodak Retina, first of a series of 35-mm-load cameras aimed at home photographers. (*Photograph courtesy of Eastman Kodak Company*)

of the sports or nature photographer for sequence photography. Both cameras were unusual in that the picture area was a 1-inch (24-millimeter) square. Of the two, the Robot was by far the more interesting since it not only had provision for interchangeability of lenses, it also had a spring wind making it possible to take up to 24 exposures before winding the mainspring for the next sequence. (This feature had appeared in earlier cameras including the 35-mm Sept from France in the 1920s.) Robot photos could be taken as fast as the finger could touch the shutter release, but it was not a filmed sequence as with a motion-picture camera. The camera was small, easily pocketable, and remains popular in its more advanced models of the present.

The Zeiss Tenax (not to be confused with the large Tenax of the 1920s) had no spring wind; it offered a two-lever system. One hand's trigger finger pressed down to advance the film while the other hand's trigger finger tripped the release.

With either of these cameras, it is said, three, four, and five frames *per second* could be taken during final instants at a high-speed event such as a high jump. Since the short-focal-length lens offered extreme depth of field (deep field in focus), it was possible to catch the runner approaching the bar, the start of the jump, the lift, the cross-over, and then the descent or fall—in a complete sequence.

Argus sought to introduce this auto-advance feature into a little-known prototype model: the Argus D. But the engineers could never seem to get it to function properly, and ultimately the body dies were used to make the later camera, the Argus K, a model introduced in 1939 for the Daguerre Centennial (of the announcement of the invention of photography). As a result, the Argus K is a rare model, eagerly sought by 35-mm collectors, both for its design difference and for the centennial tie-in nostalgia.

The Zeiss Tenax was made in models I and II (with interchangeable lenses) but was never produced after the 1930s. On the other hand, the Robot became a wartime camera for the intelligence purposes of the German Air Force; by the 1950s, it appeared again but in a version that permitted the use of standard 35-mm cartridges and took standard 24-by-36-millimeter frames, not the 24-by-24-millimeter of the first models.

The Bolta Photavit was another example of a 35-mm camera designed around the square frame, but it had no sequence capability.

Collectors of folding cameras will find a number of folding 35-mm cameras from Germany in addition to the folding Kodak Retinas. The Zeiss Ikon 24 × 36, the Balda Baldini and Baldinette cameras, and a few other petite folding cameras of the period are among the most compact 35-mm cameras ever made. Without the advantages of interchangeable ultrafast lenses of the Leica and Contax, they appealed primarily only to the family photographer. With few distinguishing design or performance features, they attract little interest in the collector market.

It took another American company with experience in 39¢ plastic box cameras and a $9.95 metal movie camera to make one of the most interesting collectible 35-mm cameras of the late 1930s. In November 1938, the Universal Camera Corporation, which had made the tiny Univex sold in drugstores and at tobacco counters with 10¢ rolls of film, introduced the Univex Mercury I. As with the Robot, the camera could only be loaded with the special cassettes provided by the camera maker. The engineers deliberately created a camera that would not accept the standard Kodak 35-mm cartridges; but, since dealers protested as loudly as consumers at the inconvenience of not being able to find the specially spooled Univex films, the camera was altered with the Mercury II to accommodate the readily available Kodak film. The design features for this unusual camera make it a collectible camera of today. It made photographs of single-frame size (¾ by 1 inch) and used a whirling rotary shutter to create speeds up to $\frac{1}{1000}$ second (up to $\frac{1}{1500}$ second in models made in 1939).

The single-frame format as much as the slightly strange shape ultimately would end this camera when the company went into wartime production (of binoculars) and directed its postwar attention to more standard 35-mm–design cameras. The problem in 1938–1939 was that Kodak would process the Mercury-exposed Kodachrome film in its full length, unmounted. It was then up to the camera owner, or the dealer, to individually mount each frame in the 2-by-2-inch cardboard mount to ready it for projection. This not only added to the per-picture cost, it delayed the pleasure of seeing the slides on the home screen. Few owners of the camera used it for black and white since this made each roll a costly printing venture (72 prints).

Universal Mercury cameras were equipped with the first "hot shoe" flash connection (a snap-on flash attachment connecting and synchronizing the shutter to the firing of the now-popular flashbulb). The first models with f/3.5 lenses were sold first for $25, then $29.75; later models sold at higher prices with f/2.7 and even f/2 lenses. It is the models with the f/2 lenses and the $\frac{1}{1500}$-second shutter that are the rara avis for collectors of this photographic bird.*

In the year of the first Mercury, 1938, Kodak made its debut with the Kodak 35. This featureless

* Postcard "boardwalk" photographers were the first after World War II to buy used Mercury II cameras from the pawnshops and used-camera shelves of camera stores for "street photography" at tourist sites.

Kodak product was expected to compete with the Argus C-3, which was a step ahead with flash synchronization and a yard ahead with a coupled range finder. When Kodak modified the Kodak 35 to add these performance features, the resultant camera looked as though Ma and Pa Kettle were on the way West in a photographic jalopy. Bulging wheels and pointed extensions (to catch into the skin and to snag on the camera carrying case) marred the once-simple lines of the first Kodak 35. Collectors look for the later cluttered-look Kodak 35 cameras as a way to laugh at the folly of man.*

Still other American camera makers sought to enter the 35-mm market prior to World War II with cameras in the general appearance of the Leica. The Perfex 35-mm Speed Candid was styled along the lines of the Argus A but with a superior lens and a faster shutter. The Perfex sold for $25 and offered an f/3.5 lens and a shutter to ⅟₅₀₀ second. It even featured an interchangeable-lens capability. Its focal-plane shutter of the curtain type was the first in a 35-mm size in an American camera (other American cameras such as the Graphic and the Graflex cameras from the earliest days of twentieth century had employed the curtain-shutter system).

The Perfex Speed Candid was followed by the Perfex 44, which won greater attention, and finally by a further group of both improved and stripped-

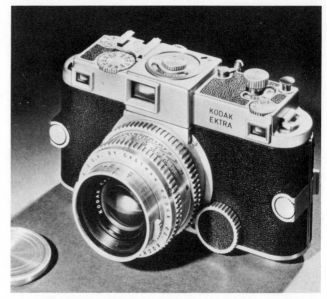

The finest 35-mm camera ever made in America is a leading Kodak collectible—the 1940 Kodak Ektra. It had such unique features in a precision 35-mm design as interchangeable backs and a close-up capability unavailable in either the Leica or the Contax. *(Photograph courtesy of Eastman Kodak Company)*

model cameras to compete with the ever-successful Argus cameras: the Perfex 22, 33, and 55.*

It is likely that somewhere on Sunday, December 7, 1941, someone was puzzling over which 35-mm camera to buy when the radio flashed news of a bombing in faraway Pearl Harbor. If he delayed the purchase of the 35-mm camera till after the war, the chances were that he wound up buying one made in Japan, the country that took over the photo-optical production of the world in an unsuspected industrial surge that brought quality cameras from the Orient to every corner of the world. The drama of the Japanese conquest of the camera industry is all the more enhanced in that in this book, for example, there is not a single bit of evidence of the coming Japanese technological capability that emerged from the ashes of Hiroshima and Nagasaki after 1950.

---

* Kodak's prestige entry into the 35-mm market with the Kodak Ektra in 1941 won more favorable attention. This unique camera system had features unknown to the Leica-Contax-Exakta competition. For example, the entire back could be removed with the film without a loss of even a single exposure so that another back with a different film could be used without waiting to unload the camera. The f/1.9 lens could focus down to 3½ feet, but a further button released the lens for use down to eighteen inches for closeups with an accessory range/viewfinder. Models were offered at $235 with f/3.5 lens and at $300 with f/1.9. Approximately 2,000 were made, suggests K. Lahue and J. Bailey, the authors of *Glass, Brass and Chrome*, p. 216, before the dies were put into storage for the war. At war's end, an analysis of costs showed that the camera would have to be reintroduced at a price of $700, nearly double the cost of the postwar Leica making a market reentry at the time. The Ektra was never made again. A limited-edition collectible for the 35-mm fan had been born. An Ektra today brings over $200 in the collector market with some Ektra accessory lenses (as the rare 153-mm Ektar lens) bringing even double that price.

* After World War II, the new models were the Perfex Deluxe, the One-0-One, One-0-Two, and finally the Cee-Ay 35. The Cee-Ay 35 ultimately became the Ciro 35 of 1949 when the dies were sold to a new company entering with the Ciro line of cameras.

9
Cinematography

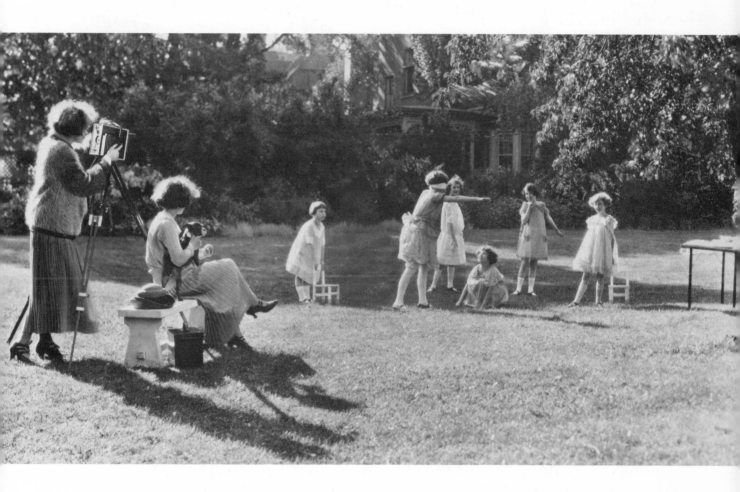

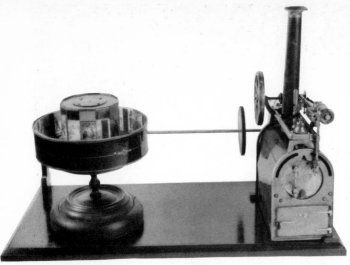

Steam-driven Praxinoscope, ca. 1885, combined two children's toys for parlor motion illusion. *(From the collection of George Skelly)*

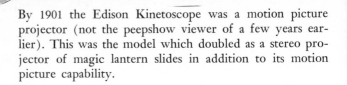

By 1901 the Edison Kinetoscope was a motion picture projector (not the peepshow viewer of a few years earlier). This was the model which doubled as a stereo projector of magic lantern slides in addition to its motion picture capability.

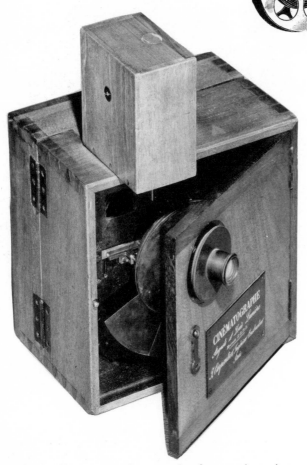

Lumiere's Cinematographe was the first motion picture projector to entertain audiences; Paris, December 1895. *(Photograph courtesy of Eastman Kodak Company)*

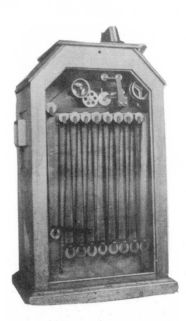

In 1894 the Edison Kinetoscope (peepshow) provided viewing devices for the kinetoscope parlor. Rows of machines entertained individual viewers. *(From the collection of Ernie Siegel)*

148

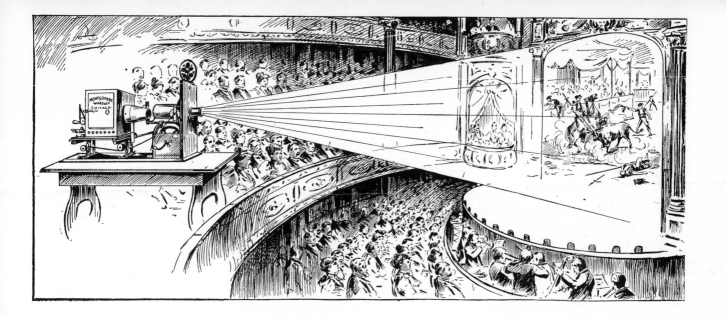

T. H. McALLISTER, OPTICIAN, 49 NASSAU STREET, N. Y.

ZOETROPE.

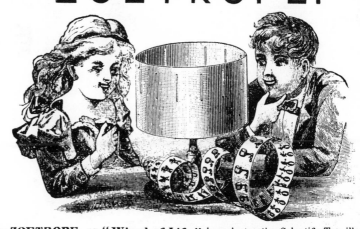

Novelty devices like the zoetrope provided pre-motion picture animation in the home, starting from the 1830s.

The **ZOETROPE, or "Wheel of Life,"** is an instructive Scientific Toy, illustrating in an attractive manner the persistence of an image on the retina of the eye; it consists of a card-board cylinder, about 12 inches diameter, and 8 inches deep, with 13 equidistant narrow openings, each about 3 inches long, arranged near the top as shown in the engraving. The lower end rests on an iron shaft, rising from a substantial wood base; on strips of paper, about 3½ inches wide, 36 inches long, are printed figures of men, animals, etc., in different positions, which are placed in the cylinder. By revolving the cylinder by the hand, and looking through the openings, the images passing rapidly before the eye are blended, so as to give the figures the motions of life in the most natural manner. As many persons as can stand around the Zoetrope can see the movements at the same time.

PRICE OF THE ZOETROPE, $2.50.

Including following series of 12 amusing pictures: Base-ball Player, Chewing Gum, Dolphin Swimming, Donnybrook Fair, Gymnast, Hash Machine, Jig Dancer, Johnny Jumper, Keep the Ball Rolling, Kick her up, Old Dog Tray, Raining Pitchforks.

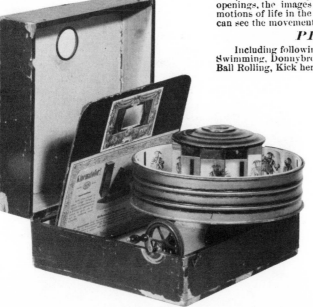

The Praxinoscope, ca. 1887, in hand-turned toy version was known in Germany as the Kinematofor. It depended on persistence of vision to create the motion illusion of specially created drawings. (*From the collection of Alan and Paulette Cotter*)

149

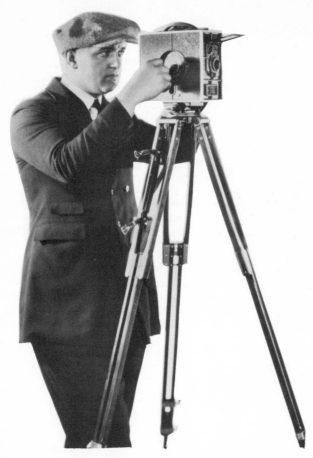

The Cine-Kodak Model A of 1923: first of the many Kodak movie cameras. It is the most sought after cine collectible. *(Photograph courtesy of Eastman Kodak Company)*

The Kodascope model C 16-mm motion picture projector for the 16-mm home movies of the 1920s and 1930s. Most collectors today eschew interest in projecting machines. *(Photograph courtesy of Eastman Kodak Company)*

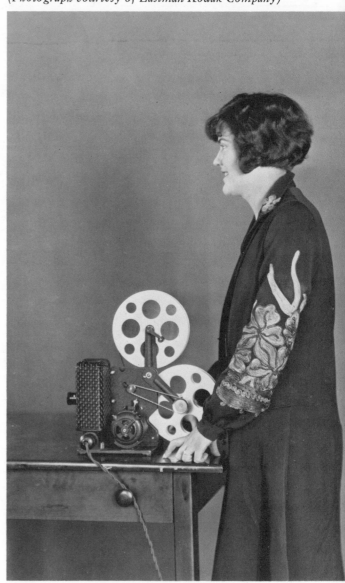

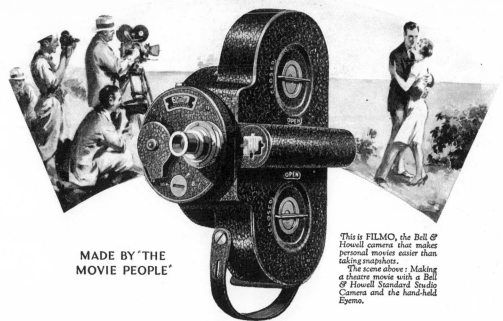

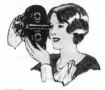

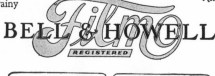

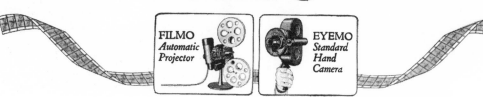

A 1927 advertisement for the Bell & Howell Filmo in the family size for 16-mm film. Professionals used a similar-looking camera in 35-mm size for newsreel photography.

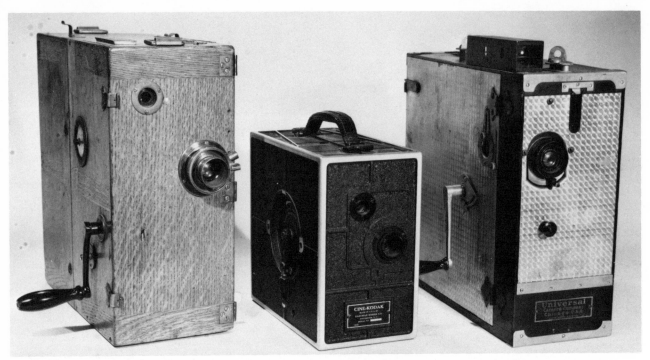

The Cine-Kodak Model, ca. 1923 *(center)*, loaded with 16-mm film and was crank wound like the 35-mm professional cameras of the earlier days. All-wood body *(left)* was typical of earliest professional cameras, pre-World War I. Universal *(right)* represents later generation of the pre-electric professional cameras. *(From the collection of Louis S. Marcus)*

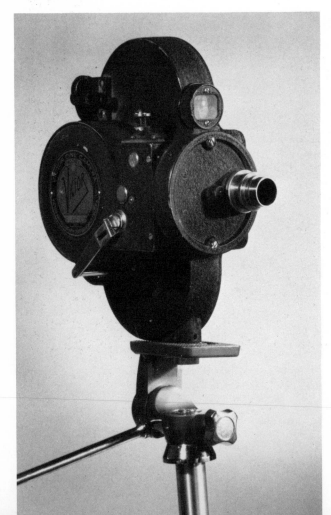

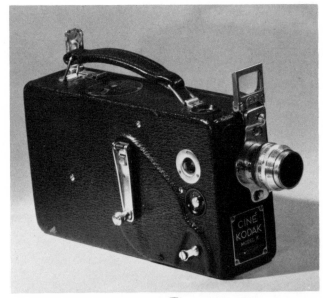

Cine-Kodak Model K was the traveler's compact 16-mm camera by the 1930s. *(From the collection of the author)*

Victor Model 3, ca. 1930, was a hand-held family 16-mm camera. *(From the collection of the author)*

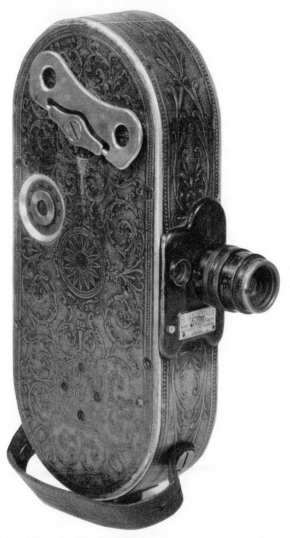

Bell & Howell Filmo Model 75, ca. 1928, was an early compact 16-mm family camera with a simulated-tooled-leather finish. *(From the collection of Matthew R. Isenberg)*

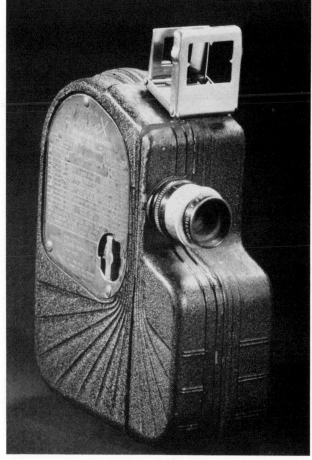

The most amazing movie camera of the 1930s, the Univex Cine–8, which sold for $9.95. *(From the collection of the author)*

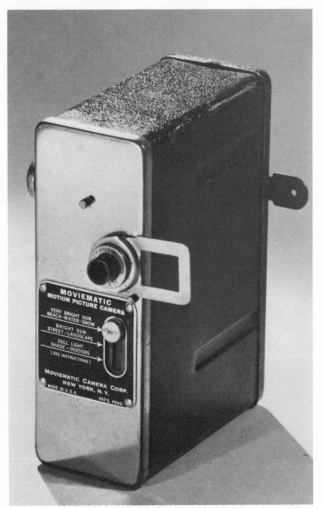

Low-cost "tin-can" Moviematic 16-mm motion picture camera of the 1930s could also take still pictures. It was found in a junk-tique shop for $2. *(From the collection of the author)*

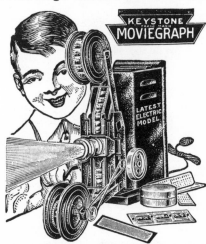
Keystone Motion Picture Projectors with Magic Lantern capability were a Christmas gift introduction to movies for thousands of American youngsters, ca. 1929, at $5.75 with film. *(From* Photographic Advertising from A-Z)

10
In the Darkroom

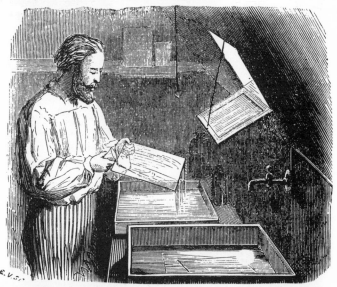

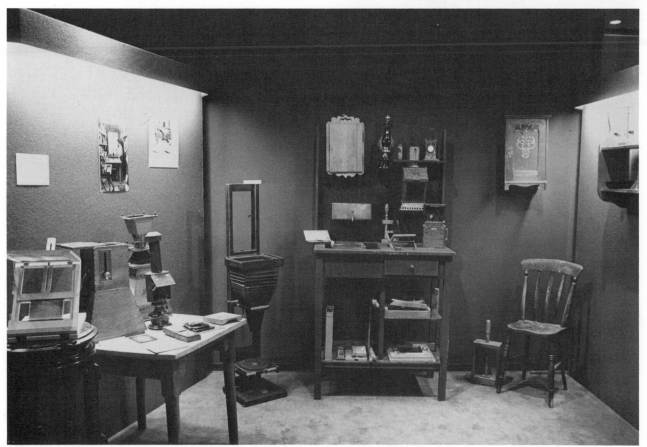

Agfa Historama in Leverkusen, Germany, displays reconstructed darkroom of the mid-1880s. (*Photograph courtesy Agfa*)

SERIES "B" DEVELOPING, FINISHING AND MATERIAL OUTFITS FOR EITHER PLATE CAMERAS OR FILM CAMERAS.

$2.10 TO $4.75 ACCORDING TO SIZE.

OUR SERIES "B" Developing, Finishing and Material Outfits are the largest, the best and the most complete outfits ever offered. They are suitable for use with every 4x5, 5x7, 6½x8½ and 8x10 camera which we sell and we strongly advise everyone who buys a 4x5 or larger camera to order one of these outfits and thus secure this big assortment of necessary supplies and apparatus for less than one-half the money these same goods would cost if purchased separately from the regular dealers in photographic supplies. Every item contained in our big Series "B" Outfits is extra high grade, the best the market affords, suitable for use with our very best cameras. Not an unnecessary item is included. You will need everything contained in these outfits when you commence making pictures. Arranged for plate cameras; each outfit contains the following items.

1 High Grade Metal Ruby Lamp with Oil Burner.
25 Card Mounts.
1 Compressed Fiber Tray for developing.
1 Compressed Fiber Tray for fixing.
1 Compressed Fiber Tray for toning.
1 Folding Negative Rack to hold 24 plates.

1 8-Ounce Cone Shaped Graduate.
1 Heavy Printing Frame.
1 Paste Brush.
1 Fine Gossamer Focus Cloth.
1 Dozen Extra Rapid Roebuck Dry Plates.
1 Package Toning and Fixing Powders (makes 24 ounces of toner).

1 Package Hydro-Metol Developing Powders (makes 24 ounces developer).
1 Pound Hyposulphite of Soda.
1 Print Roller.
1 Dozen Sheets DuVoll's Sensitized Paper.
1 Jar Photo Paste.
1 Copy of "Complete Instructions in Photography."

Outfits for Plate Cameras.

No. 20K630 Series "B" Outfit for 4x5 plate camera. Price................$2.25
No. 20K631 Series "B" Outfit for 5x7 plate camera. Price................ 3.10
No. 20K632 Series "B" Outfit for 6½x8½ plate camera. Price............. 3.65
No. 20K633 Series "B" Outfit for 8x10 plate camera. Price................ 4.75
There is no Camera included with these Outfits.

Outfits for Film Cameras.

We also put up these Series "B" Outfits arranged for film cameras, the list of items being the same as included in the outfits for plate cameras, except that we put in one roll of film (12 exposures) in place of the dry plates, a box of push pins in place of the negative rack; the focus cloth is omitted and the printing frame is provided with a glass.

No. 20K639 Series "B" Outfit for 3½x3½ film camera. Price. $2.10
No. 20K640 Series "B" Outfit for 3¼x4¼ film camera. Price. 2.20
No. 20K641 Series "B" Outfit for 4x5 film camera. Price..... 2.35
There is no Camera included with these Outfits.

With both the 3½x3½ and 3¼x4¼ outfits for film cameras we furnish 4x5 trays and printing frame, as this size is more convenient to work with.

Darkroom tools are sought by collectors as mementoes of earliest processing procedures. Sears, Roebuck & Company catalogue of 1908 shows typical safelight, printing frame, trays, and chemicals.

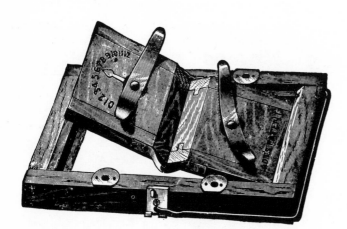

Printing frame has remained in its basic design for nearly one hundred years.

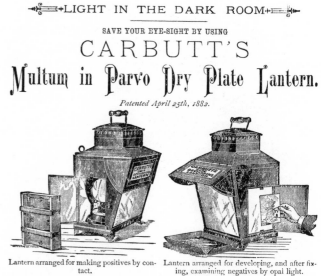

LIGHT IN THE DARK ROOM

SAVE YOUR EYE-SIGHT BY USING

CARBUTT'S
Multum in Parvo Dry Plate Lantern.

Patented April 25th, 1882.

Lantern arranged for making positives by contact.

Lantern arranged for developing, and after fixing, examining negatives by opal light.

Kerosene and candlelight were pre-electric darkroom light sources.

156

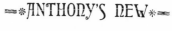

ENLARGING CAMERA.

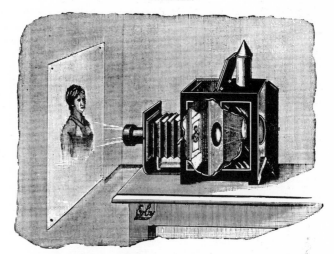

Metal Dallon plate developing tank was popular in the 1920s.

The great merit of this new enlarging camera is its simplicity of construction, economy, and practical usefulness.

It is intended for making enlargements on gelatino-bromide rapid printing paper by artificial light, requiring only from *thirty to sixty seconds'* exposure for a life-size head.

Another purpose for which it admirably serves is that of a dark room lantern. Some of them are provided with non-actinic glass panels in the sides of the camera. It can also be used as a copying camera for making lantern transparencies.

Grooves in the interior admit of changing the relative positions of the negative and condensing lens. It is very compact, the size being 18 x 15 x 8 inches.

PRICES :

Enlarging Camera, Complete (except Lens,) . . $20 00
Including one quarter-size E. A. portrait lens, 28 75

E. & H. T. ANTHONY and CO., MANUFACTURERS.

591 Broadway, NEW YORK.

The Anthony Enlarging Camera was used as a horizontal projecting device, a popular system until the 1930s.

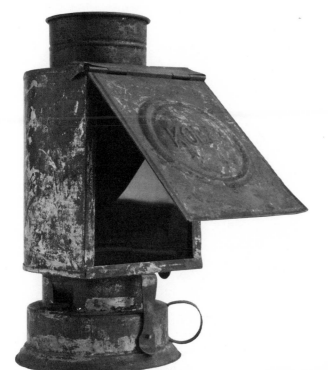

Kodak safelight of the late 1800s.

A roll-film processing system used roll-up systems for film rolls.

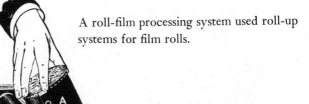

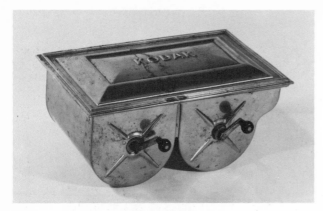

Two-part stainless steel developing tank.

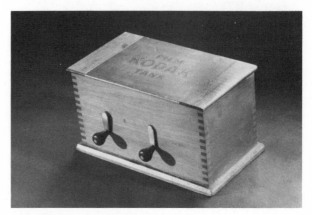

Polished wood box from Kodak darkroom system available up to the 1920s.

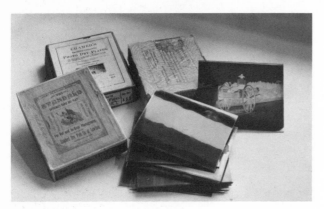

Early glass plates were most often stored in original light-tight plate boxes.

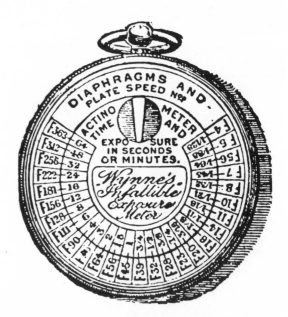

Wynne's Infallible Exposure Meter was an early system for light measurement using sensitized paper which darkened in bright sunlight.

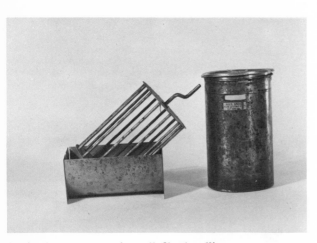

Squirrel-cage system for roll-film handling.

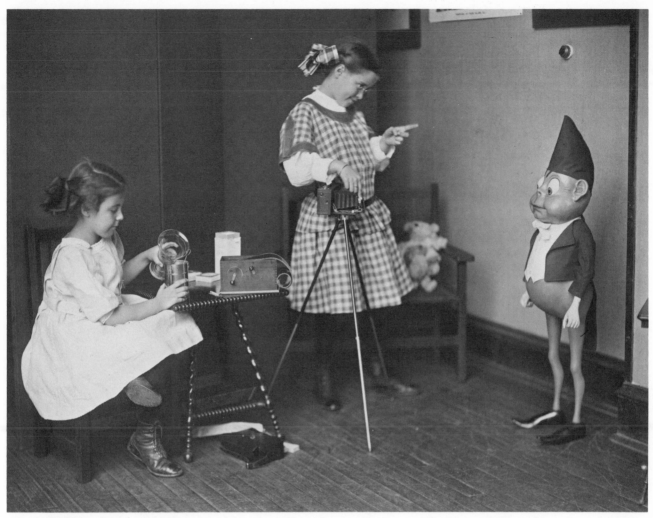

Photography and home processing, suggests this Kodak photograph, were simple enough for young children. *(Photograph courtesy of Eastman Kodak Company)*

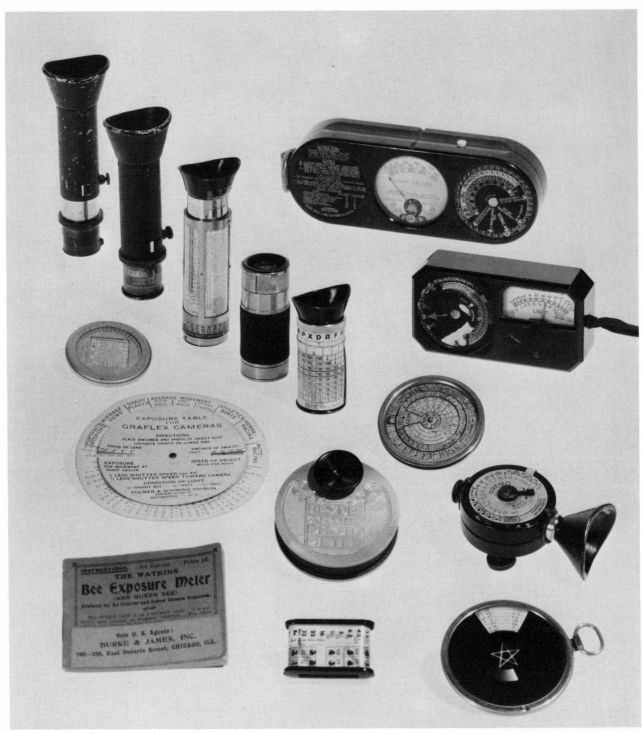

A variety of systems to measure light and to guide proper exposure range from extinction devices (dark tubes) through charts, tables, and finally in the early 1930s the photo-electric eye activated by light-sensitive selenium. *(From the collection of Nat Kameny)*

11
Magic Lanterns, Albums, and Viewers

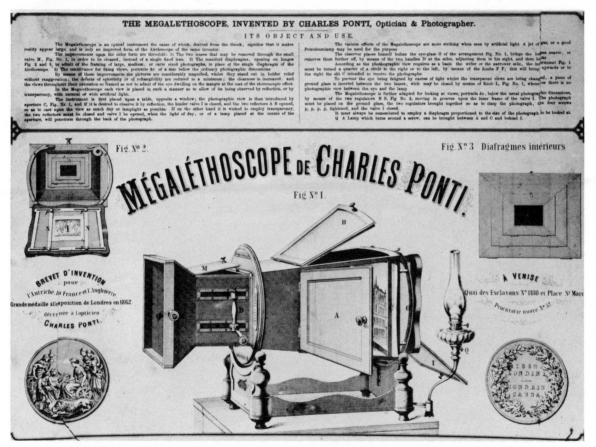

A parlor device for the wealthier families of the world, presenting optically magnified views of drawings.

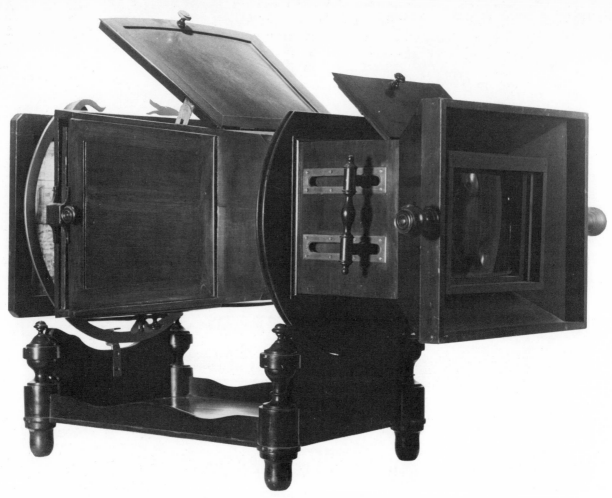

A fine example of a megalethoscope with a mahogany finish. Ornate versions with costly inlays have sold at auction for over $1,500. *(From the collection of Bruce C. Vaughn)*

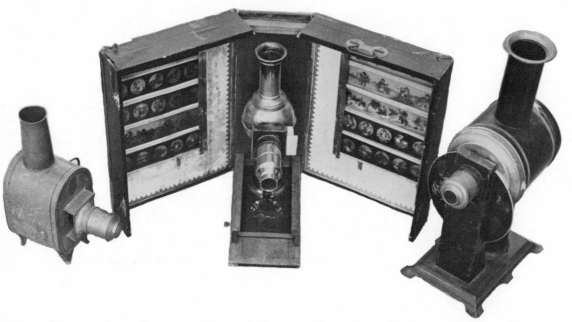

Three versions of representative magic lanterns. *(From the collection of Marvin and Katrinka Kreisman)*

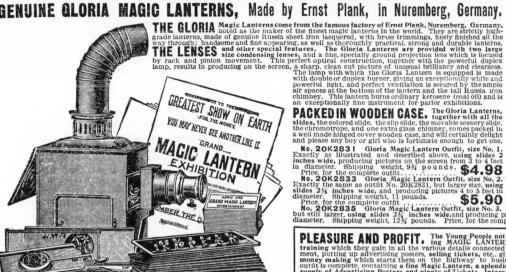

THE GLORIA MAGIC LANTERN OUTFITS $4⁹⁸ $6⁸⁵

GENUINE GLORIA MAGIC LANTERNS, Made by Ernst Plank, in Nuremberg, Germany.

THE GLORIA Magic Lanterns come from the famous factory of Ernst Plank, Nuremberg, Germany, noted as the maker of the finest magic lanterns in the world. They are strictly high-grade lanterns, made of genuine Russia sheet iron lacquered, with brass trimmings, finely finished all the way through; handsome and fine appearing, as well as thoroughly practical, strong and durable lanterns.

THE LENSES and other special features. The Gloria Lanterns are provided with two large size condensing lenses, and a fine, specially ground projection lens which is focused by rack and pinion movement. This perfect optical construction, together with the powerful duplex lamp, results in producing on the screen, a sharp, clean cut picture of unusual brilliancy and clearness. The lamp with which the Gloria Lantern is equipped is made with double or duplex burner, giving an exceptionally white and powerful light, and perfect ventilation is secured by the ample air spaces at the bottom of the lantern and the tall Russia iron chimney. This lantern burns ordinary kerosene (coal oil) and is an exceptionally fine instrument for parlor exhibitions.

PACKED IN WOODEN CASE. The Gloria Lanterns, together with all the slides, the colored slide, the slip slide, the movable scenery slide, the chromotrope, and one extra glass chimney, comes packed in a well made hinged cover wooden case, and will certainly delight and please any boy or girl who is fortunate enough to get one.

No. 20K2831 Gloria Magic Lantern Outfit, size No. 1. Exactly as illustrated and described above, using slides 2 inches wide, producing pictures on the screen from 3 to 4 feet in diameter. Shipping weight, 9¾ pounds. **$4.98** Price, for the complete outfit.

No. 20K2833 Gloria Magic Lantern Outfit, size No. 2. Exactly the same as outfit No. 20K2831, but larger size, using slides 2¼ inches wide, and producing pictures 4 to 5 feet in diameter. Shipping weight, 11 pounds. **$5.90** Price, for the complete outfit.

No. 20K2835 Gloria Magic Lantern Outfit, size No. 3. Exactly the same as outfit No. 20K2831, but still larger, using slides 2½ inches wide, and producing pictures from 5 to 6 feet in diameter. Shipping weight, 12¾ pounds. Price, for the complete outfit **$6.85**

> **EACH GLORIA MAGIC LANTERN OUTFIT CONTAINS OUR GLORIA MAGIC LANTERN,**
> **TWELVE COLORED SLIDES** with four pictures on each slide, making 48 different pictures.
> **ONE COMIC SLIP SLIDE** producing most amusing effects.
> **ONE MOVABLE SCENERY SLIDE** always an interesting feature to the youngsters.
> **ONE BRILLIANT CHROMOTROPE** or artificial fire works slide.
> **FIFTY ADVERTISING POSTERS** large size, sure to bring out a big audience.
> **FIFTY ADMISSION TICKETS** regular full size tickets.

PLEASURE AND PROFIT. The Young People not only derive great pleasure from giving MAGIC LANTERN EXHIBITIONS, but the business training which they gain in all the various details connected with the management of an entertainment, putting up advertising posters, selling tickets, etc., gives them ideas of the rudiments of money making which starts them on the highway to business success. REMEMBER that each outfit is complete, containing a fine Magic Lantern, a splendid assortment of Colored Views, a large supply of Advertising Posters and plenty of Tickets. Interesting, instructive and profitable. You will easily make the original cost of the outfit in your first exhibition; after that it's all profit.

THE HOME MAGIC LANTERN OUTFITS.

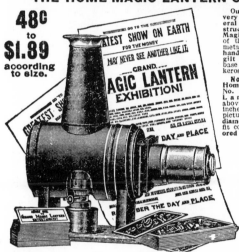

48c to $1.89 according to size.

Our illustration gives a very exact idea of the general appearance and construction of the Home Magic Lantern. The body of this lantern is made of metal, japanned in black, handsomely decorated in gilt and mounted on wood base board. Burns ordinary kerosene or coal oil.

No. 20K2805 The Home Magic Lantern Outfit No. 1, with Home Magic Lantern as described above, using slides 3-16 inches wide, and magnifying pictures to about 1 foot in diameter. The complete outfit contains lantern, six colored slides, three to four pictures on each slide, twenty-five advertising posters and twenty-five admission tickets. Price, complete. **48c** If by mail, postage extra, 24 cents.

No. 20K2808 Home Magic Lantern Outfit No. 2, same as No. 20K2805, but using slides 1 9-16 inches wide, magnifying pictures to 2 feet and including twelve colored slides instead of six. Price, complete (If by mail, postage extra, 52c.) **$1.25**

No. 20K2811 Home Magic Lantern Outfit No. 3, same as No. 20K2805, but using slides 2 inches wide, magnifying pictures to about 3 feet in diameter. Price, complete **$1.89**

Shipping weight, 4½ pounds.

THE BRILLIANT MAGIC LANTERN OUTFITS.

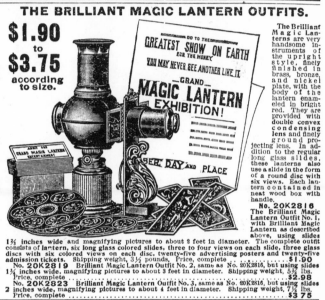

$1.90 to $3.75 according to size.

The Brilliant Magic Lanterns are very handsome instruments of the upright style, finely finished in brass, bronze, and nickel plate, with the body of the lantern enameled in bright red. They are provided with double convex condensing lens and finely ground projecting lens. In addition to the regular long glass slides, these lanterns also use a slide in the form of a round disc with six views. Each lantern contained in neat wood box with handle.

No. 20K2816 The Brilliant Magic Lantern Outfit No. 1, with Brilliant Magic Lantern as described above. The complete outfit consists of lantern, six long glass colored slides, three to four views on each slide, three glass discs with six colored views on each disc, twenty-five advertising posters and twenty-five admission tickets. Shipping weight, 3½ pounds. Price, complete **$1.90**

No. 20K2819 Brilliant Magic Lantern Outfit No. 2, same as No. 20K2816, but using slides 1¾ inches wide, magnifying pictures to about 3 feet in diameter. Shipping weight, 5½ lbs. Price, complete **$2.98**

No. 20K2823 Brilliant Magic Lantern Outfit No. 3, same as No. 20K2816, but using slides 2 inches wide, magnifying pictures to about 4 feet in diameter. Shipping weight, 7½ lbs. Price, complete **$3.75**

Magic lantern outfits sold for as little as 48¢ in 1908. (*From the* Catalogue of Sears, Roebuck & Company—1908)

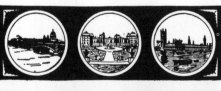
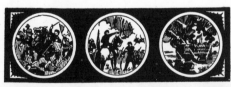
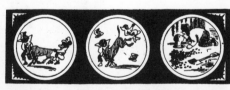

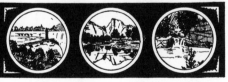
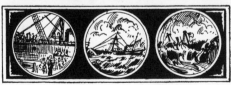
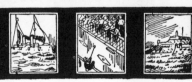

Typical slides for magic lanterns are glass-bound views.

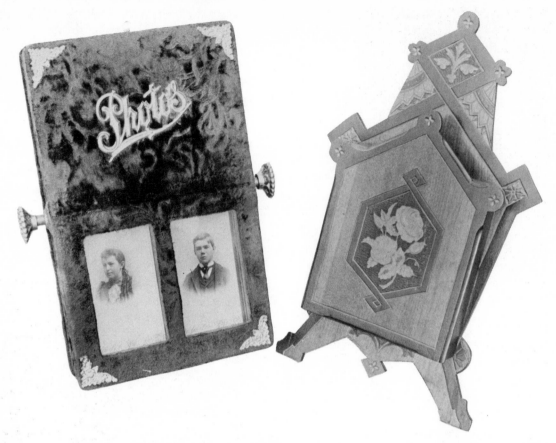

Left: an unusual photo album with a system of changing photographs set in a velvet standing album. *Right:* wood easel-album with ornate carving had drop front to reveal cabinet photographs. *(From the collection of Marvin and Katrinka Kreisman)*

Most common Victorian album with plush velvet cover and unidentified portraits generally sells for $10 and up. *(Photograph courtesy of Eastman Kodak Company)*

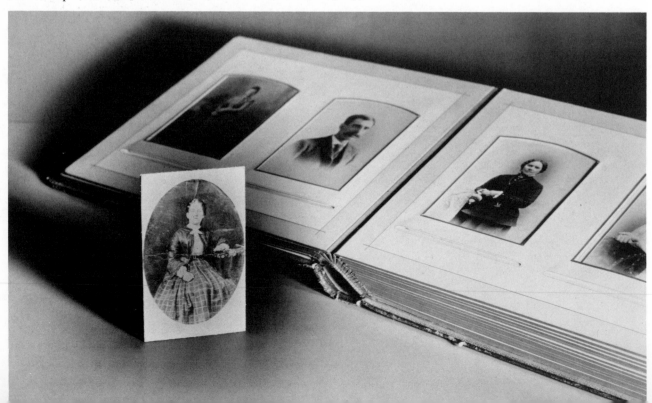

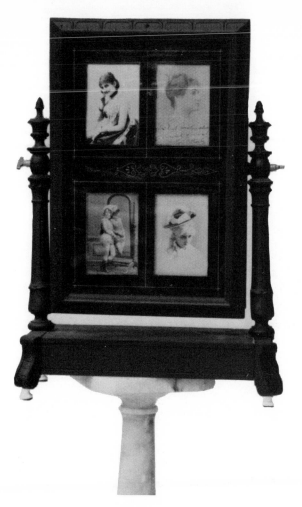

Victorian frame on a pedestal displays four cabinet photos.

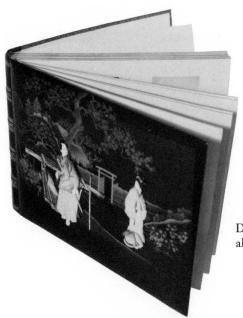

Folding viewer for cartes de visite provide magnified image of card set in sliding holder. *(From the collection of the author)*

Dimensional figurines in ivory adorn ornate Victorian album. *(From the collection of Jerry and Shirley Sprung)*

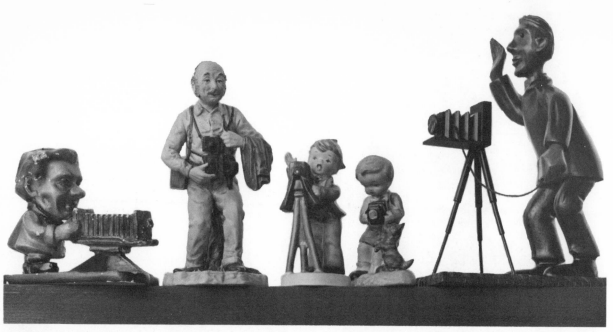

Novelty figurines of the photographer have been created by artisans of Germany, Japan, Italy, and other ceramics centers. *(From the collection of Marvin and Katrinka Kreisman)*

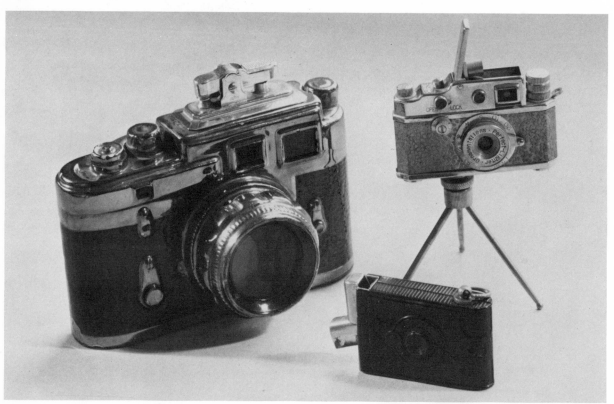

Cigarette lighters in actual camera shapes are among novelties sought by collectors of photographica. *(From the collection of the author)*

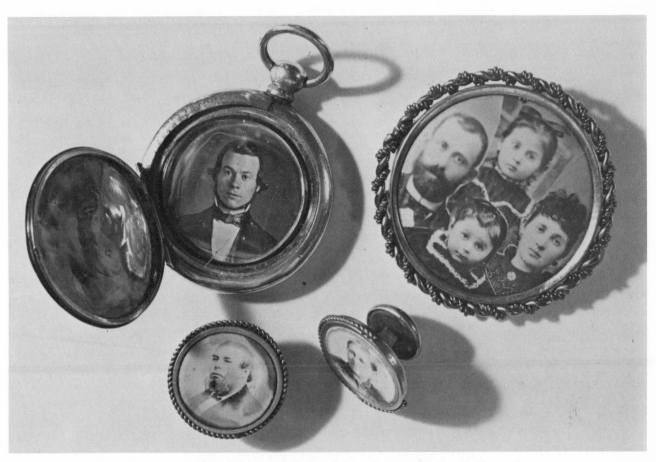

Daguerrean and later images are often hidden or displayed in such Victorian jewelry as lockets, cuff links, and photo buttons. *(Photograph courtesy of* Graphic Antiquarian *and Carole G. Honigsfeld)*

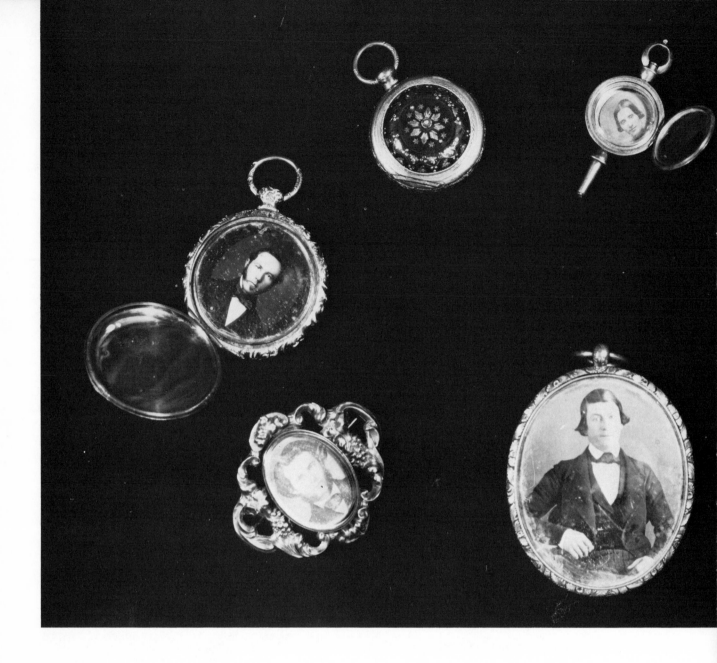

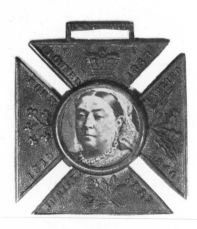

Albumen print is set into a memorial medallion honoring
Queen Victoria. *(From the collection of the author)*

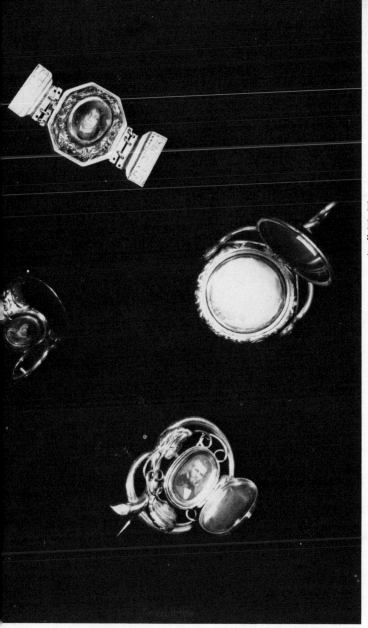

Daguerrean and later images are often hidden or displayed in such Victorian jewelry as lockets, cuff links, and photo buttons. *(Photograph courtesy of* Graphic Antiquarian *and Carole G. Honigsfeld)*

Photo Garter Buckles

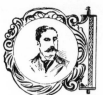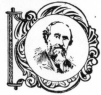

K 1716 The very latest novelty in photo jewelry. It is now quite a fad for the ladies to wear the picture of the favored one on her garter. Buckles are of best rolled gold, handsome in appearance and wear well.

Price, per pair, with two pictures uncolored. **$1.50**
Price, per pair, with two pictures beautifully painted............ .... 2.20

Photo Watch Charms

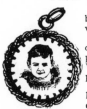

Beautiful in design, of very best rolled gold; look well and wear well.
K 1708 With same head on both sides of charm, each, pictures uncolored.....**$1.50**
With pictures hand painted 2.00
K 1710 With different heads on separate sides of charm, each, with pictures uncolored **$1.75**
With pictures hand painted.............. .. 2.25

Photo Belt Buckles

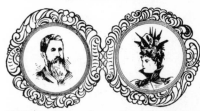

K 1714 Of very best rolled gold, handsome in design, durable and of Roman gold finish; wear well.
Price, each, with two pictures uncolored . .**$3.45**
Price, each, with two pictures beautifully hand painted......................... 4.15

Montgomery Ward catalogue of 1900 offers such novelties as garter buckles with photographs, photo belt buckles, and photo watch charms.

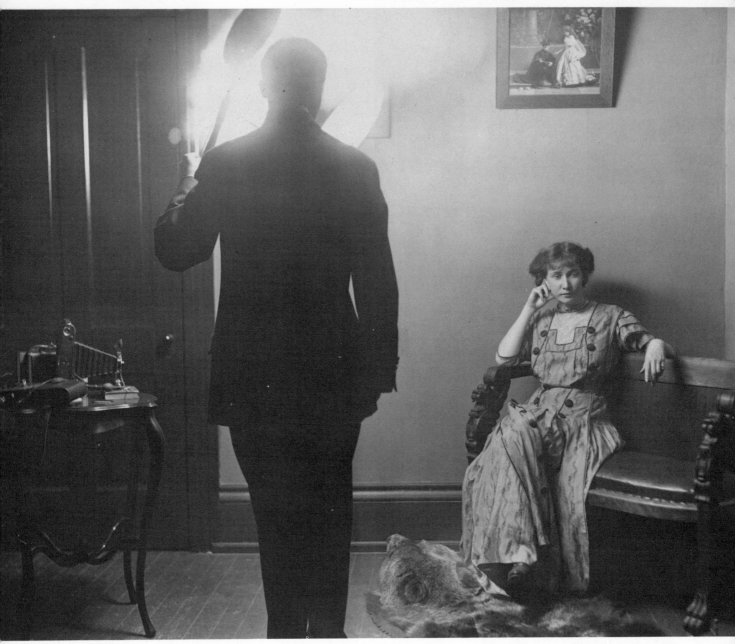

Magnesium flash for photography in the home, ca. 1910. (Photograph courtesy of Eastman Kodak Company)

12
Photographic Accessories and Other Photographica

NONCAMERA PHOTOGRAPHIC NOVELTIES

A number of novelty cameras that attract the attention of photographers and the collectors of photographica are cameras that are not cameras. They are boxes sold in novelty shops for under one dollar today and for 10¢–25¢ in the 1930s which conceal a jump-out snake or which squirt water into the face of the posing subject. "Squirt" cameras date back to the 1890s and are even tripod mounted. Most often they are cameralike cigarette lighters, sold at tobacco counters or in gift shops if they are table models. The collector of photo novelties also seeks the hidden images, the unique microminiatures of the Stanhope: tiny photo views hidden within rings, watch fobs, bracelet charms, such desk aids as a letter opener or an ink pen, but also in such tourist souvenirs as a sewing kit, a tape measure, and other small items for the home.

The Stanhope

The Stanhope is named after Lord Stanhope, an English scientist (1753–1816) who conceived the tiny glass-rod lens on which a film positive barely ⅛ inch across could be cemented. After a hole has been drilled through a ring or a letter opener (or even in the base of the bowl of a man's pipe and the cover of a cigarette holder, both of which are in the author's collection), it is possible to insert the glass rod with its image. The tiny image is quite easy to see in a magnified view through the aperture

in the ring or other carrier of the hidden lens. Images range from the Eiffel Tower of Paris to the Tomb of David in Jerusalem. Watch-fob charms concealed "fancy" photos: bathing beauties.

Collectors find Stanhopes by checking jewelry trays at antique shops and in the flea markets for the telltale ⅛-inch-wide aperture on both sides of jewelry items. Silver or gold charms in the shapes of tiny telescopes and folding cameras almost invariably conceal a Stanhope. Ivory items and especially desk ornaments are often found with the tiny hidden image. Held close to the eye, the astonishing magnification of the lens makes it possible to read captions under as many as eight separate photographs reduced to microscopic dimensions in the image area as small as the letter *o* in this w-o-r-d.

Numismatics and Philately

Two of the most active collector hobbies in the United States have long been philately (stamp collecting) and numismatics (coin collecting). A number of photographers and collectors of photographica have been able to cross their two collections with a variety of nineteenth- and twentieth-century examples of stamps and coins that add new dimensions to a photographic display.

A leading American collector of photographic numismatics, Nick Graver of Rochester, New York, for example, held an audience entranced with slide after slide during a one-hour presentation at a photo-history seminar in New York in the fall of 1972. Why? How? Collectors of images and equip-

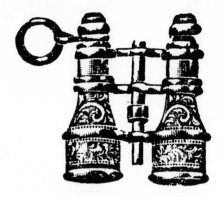

The Stanhope, an optical invention by the English scientist Lord Stanhope. He made possible a simple lens for magnification of tiny images that could be hidden in watch charms, rings, and desk accessories.

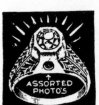
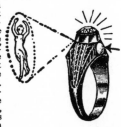
ment were shocked to learn how the economic history of America is reflected back to the 1830s (prephotography) when a company, Scovill and Feuchtwanger (later to market the tools and materials of the Daguerrean photographer), issued its own "hard-times tokens," an actual medium of exchange of the time, used exactly like money. Scovill later was to become the *sco* of *Ansco*; these hard-times tokens are among the earliest example of American photographic numismatics.

Stamp collectors have modern reflections of the growth of photography in the U.S. three-cent stamp issued in 1954 to honor the centenary of George Eastman's birth. At the same time, a number of "first-day covers" (envelopes honoring Eastman bearing the Eastman stamp and cancelled on the first day of issue) were made available to the philatelist. Stamp collectors can also display such items as photo equipment on East German stamps created for the Leipzig Trade Fair of 1972.

During the nineteenth century and early in the twentieth century, a number of camera clubs honored winners in club photo competitions with silver, and at times gold (or base metal), medals for "Best Photo." But in industrial competitions, medals were awarded for "Best Camera." Employees of the Eastman Kodak Company have been awarded medals on the occasion of twenty-five years of service. Many famous early photographic pioneers are permanently honored by sculptured likenesses on a variety of medals issued on anniversaries of various photo companies, societies, etc. The collector of

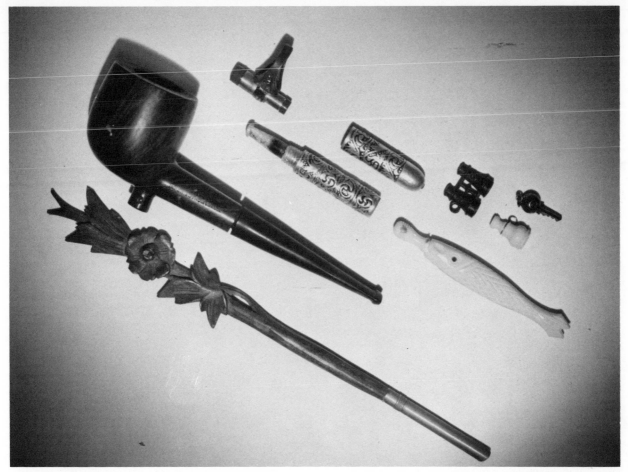

Stanhope collection of the author includes rings, cigarette holder, pipe, letter opener, and bracelet charms.

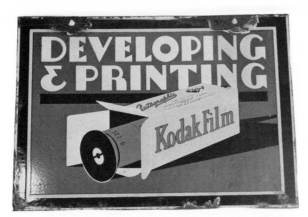

Art Deco lettering suggests that this store sign dates back to the 1920s. (*From the collection of Allen and Hilary Weiner*)

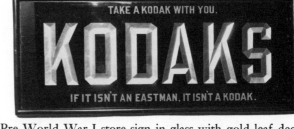

Pre-World War I store sign in glass with gold-leaf decor of incised letters. (*From the collection of Matthew R. Isenberg*)

Rare 2-foot long all-metal advertising sign for the Premo camera. (*From the collection of Eaton S. Lothrop, Jr.*)

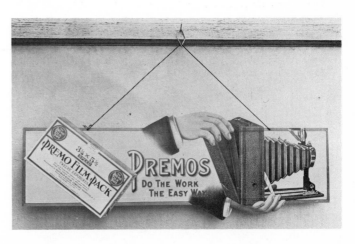

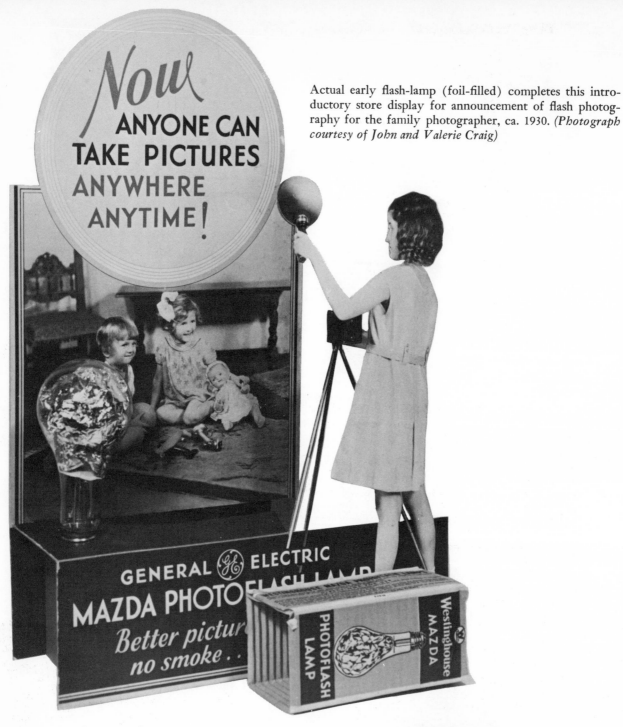

Actual early flash-lamp (foil-filled) completes this introductory store display for announcement of flash photography for the family photographer, ca. 1930. *(Photograph courtesy of John and Valerie Craig)*

Cases for pre-flashbulb flash cartridges are a memento of early twentieth century professional and home photography flash lighting systems.

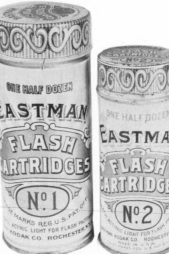
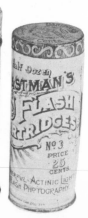

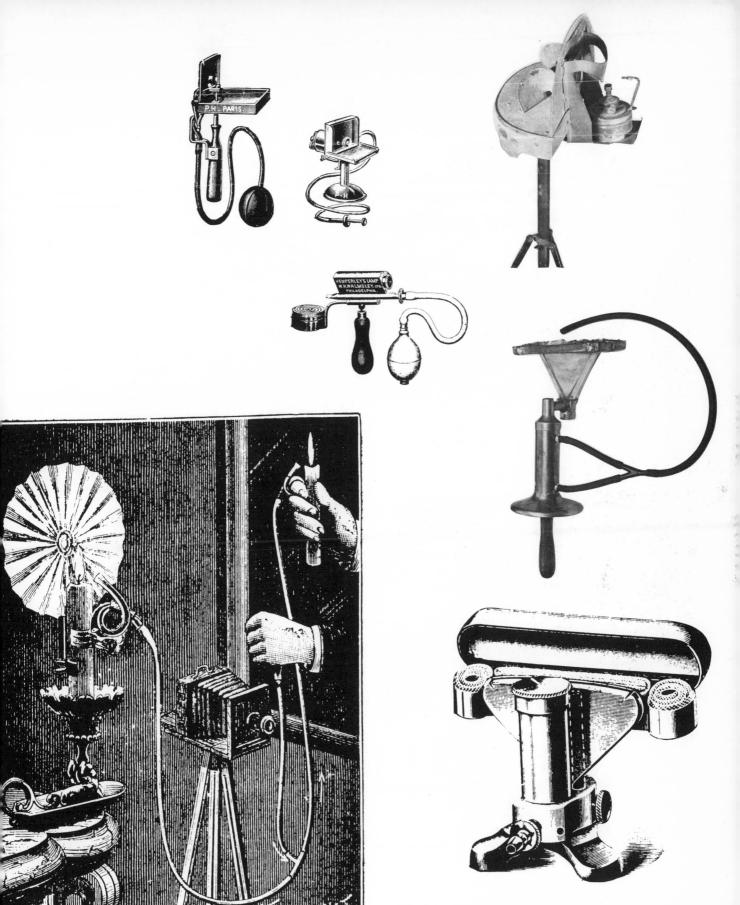

Two simultaneous flashes were produced by an air puff of magnesium powder to two candles. The process is suggested in the French illustration, ca. 1895.

Early flash photography equipment often blew magnesium powder into a flame to produce flash.

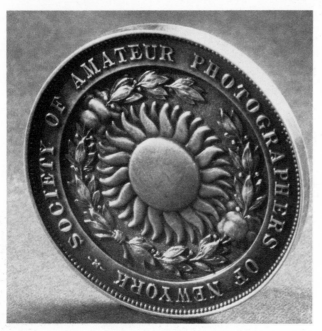

An 1895 award medal from Society of Amateur Photographers of New York. (*From the collection of the author*)

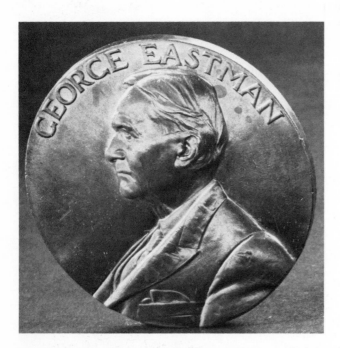

George Eastman Medal is awarded to Kodak employees after twenty-five years of service. (*From the collection of the author*)

photographica can find these medals in flea markets; but probably more easily in the coin and stamp shops across America.

Finally, political tokens issued during presidential campaigns often had tintypes incorporated within the political memento. Collectors of images may find special interest in these tiny likenesses found among the political buttons at flea markets and in antique shops.

The backs of cabinet photos often had floral designs, and some of these incorporated handsome illustrations of medals issued in connection with the studio's success in competitions among professionals. Whether it's the illustration on the card or the medal itself that attracts him or her, the photographica numismatist has a broad range of material to seek in numerous collector circles.

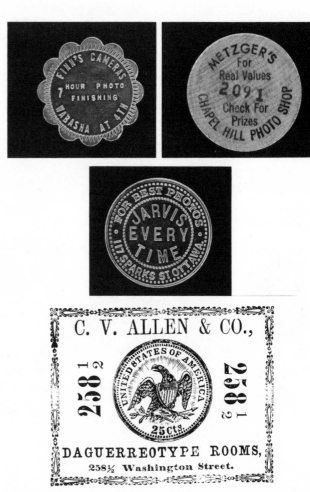

Metal and wooden tokens of the photographic retailers. (*From the collection of N. M. Graver*)

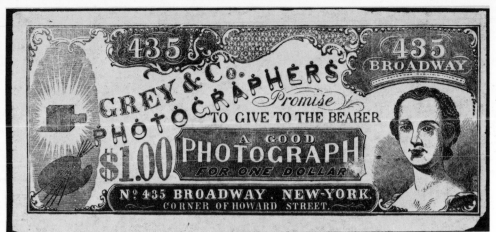

Moneylike paper token from Grey & Co. Value: $1. (*From the collection of N. M. Graver*)

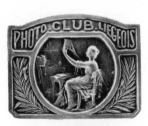

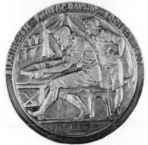

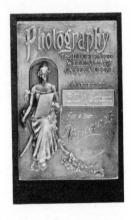

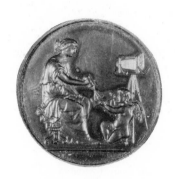

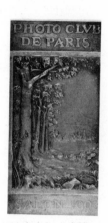

American and French photographic award medallions and plaques. (*From the collections of Jerry and Shirley Sprung; N. M. Graver*)

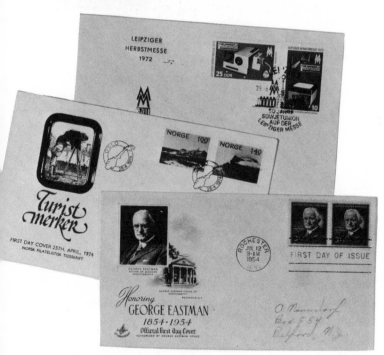

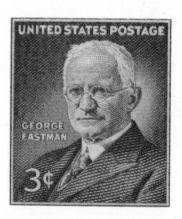

UNITED STATES POSTAGE

GEORGE EASTMAN

3¢

"First-Day Covers," letters mailed on the first day of issue of postage stamps, commemorate photographic events. (*From the collection of the author*)

3¢ George Eastman Stamp. This 1954 postage stamp issued at Rochester, New York, on July 12 honored the 100th anniversary of the birth of George Eastman, founder of Eastman Kodak Company and its predecessors. A total of 119 million were authorized. A portrait taken in England in June 1921 when Eastman was sixty-seven years old provided the original.

Professional lecturer's auditorium projectors had lenses of different focal length (magnification power) for extra on-screen effects, as titling.

. . . . . Show Any Picture— In Any Color—At Any Time

source of amusement. With it you can show a different set of pictures every night; in fact, with the RADIOPTICAN there is always something new to see and never anything to buy. In the long winter evenings snap-shots and other photos made during vacation and picture post cards showing places visited can be seen over again to bring back pleasant memories and impressions of a trip. You can arrange quite an evening's entertainment by getting together a series of pictures showing the sights of the larger cities, the Exposition, a trip to Washington, a trip through the Rockies, or to Florida, Historic Spots of the Civil War, etc. On other evenings, there can be trips to London or to Paris, a trip down the Rhine, or to Egypt, Bible Scenes, and so on. Short lectures can be given, and, if the occasion warrants it, an admission fee can be charged and is usually willingly given. Thus your RADIOPTICAN can be a source of profit as well as pleasure. If you are interested in animals or birds or electricity or postage stamps or any other subject, it is easy to find pictures that will form good illustrations for talks on the favorite topic you are interested in. For parties and entertainments, the RADIOPTICAN can be used to great advantage. Guessing contests can be arranged and prizes awarded to those giving the greatest number of correct answers. For instance pictures of well known authors, actors and actresses, public men and women, etc., are shown, and calling upon the audience to name them. Or advertising contests can be arranged. Part of an advertisement illustrating a well known article can be thrown upon the screen and the audience asked to state what it represents. It is impossible to tell you even one-tenth of the ways you can entertain yourself, your family and your friends with the RADIOPTICAN. Every bright boy or girl will be able to think of dozens of other ways in which pictures of any kind can be combined with explanations, descriptions, jokes, etc.

This RADIOPTICAN is exceptionally well made, the actual size being 11¼ inches long, 11 inches wide, 9¾ inches high; weight about 8 lbs. The illuminating in this model is double that of No. 6012 and it has the distinct advantage of a double sliding carrier for detachable backs, patent adjustable picture holders and minor refinements such as light-tight ventilators. It is fitted with a Double Plano-Convex Lens System of highest quality, that covers prints and photographs up to 6x5½ inches. The reflecting system comprises two extra large parabolic reflectors, heavily plated, converging the light rays on the subject with great intensity. There are two unique patented, adjustable picture holders mounted on metal plates which drop into a double sliding carrier, and which provide a picture changing system identical with the established standard of all high grade stereopticans. These picture holders are adjustable, so that all shapes and sizes of pictures, post cards, photographs, clippings, etc., up to 5½x6 inches in size, are instantly accommodated and held in perfect focus.

No. 6013. RADIOPTICAN. Price Postpaid............................**$15.00**

Radioptican was all-electric "magic lantern" to project snapshots and postcards onto screens in the early part of the twentieth century.

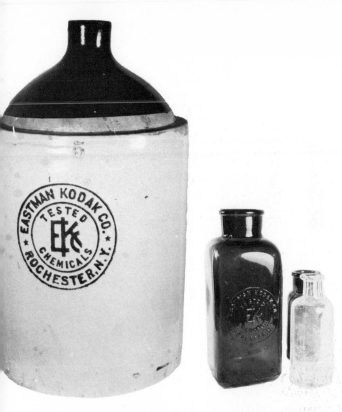

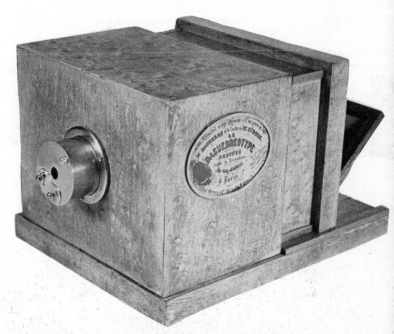

Bottle collectors have their own photographica corner with stoneware and glass examples bearing the EKC emblem (Eastman Kodak Company). *(From the collection of Dr. George Layne)*

One-third scale wood model with image-forming meniscus lens is replica of Giroux camera made for Daguerre, even to simulated seal and Daguerre signature. Model by Jerry Smith, Florissant, Mo. *(From the collection of the author)*

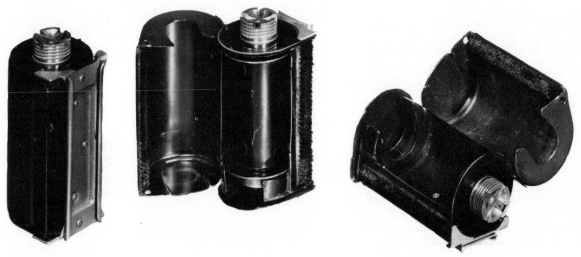

35-mm equipment collectors seek examples of early cassettes for short lengths of motion picture film loaded into the earliest 35-mm cameras. *(From the collection of Dr. R. H. Krauss)*

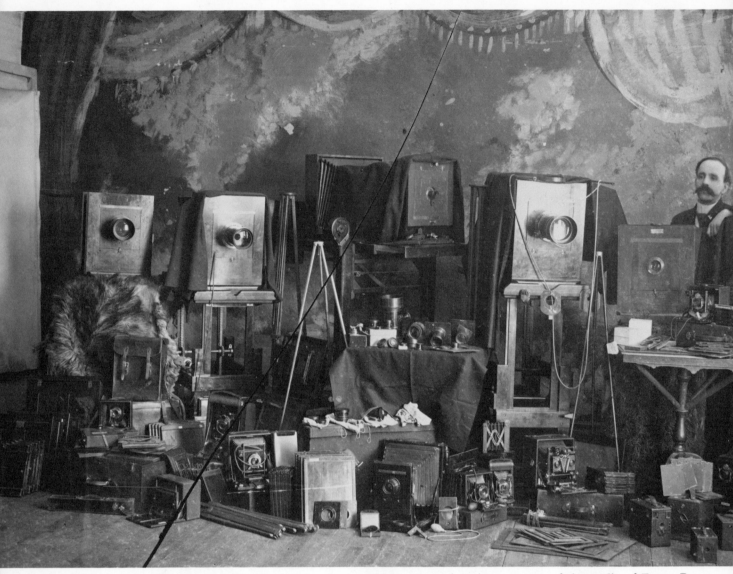

A treasure trove for the collector of early photographica: an actual equipment array of the studio of Ernest Brown, 1913. *(Photograph from the Provincial Museum and Archives of Canada)*

13
Collecting Photographica

Camera collecting, like charity, begins at home: in the attic, where not only retired cameras and framed photographs originally from grandma's home, but even more exotic apparatus or ephemera of photography may be hidden in an old barrel, trunk, or box.

Was grandfather an amateur photographer? Perhaps his view camera, tripod, and possibly even the trays and tanks of his darkroom are safely stored because no one knew what else to do with them. Was grandmother a collector of the family's heritage? There could well be the pre–Civil War Daguerreotypes and the ambrotypes of the family and its friends. Portraits of great-grandmother's older brother in his Civil War uniform and cartes de visite of his buddies from the regiment may be stored in albums or envelopes along with his military discharge.

If, like so many millions of others, the family owned an assortment of a few hundred stereo cards, there is also likely to be one or more of the hand-held Holmes-Bates viewers or the earlier Brewster viewers (see Chapter 5, "Stereo Cameras and Stereography"). In wealthier families, the stereo interest may have spurred the acquisition of a table viewer. Your search is for any hand-held or wooden-box device that apparently has been built around a pair of binocular eyepieces.

The box camera of your own youth and the slightly earlier folding cameras could be in the attics of other members of the family. It was from his mother's house that a friend found for me the Expo Watch Camera (see Chapter 4, "Detective Cameras and Later Novelty Cameras") for my collection.

The family photo album of the past will have a plethora of tintypes, cartes de visite, or cabinet photos. The album itself may be of the type that incorporates a music box or which entices interest with a delightfully enameled cover illustration on its Victorian velour book-thick cover with brass lock.

Envelopes in a trunk may hold glass plates or film negatives. Boxes may be hiding the family's first motion-picture projector and cans of the first black-and-white films. Vanity-table boxes may have a tangle of necklaces but also pieces of jewelry that conceal the Stanhope images.

Whether for images or equipment, the start of many collections will be found at home. The growth of the collection, then, may rely on one of many different sources of photographica available to the collector today.

THE NEIGHBORHOOD THRIFT SHOP

If someone has been attic–basement cleaning, he or she may have donated clothing, books, furniture —and photographic equipment—to the neighborhood Goodwill Industries, Salvation Army, or church-charity thrift shops. The display rooms and side-street shops where the highest price on anything is about $1 are an excellent starting point for searching the contents of everyone else's attics. Cameras in these sales centers are organized neatly on shelves.

Since cameras are priced here at 50¢ and slightly higher, it's easy to come away from any cautious first-time entry into such a shop with an armful of equipment. Don't forget to ask if they have a back room where cartons of cameras have been stored; very often there is no room to display everything at the same time. Although most cameras found here tend to be collectible folding cameras of the 1920s and the less-desirable plastic box cameras of the 1930s and 1940s, I have found much early equipment of the darkroom, a Weston exposure meter, folding cameras from 1908–1920, and other photographic collectibles on the shelves of thrift shops in Great Barrington, Massachusetts; Pittsfield, Massachusetts; Albany, New York; Newark, New Jersey; and in similar shops in long-forgotten smaller cities visited during the past fifteen years.

NEIGHBORHOOD JUNK-TIQUE SHOPS

There is a class of shops in poorer neighborhoods of most cities which are treasure troves for the collector. They cater to the families who can only afford a table radio for $2 and a cooking pot for 50¢. Items offered are generally used household wares, but many of the shelves offer cameras that have been acquired from estates or from families moving to other neighborhoods. In such shops, the owner is only too happy to find someone likely to purchase neglected cameras dusty with disuse.

While prices tend to be higher by a dollar or two than those in the thrift shops, these shops always seem to have a larger number of photographic items. In one such shop in Albany, New York, in the spring of 1975, I was able to acquire an Argus C-3 (see Chapter 8, "35 Millimeter") and five folding cameras of varying sizes and makes for a total of $20. It was a group with a value of four to five times that outlay.

THE NEIGHBORHOOD CAMERA SHOP

The used-camera shelves of the photographic dealer are an excellent source of major cameras of the 1920s and 1930s. There is small call today for the roll-film folding camera, and the dealer is having a hard time finding buyers for cameras with lenses slower than f/3.5 or which do not have provision for flash photography. If the camera is earlier than the 1920s, the dealer himself may have designated it an antique and, indeed, may have an entire section of the store devoted to such items. Often his prices on these shelves are much higher than the prices these cameras command in the auctions or at the fairs where photographica collectors meet.

The used-camera shelf is likely to have the Kodak Bantam, possibly even a Bantam Special (see Chapter 8, "35 Millimeter"). There is likely to be any of the Zeiss Ikonta cameras and especially the later models of the Super Ikonta line. There will be one or more of the folding plate cameras of the 6-by-9-centimeter and 9-by-12-centimeter size, like the Kodak Recomar 18 or 33, or the numerous look-alike black hand-held view cameras from Voigtländer, Ica, Zeiss, and others of Germany.

Camera dealers have inoperable cameras in drawers or in boxes in the basement, left by individuals who brought these in for repair. Often these were abandoned when the repair estimate approached the cost of a new camera. A box of such cameras may not have a single camera suitable for use, but each may be well suited for shelf display in your home museum of photography. The best price can be had by buying the entire drawer or box. Make an offer of $10 or $20; the dealer may realize this as "found" money.

If the dealer has a small repair set-up, he will be loath to sell these stored cameras since he is planning (someday!) to cannibalize one or another of them for parts. It is as unlikely that he will be asked to repair another such camera as it is that he will find time to cannibalize even a single one of the cameras he may show you. Nonetheless, don't be too disappointed if he won't sell from this group.

Dealers have basements with early merchandise they may have forgotten to sell; almost every day a collector is able to buy a camera from the 1930s still in its original box and pristine new from a basement storage shelf, most often in shops that have had frequent changes of ownership. Only after you have made friends with a dealer will you have the privilege of shopping in his basement storage area where these "goodies" lurk in dusty disarray. Many a perfect example of early twentieth-century equipment may still be found in camera stores where they lay forgotten—by all but you. But you'll have to speak up to be heard, and you'll need the courage to move long dusty boxes about in a dark basement. Bring along a flashlight and rainy-day clothing.

CAMERA-REPAIR SHOPS

Most large cities have camera-repair centers that can be located by your walking fingers in the *Yellow Pages*. It is to these centers that outlying photo shops and downtown camera stores send cameras for the typical shutter or range-finder repairs. Some of these shops have boxes of cameras that were left for estimates and then never claimed—twenty years ago. Other boxes and bins have cameras from which a knob here or a ring there have already been taken to repair someone else's identical model.

Have a talk with the shop manager or owner and make it clear that you are willing to pay for such items. Leave your card or a phone number so that if early cameras are offered for repair or abandoned, you can make an offer to purchase the equipment from the original owner. Advise the manager that you will gladly pay a finder's-fee percentage of up to 10 percent to the establishment as a way of saying "thank you" for the reference. This system actually located three cameras for me when I contacted a camera-repair shop in the city of Haifa during a two-week vacation in Israel.

ADVERTISING

If Mohammed won't go to the camera, then the camera must go to Mohammed. If there are no thrift shops, camera shops, junk shops, and camera repair shops in your living-working-vacation areas, then advertise. In many small-city newspapers, and

Used-camera shelves of leading camera stores are still a fine source of such landmark cameras of the 1930s as Leicas, Contaxes, Robots, Bantam Specials, and others.

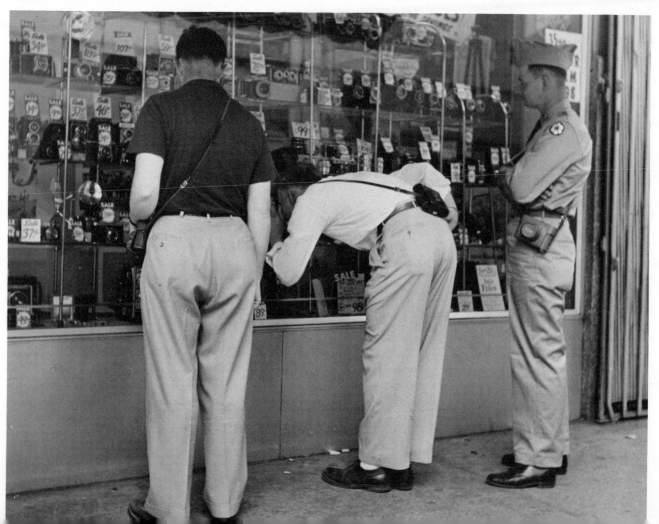

even in larger cities, the cost of a small ad in the "Antiques Wanted," or "Photography" or "Miscellany" columns will bring in numerous calls from camera owners.

This simple ad has brought a number of photographic treasures to a leading collector in New Jersey. He recommends it to his (distant) friends:

OLD CAMERAS—ANY CONDITION. Highest prices paid
in cash by local educator. Phone———.

The phone number assures instant contact and excludes the possibility of camera owners unexpectedly coming by. It also assures quick contacts without waiting for forwarded mail from the newspaper office. The ad is small and will cost but two or three dollars in most newspapers. The "educator" idea makes you look like a responsible schoolteacher in search of visual aids, and this image is likely to help you when you approach the bargaining stage. (Actually you "educate" by exhibiting your cameras and talking about your collection to any interested family members, friends, etc.)

When someone calls, ask at once for the name of the camera. Box cameras usually have to be opened (to insert film), and the name, if not on the leather handle, will be imprinted in the camera interior. Roll-film cameras have the name embossed on the leather or imprinted on a nameplate below the lens or on the camera bed; if not in these places, it is imprinted inside on the removable back. Modern smaller cameras almost invariably are identified on the camera top. Model numbers for modern cameras are rarely on the cameras. In early cameras they are included, almost always, inside the camera.

Phone calls lead to difficulties in the buy-sell relationship. There are people who believe that their very common folding camera is the equivalent of a long-lost Rembrandt. Others hate to sell part of the parental heritage and need reassurance that the camera will have an honored place in a clean home and will not be treated like a stray cat or dog.

Always ask the price people expect to be paid, but never confirm the price until you see the camera itself. One man's "first Kodak box camera" (worth to him a thousand dollars) is another man's Kodak Brownie 2A, actually worth $1 to the collector. The average person selling rarely has any knowledge of the camera, its present value in the photo antique market, or how it is operated.

ANTIQUE SHOPS

The antique shop, by and large, until the 1960s, was unable to maintain any inventory of photographic collectibles. There was little literature to guide the dealer in buying, and there was no way for the dealer to know the market value of items from groups acquired from estates or at auctions. While expert in glass, china, silver, and home decor items, antique dealers were totally at a loss as to the value of much photographica.

The exception to this has been images. Antique shops have to be thanked for their preservation of Daguerreotypes (even if countless thousands had their original images replaced so that the gutta-percha cases could find secondary use as cuff-link and button boxes) and of stereo cards, which had gone largely unnoticed for years at 5¢ and 10¢. Now these are bringing 25¢, 50¢, and in some rare instances, even slightly higher prices in the typical antique shop (see Chapter 5, "Stereo Cameras and Stereography").

Antique shops have been and still are the places to find early advertising signs of photography, Holmes-Bates and Brewster viewers, boxes of glass negatives, Kodak and other kerosene-lit darkroom lamps (which are usually misidentified as "railroad signal lanterns" because they have a ruby red glass and a fold-up cover), framed photographs, etc.

Antique shops periodically obtain view cameras in cases with lenses, filmholders, and tripods. For years, I ignored a shop outside Philadelphia, Pennsylvania, where a group of cherrywood view cameras in 5-by-7-inch and full (6½-by-8½-inch) plate were offered at $15 and $20. I was always going to buy "next time." But I didn't—and the prices of these items are now $100 and rising.

An antique shop near the Rip van Winkle Bridge in upstate New York has a Powers Animatograph No.1 35-mm projector shutter and arc-light assembly, which has gone unnoticed on the floor for ten years. The price is $65. It has not sold because, among other things, it is nearly four feet long, nearly eighteen inches high, and is covered with rust and grime accumulated since its last use (1912?). It has no great collector value, but it is a fascinating showpiece in any collection as an early movie-history relic.

For the photographica collector, antique shops break down into three major categories: likely, unlikely, and highly unlikely as a source for even a single item. But even the "highly unlikely" antique shop that caters to the audience for fine furniture and glass could have a drawer with Daguerreotypes or a small tray of Victorian jewelry that could include a ring or a watch-fob charm with a Stanhope image.

It is the catch-all, tidy-and-trim antique shop with the furnishings of middle-class homes of the past that is most apt to hold a major photographic treasure. A Megalethoscope was unnoticed for years in such a shop outside New Hope, Pennsylvania. Evidently neither the dealer nor the shop's regular customers understood the giant mahogany-wood lens device. In one such shop I was able to acquire an ebony black stereographoscope (which

Back issues of photographic magazines become a valuable data source for early equipment.

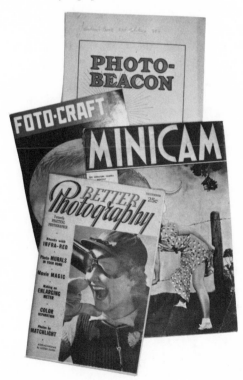

had been totally disassembled for some unknown reason) for $20. On the walls of such shops there are full-plate Daguerreotypes that would look marvelously exciting on my wall, or yours.

The typical roadside cluttered-look antique shop or barn is more apt to have the boxfuls of stereo cards, Daguerreotypes, ambrotypes, and folding cameras. Here one can find the toy magic lanterns or the lecture-type projector with its 3¼-by-4-inch glass slides. These shops have the toys and tools of the past that include the photographic heritage you seek.

Finally, the "likely" antique shop is a catch-all with parts of yesterday's automobiles next to farm implements and household gadgetry of the Depression Age. It will have a broad variety of collectible photographica: store signs, odd pamphlets and books, framed panoramic views of the Great West, and other odds and ends of photographyland.

There is a technique that has evolved to make a five-minute shopping tour of even the most elaborate shop pay off with at least one or two items. If the shop owner is busy, start a systematic eyeball tour of the establishment, walking along aisles and shelved walls, scanning for product groups. It is easy to quickly dismiss shelves of glass, china, plaster ornaments, and metal wares. Run your eyes over wall-hung items and past framed oils as you search for photography. Check the floor areas for leather or fabric cases that might contain cameras or a projector. Note where the jewelry counter is located (usually in the cash-register area) for the final moments in the shop if you are seeking Stanhopes. When you finally come upon the proprietor, make a friendly greeting and then get right to the point:

I seek examples of photography in any of its forms. Do you have cameras or parts of cameras? Any related photographic item for the darkroom or something to do with slide projectors? Do you have large photographs? Small Daguerreotypes? Any box of literature that might have a photography catalogue? Boxes of stereo cards? A stereo viewer? Does any of your jewelry have a little picture in a peephole window?

But never trust the answers of the dealer. While they look for a camera that you will find from ex-

185

perience they really can't find, finish your search of the shelves, walls, and display trays. Quick-check shelved books for photography titles.

Early full-plate holders from the 1880s were bought as a group for $2 from a shop in Sheffield, Massachusetts, where the woman owner swore there was nothing photographic in the shop. (She finally remembered these in a china-closet bottom drawer, which she had first stated contained linens.)

It was the combination of visits to thrift shops and antique shops beginning almost fifteen years ago that led to the creation of one of the most important detective- and box-camera collections in the United States by one of America's foremost collector-historians, Eaton S. Lothrop, Jr., author of *A Century of Cameras* and first president of the Photographic Historical Society of America.

Photography as an art and science, along with its tools and peripheral equipment, has been ignored by the antique shops by and large since they neither understood nor appreciated the value of this heritage until recently. Antique shops can be "too-too" shops: priced "too" high or "too" low (because the dealer does not know the market value in the photographica field that emerged only in the early 1970s). But it was in a "too-low" shop that I bought a Kodak Bantam Special for $12.50 (this camera is worth about $100, though it has brought up to $175 at auction). In another shop a puzzled owner sold me for $12 a David White Stereo Realist that he assumed was a broken stereo camera. After some effort with the mechanism, it developed that it wasn't in any way a broken camera. It was designed so that without film within to trigger a release, the key operating features do not function. This camera has a value of from $50 to $75 in today's collector market.

ANTIQUE SHOPS BY MAIL

It is possible to shop in photographic antique shops in the far corners of the United States through the pages of a number of specialized antique publications, and especially *The Antique Trader Weekly*. The columns of this fascinating publication contain ads placed by dealers who seek buyers for items that have not found local buyers.

There is a column for photographic equipment which weekly offers from ten to a hundred cameras that can be purchased by mail.

It was in the pages of *The Antique Trader Weekly* that I located a copy of Humphrey's important treatise on Daguerreotypy (1855) for $5. It is worth many times that price. It was in these same pages that I located a source of nineteenth-century clothing to create a small wardrobe for occasional portraits of friends in the costuming of photography's earlier days. This publication also lists flea markets and antique fairs where hundreds of dealers display their wares. (See other publications and dealers in "Catalogues of Mail-Order Auctions," page 198.)

ANTIQUE SHOPS ON WHEELS

Just about every weekend in America, aggressive antique-shop owners take to the road, joining with fellow dealers in antique shows and fairs in the large halls of cities across America. Churches, synagogues, American Legion halls, armories, and social halls are converted for a weekend. The small admission charged to the public usually benefits the sponsoring organization or the commercial operator of the event. These events make it possible for the collector to become friendly with anywhere from fifty to two hundred dealers in a single visit and to check with each about the possibility of photographic wares on the display tables or back at the shops that these dealers represent. Arrangements can be made to visit one or another of the dealers with an inventory of interest or to arrange for a mail-order purchase of an item or two.

Local newspapers and street signs will keep the collector abreast of such antique fairs in his own community. Such publications as *The Antique Trader Weekly* and the *Newtown Bee* (see "Mail-Order Shopping," page 190), which covers the New England area, are sources for dates and locations of shows in hundreds of communities each weekend.

Dealers at such shows tend to bring numerous small items for table display. The photographica collector will usually find it easy to find stereo cards and viewers and such small early cameras as the 1895 Pocket Kodak (see Chapter 2, "Box Cameras"), according to Shirley Sprung, treasurer of the Photographic Historical Society of New York, who is herself an antiques dealer specializing in jewelry and silverware. Dealers packing for such shows prefer to carry numerous small items rather than a few large items; fortunately for the collector of photographica, most items are "small." The Sprung collection has many important items found by Shirley on the tables of her fellow dealers, such as "tropical" (all-wood) cameras of the 1920s and photographic jewelry for herself. Since she can only be at one show per weekend, that leaves 999 shows for you and the other collectors.

FLEA MARKETS

They have been called the public sale of public garbage, and they are as much a part of the suburban weekend as the noisy lawn mower. They are a lure to the photographica collector since they provide everything photographic from the earliest periods up to last year's plastic drugstore camera.

It was as a result of buying cameras from the tables of a Connecticut flea market that John Kowalak, an executive with one of the largest film-industry laboratories, was able to buy two Daguerreotype cameras worth $5,000 and a stereo viewer—all for $20. And it was at a flea market that I found a modern $30 exposure meter for 50¢ and early photo equipment catalogues for $1.

Flea markets are something you love—or hate. The sun is hot; the field is dusty; and even with a refreshment stand loudspeaker announcing the availability of cold drinks to cool hot crowds, the combination of sun, heat, and fatigue make it work to find a treasure. Sunglasses, a hat, and patience are recommended aids for the collector.

Flea markets are listed in the pages of *The Antique Trader Weekly* and the *Newtown Bee* (see page 197 for subscription information), but also on highway signs to attract Sunday drivers.

GARAGE AND TAG SALES

The garage sale had arrived as an American phenomenon when it was given the dignity of a major photographic essay in an issue of *Life* magazine (August 18, 1972).

Garage or tag sales are held in fair weather in most parts of the country in the garages of families wishing to dispose of no-longer-needed household items, clothing, sports equipment, and, among other things, cameras. Prices are very low and usually negotiable since owners do wish to sell and buyers of used cameras are often few and far between. Garage sales are sometimes advertised in the "Miscellaneous" columns or antiques columns of local newspapers.

In 1974, in Columbia County, New York, I acquired a Victor 3 16-mm camera (see photograph on page 152), that I had located at a garage sale—for $5. Again: This was an instance in which the seller believed in all honesty that he was offering a damaged camera. After its purchase, it refused to operate even when fully wound. But it was simply thirsty for a few droplets of oil. Given this life-restoring refreshment, today it hums like a bee. Z-z-z-z-zmmmmmmmmmm.

Another garage sale provided a book, *Tom Swift and His Wizard Camera* for 25¢. The Tom Swift book series is a part of the romance of early twentieth-century youth literature; Tom's adventures with his camera are of special interest to the collector of Wizard cameras, a group of folding plate cameras made in America and sold at the turn of the century.

PAWNSHOPS

The shelves and back rooms of pawnshops in nearly every American city are the long-neglected resting places for numerous quality cameras of the 1920s and 1930s. Leicas, Contaxes, Rolleis, and similar highly collectible cameras may be had for prices equal to the prices for these items when purchased from shelves of used cameras at larger camera stores.

It was in the side-street pawnshop of Albuquerque, New Mexico, that I acquired a Robot of the mid-1930s for $12. Until I spotted the tiny sequence camera on a long shelf, the shop had found it literally unsalable since it could not be loaded with any film obtained at a typical film counter.

The Robot in its early formats was loaded with 35-mm bulk film in special Robot-made cassettes in the photographer's own darkroom before each day's trip with the camera (see Chapter 8, "35 Millimeter").

It was in the window of a pawnship of Charlotte, North Carolina, that one morning I spotted a 35-mm Universal Mercury equipped with a bizarre lens, obviously a homemade telephoto of longer-than-usual tele capability. The shop was closed; I planned to return to the store en route to the airport for departure from the city, but time did not permit the return trip. Months later, a friend was scheduled for a Thanksgiving visit to her home: Charlotte, North Carolina. She vaguely remembered that a pawnshop was located near the local burlesque house. (That was the only way I could identify the store's location.) A sketch was her guide to the camera and its unusual lens. The pawnshop owner was only too happy to find a buyer at last; it was a great acquisition for $10, and the telephoto capability proved to be as unique as the camera's novel appearance.

PUBLIC AUCTIONS

Auctions of every sort are held in every city of America just about every day; most are auctions of industrial properties, land sales, bankruptcy sales, etc. But auction sales of the contents of homes occur with great regularity, too. Some of these auctions are held right on the home site; others are held on the barnlike premises of the auctioneer.

If there is an opportunity to preview the auction merchandise, you can save hours of sitting through the bidding on chairs, tables, and housewares. Auctions that are well-organized and permit previews usually also permit bids by the house on your behalf. (You need not be present at the auction itself; the auctioneer includes your bid as though you were on the premises. If you have bid high above the value established at the auction, in most cases you'll have acquired the item at a few dollars above the last floor bid, but less than you had authorized.) It was in such a situation that I was able to acquire the German-made stereo folding pocket

viewer of the 1920s for $10 (see Chapter 5, "Stereo Cameras and Stereography").

In country and farm auctions, you must stand outdoors in the sun or sit in the shade of a tent on a tiny folding seat. (I'm big and that hurts.) It was at such an auction that a grocer's carton of box cameras as a group went up on the block. The site was a country home on the slopes of the Berkshire Mountains in western Massachusetts. The first bid was "Two dollars" from someone in the rear. I immediately said: "Three!" A pause and then the response, "Four dollars." I immediately offered: "Six!" A pause. New voice: "Seven dollars." I sung out at once: "Eight." A pause; then the new bidder again: "Nine." Immediately, seeking to discourage the new bidder and to show my determination: (loudly) "Eleven dollars." I hoped that it was clear from my voice that I would again raise the bid and that all further bidders would know I was planning on having that box. There were no further bids.

From the top of the box I had been able to note that there were at least four box cameras, one quite large, all obviously pre-1914. Actually the box contained seven cameras when it was brought to me. One was a Blair Detective (see Chapter 4, "Detective Cameras and Later Novelty Cameras") from the 1890s. Although it was in poor condition, it was subsequently sold to a delighted friend for $35. Five small cameras included Bull's-Eyes and Bullets (see Chapter 2, "Box Cameras"). These were all ultimately swapped at antique-photography fairs for the kind of small cameras I especially seek. The final item was too small to be noticed by anyone looking at the boxload of cameras; it was a matchbox-size Expo Police Camera of about 1916, an Expo model eagerly sought by all collectors of novelty cameras. This was swapped about six months later with a Long Island collector for a rare Steineck ABC wristwatch camera from Germany, 1948, a choice item for my collection. This was possibly the best auction buy I have enjoyed in ten years of auction going, since the value, with swaps and sales, was close to $300—for an $11 investment.

Auctions can be fun. But there is such a thing as auction fever. I have seen people buy used TV sets at the prices of new models, for example, which makes you wonder about the rationality of the consumer. Auctions are also educational. One major East Coast dealer in photographica traces his own start to a chance visit to an auction of photographic items. He was hooked.

MAIL-ORDER AUCTIONS

The most prestigious auction house in the world, Sotheby's, of London, now regularly schedules auctions of photographica that have made international headlines in the photographic and antiques press. Prices for a single item of equipment (a Sutton panoramic camera of the 1860s) reached the $25,000 level, and over $120,000 was paid for an album of photographs by Julia Margaret Cameron (1815–1879).

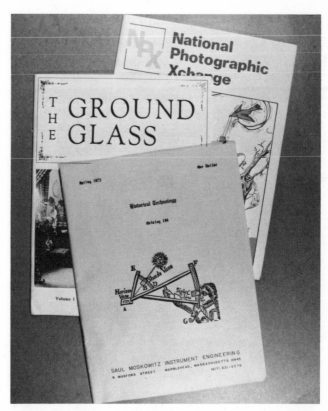

Quarterly and monthly catalogues and publications offering both early and contemporary photographic equipment make it possible to buy antique photographica by phone.

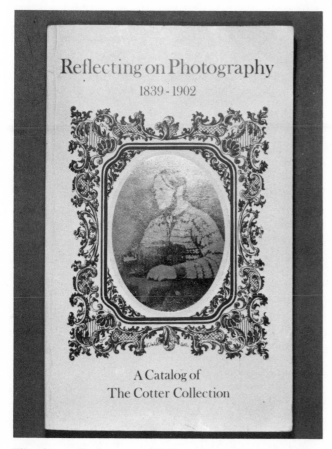

The first collectors to publish catalogues of their photographica provided a guide for quick identification of little-known items. (Reflecting on Photography *from the collection of Alan and Paulette Cotter*)

The catalogues of these auctions have themselves become collectible items relating to the history of photography. It is possible to write to Sotheby's in London and to Sotheby Parke Bernet Galleries in New York for the dates and places of photographica auctions (see page 198 for addresses). These are presently scheduled about two times a year and include numerous items that will sell for $25 and up. The illustrated catalogues, which are sold for $3 or $4, contain background and historical information, which are an education for the novice collector, along with information on how to bid by mail.

There are a number of smaller dealers who conduct mail-order auctions on occasion. News of these events is carried in the antiques press and the publications of the photographic-collecting societies (see page 197). In addition, page 190 provides additional information on obtaining catalogues of mail-order auctions.

MAIL-ORDER SHOPPING

It has become increasingly easy to acquire items related to the history of photography and particularly cameras that are readily identifiable by name and model number. Camera listings of mail-order dealers describe condition in such evaluations as "fair," "good," "excellent," and even in the terms of numismatists who describe coinage newly emerging unblemished from the mint, as "mint." It is not uncommon to find offerings of "new, in orig. box" as items are unearthed in store basements.

The mail-order sellers are advertisers in such publications as *Shutterbug Ads, National Photo Xchange*, and in the columns of the antiques press, in which it is educational to regularly peruse offerings. Not only does it pique interest to learn what is commonly available, it is also a guide of a sort to the prevailing market prices. Buying from such offerings is not always the easiest matter. Dealers will ship on receipt of a check or money order. It is not that easy to obtain a refund should the merchandise arrive in poor condition or if the item so acquired is not the item the buyer was seeking.

There can be honest errors in mail-order shopping since the Tenax camera of the 1920s is not the Tenax camera of the 1930s (the earlier one is a plate-type folding camera while the latter is a 35-mm camera). Yet both are German made, both can be described as black, and both will be sold for about the same price. There is always a problem with the Contaflex cameras from Zeiss: The first was a twin-lens reflex (see Chapter 7, "Twin-Lens Reflex Cameras"); after World War II the name was placed on a line of single-lens reflex cameras. The recent reuse of the Contax name will lead to confusion in the years ahead: The Contax of the 1970s is a Japanese-made single-lens reflex while the Contax of the 1930s was a German-made 35-mm range-finder–type camera (see Chapter 8, 35 Millimeter"). Both are 35 mm; both have interchangeable lenses; both offer focal-plane shutters.

A new class of antiques dealers has emerged during the past decade in America, England, France, and Germany who are extremely knowledgeable of the artifacts of photography. These elite merchants of photographica have reached out internationally to locate the buyers of photographic exotica and also the collectors of the more mundane examples of equipment, images, literature, and ephemera. They are among the most reliable sources for antique photographica items, since in their ads and in their catalogues they most accurately describe their offerings. They deal by phone and usually practice a money-back guarantee if the item is not as described. Many of these dealers themselves were first collectors; their experience in trading and swapping led to the full-time activities of dealership.

On the East Coast, Tom and Elinor Burnside (specializing in the Daguerrean era) of Pawlet, Vermont, or Allen and Hilary Weiner of New York City regularly publish catalogues of offerings, which are small textbooks of photographica. On the West Coast, Mike Kessler and Alan and Paulette Cotter have been successful in extending their collecting interest into active private sales through the mail and by phone.

Lists or catalogues are available from these well-known dealers across America:

Bel-Park Photo Supply, 2837 Milwaukee Avenue, Chicago, Illinois 60618; Phone: (312)252-5700

Classic Photographic Apparatus, P.O. Box 161, Simsbury, Connecticut 06070; Phone: (203)658-5782

Daguerreian Era, Pawlet, Vermont 05761; Phone: (802) 325-3360

John Darrow, 50 Orchard Road, Akron, Ohio 44313; Phone: (216)836-4458

Thom Hindle, P.O. Box 951, Eatontown, New Jersey 07724; Phone: (201)988–9287

Leon Jacobson, 161 Genesee Park Drive, Syracuse, New York 13224; Phone: (315)446-8345

Mike Kessler, 5916 Adenmoor Avenue, Lakewood, California 90713; Phone: (213)866-1134

Karl J. Koch, 206 Port Watson Street, Cortland, New York 13045; Phone: (607)753-1817

Ed Lauten, 273 Springtown Road, New Paltz, New York 12561; Phone: (914)255-7342

Jay L. Manning, 234 Church, Ardmore, Pennsylvania 19003; Phone: (215)MI9–9681

Saul Moskowitz Instrument Engineering, Historical Technology, 6 Mugford Street, Marblehead, Massachusetts 01945; Phone: (617)631-2275

Allan and Hilary Weiner, 392 Central Park West, New York, New York 10025; Phone: (212)749-3247

Myron S. Wolf, P.O. Box 351, Lexington, Massachusetts 02173; Phone: (617)862-6041

PHOTOGRAPHIC SUPPLIERS WITH ANTIQUE DEPARTMENTS

In a number of cities the camera store has become the center of available photographic antiques. A city as small as Putnam, Connecticut has a camera store in a converted railroad station with an owner, Herbert Grube, who has developed a fine collection of antiques. Chicago's Bel-Park Photo Supply (2837 Milwaukee Avenue, Chicago) has a nationwide reputation built by the knowledgeable Barney Copeland, who with his wife visits most photographica fairs within a few hundred miles of Chicago. Their store regularly publishes a detailed catalogue of vintage cameras for the collector of twentieth-century cameras. Barney won the hearts of collectors by creating a novelty sweatshirt in the early 1970s: the Daguerre sweatshirt.

In New York City, Fotoshop on Camera Row (West Thirty-second Street) is run by the irrepressible Charlie Pellish, who is among the most knowledgeable experts on the early Leica system and the related contemporary cameras. Collectors visiting New York find a few minutes with the smiling Mr. Pellish not only startling because of the hard-to-find Leica items he may have to offer, but delightful as well, as they are regaled with the stories of "the ones that got away."

In England, Vintage Cameras, Ltd., is one of the largest retail centers of the world for sophisticated collectible photographic antiques. A visit with Tony Kowal (256, Kirkdale, London S.E. 26, England) is a memorable afternoon for the beginner or experienced photographica collector. In a Paris suburb, one may find Michel Auer, (47 Avenue Aristide Briand, Montrouge) who has established a center for photographic antiques following years of building what has been termed the finest privately owned collection of rare photographica on earth.

While the average camera store in the typical American city may have an early camera that it has taken in trade, it is more likely that the collectible cameras will be held for occasional window display as the collection of the store or its owner. Such is the case at Camera Craft, 210 North Avenue, New Rochelle, New York, where a collection of early American twentieth-century cameras is exhibited annually from the collection of shop owner Marvin Goldfluss.

PHOTOGRAPHICA FAIRS

The very easiest places in the entire world to buy early cameras are all in America. In Boston; in New York; in Chicago; in Columbus, Ohio; in St. Louis, Missouri; in Pasadena, California; and elsewhere; fairs sponsored by the collector societies in these cities are one- and two-day events at motel and hotel halls, open to the public.

These fairs will bring together anywhere from twenty-five to one hundred dealers in early cameras who will load eight-foot-long tables with every imaginable photographic item dating back from the first days (1840–1850) up to the present. At hotels like the Copley Plaza in Boston and the McAlpin in New York, it is usually a $1 donation that opens the door to instant access to 2,000 to 5,000 cameras and as many Daguerrean and later images. Plus books. Plus displays. Plus advertising signs. Plus reprints. Plus magazines. Plus more than you can imagine—all related to the collecting of photographic equipment. (See page 193 for addresses to which one may write for information on the fairs.)

These fairs are gathering points for the most knowledgeable collectors, who arrange to meet where they can swap cameras and stories in ballroom corners and hospitality suites on the evenings of the fair dates. An entire folklore of photographic collecting has emerged from such sessions, which are the fireside-chat material when, years later, collectors sit over hot stories and cold drinks.

All of these fairs permit nonmembers to reserve a table or to simply attend as a visitor, free to look, see, and buy for hours on end. The photographica fairs are in effect one- and two-day seminars on photography with up to 100 lecturers at tables feeding data and information to photography-hungry audiences. The first glimpse through the open doorway to the exhibit halls is a never-to-be-forgotten experience as tables loaded with black, chrome, and red leathers come into view for the first-time visitor-collector.

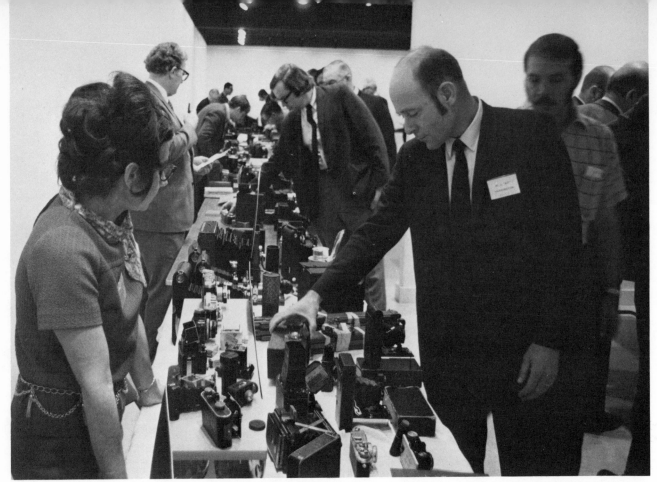

Semiannual photographica trade fairs, usually at major hotels in New York, Chicago, Columbus, and other cities, permit opportunities to select from thousands of items on display for sale or trade. *(Photograph by Mike Sullivan)*

A start in collecting at such an event may be with 25¢ for a stereo card already one hundred years old or up to $5,000 for a Daguerrean camera. It is impossible *not* to find choice examples in the area of interest of any collector. Tables are either representative samplings of the specialty interest of the dealer (as Daguerreotypes, books, or stereo cards) or they are a potpourri of cameras from all periods, along with lenses, shutters, early magazines, etc., as at a flea market. It is possible to bring a camera up to any table and to offer it in trade or for sale to a dealer, or to anyone in the aisle. These fairs are photographic free-for-alls.

The sponsoring organization customarily has a table where one may find information on the activities of the local collector group, its planned meetings, seminars or other fairs, etc. The easiest way to learn of such impending events is to initially join any of the societies around the country (see pages 193–194). Their bulletins will announce fair dates for all other societies in nearby states.

THE SOCIETIES OF THE COLLECTING FRATERNITY

Photographic societies are made up of groups of individuals who share the collecting aspect of their hobby as much as a burning interest in the overall field of photographic history. Most of the societies appeal to the cultural, educational, and social needs of the general collector. A few have been organized to meet the special interests of collectors in specific fields: the stereo buffs, the Leicaphiles, the Daguerrean-era followers.

The one national organization, the Photographic Historical Society of America, is an administrative coordinator rather than an action group. It is the local groups that have the membership meetings, fairs, publications, displays in civic centers, or social activities. Membership in the national organization entitles one to receive a quarterly newsletter (*Northlight*), which contains major essays on aspects of photographic history or equipment devel-

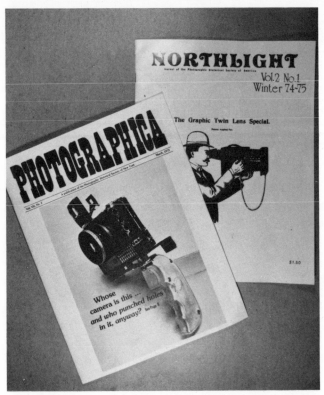

Members of the nearly thirty organizations now active in the photographic collecting field gain news of collector activities and aid in collecting from the monthly publications published by the various societies.

opment along with news of activities of the local societies.

The largest local society actually has a vast national and international membership. It is the Photographic Historical Society of New York, Inc., founded in 1969, some years after the formation of the first such group (the Photographic Historical Society of Rochester, New York). The New York group has grown from its start with a half dozen collectors, who were also photographers-writers-lecturers, to its present status of nearly six hundred members. Monthly meetings cover such topics as the equipment, companies, and technologies of early photography, along with presentations on early images, current related books, and hardware. The New York group, like its counterparts in many major cities, conducts semiannual fairs, issues reprints of significant early photo literature, and provides speakers to interest the public and today's photographers in the past of the art. The society publishes a ten-times-a-year magazine, *Photographica*, which is much prized by distant collector-

members who otherwise have little contact with active collectors.

The following listing gives the names and addresses of photographic historical and collecting groups that are active in America as well as abroad.

The Bay Area Photographica Association (greater San Francisco area)
1178 Crespi Drive
Sunnyvale, California 94086

The Cascade Photographic Historical Society (southern Washington and northern Oregon)
c/o Ron Panfilio
3155 S.W. 72nd Avenue
Portland, Oregon 97225

The Chesapeake Antiquarian Photographic Society (Delaware; Maryland; Washington, D.C.; and northern Virginia)
P.O. Box 66
Severna Park, Maryland 21146

The Chicago Photographic Collectors' Society (Chicago area)
P.O. Box 375
Winnetka, Illinois 60093

The Club Daguerre (West Germany)
c/o Dr. Vladimir Delavre
61 Daemstadt
Hindenburgstrasse 13
West Germany

The Delaware Valley Photographic Collectors Association (southern New Jersey, eastern Pennsylvania)
c/o E. H. Rifkind, Secretary
P.O. Box 74
Delanco, New Jersey

The Great Plains Photographic Historical Society (Kansas, Nebraska, and Oklahoma)
P.O. Box 13114
Ofutt AFB, Nebraska 68113

The Historical Group, The Royal Photographic Society of Great Britain (Great Britain)
14 South Audley Street
London, W1Y 5DP
England

The Historical Photographic Society of the Western Reserve (Cleveland area)
c/o Donn Rothenberg
4176 Hinsdale Road
South Euclid, Ohio 44121

The Leica Historical Society (Leica collectors everywhere)
c/o N. R. Skipper, Jr.
P.O. Box 461
Franklin, Michigan 48025

The Michigan Photographic Historical Society (Michigan, western Ohio, and southern Ontario)
P.O. Box 191
Dearborn, Michigan 48121

The Midwest Photographic Historical Society (Missouri and vicinity)
P.O. Box 882
Columbia, Missouri 65201

The National Stereoscopic Association (stereo collectors in U.S., Canada, Europe, and Africa)
R.D. #1
Fremont, New Hampshire 03044

The Ohio Camera Collectors Society (Columbus and vicinity)
P.O. Box 282
Columbus, Ohio 43216

The Photographic Collectors of Houston (Houston and vicinity)
2711 Houston Avenue
Houston, Texas 77009

The Photographic Historical Society (central New York State)
P.O. Box 9563
Rochester, New York 14604

The Photographic Historical Society of America (a national organization covering all states)
P.O. Box 41
Simsbury, Connecticut 06070

The Photographic Historical Society of Canada (a national organization for all provinces)
631 Sheppard Avenue W.
Downsview, Ontario
Canada

The Photographic Historical Society of New England (greater New England)
P.O. Box 403
Buzzards Bay, Massachusetts 02532

The Photographic Historical Society of New York (southern New York, New Jersey, Connecticut and national)
P.O. Box 1839
Radio City Station
New York, New York 10019

The Rocky Mountain Photographic Historical Society (Colorado and Wyoming)
c/o Donald Upjohn
P.O. Box 577
Aurora, Colorado 80010

The Tri-State Photographic Collectors' Society (southern Ohio, Indiana, and Kentucky)
c/o William R. Bond
8910 Cherry Avenue
Blue Ash, Ohio 45242

The Western Photographic Collectors Association (south central California)
P.O. Box 4294
Whittier, California 90607

PHOTOGRAPHICA LITERATURE
Early Catalogues and Camera Brochures

The authentic information on a specific early camera or its lenses plus an indication of related accessories would be lost to history except for the catalogues and brochures that at the time accompanied these items.

Since many of the companies are no longer in business, and since few of these booklets, catalogues, or brochures were ever provided to public libraries or technical-reference centers, the only sources for this information are those pieces of literature that have survived in "used"-book stores or in the cardboard boxes of the "paper dealers" in the antiques and flea markets.

Mixed among the piles of Atchison, Topeka, and Santa Fe Railroad timetables and Cunard Line schedules, one may find a booklet on the 3A Auto-

Basic references for collectors are catalogues of the past. Numerous reprints are now available for rare cameras and accessories.

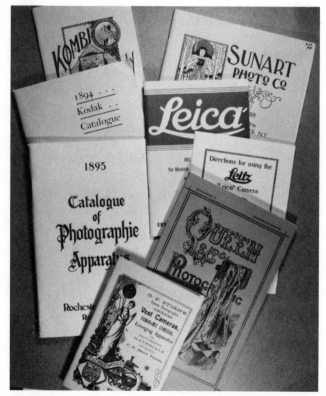

graphic Kodak or the Kombi camera. Depending on size, condition, and the individual dealer, booklets of eight to forty-eight pages are likely to be priced at anywhere from 50¢ to $5. In 1975, I paid $10 for a 1900 Montgomery Ward camera catalogue that provided some of the illustrations for this volume along with details on the Edison Stereo-Projecting Kinetoscope.

The basic value of photographic literature, whether an instruction booklet for the operation of a now obscure camera or a catalogue of offerings by a camera store fifty years ago, must be related to each collector's major field of interest. To the collector of panoramic cameras, a booklet on the operation of a Turret Panoramic camera of 1904 will have a value far higher than an even earlier booklet on a camera which does not have the panoramic capability. The collector of Leica was happy to learn that a major company (Morgan and Morgan, Inc.) had republished the nearly-impossible-to-find manual on Leica's first model; but as a reprint, this booklet has little interest to the collector of original photographic books and literature.

As the initial booklets become more difficult to obtain, there will be an increase in reprint editions by services directing products to the collector market. It is likely that this will prevent the scarce originals from ever becoming valuable collectibles.

By far the most eagerly sought booklet is the original announcement brochure written by Daguerre and translated into English and other languages for worldwide dissemination. The original, in French, is sold from time to time at $500 or more.

It was at a one-time-a-year Antique Fair and Flea Market at the Shaker Museum, outside of Chatham, New York, that I located a Panoram-Kodak booklet for 50¢. In 1969 in an antique barn in northern Pennsylvania I found a 1936 German camera brochure of the popular cameras of Germany of the time.

On a trip to Israel in 1972, I found a camera-shop owner who was happy to give me German Leitz literature and lens booklets of the 1930s. These booklets had been in a drawer for nearly forty years until this American asked if any were available. The dealer was happy to make a gift of the literature during the course of a small transac-

tion for some film simply because I was interested. It is likely that stores all over America and, indeed, the world, still have early literature on a basement shelf that can be had for the asking.

Because of the importance of this early literature, a number of collectors have taken rare booklets and pamphlets and have had these privately republished. They provide an instant library of the photographic past. Below are listed some sources for historical catalogue reprints.

Canadian Museum of Photography, P.O. Box 74, Jarvis, Ontario, Canada
> Publisher of Cummins Catalog of Anthony Photo Products of 1888.

Classic Photographic Apparatus, P.O. Box 161, Simsbury, Connecticut 06070
> This company has reproduced over one hundred catalogues of the late 1890s and early 1900s, plus numerous one-, two-, and three-page articles and reports describing early Kodak, Graflex, Expo, Poco, detective cameras, and even numerous European cameras.

D-M Enterprises, 144 Happ Road, Northfield, Illinois 60093
> Publishers of the 1897 camera catalogue of Marshall Field & Co., Chicago.

Andre Farkas, 11 Leann Drive, Norwalk, Connecticut 06851
> Publisher of the 1898 Catalogue and Price List of the Sunart Photo Co. and the French & Co. catalogue of lenses of 1887.

N. M. Graver, P.O. Box 18051, Rochester, New York 14618
> Publisher of the McAllister Optical Goods catalogue of the early 1880s.

Hove Camera Company, 34 Church Road, Hove, Sussex, England
> Publishers of the Leica General Catalogue (all models as of 1936) and the Leica Instruction Manual for Standard, IIIa, and Model 250 Leicas.

Morgan and Morgan, Inc., 400 Warburton Avenue, Hastings-on-Hudson, New York 10706
> Publishers of E. & H. T. Anthony & Co. catalogue of 1891 and the Leica A Operating Instructions, ca. 1928.

National Directory of Camera Collectors, P.O. Box 4246, Santa Barbara, California 93103
> Publishers of the National Directory, plus reprints of the C. P. Stirn catalogue (vest and wonder cameras); and the Kombi catalogue of 1895.

Photographica, 20 Stoneboat Road, Westport, Connecticut 06880
> Publishers of a reprint of the E. & H. T. Anthony & Co. catalogue of 1877.

Photo-Historical Reprints, 1545 East 13th Street, Brooklyn, New York 11230
> Publishers of Bull's-Eye camera flyers; Leica cartoon compilations; "Travelling Photographer" cartoons; Amateur Photography cartoons, etc.

The Pyne Press, Lower Pyne Building, Nassau Street, Princeton, New Jersey 08540

    Publisher of the Rochester Optical Co. catalogue of Premo Cameras of 1898.

Western Photographic Collectors Association, P.O. Box 4294, Whittier, California 90607

    Publishers of a reprint catalogue of Graflex products of 1904.

Other Reference Literature

A variety of publications provide illustrations and details on early and classic cameras that might otherwise be lost to history. One of the most interesting of these reference works is the two-volume publication by Yesterday's Cameras, a camera-collector information service originally founded by the author.

These basic references are *Photographic Advertising from A–Z* and *More Photographic Advertising from A–Z*, containing page-by-page reproductions of the early advertising on cameras of America and Europe as these were advertised in the photographic or popular press of the times from the Kodak (1888) to the Leica (1926). Both books are available from Porter's, P.O. Box 628, Cedar Falls, Iowa 50613 for $8.95 each.

Other compilations from directories of cameras from the 1930–1950 period have been published as the *Directory of Collectable Cameras*, volumes I ($5.95) and II ($8.95). These are available from: Myron S. Wolf, P.O. Box 351, Lexington, Massachusetts 02173.

The basic reference work on 130 classic cameras from the Giroux Daguerreotype camera of 1839 up to the Minox of 1940 was assembled by Eaton S. Lothrop, Jr., editor of the *Photographic Collectors' Newsletter*. His book, *A Century of Cameras* published by Morgan & Morgan, Inc., is available at bookshops (for $12.00) and libraries.

Aside from the published works cited, there is a further valuable source for information on early photography, the monthly mailings in the form of newsletters and magazines published by camera companies and photo-products distributors which can be found at flea markets and from dealers in photographic literature.

The Ohio Camera Collector's Association provided this list to its members as a guide to the search for information on photo products of the past:

"Rexo Dealer Bulletin" by Burke and James, Inc., Chicago, Illinois, 12 pages.

"Thru the Darkroom Door" by the Cleveland Photographic Society, Inc., 28 pages, started 1926.

"Lensology and Shutterisms" by the Wollensak Optical Co., Rochester, 14 pages, started 1912.

"Developments" by the Master Photo-Finishers of America, 26 pages, started 1925.

"Snap Shots" by George Murphy, Inc., New York, 34 pages, started 1888.

"Liebers Photo News" by the H. Lieber Co., Indianapolis, 26 pages, started 1924.

"The Professional Photographer" the Official Journal of the Photographer's Association of America, 36 pages, started 1875.

"The Ansco Dealer" by Ansco Co., Binghamton, 14 pages, started 1913.

"Studio Light" by Eastman Kodak Co., Rochester, 34 pages, started 1908.

"Photographic Review" by Eastman Kodak Stores, Inc., Cleveland, 34 pages, started 1921.

"Kodakery" by Eastman Kodak Co., Rochester, 34 pages, started 1912.

"Photographic Chimes" by Eastman Kodak Stores, Pittsburgh, Pa., 34 pages, started 1922.

"The Gevaert Sensitizer" by Gevaert Co. of America, New York, 12 pages, started 1933.

"The Fowler and Slater Co. Photo News" by Fowler and Slater, Cleveland, Detroit, Youngstown, 34 pages, started 1903.

"Photographic Dealer," Hollywood, California, 8 pages.

"Defender Trade Bulletin" by Defender Photo Supply Co., Rochester, 16 pages, started 1916. Defender also supplied booklets of their films and photo papers.

Contemporary Publications on Collecting and Antiques

By and large, the collecting of photographica attracts only modest interest in the major publications of the antiques field. These publications primarily serve the interests of the collectors of quality furniture, china, glass, etc. The world of technology has generally been of small interest to the editors of the magazines, who, when showing token interest in photographica, are primarily devoting themselves to image collecting.

As a result, a number of special-interest publications have been created to serve the photographica collector. The active collectors subscribe to almost all of these weekly and monthly publications as sources for advertised collectibles, for news of forthcoming collector-oriented flea markets and antique shows, and news of the auctions, new publications, special finds, and the like.

Antiques and Art Weekly (*The Newtown Bee*), Newtown, Connecticut 06470

> This is a special weekly supplement to *The Newtown Bee*, serving the antiques-collector market for all of New England, listing auctions, flea markets, etc. $8 per year.

Antique Trader Weekly, P.O. Box 1050, Dubuque, Iowa 52001

> This is a newspaper with an amazing vitality, featuring news of numerous collecting areas, national listing by regions of all forthcoming markets and shows, and offering columns in which buyers and sellers of photographic items may find each other. Published weekly; annual subscriptions (as of fall 1975), $9.50.

National Photo Xchange, P.O. Box 706, Cortland, New York 13045

> This is an 8½-by-11-inch magazine of up to twenty-four pages, featuring articles on early photo items and offering advertising space to dealers in early photo equipment along with classified columns for buyers and sellers of photographica. Published monthly; $4 per year.

Shutterbug Ads, P.O. Box 730, Titusville, Florida 32780

> This is a monthly tabloid newspaper that addresses itself exclusively to the photographer, and incidentally to the collector of photographica. While much of the offerings are contemporary, a number of early photographic items appear in each issue. $5 per year.

There are special publications for the collectors of 8- and 16-mm motion pictures of the past, along with the esoterica of filmdom (photos of stars, film advertising, posters, theater decorations, etc.):

Classic 8/16 Collector, c/o Samuel K. Rubin, 734 Philadelphia Street, Indiana, Pennsylvania 15701

> This is a 64-page and larger tabloid newspaper published quarterly that is packed with the news of past films and the present availability of reprints for the film collector. Advertisers are the laboratories that are duplicating early classics and films by past stars; a classified page makes it possible for buyers and sellers of films and equipment to find each other. $6 per year.

The publications issued by the various photographic historical societies are sources of news of these societies who are the primary sponsors of the photographic flea markets around the country. The

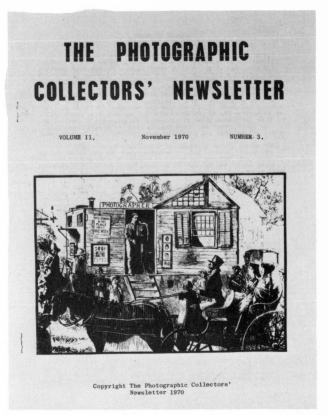

Copyright The Photographic Collectors' Newsletter 1970

The photographic collector's bible for many years has been this authoritative newsletter. It's published as an avocation by a science teacher with a fascination for the history of photographic equipment.

pages of these publications carry valuable reference guides to the equipment and companies of the past.

Northlight, P.O. Box 41, Simsbury, Connecticut 06070

> This is the quarterly publication of the Photographic Historical Society of America (PHSA). It carries news of early technology along with announcements of all planned flea markets, auctions, and events of interest to the photographic collector. PHSA membership ($8.00 per year; $6.00 if member of any affiliated society) includes a subscription to *Northlight*.

The Photographic Collectors' Newsletter, 1545 East 13th Street, Brooklyn, New York 11230

> Less than twenty issues of this vital newsletter were published between 1968 and 1975. Issues of 36 to 48 pages have been rich with technical details on little-known aspects of major cameras of the past along with the background on their inventors, makers, etc. Publication was suspended in August 1975. Back issues are available at $2 each from the publisher; the serious collector should acquire the entire set.

197

Photographica, P.O. Box 1839, Radio City Station, New York, New York 10019

> Published monthly, this is the publication of the largest regional photo-history group active in the country, The Photographic Historical Society of New York (PHSNY). It features activities of special interest to PHSNY members, detailed studies of key products or personalities of photography's past, news of forthcoming events, etc. A subscription is included with annual membership: $15 per year.

The Viewfinder, P.O. Box 461, Franklin, Michigan 48025

> This publication is the house organ of the Leica Historical Society of America and is exclusively devoted to provide Leica collectors with all new data on past Leica equipment or personalities. Published quarterly. Included in your membership; $10 per year.

Contemporary Magazine Articles on Photographic Collecting

Four magazines of the photographic field regularly run columns on aspects of photographic collecting that are of interest to the collector audience. The columns are:

"The Camera Collector" by Jason Schneider, a monthly feature in *Modern Photography* magazine.

"Time Exposure" by Eaton S. Lothrop, Jr., a six-times-a-year feature in *Popular Photography* magazine.

Articles by Norbert Nelson, a monthly feature in *Camera 35* magazine.

Irregularly appearing articles by Carole G. Honigsfeld and Bruce C. Vaughn in *PSA Journal*, which is published by the Photographic Society of America, 2005 Walnut Street, Philadelphia, Penna. 19103.

Catalogues of Mail-Order Auctions

Collectors of photographica who wish to participate in mail-order auctions should acquire the occasionally published catalogues from these auction centers:

Americana Mail Auctions, 10 Lilian Road Ext., Framingham, Massachusetts 01701

Montreal Book Auctions, Ltd., 1529 Sherbrooke Street West, Montreal, Canada

George M. Rinsland, 4015 Kilmer Avenue, Allentown, Pennsylvania 18104

Sotheby Parke Bernet Galleries, 910 Madison Avenue, New York, New York 10021

Sotheby Parke Bernet Galleries, 34-35 New Bond Street, London W1A2AA England

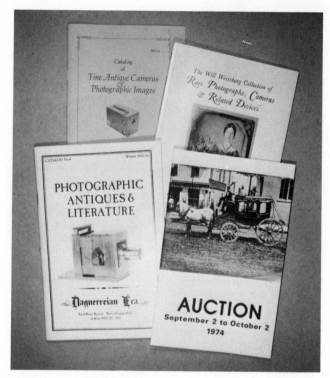

Auctions and sales conducted by mail by specialist dealers in antique photographic items are periodically announced in catalogues which then become valuable reference guides and data sources.

Serving the Collector of Images

A number of dealers in American graphics have developed a substantial operation in display and sales of American photographic images, first as a supplement, then as the mainstay of gallery operations, which are important sources for collectors of photographic images.

The well-known Witkin (243 East 60th Street, N.Y.C., 10022) and Neikrug (224 East 68th Street, N.Y.C., 10021) galleries in New York City and the mail-order–sales operation by George R. Rinhart of Litchfield, Connecticut in the East or by Bruce Duncan Galleries (303 Happ Road, Northfield, Ill. 60093) and Cliff Krainik (P.O. Drawer 1234, Arlington Heights, Ill. 60006) in the Midwest are examples of such important centers.

The collector of stereo images should be aware of the Lightfoot Collection (11 Court Drive, Huntington Station, N.Y. 11746).

In addition, these dealers issue catalogues that are available by mail:

Classic Photo Apparatus, P.O. Box 161, Simsbury, Connecticut 06070

Daguerreian Era, Pawlet, Vermont 05761

Howard C. Daitz, P.O. Box 530, Old Chelsea Station, New York, New York 10011

Lewis G. Lehr, 45 East 85th Street, New York, New York 10028

Allen and Hilary Weiner, 392 Central Park West, New York, New York 10025

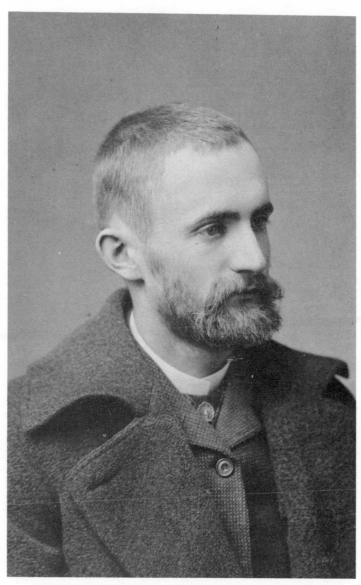

Cabinet photo of George Eastman in 1882 is imprinted: "Negative by Mr. J. H. Kent, Rochester, N.Y.; Made on Eastman's Special Dry Plate." Kent was an early stockholder. *(From the collection of Alfred Lowenherz)*

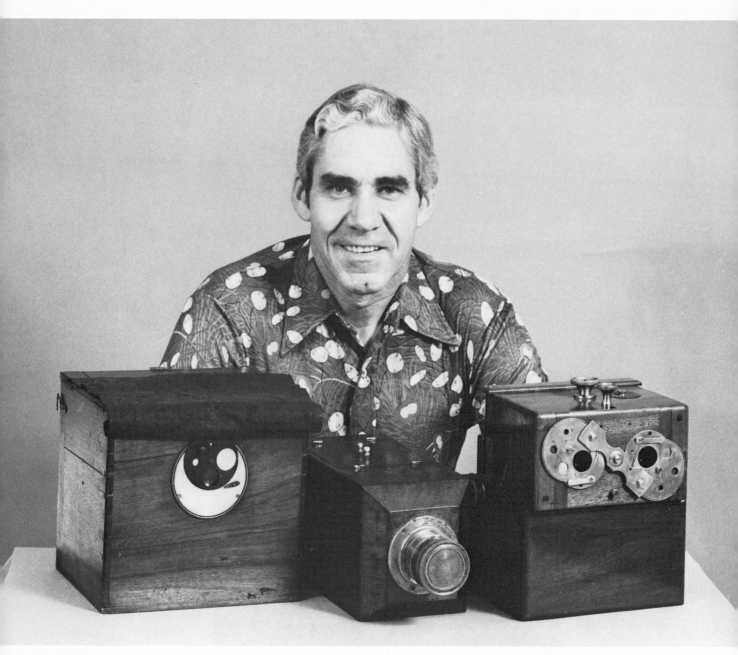

Matthew R. Isenberg and some of his major Daguerrean era items. *(Photograph by Michele Fleisher)*

14
Meet the Collectors

Until 1968, there was one photographic society in the United States (in fact, in the world) centering its interest in the equipment aspect of photography, and that was a group of engineers and camera designers of the photographic companies in Rochester, New York. If there were other collectors of photographica, no one knew of them, and consequently, they found a wide-open opportunity to accumulate literally unwanted treasures for the asking.

But in 1968, when a collector of cameras who was a novice historian announced in the photographic press that there would be a meeting of collectors on the campus of Ohio State University in Columbus, to his delight and surprise collectors drove, flew, or thumbed rides to come for the conclave. Collectors were meeting each other, and they liked what they saw. They promised to keep in touch, and the mails and phones were the first avenues. Not content with occasional contact, they met in small groups in New York; Chicago; Columbus; Riverside, California; and formal organizations resulted.

Those who have attempted to compile lists of known major collectors suggest that somewhere between 5,000 and 10,000 individuals are now collecting cameras, books, images, or something else related to photography.

They were doctors, lawyers, schoolteachers, and professional or amateur photographers. They were shopkeepers and students, men and women. In the main, they seem to have more education than a group their own size seated at a ball game; and they probably have more ready cash for their avocation, since camera collecting is on the whole more costly per year than bowling, fishing, or Sunday painting.

In the following pages we present a cross section of collectors, who are presented because of such reasons as their total dedication to photography (one has a son named after Mathew Brady, for example) or for their ability to define a specialty within the broad panorama of the photographic field (such as a man who collects only numismatically related photographica). I am pleased to number many of these collectors as friends. With others I have never crossed photographic paths; but all have known of each other through the pages of the newsletters and publications of the collecting societies.

Some of the collectors presented in these pages have giant collections (more than two thousand individual, catalogued items); others number their collection in a few dozens of examples of their field of interest. Because their diversity in age, range of interests, and dedication are such a patchwork quilt of colors and patterns, we take great pride in asking you to "meet the collectors."

AMERICA'S MOST REMARKABLE COLLECTOR

Matt Isenberg has become a household name in the field of photographic collecting, not only for having built what is possibly the most significant private collection in the United States, but because he has been willing to share his vast knowledge with collectors across the country.

Within the last five years, he organized in his two-hundred-year-old suburban Connecticut home, displays of early equipment, a fine reference library, and a vast assortment of ephemera relating to nineteenth-century photography. His specialty collection-within-a-collection centers around the first twenty years of photography and is comparable to that of any major museum collection in the world. Almost one dozen Daguerrean cameras and nearly two dozen wet-plate cameras, plus related equipment claim chosen vantage points in his living room.

The vast collection, assembled largely in the United States, now includes key cameras from every decade including multi-lens cameras, detective cameras, early color equipment, the entire progression of Leica cameras, and most of the "black-and-whites," as he calls the twentieth-century leather and chrome cameras.

The history of cameras and their manufacturers is as important to Isenberg as the equipment itself. Not content with the available literature in the United States, he undertook an extended visit to Europe to research original source documentation. With this material as a base, he has built one of the world's finest libraries on the subject of both European and American Daguerrean equipment, manufacturers, and photographers.

Says Isenberg, "Large or small, expensive or a bargain, buy things that tell the story of photo history if you really want to enjoy your collection over many years."

A SLEUTH OF THE DETECTIVE CAMERA ERA

After Mike Kessler had been collecting cameras for over eight years, he settled on his specialty: collecting only the finest examples of the pre-1900 cameras and their related literature. His emphasis was on the box or detective camera. But when friends ask why his collection also includes choice examples of folding plate cameras with bellows, Kessler explains that his background as a graphic designer didn't allow him to overlook the beauty of polished woods and gleaming brass.

The Kessler collection is made up of about 125 choice pieces. Says Kessler, "Although there are many collections with far more cameras, I would rather have the select (even if costly) few items for their unique character or historic role in equipment development." His earliest camera is one from the Daguerrean era, an American chamfered box-style Daguerreotype camera, complete with tripod. There are several wet-plate items, including an English and an American stereo camera, both dating from the 1860s. He also has a much-sought Dubroni.

The vast majority of Kessler's items are dry-plate hand-held cameras dating from 1883 to 1900. These include the Anthony Climax, the Tom Thumb, Schmid, Kamarette, Genie, Tisdell, Waterbury, and Hawk-Eye. From Europe he has the rare Photosphere and the Kinegraph.

Says Mike: "I have all but two of the String-Set Kodaks, including an original. It is possible that my eight Wing cameras represent the largest assortment of different Wing cameras in a single collection. The most treasured of these is a four-lens studio camera dating from the late 1860s. It is documented to be the personal instrument of Simon Wing himself."

EUROPE'S NO. 1 COLLECTOR

Michel Auer, now a resident of both France and Switzerland, in earlier days started his photographic career in Geneva, where he operated a major photographic establishment in the photofinishing and photomural business.

The fascination with the photographic field's earliest days captured his imagination in 1961. Within ten years, traveling all over Europe, he assembled a four-thousand-piece collection including some of the most rare items in photography. His first catalogue (1972, printed in French and English) of nearly one thousand of his own cameras was acquired by collectors all over the world as Auer made friends with whom he could swap items and share early-camera lore. This catalogue's scope has not since been equaled by any other collector.

A true student and a voracious collector of information about the early equipment, its owners, and makers have made this most knowledgeable

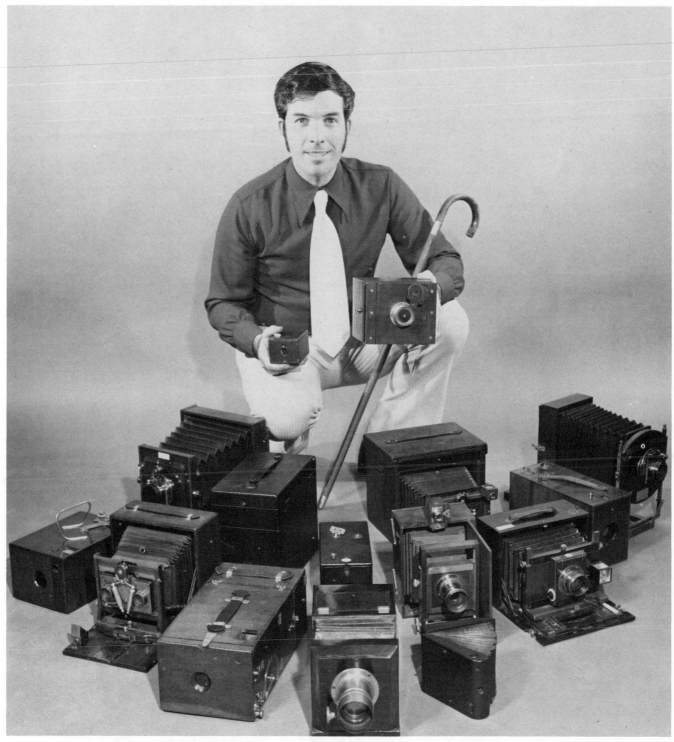

Mike Kessler holds (in his left hand) a camera once the property of Thomas Alva Edison. In his right hand is an 1895 Pocket Kodak, Eastman's first miniature. *(Photograph by Darrell Dearmore)*

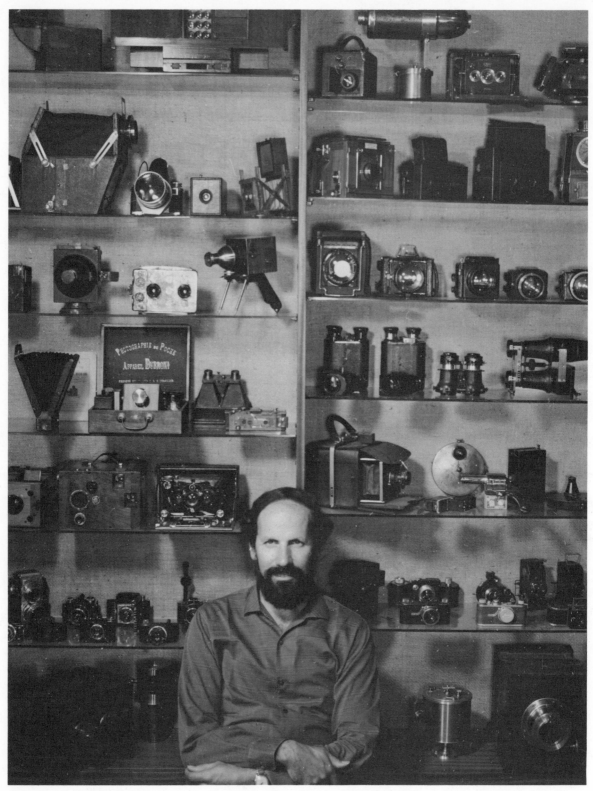

Michel Auer of Europe.

and vastly successful collector possibly the world's (and surely Europe's) foremost collector of photographica. His numerous visits to the U.S. have been rich with legendary moments for all collectors he meets.

Auer has a comfortable familiarity with unusual cameras of the 1850s and 1860s that most Americans will never see and which few books will reflect. A major section of his collection has become the basis for one of the largest of Europe's museums of photography (see Appendix F, "Photographica Museums"). He advises beginners in collecting: "Seek quality, not quantity; and pay the price, even a high one, since it is possible that you have the find of a lifetime."

AMERICA'S BEST-KNOWN PHOTOGRAPHIC COLLECTOR/HISTORIAN

Eaton S. Lothrop, Jr., is a schoolteacher by profession and has built a simultaneous "second life" as a student. He studies photographic history to the point where he has a working familiarity with the early names of cameras, companies, photographers, and related accessories that is unmatched among his collector contemporaries.

In order to bring some of this information to other collectors and groups around the country, Lothrop single-handedly created and published *The Photographic Collector's Newsletter*, issued as time has permitted but approximately quarterly since 1969. With the friends he made in the field as he visited collector groups (where he was often the speaker at meetings or photographica fairs on such subjects as the American detective cameras or the writing of his book, *A Century of Cameras*, which details the landmark cameras in the collection at the George Eastman House), Lothrop helped launch the Photographic Historical Society of America, and he was elected the group's first president. Earlier he became active in the leadership of the collecting/history group in the New York area.

Lothrop's column, "Time Exposure," is published on a bi-monthly basis in the largest photographic magazine in the world, *Popular Photography*, and in interesting articles, he has traced the development of major groups of early but long-forgotten cameras and the amusing anecdotes and legends that accompany these hardly-known items of the photographic past.

Lothrop began his now-mammoth collection of box cameras on a cross-county tour at a time when 25¢ and 50¢ bought cameras in thrift shops and

Eaton S. Lothrop, Jr. *(Photograph by N. M. Graver)*

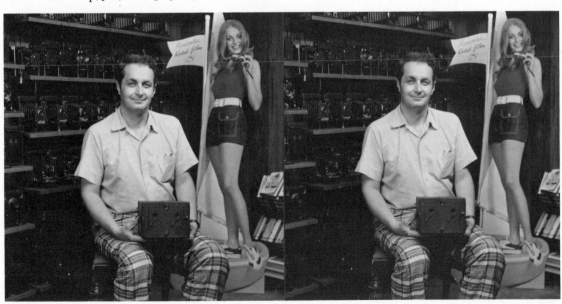

junk stores. He found numerous treasures, which have been the basis for many Lothrop articles and presentations. His interest in photography is very broad, and he has collected a Daguerreotype camera of the earliest period and landmark cameras of the Kodak line and others that are displayed in cabinets in the Brooklyn, New York, living room of the Lothrop family.

A BURNING INTEREST IN THE NINETEENTH CENTURY

If Allen Weiner was not the finest trout fisherman in America, he and his wife, Hilary, would probably not be living in New York City off sumptuous Central Park West amidst the splendor of nineteenth-century photographica. Their apartment is literally a live-in museum of the Victorian past of Daguerrean studios and Victorian parlors.

Weiner needed photos to show friends exactly the kind of insects that make the best trout lures; someone recommended a Nikon, and Weiner began to study photography. A year later, in 1970, when he should have been making efforts to locate another job as a schoolteacher, he sat in on the now famous Strober Auction at the Sotheby Parke Bernet Galleries in New York. He bought a Kodak Bantam Special (the Walter Dorwin Teague–designed miniature folding camera) for $100. With this purchase a collector was born.

His second camera was a Valentine's Day gift from his wife a few weeks later: a triple-extension–bellows German folding plate camera of the 1920s. Now both cameras are gone to other collectors in trades, and the Weiners are known coast to coast as the publishers of a quarterly catalogue loaded with photographic items.

The Weiners search for the nineteenth century in the flea markets, antique shops, and other possible sources of photographic hardware or images. They go to auctions; they visit old studios. Their best discovery to date was all of the equipment of a wet-plate studio (1855–1875), which started with a purchase at 3:00 A.M. by flashlight at the now-famous Brimfield, Massachusetts, weekend flea markets.

Today their home is a private museum and also

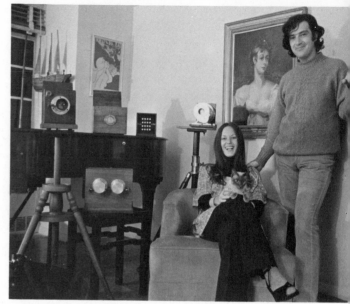

Allen and Hilary Weiner. (*Photograph by N. M. Graver*)

the center for endless mail, phone calls, and package exchanges, which have become their life. America lost a schoolteacher and gained a successful photographic-history sleuth.

The Weiners have collected items for as little as 50¢ (stereo cards), but also up into the thousands of dollars for Daguerrean equipment. If it's Victorian or earlier, an optical-effects toy or a rare studio item (such as a camera which took sixteen tiny tintypes in a single exposure), either the Weiners have it or will know how and where to find it for you.

A COLLECTOR OF TIN (TYPE) SOLDIERS

In any handful of tintypes, a picture of the Zouave of the Civil War in full military regalia stands out as no other. With gun and bayonet capturing the eye, with the military uniform establishing the time and place, military portraits are a special standout. For photographer Herb Peck, Jr., of Nashville, Tennessee, they hold a fascination that has kept him traipsing like an army scout in endless pursuit of the man in uniform, hidden amid endless unidentified portraits in closed Daguerrean

206

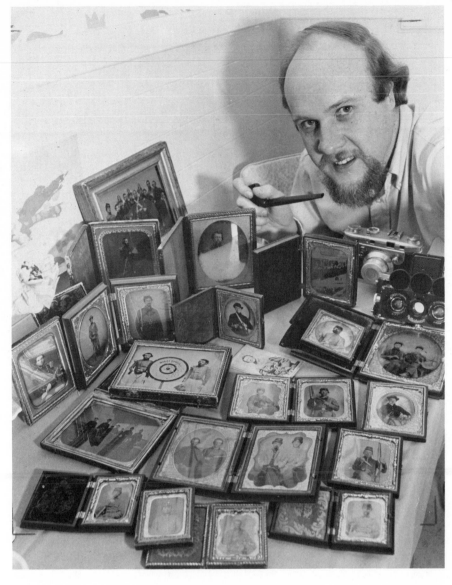

Herb Peck, Jr., Nashville, Tennessee.

gutta-percha cases or in photo albums of tintypes.

Peck started his search for the military past with weapon collecting as a youngster. But today, he collects the soldiers—their images, that is. Some of his "finds" go back to the period before the Civil War. One whole-plate ambrotype (6½ by 8½ inches) depicts a group of six firemen and four militiamen. A half-plate view of two Alabama cadets standing by a large bull's-eye target pierced with musketball holes is another, relates Peck in describing choice specimens from his collection.

In his endless search for images, Peck continually locates other photographica; he invariably acquires these and brings them to photographica fairs where he can trade cameras, magazines, catalogues, and other items of interest with the general collector who just might have one more soldier boy in uniform.

A DAGUERREAN-JEWELRY COLLECTOR

Among the most interesting items of photographica are the photographic jewelry of the Daguerrean era. While most Americans have seen photographs in brooches and round or heart-shaped lockets, few are aware that tiny Daguerrean images were set by jewelers of the 1840s and 1850s into rings, cuff links, watch-case covers, bracelet charms, watch-fob charms, and in other items of gold.

Inevitably, these items come into the hands of the antique dealers in Victorian jewelry. Shirley Sprung of Teaneck, New Jersey, is known among these dealers as someone who will appreciate their historic value. She makes it her business to be friendly with these dealers as part of her own business in the antiques field, where she is a specialist in the American silverware of that same period.

Since so few dealers know the difference between one kind of tiny photograph and another, Sprung makes certain that other dealers know that if there is a photograph in a precious-metal setting, she is apt to buy it. If these same dealers happen to have interesting Daguerrean portraits or outdoor

Shirley Sprung, Daguerrean jewelry specialist.

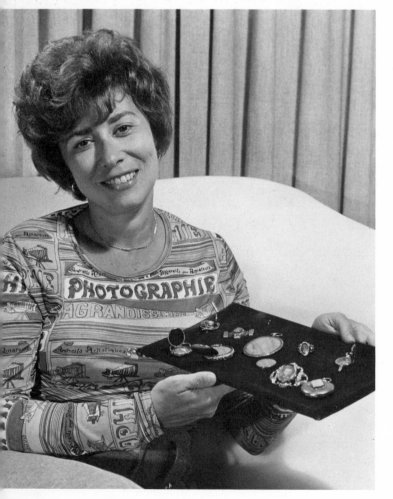

scenes, or even the thermoplastic protective cases of the period, she adds one or two more items to the growing image collection which has become a major element of the Sprung family interest in photography's early days. The Sprungs make it a point to research the portraits where there are clues to personality identification; a portrait of the nineteenth-century actor Edwin Forrest and one of an early mayor of New York City are among their "finds."

For over five years, Sprung has been the driving force behind the semiannual fairs of the Photographic Historical Society of New York. A collector in her own right, she is respected by other collectors who have learned to rely upon her judgment and information on little-known corners of the photographic scene.

HE STUMBLED UPON THE EARLIEST COMPLETE DAGUERREOTYPE SYSTEM

Jerry Sprung for many years has been a fine amateur photographer with a keen eye for the dramatic detail that one can capture with a telelens or in an ultra close-up. Thus, when the idea of collecting cameras occurred to Sprung, it was with an eye to the interesting smaller cameras of the twentieth century. He found particular delight in the meticulously made all-wood cameras of Germany and England that in folding plate designs are known as the tropical cameras. With honey-colored woods and rich, red leathers, they are handsome display items.

Finding unusual cameras became almost a weekly occurrence when his wife began to share her husband's interest in locating early photographica. But it is Sprung's delight that on a tour by himself he noted a camera on a tripod in the window of an antique-armaments shop just outside New York City. The next day the ensemble which the shop identified as a "Civil War" camera was his. He had located the earliest dated (1842), complete, portable Daguerreotype system. The camera, unipod, sensitizing box, mercury chamber, and holders are a perfect example of the earliest type of American-made equipment. Seals on the

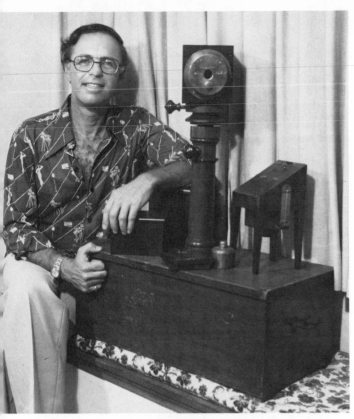

Jerry Sprung with his Butler Daguerreotype camera, ca. 1842.

chest in which it was originally maintained attest to its having been on display at the 1933 Chicago Century of Progress World's Fair. Now visiting collectors and historians from across America and from Europe make a stop at the Sprung home for the chance to see such a system at first hand.

Sprung has long been an officer of the Photographic Historical Society of New York and is well known as a speaker on the equipment aspect of photographic history at camera clubs and social groups in New Jersey and New York City.

PHOTO HISTORY COMBINED WITH COIN COLLECTING

Professional photographer Nicholas M. Graver traces the beginning of his interest in photographic history and collecting to 1967, but his coin collecting dates from his youth. Naturally, one interest began to merge with another. Although he has built a fine collection of photographic literature,

equipment, images, and miscellany of the photographic art, among his collector friends, he is known for his endless curiosity about the art and business of photography as depicted in medals and tokens.

Nicholas M. Graver. (*Photograph by Marilyn A. Graver*)

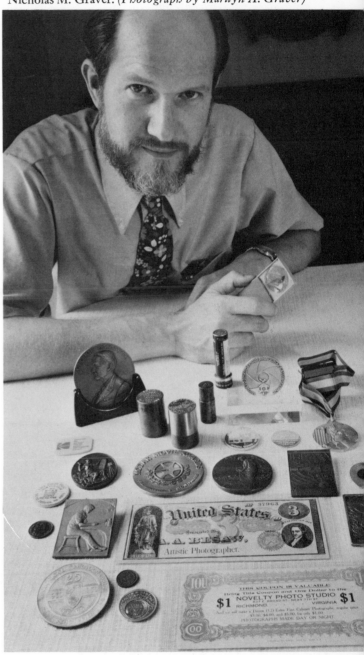

In 1972, Graver came to New York City from his Rochester home to give a special presentation at a weekend seminar of photographic historians on the theme of photographic numismatics. His talk pointed out that photographic salons issued business tokens, that special medals were awarded to prizewinners in photo contests, that a variety of companies honored special occasions in the field of photography with further medallic creations, and that all of these are found at coin conventions and in coin dealer shops, if not in trays at antique shops.

When he can, Graver travels to fairs. Here he meets other collectors, and he often takes stereo photographs in black and white, which he mails to the collectors met on these occasions. It has become a point of pride among collectors to be able to show a Graver-made stereo card to other collectors. He is a frequent contributor to the publications of the various photographic historical societies in which he enjoys membership.

A PUBLISHER OF PHOTOGRAPHICA

John and Valerie Craig started as collectors of interesting cameras, a hobby that grew logically out of a lifetime interest and profession in photography. Becoming the world's largest reprint publisher of materials relating to early photography was an entirely different matter.

Like many collectors, John had located instruction booklets for a variety of cameras and other publications on photography at various flea markets and in antique shops and bookstores. At first he tried providing a copy to a friend here and another one there. It was after he had formed his antique camera effort under the name of Classic Photographic Apparatus in a small city in central Connecticut that he decided that he could provide a major service to collectors everywhere by a concerted effort to re-create hard-to-find catalogues, instruction booklets, and manufacturer data sheets on a broad variety of American and European cameras.

In the course of distributing these items across America and with his interest in reproduction processes, the Craigs volunteered to assist with preparation of a scholarly quarterly on photographic his-

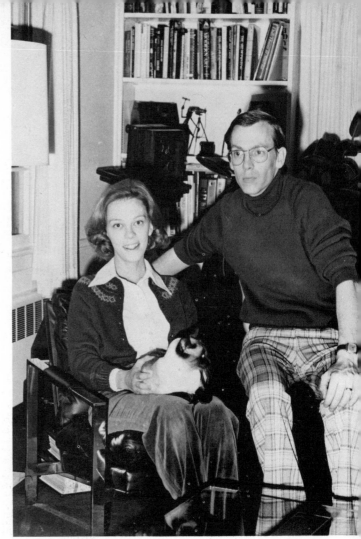

John and Valerie Craig.

tory, during the founding of the national organization of collectors. Today *Northlight* is well known to collectors as a vital source of background and history on photographers and their equipment.

In addition to playing a leading role in the national Photographic Historical Society of America, the Craigs have been key figures in the New England Photographic Historical Society, providing both the energy and organizational know-how that has sparked growth of the collecting group in greater New England.

AMERICANA COLLECTION

John Dobran is an advertising/marketing executive who owns a suburban Connecticut home that started out as a trim cottage amid the trees and shrubs of a shady lane. No more; Dobran's trips to

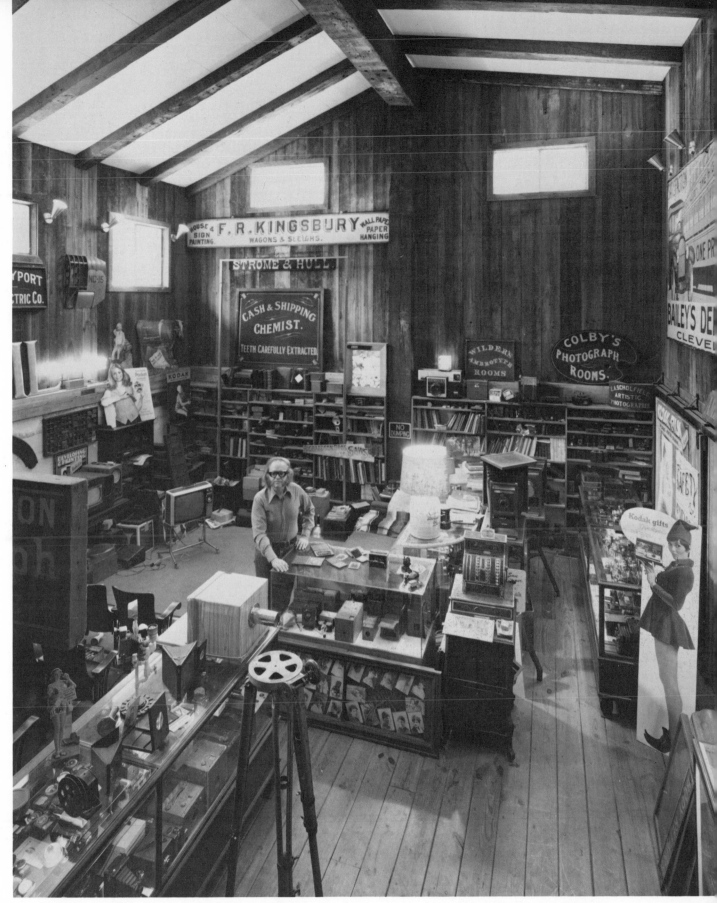

John Dobran, Connecticut, collector of Americana and photographica. *(Photograph by Donald Roberts)*

antique shops and flea markets, where he acquired an endless fascination for the signs and wall placards of the nineteenth century, turned his home into a museum-like studio that is filled today with store showcases laden with every evidence of America's photographic past. The living room is a display center for an entire Victorian photographer's studio, and other cases on walls and in hallways are rich with books, images, and display items.

"I'm living with what I love," says Dobran of his collection. Most types of cameras, viewers, studio accessories, frames, wall posters, plus curiosities like a machine-gun camera and a fifteen-foot outdoor photographer's sign are represented in the vast collection.

"The way to build a collection is to travel. It won't come to you; you must go to it," says Dobran. Within a five-state area, he knows where all flea markets and antique shows are being held. He makes it a point to get to as many as his schedule permits. He has been known to be at three shows in a single day, even if they are located in cities one hundred miles apart.

Cyril Permutt, England's foremost stereo collector. (*Photoraph by* Hendon Times, *London*)

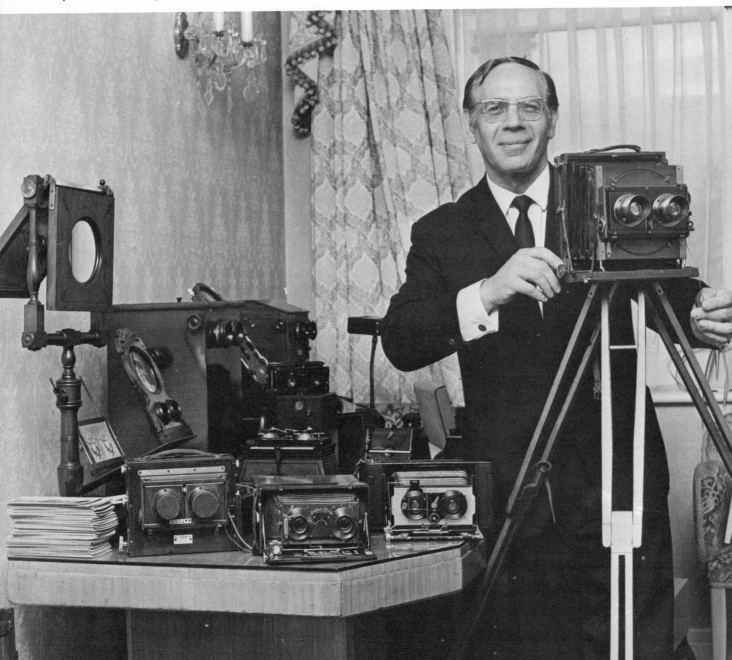

ENGLAND'S MR. STEREO

In an age of specialists, Cyril Permutt of England is a natural standout. He sees double; he collects double: He is a specialist in the stereo cameras of the past.

Though stereo viewing as a phenomenon was not truly understood until the nineteenth century, his collection of early stereo-related items dates back to a device ca. 1750. His earliest stereo camera dates back to the 1860s, the beginning of the vast sweep of interest in the three-dimensional photograph that swept the world.

Collecting the cameras is only a part of the history of photography. Permutt, naturally, also collects stereo slides and has made diligent efforts to identify the early photographers who made them. As contemporary stereo cameras appear, he acquires an example of each to maintain a total collection, one which will show the new and the old. The result of all this diligent effort is that he is credited with being the owner of one of the finest camera collections in Britain.

He is a founder member of the Historical Group of the Royal Photographic Society and was one of the earliest overseas members of the Photographic Historical Society of New York. Items from the Permutt collection are regularly shown in exhibitions, in such museums, as the Fox Talbot Museum (see Appendix F, "Museums of Photography Abroad"), and on television. He is the author of the book *Collecting Old Cameras*, a planned addition to the photographic library of the English collector.

Permutt is quick to point out: "The photograph we know is phasing away before the ultimate impact of holography, which uses laser beams. Cameras as we know them today will slowly disappear. Now is the time to find them and care for them before they are all lost."

HIS FIRST CAMERA CAME FROM THE TRENCHES OF WORLD WAR I

In the 1890s, the father of Alfred Lowenherz, vice-president of the Camera Club of New York (the club of Alfred Stieglitz), was a professional photographer in Germany; it was natural that as a drafted soldier in the Kaiser's army in World War I he would carry a pocketable camera with him into the trenches.

Today Lowenherz, a retired American businessman and a founder of the Photographic Historical Society of New York, is an avid collector of cameras. His collection's cornerstone is that 4.5-by-6-centimeter pocket camera that had become part of the family's heritage when in the 1920s his father at last joined the family in the U.S., almost 30 years after the Lowenherz clan took root in America.

The Lowenherz collection centers about a group of miniature folding plate cameras. Along with books, literature, and pamphlets, all meticulously filed for reference, Lowenherz maintains a personal workshop in his home, which has been the joy of numerous collectors who know that he can't resist the challenge of re-creating a lost camera part. One of the hardest to find of all of landmark-camera lore is the winding key for the Kodak #2 and #3. Lowenherz's reproductions of these keys have brought joy to collectors across the country who had despaired of ever seeing the camera in its complete state.

"NEVER PASS UP AN ITEM"

Once a commercial-fashion photographer, and more recently an instructor in photography at the army signal school and a studio owner in New Jersey, Thom Hindle has enjoyed a varied career in photography.

As a collector Thom frequently participates at photo fairs around the country and he has run several museum exhibits. He recently gained national recognition through an article featured in *Yankee Magazine*. In another article about him, which appeared in the *Graphic Antiquarian*, Thom cited a number of early Kodak cameras such as the No.2 string set, Panoramics (which he uses) and wood and brass plate cameras as favorites. A special favorite is his ¼-plate Daguerrean camera which he found on his honeymoon. (Thom and Mira were married by their close friend and fellow collector, Rev. Steve Shuart). Thom's collection consists of mostly pre-1910 items and includes a few fine images, darkroom and flash apparatus and literature. Some early pieces are his S. Wing multiple

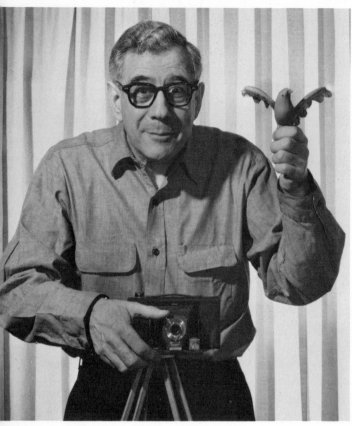

Alfred Lowenherz. His collection started with a family camera.

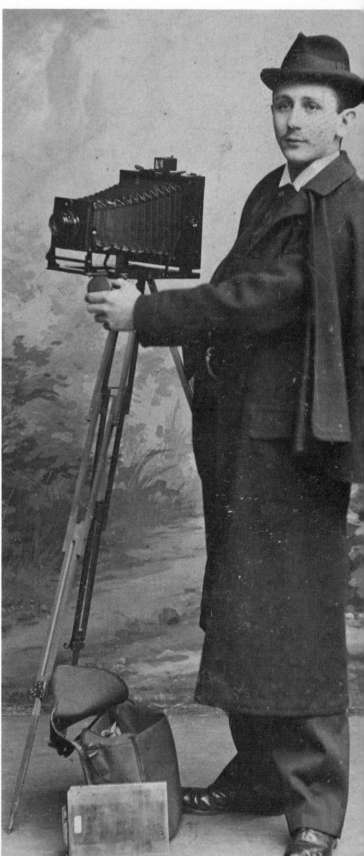

The photographer-father who brought the Lowenherz family and the Tell camera to America.

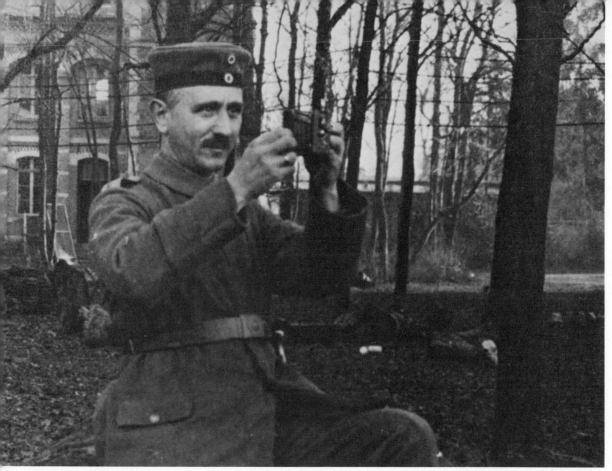

The Tell folding camera in the hands of soldier-father.

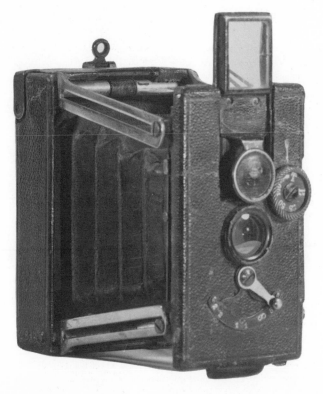

4½-by-6-cm Tell folding camera, which saw duty in World War I trenches.

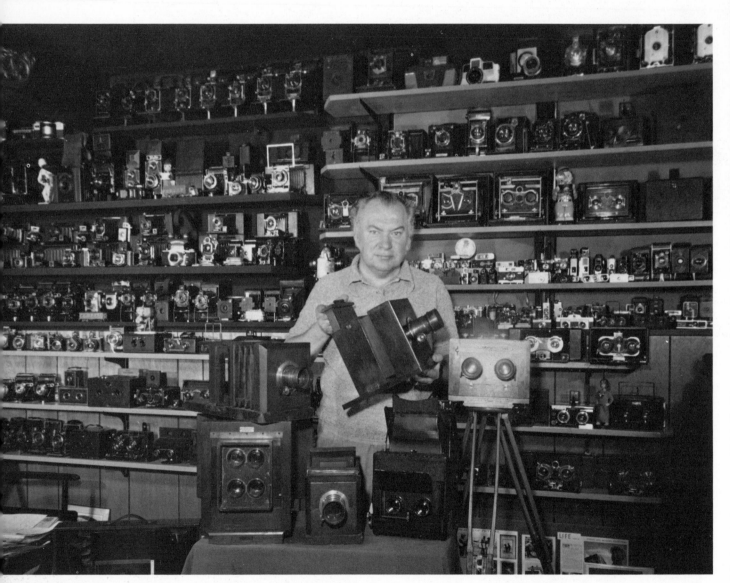

A camera from his youth started the John Kowalak collection.

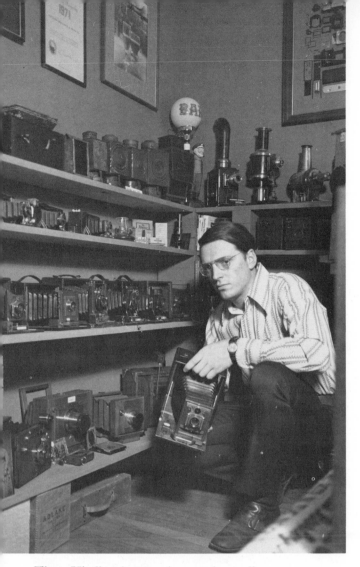

Thom Hindle; photographer–teacher–collector.

camera, a Blair Kamaret, Nodark, Expo and Ticka watch cameras, a #2 Stereo Kodak box and viewers.

When he was asked why he had become a collector, Hindle found it easy to answer: "It's my way of showing some appreciation to the photographic pioneers who made photography possible and who enabled me to have such a fine profession." His advice to new collectors: "Never pass up an item you want, thinking you'll find another or go back later—you never do."

AN ENDLESS SEARCHER
FOR THE 1840'S

Cliff and Michele Krainik of Arlington Heights, Illinois, are deeply involved in America's photographic past. A visit to their home—rich with the art of Daguerreotypy and other evidences of the early photographic art on walls, tables, shelves, everywhere—is proof of their commitment to their love of photographic lore. Indeed, their son is named Matthew Brady Krainik, after the famed Civil War photographer.

The Krainiks share the search for historic images, and they have located at one time or another such important examples of early photography as an 1851 full-plate (6½-by-8½-inch) view of Sacramento, California, plus scenes of California's "fortyniners" at work. They have assembled an impres-

Left: Matthew Brady Krainik; his father and mother are dedicated to collecting items from the 1840s. (*Photograph by B. F. Stein*)

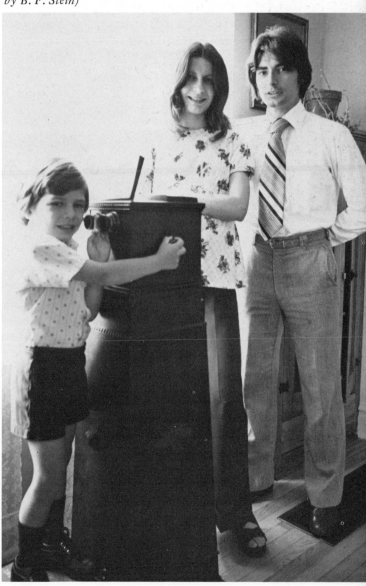

sive army of military personages in the uniforms of the period.

"Daguerreotypes come in all sizes," says Cliff, "and we have managed to acquire examples as small as seven sixteenths of an inch up to the largest one any of our collector friends have ever seen: an eleven-by-fourteen-inch plate which was created at the graduation ceremony of the Rutger's Female Institute." Locating unusual and often extremely rare images has become such an active business that he organized his efforts in selling these many items under the catch-all name of Graphic Antiquity, a venture he shares with Michele.

Studying the Daguerreotype era in an organized manner has led to Krainik's authorship of a directory of over five hundred Daguerrean artists, which he has been expanding with the help of other collectors. He helped to found and is active in the Chicago Photographic Collector's Society. He is editor of the group's quarterly journal, *By Daylight*.

His scholarly and careful approach to the history of photography led to his contributing editorship on *The New Daguerreian Journal* and as a writer on photographic-history–related subjects for the publications in the antiques field, the *Chicago Tribune Magazine*, and in *Graphic Antiquarian*. In 1974, he was the recipient of the Donelson Award from the University of the Pacific, Stockton, California, for outstanding excellence in writing and researching in American history. It was in recognition of his effort in creating a concise biography of John Plumbe, Jr., a pioneer American photographer.

CINE COLLECTOR

As an eight-year-old, Samuel K. Rubin, today a furniture and appliance dealer in Indiana, Pennsylvania, saw the film *The Lost World*. Years later, when he saw this film advertised in a photography magazine, he bought it—and now he owns far more than one hundred of such silent-screen classics and the related items of motion-picture photographica.

Occasional evenings with friends and family are filled with the derring-do adventures of Lon

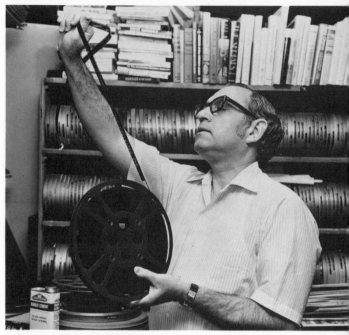

Samuel K. Rubin collects photographs of galloping cowboys and silent-film queens.

Chaney and Douglas Fairbanks; his guests once again laugh at the misadventures of Charles Chaplin and suffer the pangs of love of Lillian Gish. Cowboys William S. Hart and Hoot Gibson leave a hoofprint trail across his home movie screen.

His love for these cine gems led him to correspondence with other collectors. It was only natural that he used his spare time in 1962 to create a six-page newsletter, which has grown to today's sixty-four-page quarterly tabloid newspaper *Classic Film Collector* (see Chapter 13, "Collecting Photographica," Contemporary Publications on Collecting and Antiques). It is eagerly awaited by film collectors of silent and sound movies in 8 mm and 16 mm and even in the European size, 9.5 mm.

Among problems in building such collections are the ownership rights of early films. Some owned outright by the studios have only recently been released for the home market and are sold to collectors by distributors across the country, says Rubin. Others are owned by the actors or actresses. Many may be legally reproduced as their twenty-eight-year copyright expires; these are sold by about a dozen film reprint houses.

"Mary Pickford," a Rubin favorite, "retained the title to her later movies, so they're not available to collectors. Harold Lloyd, before he died, preferred showing his own movies himself, and he toured with them to college campuses." Time-Life recently acquired rights to the Lloyd films and plans to make these available to the film-collector public.

Film collectors, says Rubin, seek the movie photos, the outdoor posters, the window cards, and the other film promotion materials that assure proper dating of the film and identification of the cast members, cameramen, producers, and others involved in the promotion. Studying these materi-als is an area of photography's history that has more than its share of amateur aficionados. Thousands, says Rubin.

Sharing their hobby with folks in hospitals and old-age centers and youngsters (of all ages), film collectors are actively involved in a living history, made all the more interesting by the editorial and publishing efforts of the small-town Pennsylvania publisher.

MIDWEST COLLECTION

"If it once had a part in the taking or finishing of a picture, it goes into my collection," says Victor

Victor Wesselhoft prefers German 35-mm cameras but collects everything.

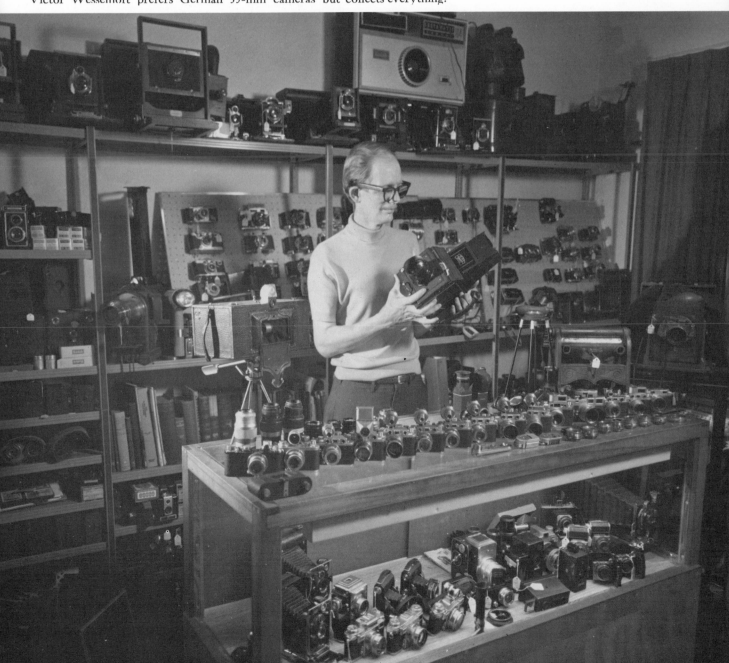

Wesselhoft of Elkhart, Indiana, a collector of everything photographic from the Daguerrean era to the modern period. Proof? Among his most choice pieces at one time were the modern classic twin-lens Zeiss Contaflex of the 1930s and the turn-of-the-century Panoram-Kodak, representing totally different worlds of photography.

Wesselhoft started as a collector in the early 1960s, and his hundreds of cameras acquired since then are proof of his dedication to this interest. He relates that the collecting started with a gift of an early 4-by-5-inch folding plate camera from a shop owner moving a camera store. Wesselhoft searched the barely available literature on early cameras and quickly learned that he had much to be curious about.

He points out that once having begun to share this interest with other collectors, he was not only gaining a knowledge of photography's first days, he was having fun.

Wesselhoft takes a special interest in the most modern period when 35-mm cameras began to change the world of photography. He owns a broad assortment of Leica and Contax cameras from Germany.

THE SHOPPING-BAG CAMERA BUYER

John Kowalak is a leading executive of the motion-picture industry whose work is the peculiar mix of quality control and deadline work that ought to leave a man weak by Friday, fit only for a weekend of rest before facing the grind on Monday morning. Instead, it's the ability to look forward to a weekend in photographic collecting that makes his hectic Monday-through-Friday a fine way to pass the week.

It all began a few years ago when Kowalak chanced upon the folding camera he remembered from his very early youth when photography was an element of any family picnic. He was intrigued by the fact of its existence in prime condition to this day. When he found another camera from the same period, it naturally had to join its brother on the back of the desk.

Now the Kowalak collection is pouring over thirty shelves in his suburban New Jersey home, a reflection of his wildly enthusiastic start as a collector "completely without discrimination," explains Kowalak. "If it was photographic, I wanted it. If it even looked like a camera and was really a cigarette lighter, I had to have it."

At some flea markets, he bought nearly every camera on any table, coming to be known as the shopping-bag camera buyer, loading up shopping bags with the photographic odds and ends one finds when one hundred to two hundred dealers share a department-store parking lot for a weekend. If the flea market was in another city or another state, well, that was reason for a Saturday drive and a new adventure of searching for photography's past.

It was at a Connecticut flea market that a farmer stopped the shopping-bag camera buyer. He proposed that Kowalak follow him to his farmhouse for "an old camera." When Kowalak saw the barn-dirty wooden boxes that were offered, he refused them at first. For $20 he insisted the farmer also include a stereo viewer. Only when he was home and had cleared away the mold and grime of over one hundred years did he learn that he had become part of the elite of camera collectors who own authentic Daguerrean-era equipment.

While his vast collection represents a broad variety of camera types and makes, he has made a minor specialty of learning about the cameras made by Kodak after the company had acquired the Stuttgart Nagel works in Germany. The varieties in such cameras as the Vollenda and the Pupille of the 1930s, German-made cameras bearing the Kodak label, is the one subject Kowalak probably knows more about than anything else photographic. Why Nagel cameras? You probably guessed that it was a camera from this plant that was the camera of his youth.

THE HONEYMOON COLLECTION

Marvin Kreisman started his collection of photographica with a box camera fifteen years ago. But it was on his honeymoon with Katrinka that this

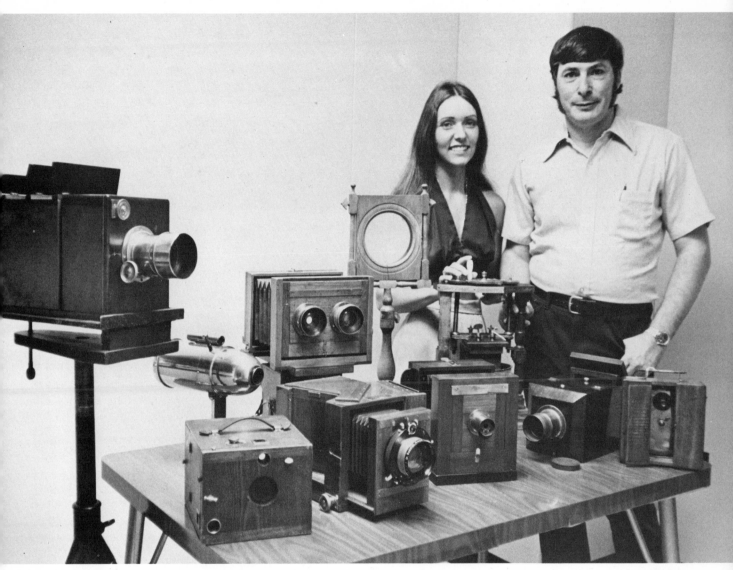

Marvin and Katrinka Kreisman amid their future museum.

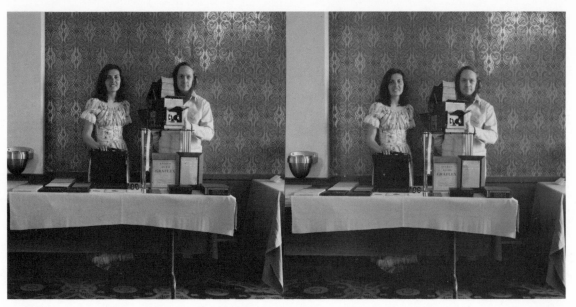

Paulette and Alan Cotter and a prizewinning display. *(Photograph by N. M. Graver)*

photographically involved couple began the intensive search that has ultimately led to the Kreisman collection of well over two thousand items of photographica.

All of it, they say, will be placed in the "Ringling House" at Baraboo, Wisconsin, which they recently purchased and will open as a Photograpic Museum in 1976. Previously, Marvin was head of the photography department at a private Missouri women's college.

Their most prized items are two Daguerrean cameras, ca. 1842 and 1850. One is the famed half-plate camera sold at auction in New York City in 1970 for over $2,500. Other key items in the collection are wet-plate–period cameras, eighteenth-century optical viewers, a variety of magic lanterns (see Glossary), and images in every style and size and process.

The Kreismans helped form the Midwest Photographic Historical Society, where with friends they organized meetings, fairs, and forums to explore the little-known byways of yesterday's cameraland. When the national organization of collectors was formed, Marvin assisted in its growth as a member of the Board of Directors and Katrinka was appointed as its librarian.

The thrust of the Kreisman collection is the emphasis on a chronological history of photography's development. Once their museum becomes a reality, they say, they are going on to the bigger challenge: to educate the public about the importance of photography in the past and future.

COLLECTORS OF COLLECTORS

Alan and Paulette Cotter of Santa Barbara, California, are the team who published three editions of the *National Directory of Camera Collectors*, a unique listing of over 1,000 known collectors around the world. This amazing directory has made it possible for collectors in an area to locate one another and for those who seek fellow specialists to make mail contact (see listing on page 195).

With a talent for organizing the endless detail necessary to conduct the massive project of locating and identifying some of the most active photographic collectors, it is no wonder that they are also one of the few teams who has created a valuable reference work on early photography; an illustrated catalogue of the most significant pre-1900 items in their own photographic collection—including images, viewers, cameras, magic lanterns and other ephemera of the photographica world.

They are active in the circle of collectors in California and in constant contact with members of the collecting fraternity across the country. An endless series of swaps, buys, and great finds have made the Cotter collection a basic collection of photography's development, one which includes a number of truly rare items and some incredibly fine examples of landmark cameras.

Intrigued by the Kombi of the 1890s, the Cotters made a reprint of an early Kombi camera catalogue, which makes it possible for everyone to understand the appeal and magic of a $3 tiny metal camera-viewer that had its own darkroom system, tripod, album, and a variety of other accessories. They also reprinted a unique catalogue of the Stirn Vest Concealed Detective Camera.

Few hobbies have the husband-wife teams that are so educationally and organizationally productive as camera collecting. The Cotters are an ideal example of this commitment to a boundless interest in expanding the collecting fraternity.

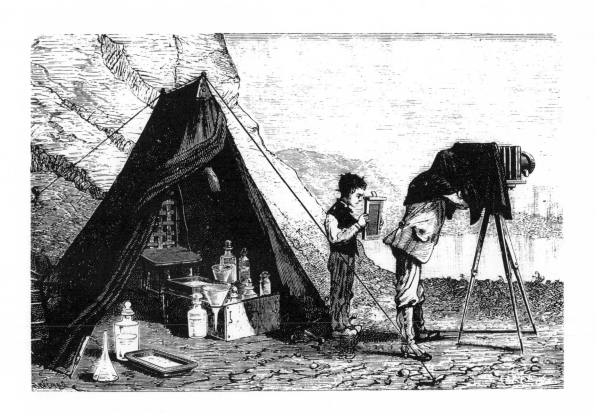

Appendixes

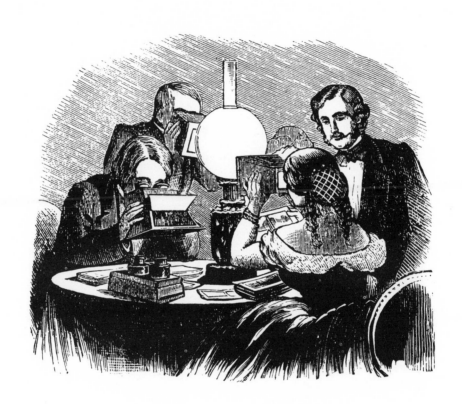

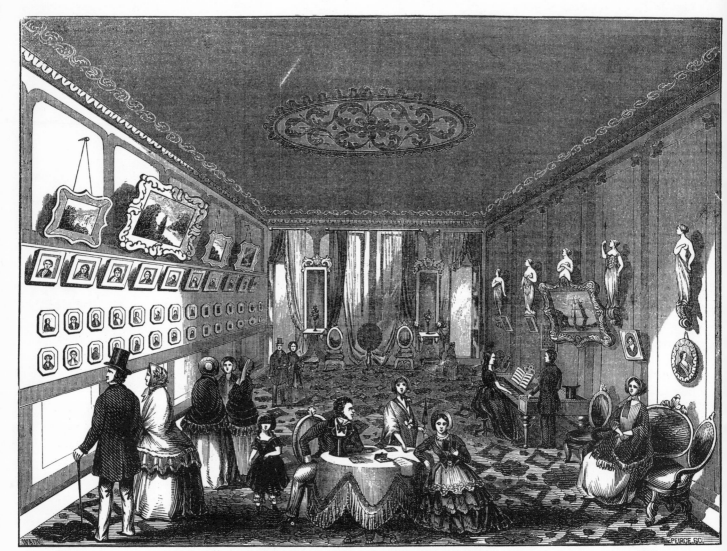

BALL'S GREAT DAGUERRIAN GALLERY OF THE WEST.   Cincinnati,   **1854.**

Appendix A
Chronology of
Photographic History

The history of photography spans the centuries, but generally within a sixty-year period between the French Revolution and the start of the Victorian age, it was the gentlemen scientists of England (William Henry Fox Talbot, Sir David Brewster, Rev. Joseph Bancroft Reade, Sir John Herschel) and the bourgeois intellectuals of France (Nicéphore Niépce, Hippolyte Bayard, Louis Jacques Mandé Daguerre) who made the breakthroughs that resulted in the form of photography as we know it today.

Daguerreotypy, whose flame glowed from just before 1839 to just about 1860, was a peculiarly French development, but the present system for negative and positive prints was the ultimately more versatile process contributed to the world by the English. In the years that followed, it was giant leaps on both sides of the English Channel that took photography up into the skies, into stereo for lifelike depth, into pictures with motion, into scientific and exploratory photography as the tool of all sciences and arts. This is all no surprise to anyone who has read the stirring document presented to the French Chamber of Deputies in 1839 to convince this body to award Daguerre and Niépce's son (heir to the development agreement between Daguerre and Niépce) French government lifelong pensions in return for their gift of photography to the world.

America's first telegraphist, Samuel F. B. Morse, was the first American to see a Daguerreotype (on an 1839 visit to Daguerre's establishment in Paris), though he was not the first American to take a Daguerreotype. News of the published process reached America by boat in the fall of 1839. By 1840, there were both photo galleries and portrait studios in New York City and also elsewhere in the world.

The development of the equipment to new sophisticated capabilities, the new chemistry, the improved lenses, and then the application of the photographic phenomenon to the only recently understood principles of stereoscopy were only to precede concepts of color photography and motion pictures by twenty or thirty years. In the postnatal stages, contributions by Americans and Germans were added to the prolific outpourings of the French and English practitioners.

The real breakthrough years for American participation in the maturation of photography may be said to begin with the successes of George Eastman. No other individual was to organize enough industrial strengths to improve photography to the degree that Eastman did until the emergence seventy years later of another science-minded American, Dr. E. H. Land. By the end of the 1960s, Land's Polaroid Corporation was selling more cameras over $100 than *all other* camera companies in the world (*Time*, June 26, 1972).

Between 20,000 and 30,000 different cameras were introduced after the Giroux of 1839. The following chronology lists both landmark and representative models. Unfortunately space does not permit the dating or listing of numerous items of picture-taking equipment, especially the novelty cameras that have for decades intrigued me personally.

The chronology could not have been assembled without the earlier painstaking investigations of a leading American collector with a special interest in the motion pictures, Louis S. Marcus of Long Island, New York. I wish to acknowledge use of such basic sources of information on the earliest days of photography from the histories developed by the scholarship of Helmut and Alison Gernsheim (*The History of Photography, 1685–1914*) and Beaumont Newhall (*The History of Photography from 1839 to the Present Day*) whose works are the standard references available to historians and collectors today.

Tenth century	Hassan Ibn Hassan (Alhazen), Arabian scholar, describes a camera obscura and comments on how the phenomenon assists observance of an eclipse. The optical principle was already established by Aristotle (384–322 B.C.)
1342	A camera obscura to view an eclipse is again described (in Hebrew) by a Jewish philosopher-mathematician of Arles, France.
ca. 1490	Leonardo da Vinci gives two descriptions of camera obscuras in the *Codex Atlanticus* (with diagram) and in *Manuscript D* (in Institut de France, Paris).
ca. 1558	Giambattista della Porta describes the camera obscura in greater detail and suggests its use as a drawing aid.
Seventeenth century	German schoolmaster J. C. Kohlans disguises a camera obscura in a book. (A book-disguised camera will be popular in Germany two hundred years later.)
1676	Johann Christoph Sturm describes a reflex-model portable camera obscura with a piece of oiled paper as a ground glass to which he added a hood to improve visibility. (The principle will be used in 1884 to make the world's first successfully marketed single-lens reflex camera.)
1671	Chérubin d'Orléans writes of his concepts of a binocular-vision (stereo) telescope and microscope.
September 4, 1694	Wilhelm Homberg exhibits an example of the blackening of silver exposed to sunlight.
December 19, 1694	Robert Hooke writes a description of a portable camera obscura. He calls it "a small picture box."
August 14, 1773	Josiah Wedgwood orders a camera obscura. (The Wedgwood family will enter history primarily as makers of tasteful pottery.)
June 24, 1775	A British patent (Number 1100) is granted to Sarah Harrington for drawing profiles by throwing a shadow of sunlight through an aperture.
November 18, 1787	The man most frequently honored as the father of photography, Louis Jacques Mandé Daguerre, is born.
ca. 1800	Images of leaves and ferns are obtained on leather sensitized with silver nitrate (an early photogram) by Thomas Wedgwood, son of Josiah.
June 1, 1802	Wedgewood's sun-print process (see Glossary) is published.
April 1, 1816	Nicéphore Niépce writes a letter in which he reviews the possibility of "making drawings by means of light."
May 9, 1816	Niépce makes his own camera, which he fits with a microscope lens.

July 19, 1822	Claude Niépce writes of his brother's apparent success in heliography (see Glossary), experiments with the light-sensitive bitumen of Judea, then commonly used in etching.
September 16, 1824	Nicéphore Niépce writes of his experiments with the camera obscura to his brother, Claude.
December 9, 1824	Peter Mark Roget reads a paper on his theories of the persistence of vision. (This is the phenomenon that will permit "motion pictures" sixty-five years later.)
June 4, 1827	Nicéphore Niépce writes to Daguerre requesting examples of photographic results.
October 25, 1829	Niépce writes of his need for a better camera to shorten exposure.
December 14, 1829	A ten-year partnership agreement is formed between N. Niépce and L. Daguerre for the purposes of heliography.
———— 1832	Sir Charles Wheatstone orders two stereoscopes to be built by a London optical house. One uses reflecting mirrors; the other functions with refracting prisms.
January 20, 1833	J. A. F. Plateau introduces the "Phenakistiscope" (see Glossary), a toylike instrument whose optical effect of animation depends on the persistence of vision. The zoetrope (see Glossary) follows in 1835 with moving images, also "seen" through slits.
February 1834	The first successful negatives on paper (photograms) are made in England by W. H. Fox Talbot; he has rediscovered Wedgwood's discovery. In 1835 he makes negatives on paper in a camera made for the purpose.
———— 1835	Daguerre produces an image after treatment of exposed silver iodide plate with mercury vapor.
June 1838	Announcement of the invention of the stereoscope by Sir Charles Wheatstone who reports to the Royal Society in England on the phenomenon of "binocular vision," successfully achieved with several forms of stereoscopic instruments.
January 7, 1839	François Arago in France announces that Daguerre has discovered a means to "fix" the photographic image. This is the first announcement of Daguerre's invention.
January 31, 1839	Talbot in England reports his earlier photographic discoveries to the Royal Society.
February 1, 1839	Sir John Herschel demonstrates "fixing" with hypo (sodium thiosulfate) to Talbot.
February 28, 1839	Herschel makes early use of the word *photography* in a letter to Talbot. (A German astronomer, Johann Heinrich von Mädler, used the word earlier in 1839 in a science article.)
March 7, 1839	Samuel F. B. Morse, father of the telegraph, is the first American to see a Daguerreotype when he calls on Daguerre.
March 14, 1839	Herschel reports on the use of hypo, the making of copies, and other photographic phenomena to the Royal Society.

March 20, 1839	Hippolyte Bayard makes direct-positive photographs on paper in his camera. (Street cameras will use this idea in the early 1900s.)
April 1, 1839	Rev. J. B. Reade writes that he has discovered a way to fix images permanently.
June 24, 1839	First photographic exhibit in history: by Bayard in Paris.
August 7, 1839	L. Daguerre and I. Niépce (son of Nicéphore) awarded pensions for life by both chambers of the French government; it is both an honor and a compensation for the agreement to publish the process for all to use.
August 19, 1839	Five days after a patent on Daguerreotypy has been issued in England, the Daguerreotype process is given "free to the world."
September 9, 1839	Herschel takes a photograph of a forty-foot telescope; it is the earliest surviving photograph on glass.
September 16, 1839	D. W. Seager states that he has taken the first Daguerreotype in America. (Its whereabouts today is unknown.)
October 14, 1839	*The New York Star* publishes an extensive account of Daguerre's process.
October 14, 1839	In Germany, Dr. Alfred Donne exhibits his Daguerreotype portrait. It is the first documented portrait by photography in Europe.
October 16, 1839	Joseph Saxton takes a 1-by-1½-inch Daguerreotype of Central High School in Philadelphia using a "seegar box and a magnifying lens." It is the only existing American Daguerreotype documented as having been taken in 1839. A portrait by Draper in summer, 1840, may be the first documented portrait.
November 20, 1839	H. Vernet and G. Fesquet take a Daguerreotype of the pyramids in Egypt.
February 16, 1840	The Daguerreotype gallery (to exhibit French-made Daguerreotypes) is opened in New York by R. Cornelius.
March 4, 1840	The first Daguerreotype parlor (a studio) in New York is opened, reports *The New York Sun*. The proprietor is Alexander S. Wolcott, who designs a new concept in lenses for the camera.
March 23, 1840	J. W. Draper announces that he has taken a Daguerreotype of the moon's surface.
May 8, 1840	The first photographic patent to be issued in America is issued to Alexander S. Wolcott for the method of taking portraits by the use of a concave reflector in lieu of the camera-obscura lenses of the time.
August 19, 1840	The Yale Class Photo is taken by Samuel F. B. Morse; it is the first such school photograph in history.
September 20, 1840	The phenomenon of the latent image is discovered by Talbot; calotypes (on paper) have been taken with eight-second exposures. The calotype (or Talbotype), more than the Daguerreotype, will set the base for the photography of the nineteenth and twentieth centuries.
January 1, 1841	Peter von Voigtländer (Germany) introduces the all-metal Daguerreotype camera.
February 4, 1841	Levi Hill describes his Daguerreotypes "in color" to Snelling.
——— 1841	Wheatstone commissions stereophotography by Daguerreotypy and calotypy.

December 8, 1841	Antoine François Jean Claudet patents the idea of a darkroom light.
March 28, 1842	The first patent for the coloring of Daguerreotypes is issued to B. F. Stevens and L. Morse.
May 14, 1842	Forty Daguerreotypes of a disastrous Hamburg, Germany, fire are taken by Hermann Biow: the first news photos.
June 16, 1842	Herschel process for the cyanotype (or blueprint; see Glossary) is announced.
June 1844	First photographically illustrated book, *The Pencil of Nature*, by W. H. Fox Talbot is published. Each of the two hundred copies contains five prints made on print-out chloride paper. The book is subsequently expanded in six installments with a final total of twenty-four prints.
June 1, 1844	The Energiatype (ferrotype; see Glossary) is invented and communicated to *The Athenaeum* by Robert Hunt.
June 30, 1845	Friedrich von Martens's panoramic camera taking a photograph 4¾ inches by 5 inches on a curved plate is introduced.
October 31, 1846	*The New York Mirror* publishes an account of what is possibly the first traveling photographic studio, a Daguerrean salon on wheels, pulled by a horse.
October 25, 1847	Abel Niépce de St. Victor announces his discovery of making an albumen negative on a glass support.
November 9, 1848	A Daguerreotype portrait of Edgar Allan Poe is taken by Henry N. or Edward H. Manchester. It will be erroneously reproduced as a work of Mathew B. Brady, famed Civil War photographer.
February 23, 1849	The first photographic Daguerreotype record of a battlefield: "Buena Vista" (Mexican War).
———— 1849	Sir David Brewster suggests a binocular (or twin-lens) camera for stereo photography. (All prior stereo photography has been accomplished with two successive exposures with a single lens, moved to one side for the second exposure.)
May 27, 1850	L. D. Blanquart-Evrard reveals his albumen-paper process. It becomes the basis for millions and millions of photographic prints for the next forty-odd years.
February 1, 1851	S. C. McIntyre's Daguerreotype panorama of San Francisco is described as the first of its kind.
November 11, 1851	A Daguerreotype camera with bellows is patented by W. H. and H. J. Lewis in the United States.
———— 1851	Frederick Scott Archer introduces the wet-plate or wet-collodion process with exposures from ten to ninety seconds. This on-glass process will sweep the world of photography until the mid-1870s.
February 16, 1852	Jules Duboseq patents his "stereoscope."
June 10, 1852	J. F. Mascher makes his first stereoscopic Daguerreotypes. His description of a box stereoscope for half-plate Daguerreotypes is published a few days later (June 13) in *Scientific American*.

July 20, 1852	The collodion process is published, and all photographers are introduced to the new photographic world (of negatives, prints later at any time, enlargements, reductions, etc.—all of which were not obtainable from the negative-less Daguerrean system).
November 24, 1852	E. Brown, Daguerrotypist, leaves with Commodore Perry's expedition to Japan. (The first Daguerreotype has already been taken in Japan ten years earlier.)
January 12, 1853	In England, William Edward Kilburn's stereoscope and case for Daguerreotypes is patented.
March 8, 1853	In America, a patent for J. F. Mascher's stereo Daguerreotype case is issued, very much like the Kilburn case but without sides.
July 1, 1853	Start of the contest for the best whole-plate Daguerreotype, sponsored by E. Anthony, leading photo-supplies merchant. The contest was won by Jeremiah Gurney with a second prize to Marcus Root.
——— 1853	Introduction to the public of the ferrotype (tintype) process by A. A. Martin.
——— 1853	A. Quinet of Paris produces the Quinetoscope: first binocular-style stereo camera (see Glossary).
May 22, 1854	A patent is issued to Arthur James Melhuish and J. B. Spencer for a camera roll holder loaded with sensitized paper.
July 11, 1854	James Ambrose Cutting's patent for the ambrotype (a negative on glass that is viewed as a positive) and for the use of bromide in collodion.
July 12, 1854	George Eastman is born.
October 3, 1854	A plastic Daguerreotype case is patented by Samuel Peck.
November 27, 1854	André Adolphe Eugène Disdéri applies for a patent for the carte-de-visite system, using eight to twelve lenses photographing on one plate.
December 13, 1854	Bulot and Cattin patent a system for fixing an image permanently to porcelain or enamel. The result will be portraits on vases, jewelry, etc.
May 17, 1855	The roll holder of M. Relandrin is introduced in France.
June 19, 1855	Albert Sands Southworth and Josiah Johnson Hawes patent their stereoscopic device.
June 23, 1855	Roger Fenton writes that he is returning to England from the war in Crimea with 360 photographic plates, an historic documentation.
August 7, 1855	H. Halvorson receives a patent for his "genuine Union case." (These cases were necessary to protect the glass protecting Daguerreotypes and the on-glass image of the ambrotype.)
——— 1855	Introduction of the collotype and carbon-print process (see Glossary) by Alphone Louis Poitevin.
June 1856	The first pistol camera is introduced by Thomas Skaife of England who is nearly arrested when he aims it at Queen Victoria. A French version is introduced in July 1856 by M. Millotbrulé.
February 24, 1857	D. A. Woodward patents a camera enlarger.

December 8, 1857	A. E. Becquerel's theories are reported to the Academie des Sciences, marking the beginning of color photography.
May 16, 1858	James Ambrose Cutting and William Bradford patent a process of photo lithography. (It will ultimately be possible to reproduce images on paper from plates made photographically from negatives.)
May 28, 1858	Charles Chevalier (lens maker to Daguerre) states that in 1840 he was the first to use an iris diaphragm (see Glossary).
June 21, 1858	The Waterhouse system is introduced. It is a simple way to change the aperture of the lens using a disc or a straight blade of metal with predrilled holes. Millions of box cameras will use this system during the first seventy-five years of family photography (1888–1963).
——— 1858	Nadar: Gaspard Félix Tournachon takes the first photographs from the air (in a balloon over Paris).
——— 1858	A "pocket" stereo camera is introduced by the London Stereoscopic Company. Folded, it is 8 by 4¾ by 2 inches deep.
May 21, 1859	First portrait engraving from a photograph, on wood, is published in *Scientific American*.
August 30, 1859	T. Morris in England creates a miniature "wet-plate" camera system with a tiny camera (only 2 by 1½ by 1½ inches). It is to be used to take ¾-inch locket pictures. It is only slightly smaller than the test cameras of Talbot that took the famous negative views of Leacock Abbey on treated writing paper.
November 27, 1859	William Sutton's panoramic camera is patented. (One sells in 1974 for nearly $30,000 at auction.)
January 7, 1860	Earliest reference in America to the carte de visite: It is in an ad in *Leslie's Weekly* by S. A. Holmes.
February 21, 1860	Abraham Lincoln is photographed by Mathew B. Brady prior to the Cooper Union address in New York City.
June 15, 1860	Adolphe Bertsch's fixed-focus camera is introduced.
October 13, 1860	The first successful aerial view in America is taken by S. A. King and J. W. Black. It shows the Boston Harbor as it is seen from a captive balloon at 1,200 feet.
December 4, 1860	A sliding plateholder and a camera patent is issued to Simon Wing. Wing cameras will become internationally acclaimed as versatile studio cameras.
——— 1860	Introduction of the Dagron Microphotographic Camera with twenty-five lenses. It took 450 exposures (each 2 by 2 millimeters on wet collodion plates: images for Stanhopes). In 1870, Dagron-made microphotographic photo messages will be flown to besieged Paris by carrier pigeon.
February 5, 1861	Coleman Seller's patent for the kinematoscope, or motoscope (see Glossary), is granted.
May 14, 1861	The first patent for a photograph album is issued to F. R. Grumel.
October 25, 1861	The *American Journal of Photography* publishes "an obituary": The Daguerreotype has died. Glass plates, ambrotypes, tintypes, cartes de viste, are all mass-produced by this date.

September 5, 1862	The Pantoscopic camera for panoramic photography invented.
October 3, 1862	Mathew Brady photographs President Lincoln in the field with Gen. George McClellan.
July 4, 1863	"The Harvest of Death" is photographed at Gettysburg by Timothy H. O'Sullivan.
July 5, 1863	"Death of a Rebel Sniper" photographed by Alexander Gardner.
November 15, 1863	Gardner photographs Abraham Lincoln.
December 15, 1863	The first edition of *The Silver Sunbeam* is issued by Dr. John Towler. It is a workbook for the photographer detailing every extant photographic process.
August 6, 1864	Cartes de visite on porcelain by Disdéri announced by *Scientific American*.
September 23, 1864	W. B. Woodbury patents photo-relief printing (Woodburytype process—see Glossary).
December 21, 1864	An English patent is secured for the Dubroni, a boxlike small camera made in five sizes for "in-camera" processing. Eighty-four years later, Polaroid Corporation will announce an in-camera–processing camera.
April 9, 1865	Gardner photographs Abraham Lincoln five days before he is assassinated.
July 7, 1865	Gardner photographs the execution of the Lincoln conspirators.
October 26, 1865	Early attempt at magnesium-light (flare-flash) photography (see Glossary).
May 18, 1866	F. R. Window's cabinet-portrait format is announced. It becomes the standard size for "family portraits" until into the twentieth century.
April 23, 1867	The zoetrope ("Wheel of Life") patented by W. Lincoln. This is the earliest introduction of the animated cartoon to the United States.
January 17, 1868	W. H. Harrison and Dr. Richard Leach Maddox publish a descripion of a gelatin dry-plate process. It is literally the obituary for the cumbersome wet-plate process.
November 23, 1868	L. Ducos Du Hauron receives a patent for making a three-color photograph.
May 7, 1869	Du Hauron and Charles Cros describe almost identical subtractive-system color theories—without knowing each other!
June 15, 1869	J. W. Hyatt is issued a patent for the invention of celluloid, combining collodion and camphor. The era of low-cost roll film to fit anyone's camera is in gestation.
November 30, 1869	J. Albert patents his Albertype (collotype—see Glossary).
December 15, 1869	First issue of *The British Journal Photographic Almanac* is published. Its annual volumes are the documentation of the artistic, technical, and equipment progress of photography.
February 5, 1870	First public exhibition of Henry Heyl's phasmatrope (see Glossary). It used persistence of vision to obtain a motion effect from still photographs.
July 15, 1871	W. H. Jackson takes one of the first photographs of Yellowstone National Park.
September 8, 1871	Dr. R. L. Maddox publishes his experiments, which led to the gelatine dry plate.

January 30, 1872	Jackson photographs shown to Congress are credited with helping to pass the Yellowstone National Park Bill in the Senate. This is the first example of the role of photography as an influence on social legislation.
———— 1872	First photographic investigations of animal movement by Eadweard Muybridge.
June 5, 1873	Platinotype process patented by W. Willis.
July 18, 1873	The first advertisement for a commercially available "gelatine emulsion ready for use" appears in *The British Journal Photographic Almanac*.
June 19, 1874	Richard Kennet introduces ready-prepared plates in London, England.
July 31, 1874	The U.S. War Department purchases Mathew Brady's collection of negatives at auction.
November 9, 1876	An English patent is issued to W. Donisthorpe for his kineoscography (see Glossary). A pack of glass plates are exposed at the rate of eight per second.
November 13, 1877	At age twenty-four George Eastman becomes interested in photography. In order to photograph a planned vacation, he purchases his first photographic outfit.
June 15, 1878	Muybridge photographs Leland Stanford's running horse to settle a bet. He proves that the four hooves of a running horse leave the ground at the same time.
———— 1878	Charles Bennett perfects a way to mature emulsions. The process has the effect of permitting photography at $\frac{1}{25}$ second. Hand-held cameras can now become a reality. (Only forty years earlier, the Daguerre exposures were of from two to twenty minutes; wet-plate exposures were typically four to forty seconds.)
———— 1879	George Eastman obtains a patent for a mass-produced glass-plate–coating machine.
March 4, 1880	The first half-tone print is reproduced in *The Daily Graphic* by the S. H. Horgan method. Mass reproduction of the photographic image by a high-speed printing system has become a reality. Until this time, line artwork (engravings or woodcuts) only could be reproduced on a newsprint press where type was pressed against paper.
ca. 1880	Census of 1880 reports that 10,000 Americans earn their livelihood as professional photographers.
June 4, 1880	Emile Reynaud demonstrates his electrical-drive praxinoscope device (see Glossary), which depicts motion effects of actual photographs taken in sequence.
September 1881	George Eastman leaves the bank where he had been working in order to join the Eastman Dry Plate Co. he had formed with a partner on January 1, 1880, in Rochester, New York.
May 27, 1882	American photographers learn of the French invention, Marey's Photographic Gun, for high-speed action photographs of birds in an account in *Harper's Weekly*.
January 2, 1883	William Schmid is issued a patent for his "detective" camera: the first hand-held camera of its type. It takes pictures on the now widely available glass plates.

October 9, 1883	Kilburn's Gun Camera patent is issued to B. J. Kilburn. It is a design for a rifle-stock stereo camera: a view camera on a rifle.
May 30, 1884	*The Photographic News* publishes a photograph taken by magnesium light. The era of "flashlight" photography has begun.
June 13, 1884	Ernest Mach describes the use of an electric spark to photograph a bullet in flight.
June 27, 1884	W. H. Walker and George Eastman apply for a patent for a film-stripping process. A tough layer of "Eastman American" film is peeled away from a roll-of-paper support.
July 1, 1884	C. R. Smith issued a patent in America for the first single-lens reflex camera: the Monocular Duplex Camera.
April 28, 1885	Patenting of the Parsell Detective Camera "intended to resemble a lady's reticule (handbag) or a case such as physicians frequently carry."
May 5, 1885	Walker and Eastman are issued a patent for a roll holder to load with the flexible "Eastman American" film introduced later in the year. It will fit cameras previously loaded with glass plates.
July 27, 1886	C. P. Stirn's Patented Concealed Vest Camera is introduced. With its lens peeking through a buttonhole, it took six exposures on a saucer-size glass plate. Eighteen thousand were sold by 1890.
August 12, 1886	Improvement of the lantern-slide projector (dating back to 1849) with the introduction of the double-slide carrier. It permitted the operator of the magic lantern to change slide number one while showing slide number two.
August 16, 1886	A photo process for printing in colors is patented.
November 27, 1886	A combination camera, enlarger, and magic lantern is patented by W. P. O'Reilly. (Thirty-five years later, a small French movie camera, the Sept, which is also a still camera, offers this combination concept for 35-mm photography.)
May 2, 1887	The Reverend Hannibal Goodwin files an application for a photographic pellicle (see Glossary) patent. Goodwin will get his patent; and nearly thirty years later, Goodwin's heirs and the Ansco Company will get $5 million from Kodak in settlement of the infringements, which will start with the Kodak Daylight Loading Camera of 1890.
May 3, 1887	C. P. Stirn receives a German patent for his "American Detective Camera": the first camera produced to accept roll film only. A year later, George Eastman's camera with this roll-film idea sweeps the world of photography.
July 12, 1887	John Wesley Hyatt's stamp portrait (multilensed) camera is patented.
——— 1888	Boston Camera Company introduces the Hawk-Eye Detective Camera. It can be optionally loaded with plates or fitted with an accessory 100-shot roll holder.
January 6, 1888	W. F. Stanley is granted a patent for "explosives and apparatus for producing instantaneous light."
January 10, 1888	L. A. A. LePrince is issued a patent for his method and apparatus for producing animated pictures.

February 27, 1888	Muybridge consults with Thomas Alva Edison on the possibility of combining his projector with Edison's phonograph: an early portent of the "talkies" to come alive commercially in 1926.
June 13, 1888	The Kodak roll-film camera is introduced. The era of family photography has begun.
October 8, 1888	Edison writes to announce his preliminary experiments on a motion-picture device, the kinetograph (see Glossary), using a roll of Eastman film costing $1.50.
November 16, 1888	L. A. A. LePrince is granted a patent for a motion-picture camera and projector.
January 23, 1889	A British patent is issued to Henry Good for a box-type roll-film camera. His design will be the basis for the Blair Kamaret and the Boston Camera Company's Bull's-Eye. Eastman will buy the American patent covering the little red window counter system in 1895.
June 21, 1889	W. Friese-Greene patents a cinematograph camera (see Glossary), which uses perforated film.
August 27, 1889	Eastman's transparent film is made available. It ends the era of "film-stripping" (off a paper support) and so permits the amateur to develop the film himself.
———— 1889	Introduction of the E. & H. T. Anthony & Co. Lilliput, a petite detective camera in an over-the-shoulder boxy bag; the camera is only 4 by 4 by 6 inches.
August 14, 1890	E. Bloch is issued a British patent for a cravat camera.
December 23, 1890	A patent is issued to Ferdinand Jekeli for Adams & Co.'s Hat Camera.
———— 1890	The Eastman Company (later to become the Eastman Kodak Company) introduces its first folding camera: A 4-by-5-inch No.4 Folding Kodak camera. It is built into a satchellike case and is loaded with the Walker Roll Holder (only in a darkroom).
May 20, 1891	First public announcement of the "peep-show" Kinetoscope Motion Picture Viewer by Thomas Alva Edison; a fifty-foot reel in an endless loop runs between a rotating shutter and an electric light.
September 15, 1891	The stereo anaglyph process (see Glossary) is patented by Louis Ducos Du Hauron, though the phenomenon had been reported earlier.
———— 1891	Frederic Eugene Ives introduces the photochromoscope color camera. It takes three images through three color filters. After development, the images are again viewed through the filters as a full-color photograph.
———— 1891	Introduction of the Kodak Daylight Load Camera, the first roll-film camera to be loaded in full daylight.
October 4, 1892	Dr. Scott's exposure calculator is patented. It is based on the slide rule.
February 1, 1893	Edison's "Black Maria," the world's first motion-picture studio, is completed.
March 18, 1893	J. Damerceau is issued a British patent for his Cyclographe panoramic camera.
June 29, 1893	Etienne Jules Marey is granted a French patent for his chronophotographic apparatus of 1887. It takes sixty pictures in a second for scientific observations of birds in motion, etc., on a celluloid band.

November 13, 1893	H. D. Taylor describes the Cooke triplet lens to the Royal Photographic Society, an advancement in optical design which led to the popular Tessar design of the twentieth century still in wide use today.
—— 1894	Creation of the phantascope by C. F. Jenkins and T. Armat. It is the first true motion-picture projector with electric light and reels.
—— 1894	Introduction of the gum-print (or gum-bichromate) process.
—— 1894	Introduction of the Kombi all-metal tiny box camera, which loads roll film.
September 1894	Introduction of the Verascope by Jules Richard, Paris. This all-metal stereo camera will then be produced continually with all but minor changes, longer than any other camera in history (1894 to mid-1920s).
February 13, 1895	L. Lumière's Cinematographe is patented in France. It is loaded with 35-mm film that is perforated with two notches per frame to facilitate advancement through the projector.
—— 1895	George Eastman acquires patents for the roll-film system of the Bull's-Eye Camera; later in the year he introduces the Pocket Kodak, the Bullet, and his version of the Bull's-Eye—all box cameras with the ruby-red window at back for advancing film.
May 20, 1895	The first public showing at 153 Broadway, New York City, of motion pictures on a screen: a four-minute movie of a prize fight.
May 21, 1895	George Eastman is granted a patent for a daylight load spool, which was invented by S. W. Turner.
December 28, 1895	Lumière's first motion-picture showing in Paris.
December 28, 1895	W. C. Roentgen reports on his experiments and discovery of the X ray.
April 3, 1896	Demonstration of the Vitascope (see Glossary) at the Edison plant.
April 23, 1896	First U.S. exhibition of an Edison kinetoscope film in a theater, Koster & Bial's Music Hall, New York City (on site of present Macy's, Herald Square), using the Armat Vitascope projector.
September 6, 1896	*The New York Times* issues the first weekend photographic supplement.
October 1, 1896	E. Bloch patents the Physiographe, a stereoscopic metal camera in the form of field glasses.
August 31, 1897	A camera patent is issued to Edison for his strip kinetograph, the first to employ perforated film with an intermittent movement.
September 13, 1898	Goodwin is issued a patent for a flexible film.
—— 1898	Introduction of the Folding Pocket Kodak cameras, the first compact bellows-type roll-film cameras. They are the first Kodak cameras with all-metal cases.
—— 1899	The first panoramic camera from the Eastman Kodak Company is introduced. It is also the first time the company announces the role of the camera in its name (the No. 4 Panoram-Kodak). It takes 3½-by-12-inch pictures on roll film.
ca. 1900	E. & H. T. Anthony & Co. merges with Scovill—the birth of Ansco, today's GAF Corporation, longest existing photo-supplies company in America.

February 1900	The Eastman Kodak Company launches another of its landmark cameras: the "leatherette paper-covered cardboard" Brownie No.1. It sells for $1; a 6-exposure roll of film costs 15¢.
April 2, 1901	The Al Vista panoramic camera loaded with roll film is patented by Multiscope Film Co.
July 29, 1901	*Scientific American* describes Ernst Ruhmer's first device to reproduce sound on motion-picture film—the photographophone.
October 1901	The first Eastman Kodak Company stereo camera: the box-shaped No. 2 Stereo Camera is introduced. It takes two, three, or six pairs of stereo pictures and four, six, or twelve singles.
January 21, 1902	Patenting of the 3A Folding Pocket Kodak camera. Its picture size, 3½ by 5¼ inches, is to become the popular "postcard" camera size that will be widely copied in other American cameras.
——— 1902	Dr. Paul Randolph of Zeiss improves an early triplet-lens (see Glossary) design to create the most important mass-produced lens type of the twentieth century: The four-element Tessar. Its patents expire in 1922, and it is widely adopted by numerous optical firms.
September 30, 1902	Edison receives a motion-picture–film patent for a camera employing the film-perforation system still in use today.
October 14, 1903	The Ticka Watch Camera is patented in England. It is a copy of the Expo, first made in the United States.
May 3, 1904	Emile Kronke is issued a U.S. patent for his Cane-Handle camera. (Today only two are known by collectors.)
September 6, 1904	The Expo Watch Camera, the invention of Magnus Neill, is patented. It exposes on roll film through the winding stem.
——— 1904	Patenting of the first successful color-screen process of A. and L. Lumière; three years later it is introduced as Autochrome.
April 1904	The Eastman Kodak Company introduces the first folding Brownie camera: the Folding Brownie No.2.
January 17, 1905	D. A. Reavill is issued a patent for certain features of a panoramic camera. It is later manufactured by the Eastman Kodak Company as the Cirkut, the most important panoramic camera of the first half of the twentieth century.
April 1905	The Eastman Kodak Company adds a stereo box camera to the Brownie line: the folding No. 2 Stereo Brownie.
May 16, 1906	An exhibition of photographs at the modernist Photo-Secession gallery on Fifth Avenue in New York by Edward Steichen includes experiments in three-color photography.
January 22, 1908	Eduard Belin transmits a photograph over a telephone line (belinograph; see Glossary).
April 1912	The Vest Pocket Kodak is introduced; it is an easily pocketable (flat when folded) bellows-type design that is loaded with #127 film to take photos 1⅝ by 2¼ inches. This basic design is produced in a variety of models—and even colors—until 1935.

September 24, 1912	One of several patents is secured for the Ansco Automatic and Semi-Automatic camera (an early noncine family-use auto-advance still camera).
——— 1912	Guy Smith of Missouri creates a prototype of a still camera loaded with 35-mm cine film. It proposed to take photos on the area ordinarily used for two cine frames. This is the first U.S. designed 35-mm camera and the first use of the double frame, which subsequently became the world standard for 35-mm still photography: 24 by 36 millimeters.
September 20, 1913	A patent is granted for a stereo camera made by Jules Richard of Paris: the Homeos, first stereo camera to use 35-mm film. About 1,500 were made.
——— 1913	Oskar Barnack (Germany) constructs the first working prototype of the Leica camera. He proposes to use a double-frame area: 24 by 36 millimeters.
——— 1913	The Mandel-Ette Street Camera is introduced, typical of the Mandel-designed and produced street cameras of 1910–1915. It made exposures on direct-positive paper, and the card print was developed in the camera's developing tank stored below.
——— 1914	The Tourist Multiple 35-mm camera system is introduced. It loads with a fifty-foot roll and will take 750 black-and-white positive single frames (18 by 24 millimeters) to be shown by a Tourist Projector. About 1,000 are made before it is discontinued as a financial failure.
——— 1914	Introduction of the Simplex Multi-Exposure camera. It loads with fifty feet of 35-mm film and will take either single- or double-frame sizes of pictures.
May 27, 1914	George Eastman settles the patent-infringement suit with Ansco and the heirs of Goodwin for $5 million.
December 1914	The first No.1 Autographic Kodak Jr. cameras are introduced. They permit the photographer to "write on the film" (date, name, place) after each exposure. Autographic cameras will be made (only by Kodak) in all popular film sizes up until 1934.
——— 1916	Introduction of the first camera in the world with built-in coupled range finder: the 3A Kodak Special camera.
April 1917	Introduction of the Stereo Kodak Model I.
——— 1921	Introduction in Germany of the Heidoscope all-metal stereo camera. It takes stereo pairs on 45-by-107-millimeter glass plates loaded in a magazine attached to the camera.
August 5, 1921	The first transmission of a photograph by radio: the belinogramme (see Glossary).
——— 1922	Introduction of the Sept, a French still and movie combination camera. It loads with 35-mm film to take single frames; it also performs as an enlarger and film projector.
November 26, 1922	First showing of the first technicolor production (subtractive color process, see Glossary) at the Rialto Theater: *The Toll of the Sea*.
January 8, 1923	Introduction of the Cine-Kodak 16-mm reversal process (for black-and-white movies).

———— 1923	Introduction of the Model A Kodak Cine Camera, which loads with 16-mm reversal film to permit amateur home movies on new Kodascope projections. Bell & Howell, Victor, and others are given the freedom to introduce 16-mm–loaded cameras at the same time.
———— 1923	The Pathé Company in Paris bids for the amateur-movie market with a smaller size film: 9.5 millimeters wide. It will have only limited success in the United States, and the introduction of 8-mm film in 1932 will totally block its U.S. potential.
———— 1924	First commercial-type 35-mm cameras (serial nos. 100–130) are handmade by E. Leitz in Germany. They carry the new trademark, "Leica."
———— 1924	Introduction in Germany of the plate-loaded 4.5-by-6-millimeter Ermanox with high speed (f/1.8 and f/2) lenses. This newest model from the Ernemann Company opens the door to "candid photography." It is the choice of Erich Salomon, photographer of diplomats at the League of Nations.
———— 1925	Introduction of the Leica A with 50-mm Elmax f/3.5 lens (three hundred made); later with Elmar f/3.5 (thousands made up to 1930).
———— 1925	Introduction in France of the EKA, a precision miniature camera by M. E. Krauss, Paris, loaded with unperforated 35-mm film.
———— 1926	Introduction of the Rolleidoscop reflex stereo camera in Germany. It is loaded with roll film. (It arrives on stage at the fading moments of the stereo era.)
August 6, 1926	The first commercially successful talking picture, *Don Juan*, is shown in New York.
December 1926	Introduction of the Ansco Memo I, a twelve-ounce oblong box-shaped 35-mm camera that exposes single frames. It is a totally simplified version of the Simplex Multi-Exposure and Tourist Multiple cameras of a dozen years earlier.
———— 1926	Ansco introduces the Photo Vanity: a ladies makeup kit in an attaché case that conceals a camera operable when the case is closed. It is the first concealed camera made since the detective-camera era (1884–1895).
October 6, 1927	*The Jazz Singer* is shown in New York: The talkies are dramatically on screen across America.
———— 1928	Introduction of Kodacolor film, a 16-mm film based on the lenticular process (see Glossary) of the Eastman Kodak Company.
April 1928	Kodak reflects the Art Deco period with body designs and packagings on such cameras as the Vanity Kodak Vest Pocket Series II (made available in a range of colors, some sold with matched cases of lipstick and makeup aids to appeal to women).
———— 1928	An all-Bakelite QRS Kamra is introduced by the DeVry Corporation in the United States. It has the boxy vertical shape of the Ansco Memo of 1926, but it is three times larger and takes the "double-frame" picture size of the Leica.
———— 1929	J. Ostermeier in Germany invents magnesium flash bulbs in which the intense burning of a thin aluminum foil or wire lights the photograph.

——— 1929	Introduction of the Rolleiflex I 6-by-6-centimeter camera (serial nos. 1–199,999) from the company that had made the Rolleidoscop and Heidoscop cameras. It is the first truly practical twin-lens reflex. Millions of Rollei cameras will be made until the 1960s.
August 1, 1930	General Electric Company introduces the GE No.20 Photoflash, the first flashbulb for the American professional and amateur photography market.
——— 1930	Introduction of the miniature version of the Rolleiflex camera: the 4-by-4-centimeter Rolleiflex (serial nos. 135,000–523,000), which loads with #127 film.
——— 1930	E. Leitz introduces the first Leica with interchangeable lenses. The true precision miniature camera system has arrived.
——— 1930	Introduction of the Zeiss Kolibri, a rigid-bodied compact miniature camera that takes pictures on #127 roll film.
July 15, 1931	Leopold Mannes and Leopold Godowsky begin experiments at Eastman Kodak that will lead to the world's first high-quality color film: Kodachrome.
——— 1932	The Eastman Kodak Company launches 8-mm cine film along with cameras and projectors for the amateur market.
——— 1932	The first commercially produced photoelectric exposure meter is offered by the Weston Instrument Company.
——— 1932	The Leica II series is introduced. It features a built-in (coupled) range finder and a family of lenses along with related shooting, developing, and projection accessories.
July 1932	Introduction in America of the first Kodak-named products from the Kodak-owned Nagel plant in Stuttgart, Germany: the Pupille, Ranca, and Vollenda cameras, all loaded with roll film.
——— 1932	Introduction of the Zeiss Contax I, the first 35-mm camera from Zeiss. (Advanced models are introduced in 1936: the Contax II and the Contax III.)
October 1933	Introduction of the tiniest of American-made all-plastic novelty cameras: the Univex A. At 39¢ (later 50¢) it will sell 3 million in three years.
——— 1933	Introduction of the Rolleicord I (a lower-cost version of the popular Rolleiflex).
——— 1933	Introduction of the National Graflex I; it is a miniature version of the bulky press-preferred Graflex single-lens reflex camera made in a number of sizes starting in 1907.
——— 1934	Introduction in Germany of the four-pictures-a-second Robot 35-mm spring-loaded sequence camera with interchangeable lenses.
December 1934	Introduction of Kodak's first 35-mm camera, the Kodak Retina I, a folding-design compact 35-mm camera made in Germany.
April 12, 1935	Eastman Kodak Company introduces Kodachrome. It makes possible low-cost color photography with slides and prints for millions of amateurs and professionals.

———— 1935	The Eastman Kodak Company announces Kodak Bantam cameras: They offer the shape of the miniature camera while using a new smaller roll film (#828) to take pictures slightly larger than a double-frame 35-mm.
———— 1935	First edition of *The Leica Manual* by Willard D. Morgan and Henry J. Lester. It teaches photography to a generation of photographers in its annual revised editions.
———— 1935	Introduction of the most sophisticated Zeiss folding cameras in history, led by the Super Ikonta B. They include coupled range finders and even built-in exposure meters (not coupled) in the Model BX (of 1937).
———— 1935	Introduction of the world's most sophisticated 35-mm miniature camera for twin-lens photography: the Zeiss Contaflex, which uses the Contax system of interchangeable lenses and which incorporates a built-in photoelectric exposure meter.
———— 1936	Introduction of the Kodak 16-mm magazine-loaded amateur cine cameras: the first drop-in–load cameras, which presage post–World War II drop-in magazines for all Kodak cameras of the future.
May 1936	Introduction of the Argus A 35-mm camera at $9.95 (and later $12.50). It is the first low-cost camera that can be loaded with the new Kodachrome. This camera and its improved models single-handedly launch the American 35-mm camera boom; 30,000 Argus A cameras were sold in a few weeks during the worst depression in U.S. history.
August 1936	The Eastman Kodak Company announces its prestige camera in the miniature field: the Kodak Bantam Special, the second camera to be designed by Walter Dorwin Teague for Kodak. (His first was the Kodak 127 Baby Brownie.)
October 1936	Universal Camera Corporation launches a mini-boom in home movies with the Univex Cine 8 movie camera at $9.95. The companion projector sold for $14.95. A quarter-million sets are sold in two years.
———— 1936	Introduction of the Exakta single-lens reflex camera, which loads with #127 roll film. It opens a new system of photography, especially when Exakta 35-mm–loading models are introduced.
May 6, 1937	The burning dirigible *Hindenberg* is photographed in still and motion pictures, which is the most unique news-photography coverage of the pre–World War II era.
———— 1937	Introduction in Europe of the Minox, a stainless steel camera about the size of a chewing-gum package, made in Riga, Latvia. It takes fifty 8-by-11-millimeter pictures on 9.5-mm film. (Serial nos. 1–20,000 were made until 1942. Later Minox cameras are German-made.)
———— 1937	Introduction of the Compass, one of the most amazing miniature cameras of the twentieth century. The tiny, all-metal camera is the size of a cigarette package; it takes both roll film and plates. Designed in England and produced in a Swiss watchworks, it is more camera per ounce or per inch than any other camera in history. Only 5,000 were made.

——— 1938	Argus introduces a brick-shaped Argus C (to be followed in 1939 by the Argus C-3). Over 2 million will be sold in the following twenty-eight years.
——— 1938	The Eastman Kodak Company introduces the Kodak 35, a low-priced 35-mm camera to compete with the increasingly popular Argus cameras. The Kodak 35 is the first 35-mm Kodak made in America.
July 1938	Kodak launches another landmark camera, the Super Kodak Six-20, a folding camera that is the world's first to feature a built-in photoelectric automatic exposure control.
November 1938	Introduction of an all-metal 35-mm Univex Mercury with interchangeable lenses and a shutter speed to 1/1000 second (1/1500 second in subsequent models).
——— 1939	H. E. Edgerton improves electronic flash tubes and provides dramatic action-stopping photographs of scientific, industrial, and sports subjects.
——— 1939	Bell & Howell, famed for two generations for motion-picture cameras and projectors, enters the still-camera field with a spring-driven 35-mm camera: the Foton, which sells for $700. Bell & Howell produces 16,900 before the model is discontinued in 1950.
Fall 1941	Kodak introduces the landmark 35-mm precision camera: the Kodak Ektra. It features interchangeable lenses, interchangeable backs, and other advanced features.
October 28, 1942	Centennial of E. & H. T. Anthony & Co., Inc., America's oldest photographic firm; known today as GAF Corporation.
——— 1944	Introduction of Anscochrome, the first American-made color film that could be processed by anyone with a darkroom.
February 21, 1947	E. H. Land announces the Polaroid Land Camera and film.
——— 1947	A new surge of interest in stereo is stirred by a new company in the photographic field, the David White Instrument Co. of Milwaukee, Wisconsin. The camera is a precision 35-mm camera, the Stereo Realist.
November 1952	The Eastman Kodak Company is among the last to enter the five-year-old stereo boomlet started with the Stereo Realist. Kodak announces its first stereo camera since 1917: the 35-mm Kodak Stereo.
March 17, 1954	A complete set of the eleven-volume work, *Animal Locomotion*, by Eadweard Muybridge, is auctioned at Christies' in London for £175.
July 12, 1954	One hundredth anniversary of the date of birth of George Eastman: a 3¢ U.S. postage stamp is issued.
——— 1954	First light-activated, non-battery electric-eye control of exposure in an amateur 8-mm movie camera: the Bell & Howell Electric Eye Model 270.
December 12, 1957	E. H. Land announces that full-color Polaroid pictures are being made.
April 12, 1960	Demonstration of Polaroid Land color film at a meeting of the corporation's stockholders.

February 28, 1963	The Eastman Kodak Company launches its most popular series of modern cameras: the Instamatic. Its Kodapak drop-in loads with specially perforated 35-mm film. 7.5 million are sold in twenty-four months and 70 million during the following ten years. Successor (smaller) Pocket Instamatics are introduced in 1973.
———— 1967	The first color pictures of the full earth are taken from satellite *Dodge*.
October 1968	First U.S. meeting of photographic collectors and historians is held in Columbus, Ohio, as photographic collecting comes of age. Twenty collector societies will form in the next six years.
February 7, 1970	The first "meaningful" auction specifically held for image and equipment collectors of the photographic world, the Sidney Strober Auction, is held at the Sotheby Parke Bernet Galleries in New York City.

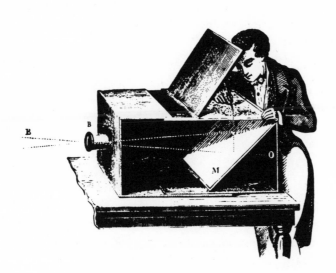

Appendix B
Dating Photographic Equipment

Our questions emerge after anyone acquires a camera, lens, or other item for a collection:

> What is it?
> What did it cost?
> How old is it?
> What is it worth today?

The answer to the first question, identification, is 99-percent potentially available.

The question of its original cost is about 90-percent available from catalogues and early advertising now accessible to the collector.

Its age will be determined when the item has been located in the catalogues.

As to its worth, there is a fifty-fifty chance of determining its value.

WHAT IS IT?

Almost all cameras and lenses made from the period of the detective cameras (1880s and 1890s) are reasonably easy to identify. By that time, makers had begun to place their names on their products; they often also incorporated camera name, film size, and other technical data (patents, operating instructions, shutter-speed guides, etc.) either on the camera body or in the removable cover at back or top. Lenses often provide three kinds of information: the maker's name, a serial number, and an indication of the lens type.

Shutters were made by specialist companies for many popular cameras so that a camera may have its own name, plus the name of the lens, plus the make of the shutter. It is the combination of these facts, even without the name of the camera on the nameplate or the carry strap, which are the guides to the most specific dating. The collector has but to refer to the catalogues and available reference works available from a broad variety of sources. (See "Early Catalogues and Camera Brochures," pages 194–196.)

Some confusion in identification is introduced by systems of chronological development which do not use sequential coding. The Leica A preceded the B, C, D, etc. But midway in the development of this series, Leica designated models as I, II, and III. Within these new categories, Leitz created subclassifications: Ia and Ib or IIIa and IIIb, modifications of the basic I and III series.

In the Kodak system of serialization, there are Kodak Brownie cameras Nos. 1, 2, 2A, 3, etc., which are not a chronological development; these numerals indicate differing film sizes of near-identical cameras. There is a uniformity in that all Kodak (not Brownie) products used these numbers for thirty years to identify the picture size. The entire series is as follows:

No.0	$1\frac{5}{8}'' \times 2\frac{1}{4}''$
No.1	$2\frac{1}{4}'' \times 2\frac{1}{4}''$
No.1A	$2\frac{1}{4}'' \times 4\frac{1}{4}''$
No.2	$3\frac{1}{2}'' \times 3\frac{1}{4}''$
No.2A	$2\frac{1}{4}'' \times 4\frac{1}{4}''$
No.2C	$2\frac{7}{8}'' \times 4\frac{7}{8}''$
No.3	$3\frac{1}{4}'' \times 4\frac{1}{4}''$
No.3A	$3\frac{1}{4}'' \times 5\frac{1}{2}''$ (postcard)
No.4	$4'' \times 5''$
No.4A	$4\frac{1}{2}'' \times 6\frac{1}{2}''$
No.5	$5'' \times 7''$
No.6	$6\frac{1}{2}'' \times 8\frac{1}{2}''$ (full plate)

In some German cameras—such as the Zeiss Ikon series, which included such popular family cameras as the Icarette and the Nixie roll-film cameras plus the Ideal A and B plate-film cameras—letters were used to indicate the film-size change, not the change in models. For example, the Ideal A closely resembles the larger Ideal B. One is for film 2¼ by 3¼ inches; and the other is loaded with 3¼-by-4¼-inch cut film. In the same period, Zeiss Ikonta cameras used the same *A, B, C,* and *D* to indicate progressively larger models of the basic roll-film camera design. *Super* as a prefix indicates a second-generation camera offered at a later date. Thus, the Ikontas of the 1920s were superseded by the Super Ikontas of the 1930s.

It is as important to know the difference between I and II in the Zeiss Contax cameras; in this case, the Roman numerals mean a successor camera, a total redesign.

The confusion on manufacturer coding dissipates as collectors begin to specialize in cameras by groups of sizes or by time periods. There is a lesson to be learned here from observing the children who collect postage stamps. Children collect stamps from "anywhere"; adults who collect stamps specialize in a particular area of interest: the United States commemoratives; stamps of Great Britain; etc. In his area of stamp collecting, the adult philatelist soon learns the terminology and the variants, all of which provide excitement to the collecting field. This is also true for camera collectors.

The answers to precise camera identification lie in the original or reprint catalogues of the various camera lines or in the basic reference works to early cameras. (See "Early Catalogues and Camera Brochures," page 194.)

HOW OLD IS IT?

There are a number of keys to the age of equipment. Major clues are to be found in the camera. While no camera has ever been made that has imprinted within its body the production date, most do include such guides as a serial number or a lens production number.

It is easy to date certain cameras within months and others within a few years by a number of facts. It is usually easiest to precisely date the first model of any camera; later variants require a greater knowledge of availability of certain shutters, lenses, etc., to guide exact dating.

We know from catalogues that the No. 4 Folding Hawk-Eye, which was available for $27 in 1910 with a Hawk-Eye R.R. (rapid rectilinear) lens and an Auto shutter was also available in that same year in a better model, which sold for $92: the No.4 Hawk-Eye with a No.7 Zeiss Protar lens and a Compound shutter.

In the mid-1920s, Voigtländer made a number of folding plate cameras in the popular 9-by-12-centimeter (3¼-by-4¼-inch) format. The model called the VAG was available with the Voigtländer Skopar Anastigmat lens in an Ibsor shutter. A very similar Voigtländer but with the extra photographic capabilities of lens-centering adjustments (vertical and lateral shift) plus double-extension bellows (for closeup photography) was known as the Bergheil model. It was the Voigtländer Bergheil Tourist with a Heliar lens and a Compound shutter. The two cameras on the shelf are Voigtländer 9-by-12-centimeter cameras; the differences in lenses and shutters make one a common camera, the other a more desirable, rarer collectible.

As camera systems of the 1930s developed that permitted the nonprofessional photographer the luxury of lens interchangeability, it became necessary for cameras to be identified by make, model, and lens in that order when establishing a price or a factor of rarity.

Just as it is impossible to identify a camera by calling it "a Kodak camera" since there have been Kodak cameras in continuous production in over 1,600 models since 1888, it is also impossible in most instances to identify a camera simply as a Leica, a Contax, an Exakta, a Voigtländer, etc.

The No.5 Folding Cartridge Kodak of 1898 in its first model had a wooden lens board and a wooden base on which the lens board stood. All further models for the next eight years had metal lens boards and metal bases. This makes it easy to date the No.5 with a wooden lens board, but it requires the specific information on lens and shutter to more precisely date the subsequent models of the No.5 during the nine years in which this camera was made by the Eastman Kodak Company.

The Leica A was a production camera starting in

1926; but Leica A cameras, some of which were later modified by the factory to incorporate the advances of later models, were also made during the years 1927, 1928, 1929, 1930, and 1931. The only sure way to date a Leica A or any other Leica is by the body serial number. In many instances, it has been shown that Leica lens numbers have provided a clue to dating the camera since only the professionals switched lenses and bodies to defeat this system. (See "Dating the Leica," page 250.)

In no case can the patent number found in the body of many folding cameras serve as a guide to the camera age or production date. Many twentieth-century box cameras include inscribed patent numbers dating back into the shutter or roll-film patents of the nineteenth century.

Eight Keys to Quick Dating of Early Cameras

1. Red leather bellows on folding cameras that open with a drop front? It's from the period before World War I but not much earlier than 1900. Example: Folding Pocket Kodaks.

2. A box camera that loads with glass plates in holders? It's probably from the period of the detective cameras (if it's larger than a large-ish shoe box), and it's a later camera and up to about 1910 if smaller. Examples: in the large size, the Blair Detective; small, the 3¼-by-4¼-inch Cyclone Magazine camera.

3. German cameras that are all black with black-enameled parts are prior to 1930 but could go back to 1905. With chromed tops or internal parts for an overall "modern" look, it's not earlier than about 1930 and up to the present. Examples: early (black), Voigtländer Avus or the ICA Ideal; later with chrome and a modern look, the Zeiss Contax II and later models of the Plaubel Makina.

4. German cameras with Compur shutters? If the Compur shutter is old style (top dial, side dial marked ZBT, left lever to cock, right lever to trip), introduced in 1912, then the camera dates during the period from 1912 to 1928. Compur shutter of the rim-set type? With a chromium ring that is rotated by gripping the rim edge of the total shutter mechanism? These can only be found on cameras after 1928. Examples: old-style Compur shutters are found on the KW Patent Etui, and later the same camera was available with rim-set shutters; rim-set Compur, the Kodak Recomar cameras 18 and 33.

5. Fold-open camera with wooden lens board that conceals shutter mechanism plus wooden bed on which shutter-lens assembly stands? From 1890s up to 1905. Examples: No.4 Folding Kodet, Premos, and Conleys.

6. View camera with no shutter assembly on the lens; lens cap on lens for *on-off* exposures? Cameras up to 1895 and usually from about 1880 on, plus rarer wet-plate cameras of the Civil War period and up to 1880. Look for the wet-plate stains at the bottom of the camera where the film holder is seated as one of the telltale clues.

7. Folding camera of small size with a squeeze-bulb–activated shutter, usually found with red leather bellows? Not later than about 1910 but not earlier than 1900.

8. Does the camera interior or does film still in the camera provide a film-size number? Here are the earliest possible dates for the film size as a clue to the earliest possible date for the camera:

#101 — 1895		#121 — 1902	
#102 — 1895		#122 — 1903	
#103 — 1896		#123 — 1904	
#104 — 1897		#124 — 1905	
#105 — 1898		#125 — 1905	
#106 — 1898		#126*— 1906	
#107 — 1898		#127 — 1912	
#108 — 1898		#128 — 1912	
#109 — 1898		#129 — 1912	
#110 — 1898		#130 — 1916	
#111 — 1898		#616 — 1932	
#112 — 1898		#620 — 1932	
#113 — 1898		#135 — 1934	
#114 — 1898		(35 mm)	
#115 — 1898		#828 — 1935	
#116 — 1899		(Bantam)	
#117 — 1900		#126 — 1963	
#118 — 1900		(Instamatic)	
#119 — 1900		#110 — 1973	
#120 — 1901		(Pocket Instamatic)	

* Not to be confused with #126 of 1963.

WHAT DID IT COST?

For years the average family member who had purchased a camera (a luxury purchase along with a radio, a piano, or a record player) could remember exactly how much it cost. There is hardly a collector who has not met an owner of an early camera who could not tell exactly what was paid for it thirty, forty, or fifty years earlier. But no one else in the family remembers, and as the camera became an attic item, the memory and circumstances of its original purchase have been lost.

But the prices of most early cameras have been preserved in the advertising of the manufacturer and of the early photo-supply stores as well as in some catalogues prepared by the manufacturer and for the reference use of the professionals and active amateurs of the times.

The catalogues and advertising play a further role in evaluation of the early photographic items since they identify a number of the accessories available at the time along with the ranges of lenses and shutters of one or another models and provide information that exactly dates the product. Catalogues of Sears, Roebuck & Co.; Montgomery Ward; and other major mail-order merchants provide year-by-year indications of product development and indicate the range of equipment within a given period.

Popular periodicals from the year 1880 and on provided the typical American family with advertising of cameras, stereo devices, magic lanterns—and include peripherally further information even on the lesser cameras and equipment that were offered as gifts to children who helped the magazines to find new subscribers.

It is interesting to note from the advertisements some of the salient developments within the technical aspects of certain cameras and even to note how a number of cameras were sold from the same factory under different names to different middlemen suppliers.

The mail-order catalogues of New York, Chicago, and West Coast camera dealers starting from the 1930s are especially valuable since they provide in the English language an introduction to many imported cameras, such as the Leica and Contax cameras from Germany or the Foth Derby and Fothflex from France.

A broad variety of these catalogues, especially dating to the periods just before and after the turn of the century, have been republished by individuals, by book publishers, by photo-historical groups, and even by retailers in America and England.

They provide a low-cost research tool for the collector and may be acquired as part of the research effort of any collector since in most cases these are offered for only a few dollars each. (See "Early Catalogues and Camera Brochures," page 194.)

WHAT IS IT WORTH TODAY?

The rarity of any item along with the zest for its ownership by a buyer will be the basis for the value put on any item in jewelry, in numismatics, in philately, as well as in photographica. Since Daguerrean equipment is scarce and eagerly sought, collectors will find that prices for these early examples of the photographic trade are costly, with cameras selling in the thousands of dollars. For example, a Daguerreotype camera whose one side was stained in a fire sold for $2,600 in 1970 at a New York auction to a Missouri schoolteacher of photography with a deep sense of history. (See Chapter 11, "Meet the Collectors," The Honeymoon Collection.)

Nevertheless, the collector is aided today by a work entitled *Price Guide to Antique and Still Cameras.** Its author, James McKeown, gathered auction reports, published offerings of collectors and antique dealers, and similar sources containing the selling prices of hundreds of cameras sold in America in the years 1970–1974. He entered twenty thousand data cards into a computer and then published his findings. He published the average figures that he obtained, though admittedly his average was sometimes the average of a single reported sale, or, a single offering that did not lead to a sale. Nearly one thousand cameras are listed, and this is the only overall pricing guide available covering cameras from the late 1880s up to the contemporary equipment of the used camera market (of typical camera stores). The *Guide* provides a general indication of the values that others have placed on their cameras along with an indication of condition ("poor," "fair," "very good," etc.) of the offerings.

A second source, *Price Guide to Collectable Cameras: 1930–1976* by Myron Wolf,† provides the col-

* Published by Centennial Photo Service, Grantsburg, Wisconsin, 54840; 60 pages, soft-cover, $8.95 postpaid.

† Published by Photographic Memorabilia, P.O. Box 351, Lexington, Massachusetts, 02173; 8 pages, $2.95.

lector of modern cameras with a current reference. It provides the high and low sale prices for two hundred cameras and will be updated semiannually.

Camera-store owners have, like auto dealers, a "blue book" to guide their transactions in the used-camera market, but these guides, when they are available, are primarily intended to assist the camera shop in pricing items of the past decade plus the Leica line, which dates back to 1926. The fact is, the camera-store owner does not have any more idea of the value of early cameras than any other shop-keeper on Main Street.

Then how does one learn the values of the early cameras? One part of the answer lies in a number of publications that appear monthly—including the *Shutterbug Ads*, a twenty-page monthly tabloid listing hundreds and hundreds of cameras of yesterday and today (see page 197 for subscription information); and the *National Photo Xchange*, a monthly magazine that lists offerings by active dealers within collecting circles (see page 197 for subscription information) and the mail-order catalogues from *Daguerreian Era* or the catalogues of Allen and Hilary Weiner (for either, see page 199 for subscription information). The catalogues issued by Sotheby Park Bernet's following auctions (which include the prices realized) are a guide to the values in New York and London, where the most sophisticated items of equipment, literature, and imagery are traded in semiannual auctions that win attention from collectors all over the world (see page 198 for subscription information).

Another part of the answer lies in the flame and fires of the actual transactions as they are conducted at the bustling swap-trade fairs of the photo-collectors groups in most major cities. At the tables and in the alcoves, one can share the excitement of hundreds of transactions—the marketplace where prices are actually created.

Here are some general guidelines to today's market:

• Early cameras sell for more than later cameras (*early* is pre-1914 or pre-1900, depending on the camera; *later* is post–World War I and up to World War II).

• Novelty cameras (tiny, concealed, or unique

in shape) sell for more than readily identifiable cameras.

• Rarity is most important at any camera age. The 1937 Leica Reporter camera (which loaded with thirty-three feet of film to take 250 pictures) was made in a run of one thousand and is sold or traded with a value from $750 to $1,500; other Leica cameras of 1937 sell for $100 to $250 because they were made by the thousands.

• Stereo cameras are worth more than nonstereo cameras.

• Badly battered cameras are worth one-third or less of the value of the same camera in excellent condition.

• Cameras without lenses are worth one-third to one-half of that camera with its original lens.

• A camera accompanied by its carry case or minor accessories, such as the filters, sunshade, cable release, or a tripod, is worth only slightly more than the camera alone. (Exception: a complete pre-1880 camera outfit is worth 50 to 100 percent more than the camera alone.)

• A camera in operable condition is worth more than a collectible camera that is defective; but this is going to account for only a 10 to 30 percent difference in the prices between the two cameras.

• Cameras with an earlier serial number (closer to #0001) are more highly priced than cameras with a later serial number (a higher number in the production run) but cameras with a unique serial number (such as #10,000; or #1010101) may be worth more than an earlier serial number.

• Cameras in color within a line are worth more than the run-of-the-mill all-black cameras.

• An early camera without the refinements of a range finder or additional chrome trim may attract less attention but is often worth more than the less rare but more appealing later cameras.

DATING THE LEICA

The Leica system of photography is based on a variety of cameras that break apart essentially into two lens systems: screw-in–mount cameras and bayonet-mount cameras, which started in the period after World War II. Since all Leica cameras starting from the very first production runs in 1925 were progressively serial-numbered, regardless of model within the screw-mount series, it is possible to establish the year of manufacture.

The very first Leica cameras are among the most rare, and within the groups that followed there are also models that are aggressively sought by the avid Leica collector.

Model identification for the Leica is not easy. The first Leicas were distinctly different versions known as the Leica A, B, and C, etc. Then a new designation started with the establishment of models known as the I, II, and III. To further complicate the picture, within the III series there are the IIIa, IIIb, IIIc, and IIIf. The differences within these letter subgroupings indicate such differences as a highest possible shutter speed of 1/500 second vs. 1/1000 second; or whether the aiming window is apart from or adjacent to the peep window for the coupled range finder.

There are a number of basic reference books that detail the differences that exist within the various models, but key among these is the *Leica Illustrated Guide* by James L. Lager, recently published in America in English.

The following chart of basic serial numbers for Leica bodies and lenses makes it possible to date the year of manufacture.

Leica Manufacturer's Numbers, 1913–1940

Year	Serial Number		
1913	Prototype*		
1923	100	–	130
1925	131	–	1000
1926	1001	–	2445
1926–27	2446	–	5433
1928	5434	–	5700
1926–29	5701	–	6300
1928	6301	–	13100
1929	13101	–	13300
1929	13301	–	21478
1930	21479	–	60000
1931	60001	–	71199
1932	71200	–	106000
1933	106001	–	107600
1933	108651	–	112500

* Only one of these was manufactured.

Year	Serial Number		
1933	114001	–	114052
1933	114401	–	115300
1933	116001	–	123000
1933	123851	–	124800
1933	124801	–	126800
1934	107601	–	108650
1934	112501	–	114400
1934	114053	–	114400
1934	115301	–	116000
1934	123001	–	123580
1934	126801	–	148950
1934–35	149351	–	149550
1934–35	150201	–	150850
1934–36	150001	–	150200
1935	148951	–	149350
1935	149551	–	150000
1935	150851	–	183600
1935–36	183601	–	183750
1936	183751	–	217500
1936	218301	–	220300
1936	222501	–	222300
1936	223300	–	223700
1936–37	217701	–	218300
1936–37	223701	–	234600
1937	217501	–	217700
1937	220301	–	220500
1937	222301	–	223300
1937	234601	–	240000
1937	248601	–	268000
1937	268201	–	268400
1937–38	240001	–	248600
1937–38	268001	–	268100
1938	268101	–	268200
1938	268401	–	288000
1938	290201	–	294000
1938	294601	–	309700
1938	311001	–	311200
1938–39	288001	–	290200
1938–39	309701	–	310000
1938–39	310601	–	311000
1939	294001	–	294600
1939	310501	–	310600
1939	311201	–	311400
1939	311701	–	335000
1939	337001	–	339000
1939	340001	–	341000
1939	341301	–	344000
1939–40	335001	–	337000
1939–40	339001	–	340000
1939–40	341001	–	341300
1939–40	344001	–	348600

DATING CAMERAS EQUIPPED
WITH ZEISS LENSES

Many European cameras from the period from World War I to World War II were manufactured in camera-assembly plants in a number of countries. Many of these cameras were equipped with Zeiss lenses, all of which are serial-numbered.

This chart, covering the years from 1912 up to World War II, provides the basis for rough-dating a camera to within a year of its production:

Serial Numbers of Zeiss Lenses
by Year of Manufacture

YEAR	SERIAL NUMBERS	
1912	173418 thru 200520	
1913	208473	– 249350
1914	249886	– 252739
1915	282820	– —
1916	—	– —
1917	289087	– 298157
1918	298115	– 322748
1919	322799	– 351611
1920	375194	– 419823
1921	433273	– 438361
1922	422899	– 498006
1923	561270	– 578297
1924	631869	– —
1925	652230	– 681743
1926	666790	– 703198
1927	722196	– 798251
1928	903096	– —
1929	919794	– 1016885
1930	922488	– 1239697
1931	1239699	– 1365582
1932	1364483	– 1389279
1933	1436671	– 1456003
1934	1500474	– 1590000
1935	1615764	– 1752303
1936	1674882	– 1942806
1937	1930150	– 2219775
1938	2267991	– 2527984
1939	2527999	– 2651211
1940	—	– —
1941	2678326	– 2790346
1942	2799599	– —

Appendix C
Kodak Cameras and Equipment

A BRIEF HISTORY OF MOST EASTMAN AND KODAK CAMERAS, 1887–1939

CAMERA	DATES OF MANUFACTURE	DESCRIPTION
Eastman Detective camera	1887 only	4″ × 5″ box, plate loaded with optional roll holder.
The Kodak camera	June 1888 thru 1889	Factory loaded with 100 exposures, picture size 2½″ diameter. Barrel-design shutter.
No. 1 Kodak camera	1889–1895	Factory loaded with 100 exposures, picture size 2½″ diameter. Sector-type shutter.
No. 2 Kodak camera	Oct. 1889–1897	Factory loaded with 60 exposures, picture size 3½″ diameter.
No. 4 Folding Kodak camera	1890–1892	First Kodak folding camera, improved model (1893–97), 4″ × 5″.
No. 5 Folding Kodak camera	1890–1892	5″ × 7″, improved model (1893–97), roll film.
No. 3 Kodak camera	Jan. 1890–1897	Factory loaded with 60 exposures, 4¼″ × 3¼″, capacity to 100 exposures.
No. 3 Kodak Jr. camera	Jan. 1890–1897	Factory loaded with 60 exposures, 3¼″ × 4¼″.
No. 4 Kodak camera	Jan. 1890–1897	Factory loaded with 48 exposures, picture size 5″ × 4″, capacity to 100 exposures.
No. 4 Kodak Jr. camera	Jan. 1890–1897	Factory loaded with 48 exposures, picture size 4″ × 5″.
"A" Ordinary Kodak camera	1891–1895	Darkroom loading, 2¾″ × 3¼″, 24 exposures.
"A" Daylight Kodak camera	1891–1895	Daylight loading, 2¾″ × 3¼″, 24 exposures.
"B" Ordinary Kodak camera	1891–1895	Darkroom loading, 3½″ × 4″, 24 exposures.
"B" Daylight Kodak camera	1891–1895	Daylight loading, 3½″ × 4″, 24 exposures.
"C" Ordinary Kodak camera	1891–1895	Darkroom loading, 4″ × 5″, 24 exposures.
"C" Daylight Kodak camera	1891–1895	Daylight loading, 4″ × 5″, 24 exposures.
No. 6 Folding Kodak Improved camera	1893–1895	6½″ × 8½″, roll film.
No. 4 Kodet camera	1894–1897	Loaded with plate or roll, 4″ × 5″. "Specials": 1895–97.
No. 4 Kodet Jr. camera	1894–1897	Loaded with plate or roll, 4″ × 5″.
No. 2 Bullet camera	1895–1896	Box, picture size 3½″ × 3½″, #101 roll film; also Improved model made 1896 to 1900, uses roll or single-plate holder.

Camera	Dates of Manufacture	Description
No. 5 Folding Kodet camera	1895–1897	Loaded with plate or roll, 5″ × 7″. Specials made 1895–1897.
Pocket Kodak camera	1895–1900	Tiny box, picture size 1½″ × 2″, #102 roll film.
No. 4 Bull's-Eye Improved camera	1896–1904	Box, 4″ × 5″, takes #103 roll film; also Special 1898–1904.
No. 2 Bull's-Eye camera	1896–1913	Box, 3½″ × 3½″, takes #103 roll film or double-plate holder; also Special made in 1898.
No. 2 Falcon Kodak camera	1897–Dec. 1899	Box, 3½″ × 3½″, #101 roll.
No. 4 Bullet Kodet camera	1897–1900	Box, picture size 4″ × 5″, #103 roll film or single-plate holder. Specials 1898–1904.
No. 4 Cartridge Kodak camera	1897–1900	5″ × 7″, #104 roll; later models 1900–1907.
No. 2 Eureka camera	1898–1899	Box, 3½″ × 3½″, #106 roll holder; also as Eureka Jr. plate-loaded.
No. 5 Cartridge Kodak camera	1898–1900	With wood lens board and front bed, for 7″ × 5″ pictures; later models with metal lens board 1900–1907; #115 roll.
No. 1 Folding Pocket Kodak camera	1898–1904	2¼″ × 3¼″, #105 roll; later models to 1915 with Automatic shutter.
No. 4 Eureka camera	1899 only	Box, 4″ × 5″, #109 roll holder.
No. 4 Panoram-Kodak camera	1899–Nov. 1900	Panoramic swing-lens box; also in Models B, C, D to 1924. Picture 3½″ × 12″ on #103 roll film.
No. 2 Folding Pocket Kodak camera	1899–1903	3½″ × 3½″, #101 roll; second model with RR lens 1904–1909.
No. 1A Folding Pocket Kodak camera	Dec. 1899–1904	2½″ × 4¼″, #116 roll; later models with Pocket Automatic shutters to 1915. Special models to 1912.
No. 2 Flexo Kodak camera	Dec. 1899–1913	Box, 3½″ × 3½″, #101 roll.
No. 3 Cartridge Kodak camera	1900	4¼″ × 3¼″, #119 roll, later models to 1907.
No. 3 Folding Pocket Kodak camera	Apr. 1900—1903	3¼″ × 4¼″, #118 roll; later models to 1915.
No. 1 Panoram-Kodak camera	Apr. 1900–1914	Panoramic swing-lens box; also in Models B, C, D to 1914. Picture 2¼″ × 7″ on #105 roll film.
No. 3 Folding Pocket Kodak Special camera	Oct. 1901–1903	Deluxe camera with Persian morocco leather, silk bellows; 3¼″ × 4¼″, #118 roll.
No. 2 Stereo Kodak camera	Oct. 1901–1905	Box, stereo pictures 3½″ × 6″, #101 roll.
No. 0 Folding Pocket Kodak camera	Mar. 1902–1906	1⅝″ × 2½″, #121 roll.
No. 3A Folding Pocket Kodak camera	May 1903–1908	3¼″ × 5½″ (postcard), #122 roll, numerous models to 1915.
No. 4A Speed Kodak camera	Apr. 1903–1913	4¼″ × 6½″, #126 (early style), with focal-plane shutter to 1/1000. Models also with B&L, Goerz, Zeiss, and Cooke lenses.
No. 4 Screen-Focus Kodak camera	Apr. 1904–1909	4″ × 5″, #123 roll, special provision for ground-glass focusing, numerous models to 1909.
3B Quick Focus Kodak camera	Feb. 1906–Apr. 1911	Box camera with rapid-adjustment focus system, 3¼″ × 5½″ picture on #125 roll.
No. 4A Folding Kodak camera	Apr. 1906–Apr. 1915	4¼″ × 6½″, #126 (early style) roll, numerous models to 1915.
No. 4 Folding Kodak camera	Feb. 1907–1908	4″ × 5″, #123 roll, numerous models to 1915.
No. 3 Bull's-Eye camera	Mar. 1908–1913	Box, 3¼″ × 4¼″, #124 roll.

CAMERA	DATES OF MANUFACTURE	DESCRIPTION
No. 1A Speed Kodak camera	Apr. 1909–1913	2½″ × 4¼″, #116 roll, with focal-plane shutter to 1/1000. Models with Zeiss, B&L, Cooke lenses.
No. 3A Special Kodak camera	Apr. 1910–1914	3¼″ × 5½″ (postcard), #122 roll, with B&L Compound shutter.
No. 3 Special Kodak camera	Apr. 1911–1914	3¼″ × 4¼″, #118 roll.
No. 1A Special Kodak camera	Apr. 1912–1914	2½″ × 4¼″, #116 roll, with B&L Compound shutters.
Vest Pocket Kodak camera	Apr. 1912–1914	1⅝″ × 2½″, #127 roll. Models including Special to 1914.
Six-Three Kodak cameras: (3)	Apr. 1913–Apr. 1915	Models 1A, 3, and 3A with B&L shutters from 2½″ × 4¼″ up to 3¼″ × 5½″ sizes, 2¼″ × 3¼″ on #120 roll; 2½″ × 4¼″ on #116; box.
No. 1 Kodak Jr. and 1A camera	1914	No. 1: 2¼″ × 3¼″ roll film #120; No. 1A: 2¼″ × 4¼″ roll film #116.
No. 1A Autographic Kodak camera	Sept. 1914–1916	2½″ × 4¼″, #A116 roll, write-on-film camera. Many models to 1924. Jr. and Special models to 1927. Special model with coupled range finder 1917–1928.
No. 3A Autographic Kodak camera	July 1914–1924	3¼″ × 5½″ (postcard), #A122 roll, write-on-film camera. Many models plus Jr. and Special models to 1927. Special model with coupled range finder 1916–1933.
No. 1 Autographic Kodak Jr. camera	Dec. 1914–1924	2¼″ × 3¼″, #A120 roll, write-on-the film camera. Models to 1926. Special models 1915–1926.
No. 3 Autographic Kodak camera	Sept. 1914–1925	3¼″ × 4¼″, #A118 roll, write-on-film camera. Models to 1926. Special models to 1926.
Vest Pocket Autographic Kodak camera	1915–1926	1⅝″ × 2½″, #127 roll, write-on-film camera. Various models to 1926.
No. 2C Autographic Kodak camera	June 1916–1924	2⅞″ × 4⅞″, #A130 roll, write-on-film camera. Models to 1927. Jr. 1925–1927, Special 1923–1928.
Stereo Kodak, Model 1 camera	Apr. 1917–1918	Box; frame size 3⅛″ × 3³⁄₁₆″ on #101 roll; ball bearing shutter model 1919–1925.
Vest Pocket Kodak, Model B camera	Oct. 1925–1934	1⅝″ × 2½″, #127 roll. Also Series III and Special cameras to 1934.
No. 2C Pocket Kodak (incl. Series II, Specials) cameras	Oct. 1925–1932	2⅞″ × 4⅞″, #130 roll. Series III: 1924–1931; Specials: 1928–1933.
No. 3A Panoram-Kodak camera	May 1926–1928	Box with swing lens; picture size 3¼″ × 10⅜″ on #122 roll film.
No. 1 Pocket Kodak, (incl. Series II, III, Jr. and Special) cameras	May 1926–1931	2¼″ × 3¼″ folding cameras, #120 roll. First models Series II: 1922–1924, plus to 1931; Series III: 1926–1931; Special: 1926–1934; Jr. in black and color: 1929–1931; in color: 1929–1931.
No. 3 Pocket Kodak Series III (incl. Specials)	May 1926–1934	3¼″ × 4¼″, #118 roll. Specials 1926–1934.
No. 1A Pocket Kodak (incl. Series II, III, Jr. and Special, plus Gift Kodak in cedar box)	1926–1931	2½″ × 4¼″ folding cameras; #116 roll. First models Series II: 1923–1931; Series III: 1924–1931; Special: 1926–1934; Jr.: 1929–1931; Gift Kodak: 1930–1931.
No. 3A Pocket Kodak (incl. Series II, III) cameras	Feb. 1927–1933	3¼″ × 5½″ (postcard); #122 roll; later models to 1933; Series II: 1936–1941; Series III: 1941–1945.
Vanity Kodak (Vest Pocket, Series III, in color) cameras	Apr. 1928–1933	1⅝″ × 2½″, #127 roll. Also available as Vanity Kodak Ensemble with lipstick, compact, mirror, change pocket.
Kodak Petite (Vest Pocket Model B in color) cameras	June 1929–1934	1⅝″ × 2½″, #127 roll. Also available as Kodak Petite Ensemble with lipstick, compact, mirror.

Camera	Dates of Manufacture	Description
Girl Scout Kodak camera	Dec. 1929–1934	1⅝" × 2½", #127 roll.
Kodak Coquette (Kodak Petite with matching lipstick holder and compact) camera	Oct. 1930–1931	1⅝" × 2½", #127 roll.
Anniversary Kodak Box Camera	1930	2¼" × 3¼", #120 roll. Free to all children 12 years old in 1930.
Boy Scout Kodak camera	1930–1934	1⅝" × 2½", #127 roll.
Campfire Girls' Kodak camera	Apr. 1931–1934	1⅝" × 2½", #127 roll.
Kodak Six-20 (and Improved) camera	Feb. 1932–1937	2¼" × 3¼", #620 roll, six models. Improved: 1934–1937.
Kodak Six-16 camera	Feb. 1932–1936	2½" × 4¼", #616 roll.
Kodak Senior Six-16 (and Special) cameras	Feb. 1932–1936	2½" × 4¼", #616 roll. Specials 1937–1939.
Kodak Recomar cameras	June 1932–1940	Model 18 2¼" × 3¼", Model 33 3¼" × 4¼". Film-pack loading. Made in Germany.
Kodak Pupille camera	July 1932–1934	1³⁄₁₆" × 1⁹⁄₁₆", #127 roll, made in Germany.
Kodak Ranca camera	July 1932–1934	1³⁄₁₆" × 1⁹⁄₁₆", #127 roll, made in Germany.
Kodak Vollenda camera	July 1932–1937	1³⁄₁₆" × 1⁹⁄₁₆", #127 roll, made in Germany.
Jiffy Kodak Six-16 (and Series III) cameras	Apr. 1933–1937	2½" × 4¼", #616 roll. Series III: 1937–1946.
Kodak Duo Six-20 camera (and Series II)	Aug. 1934–1937	1⅝" × 2¼", #620 roll, made in Germany. Series II: 1937–1939, w/rngfdr. 1939–1940.
Kodak Retina cameras (I and II)	Dec. 1934–1937	24 mm × 36 mm, #135 (35 mm), made in Germany. Model I (second in series): 1936–1950; Model II (third in series): 1937–1950.
Kodak Junior Six-16 (and Series II, III) cameras	Feb. 1935–1937	2½" × 4¼", #616 roll. Series II: 1937–1940, Series III: 1938–1939.
Jiffy Kodak Vest Pocket camera	Apr. 1935–1942	1⅝" × 2½" roll.
Kodak Junior Six-20 camera (and Series II, III)	May 1935–1937	2¼" × 3¼", #620 roll. Series II: 1937–1940; Series III: 1938–1939.
Kodak Bantam camera	June 1935–1941	28 mm × 40 mm, #828 roll, six models with different lenses.
Kodak Bantam Special cameras	July 1936–1948	28 mm × 40 mm, #828, first model with Compur Rapid shutter to 1940, second model with Supermatic shutter 1941–1948.
Jiffy Kodak Six-20 camera (and Series II, Senior Six-20, and Special models)	June 1937–1939	2¼" × 3¼", #620 roll. Series II: 1937–1948; Senior: 1937–1939; Special: 1937–1939.
Super Kodak Six-20	July 1938–1945	First camera with built-in coupled electric eye for automatic exposure. 2¼" × 3¼", #620 roll.
Kodak 35	Sept. 1938–1951	24 mm × 36 mm, #135 (35 mm); five models w/o rngfdr to 1948; w/rgfdr July 1940–1951 in three models.
Kodak Vigilant Six-20 (and Jr.) cameras	Oct. 1939–1940	2¼" × 3¼", #620 roll. Ten models; Jr.: 1940–1948.
Kodak Monitor Six-20 cameras	Oct. 1939–1946	2¼" × 3¼", #620 roll. Models to 1948.
Kodak Vigilant Six-16 (and Jr.) cameras	Oct. 1939–1947	2½" × 4¼", #616 roll. Jr. 1940–1947.
Kodak Monitor Six-16 camera	Oct. 1939–1946	2½" × 4¼", #616 roll.
Kodak Flash Bantam camera	July 1947–1953	28 mm × 40 mm, #828, two models.
Kodak Bantam RF camera	Oct. 1953–1956	28 mm × 40 mm, #828 roll, Flash 300 shutter.

256

A BRIEF HISTORY OF THE BROWNIE CAMERAS
AND BULLET CAMERAS

CAMERA	DATES OF MANUFACTURE	DESCRIPTION
The Brownie (No. 1 Brownie) camera	Feb. 1900 thru 1915	Box camera taking pictures 2¼″ × 2¼″; first model has detachable back; second model has top metal slide lock. #117 roll film.
No. 2 Brownie camera	Oct. 1901–1924	Box camera taking pictures 2¼″ × 3¼″. Aluminum model 1924–1933; in colors 1929–1933. #120 roll.
No. 2 Folding Brownie camera	Apr. 1904–1907	Drop-front folding camera; 2¼″ × 3¼″; Model B 1907–1915; #120 roll.
No. 3 Folding Pocket Brownie camera	Apr. 1905–1909	3¼″ × 4¼″; later models 1909–1915. #124 roll.
No. 2 Stereo Brownie camera	Apr. 1905–1910	Brownie Automatic only to 1905; Pocket Automatic shutter to 1910. #125 roll.
No. 2A Brownie camera	Apr. 1907–1924	Box camera taking pictures 2¼″ × 4¼″. Aluminum model 1924–1933; in colors 1929–1933. #116 roll.
No. 3 Brownie camera	Nov. 1908–1934	Box camera taking pictures 3¼″ × 4¼″, #124 roll.
No. 3A Folding Pocket Brownie camera	Apr. 1909–1913	3¼″ × 5½″ (postcard); later models 1909–1915. #122 roll.
No. 2A Folding Pocket Brownie camera	Feb. 1910–1915	2½″ × 4¼″, #116 roll.
No. 0 Brownie camera	May 1914–1935	Box camera taking pictures 1⅝″ × 2½″, #127 roll.
No. 2 Folding Autographic Brownie camera	Sept. 1915–1923	With square ends to 1916, round ends 1917–1923; 2¼″ × 3¼″; #A120 roll; write-on-film camera. Later models to 1926.
No. 2A Folding Autographic Brownie camera	Nov. 1915–1923	2½″ × 4¼″; #A116 roll; write-on-film camera. Later models to 1926.
No. 2C Folding Autographic Brownie camera	May 1916–1924	With square ends to 1917; all others round ends. 2⅞″ × 4⅞″; write-on-film camera; models to 1926.
No. 3A Folding Autographic Brownie camera	July 1916–1924	3¼″ × 5½″ (postcard), #A122 roll; write-on-film camera; later models to 1926.
No. 2C Brownie camera	July 1917–1934	Box camera taking pictures 2⅞″ × 4⅞″, #130 roll.
Nos. 2 and 2A Beau Brownie camera	Oct. 1930–1932	2¼″ × 3¼″, #120 roll.
Boy Scout Brownie camera	1932	2¼″ × 3¼″, #120 roll.
Six-20 Boy Scout Brownie camera	Jan. 1933–1934	2¼″ × 3¼″, #620 roll.
Six-20 Brownie camera (and Jr.; Special)	Mar. 1933–1941	2¼″ × 3¼″, #620 roll; Jr. 1934–1946; Special 1938–1946.
Six-16 Brownie camera (and Jr., and Special)	Mar. 1933–1941	2¼″ × 4¼″, #616 roll; Jr. 1934–1946; Special: 1938–1946.
Baby Brownie camera	July 1934–1941	First camera designed for Kodak by W. D. Teague; 1⅝″ × 2½″, #127 roll.
Bullet camera	Oct. 1936–1946	1⅝″ × 2½″, #127 roll.
Six-20 Bull's-Eye Brownie camera	July 1938–1941	2¼″ × 3¼″, #620 roll.
New York World's Fair Bullet camera	Apr. 1939–1940	1⅝″ × 2½″, #127 roll.

Camera	Dates of Manufacture	Description
Baby Brownie Special camera	Sept. 1939–1954	1⅝″ × 2½″, #127 roll.
New York World's Fair Brownie camera	1939–1940	1⅝″ × 2½″, #127 roll.
Six-20 Flash Brownie camera	July 1946–1954	2¼″ × 3¼″, #620 roll.
✓ Target Brownie Six-20 camera	July 1946–1952	2¼″ × 3¼″, #620 roll.

A GUIDE TO DATING EARLY KODAK CAMERAS EQUIPPED WITH KODAK SHUTTERS

Name of Shutter	Dates of Manufacture	Name of Shutter	Dates of Manufacture
Automatic	1904–1919	Kodamatic (old style) small	1921–1934
Ball Bearing #0	1914–1926	Kodamatic (ring set) #1	1937–1948
Ball Bearing #1	1909–1924	Kodex #0	1924–1934
Ball Bearing #2	1909–1933	Kodex (old style) #1	1925–1933
Brownie Automatic	1904–1915	Kodex (new style) #1	1935–1945
DAK	1940–1948	Kodo #0	1929–1940
Dakar #1	1935–1936	Kodo #1	1929–1940
Dakon (2 speed)	1940–1948	Pneumatic (See Triple Action)	
Dakon (3 speed)	1946–1948	Rotary	1895–1900
Diodak #1	1932–1935	Supermatic #0	1941–1948
Diodak #2	1932–1933	Supermatic #1	1939–1948
Diodak #2A	1936–1941	Supermatic #2	1939–1947
Diomatic (top dial) #0	1924–1935	Triple Action	1897–1903
Diomatic (top dial) #1	1924–1933		
Diomatic (ring set) #1 (3 speeds)	1940–1948	*Focal-Plane Shutters*	
Diomatic (ring set) #1 (4 speeds)	1938–1948	Kodak Focal Plane (4½ × 6½ inches)	1908–1912
Diomatic (ring set) #2	1938–1939		
Eastman Automatic	1898–1906	*Stereo Shutters*	
Hawk-Eye	1923	Brownie Automatic Stereo	1905–1915
Kodal #0	1932	Stereo Ball Bearing	1919–1924
Kodal #2	1932–1940		

A GUIDE TO KODAK FILM SIZES

If little more is known about a camera than the numerical designation for the film roll required (the kind of information imprinted inside the back cover of many cameras), it is possible to determine the earliest possible date which that camera could have been manufactured. For example, one of the most popular film sizes of the first quarter of the twentieth century was the "postcard": 3¼ by 5½ inches. Cameras by Kodak, Ansco, Buster Brown, Seneca, and others were designated as "3A" to indicate this very popular picture size. The Kodak-made film for the cameras of this size was the #122, first made in 1903 for the 3A Folding Pocket Kodak.

The dates within the following chart show that no 3A camera (or any camera that required use of #122 film) could have been made prior to 1903. Kodak was still making 3A-size cameras as late as 1945 (No. 3A Pocket Kodak, Series III; see "A Brief History of Most Eastman Kodak Cameras," page 253) but other camera companies had earlier discontinued manufacture of this roll-film–size equipment.

This chart of roll-film sizes, dates, and dimensions will assist determination of the earliest possible manufacturing year of cameras where little else is known but the required film size.

Kodak Roll-Film Dimensions

Film No.	Introduction Date	Date Discontinued	Picture Area	Film No.	Introduction Date	Date Discontinued	Picture Area
101	1895	July 1956	3½″ × 3½″	119	1900	July 1940	4¼″ × 3¼″
102	1895	Sept. 1933	1½″ × 2″	120	1901		2¼″ × 3¼″
103	1896	Mar. 1949	3¾″ × 4¾″	121	1902	Nov. 1941	1⅝″ × 2½″
104	1897	Mar. 1949	4¾″ × 3¾″	122	1903		3¼″ × 5½″
105	1898	Mar. 1949	2¼″ × 3¼″	123	1904	Mar. 1949	4″ × 5″
106	1898	L.L.* 1924	3½″ × 3½″	124	1905	Aug. 1961	3¼″ × 4¼″
107	1898	L.L. 1924	3¼″ × 4¼″	125	1905	Mar. 1949	3¼″ × 2½″
108	1898	Oct. 1929	4¼″ × 3¼″	126	1906	Mar. 1949	4¼″ × 6½″
109	1898	L.L. 1924	4″ × 5″	127	1912		1⅝″ × 2½″
110	1898	Oct. 1929	5″ × 4″	128	1912	Nov. 1941	1½″ × 2¼″
111	1898	no domestic listing	6½″ × 4¾″	129	1912	Jan. 1951	1⅞″ × 3″
112	1898	L.L. 1924	7″ × 5″	130	1916	Aug. 1961	2⅞″ × 4⅞″
113	1898	no domestic listing	9 cm × 12 cm	616	1932		2½″ × 4¼″
114	1898	no domestic listing	12 cm × 9 cm	620	1932		2¼″ × 3¼″
115	1898	Mar. 1949	6¾″ × 4¾″	135	1934		24 mm × 36 mm
116	1899		2½″ × 4¼″	828	1935		28 mm × 40 mm
117	1900	Mar. 1949	2¼″ × 2¼″	126	1963 (Instamatic)		28 mm × 28 mm
118	1900	Aug. 1961	3¼″ × 4¼″				

* L.L.: Last Listing. The camera is not offered in catalogues after an "L.L." date, but Kodak knows of no official notice of discontinuance of manufacture.

Appendix D
Major Cirkut, Ciro,
Crown, Graphic, and Graflex Cameras

(Originally published by the Photographic Historical Society of Rochester, New York.)

CAMERAS (*Alphabetically listed*)	DATES OF AVAILABILITY First	Last
Auto Jr. Graflex	1914	1924
2¼″ × 3¼″ R B, (Revolving Back) Jr.	1915	1924
3¼″ × 4¼″ Auto (straight back)	1910	1923
4″ × 5″ Auto (straight back)	1910	1923
5″ × 7″ Auto (straight back)	1910	1923
5″ × 7″ Stereo Auto	1907	1922
4″ × 5″ Naturalist	1907	1921
3-A	1907	1926
1-A	1909	1925
5″ × 7″ Compact Graflex	1915	1925
3¼″ × 5½″ Compact	1915	1925
5″ × 7″ Press	1907	1923
2¼″ × 3¼″ Series B (straight back)	1925	1926
3¼″ × 4¼″ Series B (straight back)	1925	1937
4″ × 5″ Series B (straight back)	1925	1937
3¼″ × 4¼″ R B Telescopic	1915	1923
4″ × 5″ R B Telescopic	1914	1923
3¼″ × 4¼″ R B Auto	1909	1942
4″ × 5″ R B Auto	1907	1940
3¼″ × 4¼″ R\B Series C	1926	1935
3¼″ × 4¼″ R B Series D	1929	1941
4″ × 5″ R R Series D	1929	1945
5″ × 7″ R B Home Portrait	1912	1942
2¼″ × 3¼″ R B Series B	1923	1951
3¼″ × 4¼″ R B Series B	1923	1942
4″ × 5″ R B Series B	1923	1942
5″ × 7″ R B Series B	1923	1942
3¼″ × 4¼″ R B Super D–under #300,000	1941	1943
3¼″ × 4½″ R B Super D	1946	1963
4″ × 5″ R B Super D	1948	1957
#0 Graphic	1909	1923
R B Cycle prior to	1900	1923
Stereoscopic Graphic 5″ × 7″	1904	1921
3¼″ × 4¼″ Speed Graphic (1/500 top speed)	1915	1925
3¼″ × 5½″ Speed Graphic	1912	1925

CAMERAS (Alphabetically listed)	First	Last
4" × 5" Speed Graphic (3¼" × 3¼" lens board)	1912	1924
5" × 7" Speed Graphic	1912	1925
4" × 5" Speed Graphic (4" × 4" lens board)	1924	1930
4" × 5" Pre-Anniversary (handle on side)	1930	1939
5" × 7" Graphic (4" × 4" lens board)	1930	1939
2¼" × 3¼" Pre-Anniversary R B	1937	1938
3¼" × 4¼" Pre-Anniversary	1935	1939
2¼" × 3¼" Miniature Speed	1938	1947
3¼" × 4¼" Anniversary	1940	1947
4" × 5" Anniversary	1940	1947
Combat Graphic 45	1944	1946
23 Pacemaker Crown Graphic	1947	1958
23 Pacemaker Speed Graphic	1947	1958
34 Pacemaker Crown Graphic	1948	1962
34 Pacemaker Speed Graphic	1948	1963
45 Pacemaker Crown Graphic	1947	——
45 Pacemaker Speed Graphic	1947	1968
45 Electrified Crown Graphic	1956	1958
C-904 Crown 45 Special (Kalart RFDR)	1956	1958
CF-904 Crown 45 Special (Graphic RFDR)	1958	——
23 Century Graphic (Black Bellows)	1949	1954
23 Century Graphic (Red Bellows)	1954	1963
23 Century Graphic (above Ser. No. 532884 Black Bellows)	1964	——
4" × 5" Super Graphic	1958	——
#6 Cirkut Outfit	1909	1921
#8 Cirkut Outfit	1909	1921
#10 Cirkut Camera	1909	1941
#16 Cirkut Camera	1909	1921
#5 Cirkut Camera	1915	1922
#6 Cirkut Camera	1909	1943
Crown View (4" × 5") brass	Aug. 1938	1942
Crown View Chrome	Aug. 1938	Aug. 1941
Graphic View I (4" × 5")	1941	1949
Graphic View II (4" × 5")	Aug. 1949	——
Graphic View II (4" × 5") Ektalite	Aug. 1951	——
Graphic View II (4" × 5") Graflok Back	Mar. 1954	——
Ciro 35 R	Sept. 1949	Aug. 1952
Ciro 35 S	Sept. 1949	Sept. 1954
Ciro 35 T	Aug. 1951	Sept. 1953
Ciroflex B,C,D,E,F earlier than	Oct. 1951	Oct. 1952
(Ciro 35 and Ciroflex acquired by Graflex)	1951	——
National Graflex, Series I	1933	June 1935
National Graflex, Series II	Dec. 1934	1941
Graphic 70 (7 mm)	Apr. 1956	Oct. 1962
Graflex 22 (200 black)	Nov. 1952	Nov. 1955
Graflex 22 (200 gray)	Nov. 1952	Dec. 1957
Graflex 22 (400 black)	Feb. 1953	May 1956
Graflex 22 (400 gray)	Feb. 1953	Nov. 1956
Graflex 22 (400F gray)	Apr. 1953	Apr. 1956
Graphic 35 f/3.5 (single color band)	Feb. 1955	Apr. 1956
Graphic 35 f/3.5 (double color band)	Apr. 1956	May 1957
Graphic 35 f/3.5 (Universal color band)	Apr. 1956	July 1957
Graphic 35 f/2.8 (double color band)	Nov. 1955	Apr. 1956

CAMERAS (*Alphabetically listed*)	DATES OF AVAILABILITY	
	First	*Last*
Graphic 35 f/2.8 (Universal color band)	Apr. 1956	July 1957
Graphic 35 Electric	Oct. 1959	June 1963
Jet Graphic 35	Sept. 1961	Oct. 1962
Century 35 f/3.5	Oct. 1957	Sept. 1960
Century 35 f/2.8	Mar. 1958	Sept. 1960
Century 35A	May 1959	Aug. 1961
Century 35N	May 1959	Aug. 1960
Century 35 NE (meter)	Aug. 1959	Oct. 1960
Stereo Graphic 35	Sept. 1955	June 1962
8″ × 10″ Crown ER & C Camera	1900	1946

Appendix E
Maintaining the
Photographica Collection

RESTORATION OF DAGUERREOTYPES

Most Daguerreotypes are found still in the display case furnished by the original photographer. It was common for these photographers to protect the delicate image on the highly polished silver by sealing the image behind a clear small pane of glass, using paper tape to bind the glass to the copper back of the silver plate. In the more than one hundred years since Daguerreotypy ended as a widely practiced art, chemical oxidation of the silver (not unlike the oxidation that blackens silverware) has covered all or part of the image. Mold spore may have formed circular blemishes or discolorations.

This oxidation can be removed with a simple cleaning process. CAUTION: With potentially unusual or rare Daguerreotypes (outdoor scenes, work views, famous personalities, nudes, historic landmarks, very large Daguerreotypes such as book-size), cleaning should only be undertaken after consultation with experts (image dealers, museum restoration departments, etc.)

Opening the Daguerreotype Case

Remove the foil mask which is usually wrapped around the glass and plate packet. Lift the entire mask and plate by edging a knife point into the case edge where the mask meets the interior edge. The foil-wrapped packet is only force-fit into the case.

The foil is folded at back around the glass and the plate. Unfold the soft metal without bending the mask face; set aside.

The glass is bound to the plate with paper tape that may be slit with a razor at the edge. Handle the silver plate only by the edges from this point forward. The glass may be removed and washed clean with soap and water. At times, fungi have formed on this glass, and such growth or surface grime can also be removed with the soap and water. It should finally be wiped dry with a lintless cloth.

Cleaning the Daguerreotype

There are a number of way of cleaning the Daguerreotype that have been explored by those who make Daguerreotype collecting their main activity. Possibly the simplest is the use of a household cleansing agent such as Noxon Quik-Dip Silver Cleaner, a bottled variant of the Noxon silverware polish widely sold in food stores. The Noxon Quik-Dip is not as readily available but may be found in some hardware stores.

A shallow saucer may be covered with a small quantity of the liquid. The Daguerreotype is placed gently face up in the bath; the liquid is rolled up onto the Daguerreotype by slightly tipping and tilting the saucer. Within seconds, the chemical action is complete. The dark blue and gray black tarnish is chemically removed without the fingers ever touching the delicate surface of the plate.

The Noxon may be returned to the original bottle for reuse. The Daguerreotype is now lifted from the saucer, handled only by the edges, and is brought under a lightly flowing stream of cool water at the tap of a sink. Less than a minute under this flowing stream will wash away any remaining Noxon.

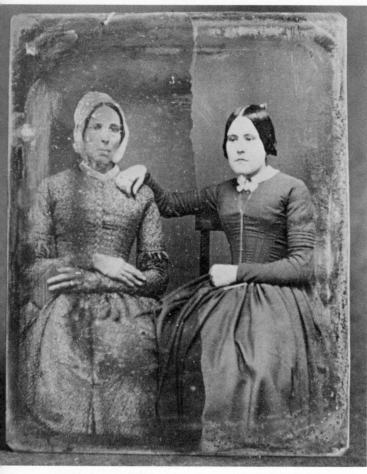

Half-cleaned Daguerreotype demonstrates effectiveness of a brief chemical bath, which almost instantly removes oxidation clouding the image.

Redrying the Daguerreotype

The problem now is the drying of the Daguerreotype without touching the surface with any material whatsoever. If a bead or droplet of water slowly evaporates when it sits on the image surface after the balance of the plate is free of water, a water spot (visible forever thereafter) is formed. The idea is to effect the drying in a matter of minutes and then to reencase the Daguerreotype in its original case with glass, mask, and new tape.

One way of drying is with a blower hairdryer now commonly available. By bringing the Daguerreotype to within ten to twelve inches of a stream of *cool* air, the air flow will push water drops sitting on the silver plate out to the edges. A few drops of a wetting agent, such as photographer's Photo-Flo, in a final water bath before drying has

the effect of preventing the formation of water bubbles. The objective is to remove all water from the surface of the plate before air-drying has time to start.

Some workers dip the cleaned plate into a dip of 95-percent grain alcohol; then the plate is dried (after draining) by the heat of a slow-burning candle ten to twelve inches beneath the plate.

Now the dry plate is joined with the newly dried glass, resealed with a slide-binding tape (available in camera-supply stores for lantern-slide binding), and then refitted to the mask.

An Alternate Procedure for the Meticulous

After experimentation with a variety of procedures, one was developed by Mrs. Ruth K. Field, assistant curator of the Missouri Historical Society. It has become a standard for museum workers.

1. Wash Daguerreotype in distilled water to remove surface dirt.

2. Drain Daguerreotype and immerse until discoloration is removed in a solution of:

> Distilled water (500 cubic centimeters)
> Thiourea (70 grams)
> Phosphoric acid (85 percent) (80 cubic centimeters)
> Nonionic wetting agent (2 cubic centimeters)
> Distilled water to make 1 litre

3. Remove Daguerreotype from bath and immediately hold under running water.

4. Place Daguerreotype in a mild soap solution (face soap) and agitate briefly.

5. Rinse thoroughly in running water, then wash in a second bath of distilled water.

6. Immerse in 95-percent grain alcohol. Drain.

7. Hold Daguerreotype high over a small flame until dry.

The advantages of this method are many. In the first place, stains are completely removed without the plate being etched.

Details of the picture are brought out clearly, and the mirrorlike quality of the silver plate is retained.

Daguerreotypes can be left in the chemical solution indefinitely without removing the image. In one experiment the plate was left in the solution for one hour and twenty minutes without visible change. Consequently, Daguerreotypes formerly considered beyond restoration because of their extensive discoloration can now be restored.

Plates can be cleaned over again as often as necessary without harm.

TREATING OLD LEATHERS

Many early cameras were leather covered; after fifty years or more, the natural lubricants within these leathers are long gone. Adhesives may have dried out, and leather is often flaking away.

Leon Jacobson of Syracuse, New York, an active dealer in early cameras, has suggested these procedures for treating old leather:

1. First, reattach loose leather, using a clear cement of the quick-dry type, after first removing mold, loose glue particles, etc.

2. If a major segment or panel of leather is detached, use a contact type cement in which the camera body and the leather section are first individually coated. Carefully rejoin leather to camera body.

3. When the glued leather is dry, a thin layer of Lexol (the Lexol Corp., W. Caldwell, New Jersey 07006; or from leather shops, shoe stores, or hardware stores) is applied to all leather with a cloth. Dry for one hour. (Do not apply to leather handles; apply to bellows only after testing a section to see if Lexol will loosen leather from the inside liner.)

4. Apply Griffin Sterling Dressing (available at shoe stores, etc.) with a cloth to all black leather and rub in, especially where leather is badly scratched. This is a shoe-preparation material that contains a black dye and polish. When dry, polish with a cloth and brush with a shoe brush. Avoid waxy shoe polishes; these tend to fill in the leather grain and provide an unnatural appearance. The Griffin solution can be wiped from metal parts with a damp cloth. Use neutral liquid shoe cleaners on tan, red, or colored leathers.

CLEANING A CAMERA WITHOUT DISASSEMBLY

Cameras may be found soiled, smudged, and even greasy from handling. Since most household cleaning agents will remove finishes from leather, wood, or other camera parts, it is usually best to wipe the camera down with a moist cloth made slightly soapy with a mild soap or with a laundry detergent such as Liquid All or Wisk.

The silicon cloth (sold in sporting goods shops to clean fishing reels or guns) is an excellent overall cleaning aid since it lubricates leather parts and will bring life back to nickel or metal parts, too. Do not use the silicon cloth on lenses. Cotton swabs and pins will help clean away corners or remove dirt from the grooves in screw heads and other tiny crevices.

Cleaning Wood Surfaces

Most collectors do not wish to disassemble a camera to refinish wood parts; total refinishing gives the old camera an unnatural "refinished" look. Polishing with a wood polish, such as Guardsman Cleaning Polish (Guardsman Chemical Coatings, Inc., Grand Rapids, Michigan), or even with a furniture polish or household cleaner such as Jubilee, produce satisfactory lusters. Brisk rubbing after application of the polishing agent brings up a rich glow.

Cleaning Brass Knobs and Struts

Camera brass was always coated with a varnish. If this film is essentially intact, clean only with a mild detergent solution. If the brass is badly tarnished and if it can be removed from the camera, Brasso (available at hardware stores) will bring life back to metal. It will be necessary to first remove the remaining varnish with a varnish remover (also available at hardware stores). After polishing, and after all traces of Brasso have been removed, a coating of automobile wax can be applied to protect the surface. (Do not use Brasso if the brass part is still attached to the camera; it tends to corrode other parts of the camera where it will seep in.)

Lenses

Unscrew the lens from the camera; then unscrew the lens itself from the brass mount or the shutter. The lens elements may now have both surfaces cleaned with a well-washed, soft cotton cloth dampened with Windex or similar glass cleaner. Polish the glass afterwards with a soft cloth and reassemble only after the lenses are dry. Clean the brass mount with Brasso (see above) if condition is poor. Otherwise, wipe the brass mount down after a mild detergent bath.

Nickel Parts

If the finish has not been removed, nickel tends to polish well. A jeweler's rouge-impregnated pad is the best item to use (available at your jewelry shop; or use Buff-n-Clean Polishing Pad sold by the Fuller Brush Company). Trichloroethylene (from hardware or paint stores) can be used to remove excess rouge after polishing. Rub nickel with a soft cloth for a high shine.

Black-Painted Metal Parts

An automobile touchup lacquer such as Duplicolor (from an auto-supply store) is available in a touch-up jar or a spray can. When lacquer is dry, rubbing compound (also available at auto-supply store) may be used to reduce the high-polish look of the touched-up area, blending the patched area with the rest of the finish. Wipe down with a soft cloth afterward.

BELLOWS

Cleaning Bellows

In most cases, washing bellows with a solution of one part household ammonia and two parts water is enough to bring the gleam and color back into the appearance of even faded bellows. Use a soft cloth and wipe one area at a time. Red bellows with faded spots may be given an improved appearance if re-

dyed with a solution made of Red Coccine Dye (used by photo retouchers) in water. Black bellows may be treated with Griffin Sterling Dressing (see above) if edges are gray or bleached.

If bellows must be replaced, bellows material (black only) is available from the National Camera Repair School, Englewood, Colorado 80110. Hopefully, the inner liner of the original bellows is still reasonably intact as a guide to size and shape. Original bellows can be separated from the original lining and stiffeners with a soak in alcohol.

Stiffeners can be recemented into place with a contact-type adhesive. If the stiffener has only partly separated from a lining, a hobbyist's razor (like the X-Acto) may be used to slit the liner from the inside to permit glue to be worked into the separated area.

To totally reconstruct a bellows is a formidable task, requiring a large form on which to build the bellows, first cutting and fitting the inner liner (using the first bellows as a size guide); then affixing stiffeners where they will be needed; then applying the new bellows leather over all. There are bellows makers who can provide bellows to your dimensions should you wish to refit an early camera with a modern bellows.

Replacement Bellows

Replacement bellows may be obtained from:
Turner Bellows, Inc., 165 North Water Street, Rochester, New York 14604
C. T. Moyse & Son, P.O. Box 228, East Rockaway, New York 11518
Western Bellows Co., 404 Agostino Road, San Gabriel, California 91776
J. Milner, 482 Griffith Street, London, Ontario, Canada

Appendix F
Photographica Museums

There was a time in America's relatively recent past when the ownership of an automobile was so novel that a "Sunday drive" was as fashionable as the Fifth Avenue stroll on Easter Day. Now the Sunday driver is going someplace. The collector-driver behind the wheel has a specific destination: flea markets, antique shows, special photographica events, and the like. They have one further travel goal: to get to the key museums and show centers where organized presentations of photography's history are on display.

In the halls of historical societies, in the corners of centers for art and technology, in the science centers, and even in corners of restorations and pioneer-day tourist sites, there are major displays of early studios, showcases of equipment, walls of images, and other photographica within the reach of a Sunday drive.

Here are the centers. The days they are open and the hours they maintain should be checked before you load the family wagon. If you're a world traveler, there's hardly a country that won't welcome your interest in its history museum of photography.

MUSEUMS OF PHOTOGRAPHY IN THE UNITED STATES

Lile Museum of Photography, 310 Lanehart Road, Little Rock, Arkansas

> A museum that includes displays from the four thousand equipment pieces, three thousand photography books, and antiques of the photography field collected by Greer and Mary Lile of Little Rock. A skylight studio is but one feature of the special building for the collection built on a two-acre site.

The Museum of Photography, University of California, Riverside, California

> Housed in the Humanities Building on the campus of the university, the museum houses the Bingham Collection of cameras along with a collection of letters, manuscripts, photographs, art, etc., of Sadakichi Hartmann reflecting the arts and letters of the period from 1880 to the early 1900s, including rare Stieglitz material (291 Gallery) and the Photo-Secessionist Movement.

California Academy of Science, Golden Gate Park, San Francisco, California

> A Museum of Photography within this general museum displays cabinets of cameras, cine equipment, early dry-plate equipment, etc.

The Mattatuck Museum, 119 West Main Street, Waterbury, Connecticut

> The Industrial Museum in the basement offers exhibits relating to Waterbury's contribution to the growth of photography. The city has long been the home of Scovill Brass Company and the original Scovill Manufacturing Company, which entered the photographic field after Daguerre's process was introduced to America.

The Museum of New Mexico, Santa Fe, New Mexico

> A collection of photographic items primarily related to the growth of the western part of the United States.

Eastman Kodak Company Patent Department Museum, Kodak Park, Rochester, New York

> Among the most complete and best organized museums of photography anywhere, it was established primarily to assist Kodak engineers and attorneys to develop their understanding of products and innovations. By appointment only; usually restricted to scholars.

The International Museum of Photography at George Eastman House, 900 East Avenue, Rochester, New York

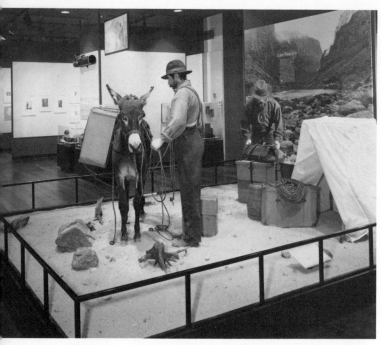

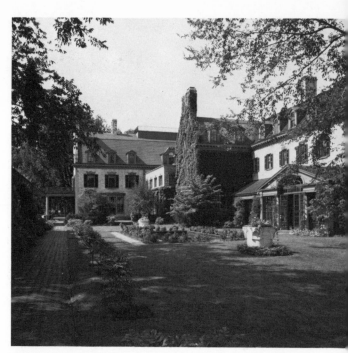

A tableau at the Smithsonian Institution's History of Photography collection depicts the wet-plate photographer with his pack mule accompanying an 1870 surveying team. An assistant is setting up the darkroom tent. *(Photograph courtesy of Smithsonian Institution)*

The home of George Eastman, founder of the Eastman Kodak Company, is now America's well-known center of early photography: the International Museum of Photography. *(Photograph courtesy International Museum of Photography)*

Originally the mansion of George Eastman, this gracious residence has long been the major center for displays relating to a variety of aspects of photography's history. A mix of infrequently changed major displays on the evolution of camera systems and hallways of minor-theme displays in window-size dioramas may be enjoyed by even the most knowledgeable collectors. Image displays may range from early photography to current experimental photography. A vast unseen collection includes the giant Cromer Collection and other major groups of rare items.

Bonanzaville, North Dakota

A ten-acre village created to depict the pioneer days of early North Dakota has established a modest photographic museum, the Photo Gallery, reflecting the equipment and images of pioneer days.

Jacksonville Museum, Courthouse Square, Jacksonville, Oregon

Maintained and administered by the Southern Oregon Historical Society, this museum is housed in a large old courthouse and two other buildings. While most displays relate to life in early Oregon, the local Indian groups, relics of children's toys, etc., a special room, the Peter Britt Gallery, is a wall-to-wall display of everything photographic covering the life and times of early photographer Britt. Daguerrean images, early

studio artifacts, and a variety of cameras make this fascinating room in a distant corner of the United States a fascinating visit for the photographic traveler.

University of Texas, Austin, Texas

Home of the photographic collection of Helmut and Alison Gernsheim, the world-famed researchers and historians on the emergence of photography.

Smithsonian Institution Museum of History and Technology, Madison Drive and Fourteenth Street, Washington, D.C.

The History of Photography Collection is housed on the third floor of the building that provides displays on numerous aspects of America's industrial and agricultural growth. The collection includes such diverse objects as the actual Daguerrean camera of Samuel F. B. Morse, Talbot's cane, and a painting by Daguerre. Displays are geared for the family groups that visit this center and do not provide an in-depth look at the vast collection of photographica in storage. The museum owns several hundred thousand images. Dioramas portray a variety of aspects of the social and cultural history of photography, such as a Victorian parlor scene, an early darkroom, etc. Open daily.

Stonefield Village, Nelson Dewey State Park, Cassville, Wisconsin

A photographic gallery has been built and equipped

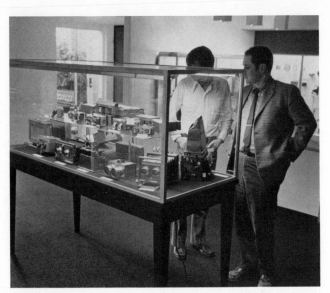

Stereo equipment in a free-standing cabinet display at the International Museum of Photography. *(Photograph by N. M. Graver)*

by the Wisconsin Professional Photographers Association, with cameras and images on display. The gallery is but one feature in a complex of a reconstructed village organized by the State Historical Society of Wisconsin and the state's Department of Natural Resources.

Galloway House Museum, Pioneer Road (between U.S. 41 and 45) Fond du Lac County, Wisconsin

> The photo gallery is a faithful re-creation of a nineteenth-century studio along with cabinets of early photographic equipment. The gallery is part of a restored-buildings complex.

Other collections of photographic equipment, major displays of images, and other evidences on display of early photography are known to be offered at the following private and public museums and cultural-entertainment centers:

Academy of Motion Picture Arts and Sciences, 9083 Melrose Avenue, Hollywood, California

Los Angeles County Museum, 900 Exposition Boulevard, Los Angeles, California

San Jacinto Photographic and Printing Equipment Museum, 147 North Franklin, Hemet, California

Florida State Museum, Gainesville, Florida

Chicago Historical Society, Chicago, Illinois

Henry Ford Museum and Greenfield Village, Dearborn, Michigan

Michigan Historical Commission Museum, Lansing, Michigan

Harold Warp's Pioneer Village, Minden, Nebraska

Missouri Historical Society, St. Louis, Missouri

New Jersey Historical Society, Newark, New Jersey

Museum of the City of New York, New York

New York Historical Society, New York, New York

Ohio Historical Society, Columbus, Ohio

The Antique Camera Museum, 1065 Jer Les Drive, Milford, Ohio

William Penn Memorial Museum, Harrisburg, Pennsylvania

Drake Well Museum, R.D. #2, Titusville, Pennsylvania

Horseless Carriage Museum, U.S. Route 16, south of Rapid City, South Dakota

Southwest Museum of Photography, 1814 North Main Avenue, San Antonio, Texas

Witte Memorial Museum, San Antonio, Texas

State Capitol Historical Museum, Olympia, Washington

Museum of History and Industry, Seattle, Washington

State Historical Society of Wisconsin, Madison, Wisconsin

MUSEUMS OF PHOTOGRAPHY ABROAD

Belgium

Museum Het Sterckshof, Hooftvunderlei 160, Deurne, Antwerp

> Originally a museum for the arts and crafts. A rapid recent expansion into the field of photography, liberally supported by Agfa-Gevaert N.V. and with assistance from the City of Antwerp, the museum has seen development of a major print room, an extensive collection of photographic literature, and a large collection of early and later photographic equipment, housed in what had been a restored manor.

Canada

Archives Publiques du Canada, 395 Wellington Street, Ottawa, Ontario

Canadian Art Academy, 1722 St. Hubert Street, Montreal, Quebec

Canadian Museum of Photography, Jarvis, Ontario

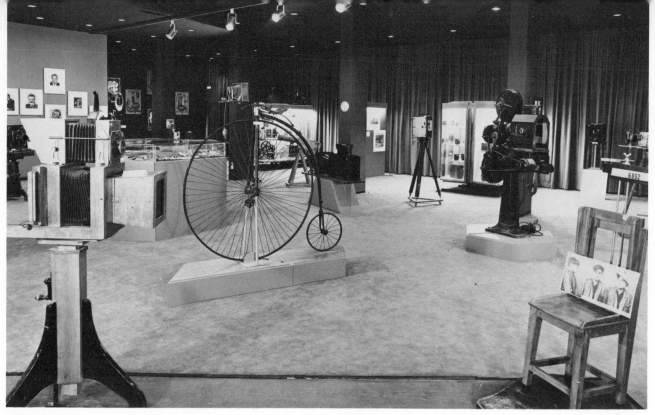

The Agfa-Gevaert Photo Historama is a 7,000-square-foot display of photographic history in the corporate head-quarters of the giant European photographic manufacturer in Leverkusen, Germany.

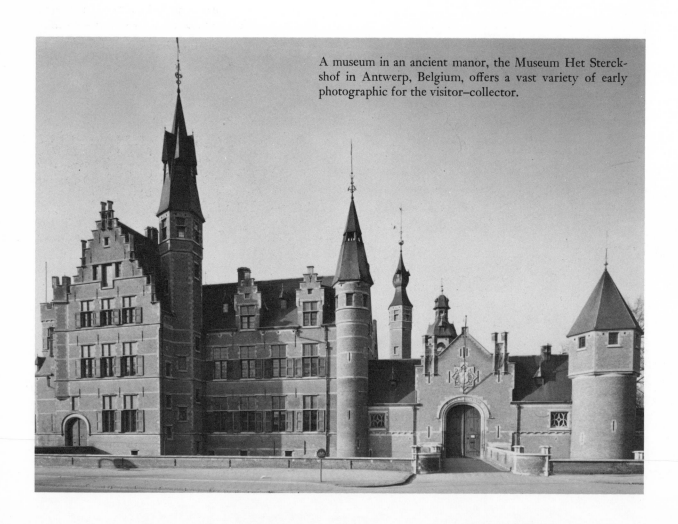

A museum in an ancient manor, the Museum Het Sterck-shof in Antwerp, Belgium, offers a vast variety of early photographic for the visitor—collector.

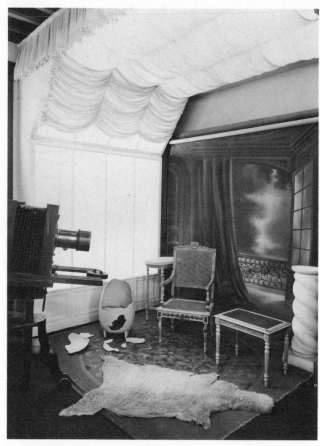

A re-creation of a nineteenth-century photographic studio at the Museum Het Sterckshof, Antwerp, Belgium.

Glenbow-Alberta Institute Museum, 902 Eleventh Avenue, S.W., Calgary, Alberta

A museum primarily dedicated to the ethnic and cultural development of western Canada. Its Photographic Section has a negative collection of over seventy-five thousand plates dating back to photography on the Canadian plains.

Maison del Vecchio Museum, Montreal, Quebec

National Museum of Science and Technology, Saint Laurent Boulevard, Smyth Road, Ottawa

Czechoslovakia

Narodny Technical Museum, Prague

The most extensive collection of photographic equipment in Eastern Europe and a significant collection of early photographic equipment by any standard. Special emphasis on cine-equipment development.

England

Fox Talbot Museum, Lacock Abbey, Wiltshire, 8 miles from Bath

The inventor's cameras and paraphernalia; open daily from February 1 to October 31.

Kodak Museum, Harrow (outskirts of London)

Located at the Kodak works. Initially an industrial museum to guide development efforts, later opened to the public and featuring major camera displays. Call for an appointment; don't be surprised if you are invited to stay for lunch.

A major presentation of the leading cameras of the world at the Pentax Gallery, Japan.

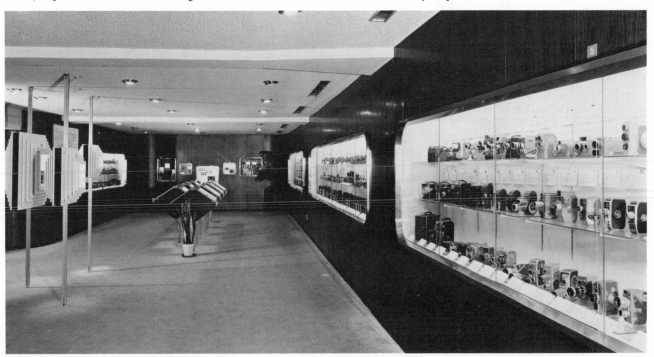

Science Museum Photography Collection, Exhibition Road, South Kensington, London

> Photography: cameras from 1835 to the present; examples of diverse processes; the evolution of exposure meters and shutters. The work of Niépce, Daguerre, and Talbot. Cinematography: origins of the cinema; the work of pioneers Muybridge, Marey, Le Prince, and Edison. Equipment.

France

Conservatoire National des Arts et Métiers, 292 Rue Saint Martin, Paris 75

> France's museum of arts and sciences, this complex of ancient buildings houses a major section on France's contribution to the world of photography. Cabinets display equipment starting from the Daguerrean era to modern times. A vast section on cinematography and a startling presentation of Daguerre's own images and such landmark photographs as an early Daguerrean panorama of Paris are among awe-inspiring presentations.

Hall of the Devon Museum, Chalon-sur-Saône (Saône-et-Loire)

> Birthplace of Isadore Niépce, this modest museum has but a few items of interest; the visit is more a "pilgrimage" to a shrine than an educational opportunity for the collector.

Bernard Mariller, 53 Rue de Cardinal Lemoine, Paris 75
Early cameras.

Musée de la Photographie du Val de Bievres, 4 Rue du Coteau, Bievres 91 (Paris)

> A small fee entitles a visitor to view a cluttered presentation of a grouping of every conceivable item related to photography in the large basement of a private home in a Parisian suburb one visits by car. Ask to see the whole-plate Daguerreotypes taken in China.

Pavillon de la Photographie du Parc Naturel Regional de Brotonne, Hôtel des Sociétés Savantes, 190 Rue Beauvoisine, Rouen

Germany

Agfa-Gevaert Photo Historama, Leverkusen (Cologne)

> A seven-thousand-square-foot museum in the top floor of the corporate headquarters of Europe's largest photographic concern houses an extensive collection of early photo equipment from all over the world, along with a special library of photographic books. The museum welcomes visitors from Monday through Fridays.

Deutsches Museum, Museumsinsel, Munich

> German Museum of Masterpieces of Natural Sciences and Technology. It highlights German contribution to the development of photography, starting with such specific German contributions as the Voigtländer camera and subsequent products.

Leica Museum, E. Leitz GMBH, Wetzlar

> History of the Leica system and the world famous "Leica Tree" to explain progression of Leica models (1912 to present).

Münchner Stadt Museum, St. Jakobsplatz, Munich

> Primarily an industrial museum but with a major display area for photography. Over twelve hundred still cameras and over one hundred cine cameras are to be seen.

Carl Zeiss Museum of Optics, Oberkochen

Italy
Museo National del Cinema, Turin

Japan
Japan Camera Inspection Institute Museum, Tokyo

> A museum of the contemporary cameras of Japan, built on samples provided by all manufacturers of postwar Japan who required JCII clearance of the products planned for export.

Pentax Gallery, 202, Kasumicho-Corp., Nishiazabu, Minato-Ku, Tokyo

> An extensive camera museum with an attached photographic exhibition hall for contemporary photography that was launched in late 1967 by the Asahi Optical Company. A permanent display of cameras primarily of the late nineteenth and early twentieth century from around the world.

South Africa
Bensusan Museum of Photography and Library, 17 Empire Road, Parktown

Appendix G
Comparative Value of
Early Cameras

In 1888 when George Eastman introduced the Kodak, it sold for $25, complete with a 100-exposure roll of film. The owner usually returned the camera with $10 to cover the cost of processing, the printing of 100 prints, and the replacement film. Was $25 too much to pay for the camera? Was 10¢ a print a good value?

By 1910 the 1A Folding Pocket Kodak Special was offered in models ranging from $15 up to $46; was this expensive for its time? More than the Kodak of 1888—or less?

One yardstick for all prices of photo equipment in the period of the family camera was the wages of the people who made it. The following figures represent the average wages of people in manufacturing industries for the years indicated.

YEAR	PER HOUR	PER WEEK
1890	.19¢ per hour	$ 9.95 for 50 hour week
1900	.21¢	10.80 for 50 hour week
1910	26¢	13.00 for 50 hour week
1920	.66¢	33.15 for 50 hour week
1930	.51¢	25.50 for 50 hour week
1940	.84¢	33.60 for 40 hour week

Obviously it took nearly two and one-half weeks of work for a factory worker to purchase the Kodak. The same two and one-half weeks of work by 1940 would purchase a Kodak Bantam Special and even a Leica.

Appendix H
Dating Guide to
Argus Cameras 1936 - 1964

Model	Introduced	Discontinued	Features
A	1936	1941	Plastic body (in black, tan, or gray). F/4.5/50mm lens. Two-position barrel for focus.
A2	1939	1950	Same as A, with extinction type exposure meter at viewfinder.
AF	1937	1938	Same as A, but with full focusing.
A2F	1939	1941	Same as A2, but with full focusing.
A3	1940	1942	Similar to A2F, but streamlined design with extensive top chrome.
K	1939	1940	Daguerre Centennial model. Shutter and lens of A, but with extinction type meter linked to lens.
AA	1940	1942	Also called Argoflash. Fixed focus, similar to A, but flash synchronized.
FA	1950	1951	Same as A2, with flash.
CC	1941	1942	Also called Colorcamera, same as A3 but with photo electric meter.
A4	1953	1956	Flat ends, knobs integral to top, F/3.5/44mm lens.
C	1938	1939	First "boxy" Argus with noncoupled range finder. No flash.
C2	1938	1942	Same as C with coupled range finder. No flash.
C3	1937	1957	Same as C and C2 but with coupled range finder and built-in flash synchronization.
C3 (standard)	1958	1966	Same as C-3, but serial numbered from No. 1921800000 up.
21	1947	1952	Round-end design with removable lens. Gunsight finder with projected reticle.
C4	1951	1957	Similar to Model 21, with coupled range finder.
C4R	1958	1958	Similar to C4, with rapid wind lever.